Thomas William Allies

The Monastic Life from the Fathers of the Desert to Charlemagne

Eighth volume of the formation of Christendom

Thomas William Allies

The Monastic Life from the Fathers of the Desert to Charlemagne
Eighth volume of the formation of Christendom

ISBN/EAN: 9783337028008

Printed in Europe, USA, Canada, Australia, Japan

Cover: Foto ©Lupo / pixelio.de

More available books at **www.hansebooks.com**

THE MONASTIC LIFE

FROM THE FATHERS OF THE
DESERT TO CHARLEMAGNE

EIGHTH VOLUME OF THE FORMATION OF CHRISTENDOM

BY

THOMAS W. ALLIES, K.C.S.G.

LONDON
KEGAN PAUL, TRENCH, TRÜBNER, & CO. L^{TD}
PATERNOSTER HOUSE, CHARING CROSS ROAD
1896

To

Aubrey de Vere

Who welcomed my first effort to trace the work of Christ in the single human soul, and year after year has cheered me with a mind which knows, and a heart which feels, the scope of the task pursued by me, I offer this last attempt to mark the completed fabric of the Divine Kingdom, when the voice of Peter, which received Cornelius, gathered Christendom together in the

MONASTIC LIFE

PREFACE

I HAVE followed in this volume the sources of history, as far as possible, by transcribing the words of those who witnessed the acts which they record. Herein I hold that no historical testimony equals in value the official authentic records of the Holy See in the government of the Christian kingdom and commonwealth. Therefore, the great collection of Mansi, in 31 vols. folio, stands first in the rank of those whom I have consulted.

S. ATHANASIUS, βίος καὶ πολιτεία τοῦ ἐν ἁγίοις πατρὸς ἡμῶν 'Αντωνίου.
ST. GREGORY, Bishop of Tours, father of Frank history.
BEDE's "*Historia Ecclesiastica Gentis Anglorum.*"
MABILLON, "*Acta Sanctorum Ordinis S. Benedicti, in sæculorum classes distributa,*" 9 vols. fol.
"*The Rule of our Most Holy Father St. Benedict,*" by a Monk of St. Benedict's Abbey, Fort Augustus, 1890.
Cardinal HERGENRÖTHER's "*Handbuch der allgemeinen Kirchengeschichte,*" 3 vols.
HEFELE's "*Conciliengeschichte,*" 7 vols.
MONTALEMBERT, "*Les Moines d'Occident,*" 7 vols.
OZANAM, "*La Civilisation au Cinquième Siècle,*" 2 vols., and "*Etudes Germaniques,*" 2 vols.
GODEFROID KURTH, "*Histoire Poétique des Merovingiens,*" 1893.
"*L'Eglise et la Science,*" by R. P. CH. DE SMEDT, S.J., 1877.
MÖHLER's "*Geschichte des Mönchthums in der Zeit seiner Enstehung und ersten Ausbildung,*" edited by Döllinger, Regensburg, 1839.
"*St. Patrick, Apostle of Ireland,*" Rev. W. B. MORRIS, 1890.
BELLESHEIM, Dr. A., "*Geschichte der katholischen Kirche in Ireland,*" 3 vols.
AUBREY DE VERE, "*Legends and Records,*" "*Legends of the Saxon Saints,*" "*St. Peter's Chains,*" "*Legends of St. Patrick.*"

To three of these authors I wish to record my special obligations. I have had ever before me Montalembert's great work, on which that fervent lover of all that is good and noble spent so many years of his life. In St. Bede's History I have found such authentic testimony to the birth of a Christian people as does not exist in the annals of any other nation for the first generation of its faith. From Aubrey de Vere, in his "Legends of St. Patrick," I first learnt the unapproachable grandeur of that saint as a converter, whose single life compassed the delivery of a nation from ancestral paganism to the Christian faith, with its full dowry of the Monastic Life.

CONTENTS

CHAPTER I

THE FATHERS OF THE DESERT

	PAGE
The moment of the Church's first triumph at the Council of Nicæa	1
Foundation of the first monastery by Pachomius on the Nile	1
Its hierarchical form of arrangement	2
A convent of nuns under the sister of Pachomius	2
Conditions for entering this monastic life	3
Antony, the first patriarch of monks, precedes Pachomius by forty years	4
St. Athanasius composes the Life of Antony	4
Having been his disciple and well acquainted with his manners	4
The youth of Antony spent in a Christian home	5
His life when left an orphan at eighteen with an only sister	5
The first fourteen years of Antony's ascetic life from twenty-one to thirty-five	6
He retires by himself to a deserted castle for twenty years	7
After twenty years of solitary life he comes forth at the call of men	8
Monasteries in the desert founded by his example	8
Antony at fifty-five years of age appears as a leader of men	9
A sermon given by him in Egyptian translated into Greek	9
Time and eternity, earth and heaven	10
The kingdom of heaven is within	12
The soul created intelligent and good	12
The number and power of our enemies the demons	13
They were created good	13
Their devices and appearances against us	14
Our Lord's coming took away their power	16
The devil received from God his power to afflict Job	18
The demons dread the ascetic life	18
They pretend to foretell, but are incapable of foreseeing, the future	19
Purity of heart gives true knowledge	20
Joy attends on the presence of good spirits, disturbance on that of evil	21
The power of working signs not to be sought for	22
Antony's own experience of demons	23

CONTENTS

	PAGE
The devil's reproach and Antony's answer	24
Demons become to us such as they find us in ourselves	25
Always to demand of the demon who he is	25
Monasteries created by the effect of Antony's words	26
Increased severity of Antony's life in his own monastery	26
Antony at Alexandria in the persecution of Maximinus	26
His dress and mode of life on his return	27
A great number healed outside his monastery	28
He retires three days' journey to a mountain in the desert	28
Lives alone in the "inner mountain," and cultivates a garden for his support	29
Is attacked by phantoms of wild beasts and demons	29
Saves his company from perishing by thirst	30
His injunction to write down privately one's faults	31
Heals Fronto by sending him away	32
Sends water to a perishing brother at a distance	33
Sees the soul of Ammon carried to heaven in triumph	34
Heals the malady of a nun at Laodicea	35
Has revealed to him the needs of those who come to him	35
Has a vision of his soul encountering "the powers of the air"	36
Antony's deference to every ecclesiastic	38
His own countenance attracted to him those who approached	38
His abomination of heresy, especially Arianism	39
The great reverence paid to him at Alexandria when Athanasius was patriarch	39
He delivers a possessed child by the name of Christ in the presence of the patriarch	40
He foils philosophers	40
He contrasts Christian truths with the impure fables of their gods	41
Deems the action of faith superior to sophistical arguments	41
The cross of Christ annulling oracles, enchantments, and magic	43
Antony delivers possessed men by the sign of the cross in the presence of philosophers	44
Constantine and his sons write to him as a father	45
Antony returns to his accustomed life in the "inner mountain"	46
Sees in vision the Arian profanations in Egypt two years before they happen	46
The promise of Christ ensures the happening of miracles	47
Antony healed not by commanding, but by praying and naming Christ	47
He foretells the death of the persecuting Duke Balacius	48
His effect upon all classes of men	49
Antony's last words to his monks	50
He absolutely forbids keeping his body unburied, in censure of Egyptian custom	50
His injunctions to the two monks to bury him secretly	51
He gives his two sheepskins to the Bishops Athanasius and Serapion	52
He expires with great joy derived from the presence of those who come to meet him	52

CONTENTS xi

	PAGE
Antony died in perfect soundness of body and mind, a hundred and five years old, living in a mountain and yet known to all the world	52
The parting words of Athanasius	53

CHAPTER II

MONASTIC LIFE IN THE FOURTH CENTURY

The death of St. Antony in 356 when the life of St. Athanasius was in danger from the attack of the Duke Syrianus	54
He was commissioned by the Emperor Constantius to seize the patriarch in his church	54
When the Life was published in 365 Athanasius had been thirty-seven years patriarch of Alexandria, and the most renowned confessor	55
This life worked a great number of conversions and had troops of imitators	56
Termed by St. Gregory Nazianzen "a code of the monastic life in the form of a narrative"	56
So by St. Chrysostom and by Möhler in our own day	56
Bearing of St. Antony's life on that of St. Athanasius	58
Who carries to Rome in 340 the knowledge of this life of the Desert Fathers, with two of their number	59
St. Jerome's account of the effect produced at Rome by the presence and teaching of Athanasius and his companions	59
Testimony of St. Augustine in 388 to the regular life of both sexes in the Italian cities	60
His institution in his own episcopal house	64
St. Jerome's praise of Pammachius, first noble of Rome and commander-in-chief of the monks	65
St. Basil's narrative of his own conversion, and the monks of Egypt, Palestine, and Mesopotamia	65
He introduces monastic life in Pontus and Cappadocia	67
His own picture of ascetic training	67-70
And what the demeanour of a monk should be	70-72
The Basilicas which he raised in his episcopal city, Cæsarea	72
St. Basil and St. Gregory encountered Julian the Apostate at the university of Athens	74
St. Gregory of Nyssa makes virginity the special beauty of the Divine Nature	74
St. Chrysostom compares the king with the monk	77-83
St. Ambrose quotes to his sister her reception as a nun in St. Peter's by Pope Liberius of blessed memory in 362	83
Emphatic commendation of Pope Liberius by his four contemporaries, Ambrose, Basil, Epiphanius, and Siricius	85
St. Martin, founder of monasteries and example of the monastic life in Gaul	85

CONTENTS

	PAGE
His house at Marmoutier the nursery of monks who become bishops	87
In seventy years from the founding of the first monastery by Pachomius, the monastic institute is planted in both sexes from Palestine to Gaul	88
St. Basil, St. Augustine, St. Benedict, the great promoters of the *Common Life*	90
Which was developed when the Church most needed it . . .	90
That the delivery from heathen persecution might be counterpoised by purity of conduct in union with strength of belief . . .	91

CHAPTER III

THE FORCE OF THE MONASTIC LIFE

The time of the fourth century for the Roman Empire, hidden then, revealed now	92
The seasonableness with which the Fathers advocated monastic life	93
How the life of Antony attracted the example of Hilarion . .	95
St. Basil finds Syrian and Mesopotamian monasteries well founded .	96
Sets himself to draw a monastic rule	96
The vast difference between an individual ascetic and an ascetic house	97
The cœnobitic life rapidly prevails over the solitary life . .	97
The greatest Fathers of the East and West active in introducing it .	98
The monastery of Lerins and its great work	99
The Sees which accepted their bishops from Lerins . . .	100
St. Cæsarius and his monastery at Arles	101
Cassian and monastic life at Marseilles	102
Cassian finds no one rule established in Eastern monasteries .	102
Quick spread of the monastic life amid much opposition . .	102
Contribution of this life to ecclesiastical learning in the Fathers .	103
It educates and supplies to the Church the worthiest bishops .	104
St. Martin founding Marmoutier	106
The founding of Condat	107
Character of the monks as bishops	108
The course of the empire from Constantine's sole monarchy in 323 .	109
First division at his death in 337 between Constantine, Constans, and Constantius	110
By the death of both brothers Constantine in 350 becomes sole emperor, and attempts to force the bishops into Arian doctrine .	110
At Valentinian's accession in 364 East and West become permanently distinct in their administration	110
Great deterioration of the empire and tyranny of Valens over Catholics in the East	111
Death of Valentinian in 375, and of Valens in 378, causes Theodosius to become emperor in the East	112
Theodosius during fifteen years suspends the fate of the empire, which collapses at his death	113

CONTENTS

	PAGE
In the fifth century the Western Empire became the prey of Northern barbarians, who were likewise Arian heretics	113
The Western Empire a course of perpetual dissolution from Constantine to Theodoric's death in 526	114
The course of the Church from the Nicene Council in 328 a new era marked by four great developments	114
Development of conciliar action elucidating the doctrine of the Incarnation	116
Efflorescence of Christian literature during this conciliar action	116
Growth of government keeps pace with expansion of learning and consolidation of doctrine	117
Leo fixes Christian doctrine, and the Western Empire is abolished	118
The position of the Pope at the abolition of the empire	118
The Arian schism mastered by Popes under hostile domination, and the infallibility of the Church proclaimed by the East to rest on the Papal See	119
The rise of the monastic life under Antony and its expansion under Benedict equally wonderful	119
The misery of Europe complete at the birth of Benedict	119
Benedict at Subiaco and at Monte Cassino	120
Delivers a captive peasant from his Gothic tormentor	122
Benedict dies just before the end of the Ostrogothic rule in Italy	123
How far the cœnobitic life had gone before Benedict	123
The four sorts of monks mentioned by the Rule of St. Benedict	123
The abbot, as a father, holds the place of Christ	125
The abbot's teaching should be twofold, by word and by example	126
He must suit himself to every disposition intrusted to him	126
He should be elected by all the brethren	127
He should consult the brethren, but act himself	127
The abbot's office the same as that seen by St. Augustine 150 years before	128
The monastery to contain all things needed by the monks	128
The whole monastic life built upon obedience	128
Private property absolutely forbidden	129
The novice to be accurately informed of the life before he is received	130
The promise of stability made after threefold examination	131
Bossuet's words on the Rule	132
Surpassed by its effect as the parent of so many generations	132

CHAPTER IV

THE BLESSING OF ST. BENEDICT

St. Benedict sends his disciple Maurus to found a house in France	134
The multitude of monasteries founded in Gaul in the sixth century	135

CONTENTS

	PAGE
The Benedictine rule finally accepted by them all	135
King Theodebert, grandson of Clovis, approves the foundation	136
The Burgundians, the Visigoths, and the Franks, and their settlement in Gaul	137
By A.D. 550 the Franks had spread through the whole land	137
Character of these barbarian invasions	137
The Roman society in Gaul destroyed by them	139
This destruction the same everywhere in the western provinces	139
The cities in some respects fortresses, but continually falling in	140
Merits and demerits of the Franks	140
Clovis treats the subjection of Aquitaine and Burgundy as a holy war	141
Merovingian munificence in giving, viciousness in life	141
The terrible barbarism of three centuries	142
Contradictons of the Merovingian race	143
St. Radegonda, her captivity, education, and married life	144
Is allowed by Clotaire to leave him and to build a monastery at Poitiers	145
Her life at the Holy Cross for more than forty years	145
The burial of St. Radegonda by St. Gregory of Tours, and the subsequent state of her monastery	147
Summing up of the Merovingian period	147
Perpetual variations of kingdoms, sovereigns, and frontiers	148
The same state introduced by the Saxon incursions in Britain	149
The similar condition of Italy and Spain	150
The Christian unity in the midst of universal instability	151
The seat of unity in the accordance of mind with mind	152
How truth and unity stand to each other	152
The unity of the Church in General Councils contrasted with the civil dissolution	152
The action of the Pope in all these Councils without parallel	153
Loss to the empire in the West of the imperial security	154
The monk entering the forest as a pilgrim and founding in it monasteries	155
Names given by the monks to their monasteries	157
The birth and education of St. Columban	157
He studies for ten years in the great monastery of Bangor	157
At thirty years of age departs with twelve monks for Gaul	158
Plants the great monastery of Luxeuil	159
Columban rebukes King Thierry for his incontinence, and is expelled	159
He is carried away first to Besançon and then to Nantes	161
He stays a time at Bregenz, then crosses the Alps to Bobbio	161
Columban's letter to Pope Boniface IV. and his death at Bobbio	162
Bertulfe, his second successor at Bobbio, obtains from Pope Honorius its exemption from episcopal jurisdiction	162
Columban's work at Luxeuil, foundation of Dissentis and of St. Gall	163
Eustatius, second abbot of Luxeuil, which becomes monastic capital of the whole region	164
Walbert, the third abbot, governs it for forty years	165
Pope John IV. bestows on it exemption from episcopal jurisdiction	165

CONTENTS

	PAGE
Its six hundred monks found religious colonies in every direction while Mohammed is commencing his religion	165
The multiplication of monasteries begins a new epoch	166
Its effect doubled by the unsettled political condition of Gaul	166
The foundation of Lure by Deole or Deicola	167
Lure doubly endowed by a rich widow and by King Clotaire II.	168
Moustier and Grandval founded by another monk from Luxeuil	169
The life of Vandregisile and St. Ouen, Archbishop of Rouen	170
Who induces him to found the Abbey of Fontenelle or St. Vandrille	171
The inhabitants of the district converted by the abbot of Fontenelle	172
Jumièges also founded by Philibert	172
The two convert and civilise the country of the Seine	173
Nine hundred monks and fifteen hundred lay brothers at Jumièges	173

CHAPTER V

ST. PATRICK AND ST. AUGUSTINE

What is that *Vita Communis* the course of which has been so long followed?	174
The Church's establishment of Christian marriage	174
Followed by another home created for the supernatural life	175
St. Benedict's answer as to what it rests upon	175
Bossuet's definition of the Benedictine Rule, how justified	176
The establishment of a monastery indicates a new power in the spiritual life equal to marriage in the civil life	176
The acceptance of such a life by vast numbers of the Teutonic and Gallo-Roman race in France from the middle of the sixth century	177
The five forces conjointly forming a new society	178
The mission of St. Patrick at the time that Gaul and Britain are lost to the Roman Empire	180
He witnesses and shares the Christian life at Marmoutier, Lerins, and Auxerre	181
At sixty years of age he is sent as missionary to Ireland	182
He establishes the monastic institute	182
The great Irish monasteries send forth missionaries to the Continent	183
Gaul, which gave Patrick to Ireland, received Columban back from her	184
Irish learning in the time of Italian and Gallic ignorance	185
The great monasteries in Wales, Bangor, Llandaff, St. David, St. Asaph found Sees	185
The conversion of Kadoc, who founds the Abbey of Llancarvan	187
Brittany converted by an immigration of British monks	188
The number of Irish monks who founded monasteries out of Ireland, and were canonised for their work in conversion	189
The conversion of England by mission from St. Gregory	191
Effect of the Saxon invasion on the Christian religion	192
Gregory's faith and courage in this mission	192

CONTENTS

	PAGE
Augustine and his monks pass through France and reach Ethelbert	193
The king, observing their life and conduct, is converted by them	194
Augustine goes to Arles to be consecrated by the archbishop	196
St. Gregory appoints him primate of all English bishops	197
And records the baptism of ten thousand Angles at Christmas, 597	198
Contemporaneous documents attest St. Augustine's mission	199
As also does the contrast between the Saxons as Pagans and as Christians	199
St. Gregory's letter to Mellitus prescribing treatment of heathen temples	201
He prescribes to the archbishop to live as a monk, with his clergy as monks	202
Special notes in the twin conversions of Ireland and of England	202
What passed in Italy while Patrick was planting the faith in Ireland	203
The state of Britain when it was converted—Burke and Lingard	204
The Archbishop of Canterbury made its primate by the Pope	205
Diocesan and National Councils and the superior Papal authority	206–208
This controlling and confirming power exerted through the seventh century	208
The archbishop the link connecting his province with the Pope	209
How the monastic institute grew from St. Anthony to St. Augustine	210

CHAPTER VI

THE MONKS MAKE ENGLAND

Bede's conclusion of his history	211
The last day of his life	211
The sources of Bede's information	212
Burke names him the Father of English learning	213
The universal character of his mind	214
His history invaluable to us—Lingard—Alfred the Great	215
Enables us to compare the Church set up by St. Augustine with the Catholic Church in the seventh century	216
And the Catholic Church of the seventh century with the Catholic Church of the nineteenth	216
And bestows on the first Anglo-Saxon century a history such as the first Christian century does not possess	217
King Edwin of Northumbria marries Ethelburga, daughter of Ethelbert	218
Letter of Pope Boniface V. to King Edwin, still a heathen	219
And to Queen Ethelburga entreating her to work for his conversion	219
Edwin converted by Paulinus, who reminds him of an old sign	220
Considers with his Witan the Christian faith and embraces it	221
Is baptized at York with a great number	221
Letter of Pope Honorius I. to Edwin, and gift of the pallium to Paulinus	222

CONTENTS

	PAGE
Death of King Edwin	223
King Oswald brings Bishop Aidan from Iona, seating him at Lindisfarne	225
Life of Aidan, the monk-bishop	225
Life and death of King Oswald	226
Kings Oswy and Oswin divide Northumbria between them	228
Oswin's gift of a horse to Aidan, and how he is treacherously slain	229
Bishop Aidan's character drawn by Bede	230
Eanfleda, Queen of Northumbria	231
Oswy's great victory over the heathen Saxon Penda	232
Bede's character of the three Cletic bishops, Aidan, Finan, and Colman	233
The congress held at the monastery of Whitby	234
King Oswy orders Colman and Wilfrid to set forth their several grounds	235
Wilfrid rests on the authority of St. Peter	236
This is accepted as decisive by Oswy and the congress	237
The birth and youth of Wilfrid and his life at Lindisfarne	237
His wish to go to Rome favoured by Queen Eanfleda	237
He is recommended to King Ercombert, and reaches Lyons	238
His first pilgrimage to Rome	239
His three years' stay with the archbishop at Lyons	240
His return to England and consecration by the Bishop of Paris	241
Ceadda made Bishop of York by King Oswy	242
Kings Oswy and Egbert write to the Pope to send them an archbishop	242
Pope Vitalian's letter to King Oswy	243
The pains taken by Pope Vitalian to find and send an archbishop	244
Archbishop Theodore received in a visitation all over England	245
Oswy prevented by death from a pilgrimage to Rome	246
English students retire to Ireland for study or devotion	247
Egbert converts Iona, with all its dependent monasteries, to the Catholic custom of celebrating Easter and the tonsure	248
The first Council convoked at Hertford in 673 by Archbishop Theodore	249
Its ten canons	250
The incidents which mark this Council	252

CHAPTER VII

THREE NUNS OF ODIN'S RACE, HILDA, ELFLEDA, AND ETHELDREDA

The work of the three martyr-kings, Edwin, Oswald, and Oswin	254
King Oswy and his wife Eanfleda	255
Eanfleda ends as a nun under her daughter Elfleda as abbess	255
The three monk-bishops throned at Lindisfarne	257

CONTENTS

	PAGE
All those who joined them or were educated by them monks	258
Aidan's vigorous work in education	258
The Anglo-Saxon maidens aspire to be brides of Christ	259
Ebba, the sister of Kings Oswald and Oswy, becomes Abbess of Coldingham	260
Bede's narrative of St. Hilda	261
She visits the monastery of Chelles, and is sent by Aidan to be abbess on the Wear, and then at Hartlepool	262
The discipline she established at Streaneshelch or Whitby	262
The five bishops who came out of Whitby monastery	263
St. Hilda becomes a light to all England	263
Her death after six continuous years of suffering	264
The vision of her death by a nun in another convent	265
Bede describes St. Hilda's thirty years at Whitby	265
No nation at its conversion so prized the virginal life	265
The great abbesses rank with bishops and abbots, and witness charters	266
Elfleda, King Oswy's daughter, ranks with St. Ebba and St. Hilda	267
Wilfrid becomes Bishop of York, with all the dominions of Oswy for his episcopate	267
He is also Abbot of Hexham and Ripon	269
His character and manners attract all to him	270
St. Etheldreda obtains leave from her husband to leave him	271
Wilfrid's ten years of laborious work in his diocese of Northumbria	272
St. Theodore in 679 appoints three bishops to divide his diocese	272
Wilfrid appeals to the Pope and goes in person to Rome	272
Preaches in Frisia, and passes by Austrasia and Lombardy to Rome	273
Pope Agatho brings the appeal of Wilfrid before his Roman Council	275
And reinstates him in the See of York	275
Wilfrid, by the Pope's command, makes confession of faith for all the Northern bishops	276
Etheldreda, being Queen of Northumbria, becomes a nun and Abbess of Ely	277
Her body sixteen years after burial disinterred and found incorrupt	278
The three queens of Northumberland, Kent, and Mercia successive Abbesses of Ely	279
The life and pilgrimages of St. Bennet Biscop	280
Is attached by Pope Vitalian to the newly-appointed primate, Theodore	282
Builds a monastery at Wearmouth by help of King Egfrid	282
And a second monastery at Jarrow	283
He dies, after sixteen years, in 690	285
English conversion due exclusively to the work of monks and nuns	285
Testimonies of Burke on this subject	286
French monasteries are the cradles of English nuns	288
The union of Church and State founded in the monastic spirit	289
The great part of woman in the conversion of the Teutonic race	289
The Fathers of the Desert lose their progeny in the East and regain it in the West	292

CONTENTS

CHAPTER VIII

ST. BONIFACE, APOSTLE OF GERMANY

	PAGE
Irregularities in the time of St. Theodore, and their correction	294
The beginning of parish priests	295
Outline of their functions	295
They are bound to continence	297
Bishops in their cathedrals live as monks with their clergy	298
The presence of women forbidden in a mass-priest's house	298
The time and action of Pope Sergius, who refuses the Trullan Council	299
And the introduction of married priests into the East	300
Which six successive Popes refuse for the West at the risk of their life from the Eastern emperor	301
Other acts of Pope Sergius in support of the English Church	302
St. Willibrord and St. Suidbert in Frisia	303
The fifty years missionary life of St. Willibrord	304
Winfrid, the Anglo-Saxon monk, appears before Pope Gregory II.	305
Who commissions him to preach to unbelieving nations	306
Winfrid joins St. Willibrord during three years	307
His second visit to Pope Gregory II., who makes him regionary bishop	308
The oath of Winfrid—Boniface to the Pope	309
The *compages* or structure of the Church seen in this oath	309
The protection, support, and counsel given by the Pope to Boniface	311
Six letters written by the Pope to commend him to Germans on the Rhine	311–314
Everything as to ordinations prescribed according to a set rule	313
Gregory II. converting the old Saxons as Gregory I. the Anglo-Saxons	313
Three foundations of the German Church given by Gregory II. to Boniface	314
Charles Martel receives and supports him	315
Boniface cuts down Thor's oak before a great multitude	315
He builds many monasteries and churches on the site of former heathen sanctuaries	316
He draws a great number of Anglo-Saxon monks and nuns from England to help him	316
Death of Pope Gregory II.	317
Pope Gregory III. confers the rank of archbishop and the pallium on Boniface, which he receives at the same time that Egbert receives that of York	318
The hierarchies of England and of Germany sprung from the Roman mission	319
The third journey to Rome of St. Boniface, A.D. 739	319

xx   CONTENTS

	PAGE
The position of Boniface on the accession of Pope Zacharias, A.D. 741	320
His profession of obedience to this Pope as his legate	321
To him he declares that Carlomann wished him to hold a Council	322
For which he requires the Pope's special authority	322
The Pope answers in detail the requests of Boniface	322
Declares that Boniface is his legate for Bavaria and the whole of Gaul	323
Answer of Pope Zacharias to a series of questions from Pepin, the bishops, abbots, and princes of the Frank realm	324
A prelude to his future decision as to changing the possessor of the royal power itself	325
Boniface presiding at councils for the restoration of discipline in France	325
Consecrates Pepin to be king on election by the nobles after Papal approval	326
The great and perpetual love with which he fostered monks and nuns	327
He sends a letter on the state of the English Church to Archbishop Cuthbert	328
Who convokes the Council of Cloveshoe in 747	328
Boniface describes the discipline of the Church as decreed in his Council of Mainz in 746	329
His anxiety for those working under him—Letters to Fulrad for them	330
He resigns his archbishopric to Lull	331
His journey down the Rhine and martyrdom	332

CHAPTER IX

THE HOLY SEE FROM ATTILA TO CHARLEMAGNE

Attila and St. Leo	333
St. Leo's confirmation of the Fourth Council	333
St. Leo and Genseric	334
The facts herein comprised	335
How St. Leo stood in a new world	335
Imperial schism ensues on Arian predominance	336
Terminated by acknowledgment that the solidity of the Christian religion rests in the Apostolic See	336
The Arian king of Italy murders the Pope	337
The deposition of a second Pope inaugurates exarchal viceroyalty	337
Justinian tries to control a third Pope as a subject	337
Exarchal viceroyalty imposed for more than two hundred years	338
Broken at last by the restoration of a Christian emperor	338
The submission of thirty-three Popes to the Byzantine oppression	339
During which they conducted with success four great contests for the Faith	340

CONTENTS

	PAGE
The example and authority of St. Gregory furthering the monastic spirit	340
The lives of Christ and of Odin encounter each other before Ethelbert	341
The ten thousand Christmas converts recorded by St. Gregory	343
The choice between Christ and Odin repeated by King Edwin	344
The great examples of Kings Oswald and Oswin	344
St. Benedict makes the West just when Mohammed desecrates the East	345
The triple impulse given by St. Gregory to this movement	346
How virgins followed martyrs in England	347
Where civil and religious government arose together	347
St. Gregory provided in the outset for a kingdom as well as a Church	348
The people through the bishops rank with the first civil powers	348
The union of the two powers running through the Gregorian conversion	349
The civil state thus arising far superior to Justinian's empire	349
The assumption of the *Vita Communis* by the Northern race the real foundation of Europe	350
The monastic spirit from the Fathers of the Desert to Boniface, the legate of four Popes	351
How witnessed by Athanasius, Basil, Augustine, and Jerome	351
Its growth in the seventh century	352
The manifold work of abbeys	353
National conversions wrought on pagan nations by the monastic spirit in both sexes	354
Its universal extent at the time it was least to be expected	354
And how far it had gone with St. Boniface	355
The duel of thirteen centuries as fought in the seventh	357
The monastery's cultivation of the interior life and the maintenance of the faith	357
The monastery as kindling the missionary spirit	358
St. Columban's blessing on St. Ouen and his brothers	359
St. Ouen founding a monastery on his inherited estate	360
He rules the whole diocese of Rouen with a spiritual sovereignty in his pontificate of forty-three years	360
Agilius another great disciple of Columban	361
Columban's influence on the great chief Agneric and his family	362
His daughter, Burgundofara, inherits Columban's spirit	363
She founds Faremoutier, which receives many Anglo-Saxons for nuns and abbesses	364
The houses of Faremoutier, Jouarre, Andelys, and Chelles help to train the first Anglo-Saxon converts	364
In all such houses servile labour gave place to free labour	364
And monks and nuns took the place of *libertini* and *libertinæ*	365
Christian cohesion humanised the broken and scattered life of barbarism	366
The Holy See as protecting and presiding over monastic life and drawing out of it a congruous monarchy	367

	PAGE
While the monasteries trained obedient subjects and wise counsellors of sovereigns	368
Monastic discipline educating a new people both of ruled and rulers	368
The civil servitude under which the Pope worked and conquered	368
In which was also the struggle between Christian and Saracenic life	369
The fourth contest of the Iconoclast heresy in the eighth century	370
The era of Leo the Great developed in that of Leo III.	371
The three contrasted monarchies which thus came forth	374

MONASTIC LIFE

CHAPTER I

THE FATHERS OF THE DESERT

THE martyrs had conquered. The sole ruler of the Roman Empire had professed the faith of Christ, and, in union with the three Sees of Peter at Rome, Alexandria, and Antioch, had summoned, for the first time in their history, the bishops of the whole Church to meet. They met, bearing many of them in their bodies the marks of confessorship. The emperor accepted their doctrinal decrees as the judgment of the Lord whose Godhead they averred, and guarded their execution with the imperial authority. It was a moment of great triumph, after ten generations of trial and of suffering.

About that same year, 325, on the site of a deserted village, one day's journey down the Nile from Thebes, Pachomius founded the first Christian monastery. Born in 292, he had, when scarcely twenty years of age, been pressed into the army at the time when Constantine was carrying on war against his colleague Maxentius. He was then a heathen. When, on the conclusion of the war, he returned home, he became a Christian, and heard of the aged anchorite Palemon, who was quite dead to the world, and led a heavenly life in the desert of the Thebaid. Pachomius induced Palemon to allow him to practise the same spiritual exercises and labours. So Pachomius lived during many years a life of great hardship. Once, searching for a complete solitude, he came to a place where a voice from above said to him interiorly in prayer, "Pachomius, this is the place where thou shalt serve Me, thou and many others. Behold!" And an angel showed him a tablet upon which were written the precepts which he afterwards gave to his monks as the rules of their Order. He submitted all to the judgment of Palemon, who went with him to Tabenna, where he helped him to erect a cell.

After the death of Palemon, when he was nearly thirty-three years old, he founded the monastery of Tabenna, and became its first abbot. Here he received all who desired to offer themselves up in sacrifice to God by a life of penance and self-denial. Before long the monks of Tabenna were reckoned by hundreds. In the end, he founded eight monasteries of men, each of which had a prior, who was subject to the Abbot of Tabenna. The hierarchical form was observed from the first beginning of the monastic life. In the various classes of his monks, all were distributed according to their various talents and capabilities, the weak in the easy occupations, and the strong in the difficult ones; but all, without exception, had to work. There was a class for each work that was required in the monastery— a class of cooks, of gardeners, of bakers, &c. The sick formed one class, and the porters another, which latter consisted of very circumspect and discreet men, because they had charge of the intercourse with the external world, and the preparatory instruction of those who wished to be received. Each class inhabited their own house, which was divided into cells, and three brethren dwelt together in each cell. But there was only one kitchen for all, and they ate in community, but in the deepest silence, and with their hoods drawn down so low over their heads that no one could see whether his neighbour ate much or little. Pachomius practised the same rule about food as about prayer; he was not too severe upon some, while he gave free scope to the zeal of others. Their usual meals consisted of bread and cheese, salt fish, olives, figs, and other fruits.

Pachomius also founded for his sister a monastery of women on the other side of the river. Except the priest, who, with his deacon, offered up the Holy Sacrifice of the Mass every Sunday, no man crossed the threshold of the monastery. The nuns had the same occupations as the monks. They prayed in community at fixed times during the day and night, reciting a certain number of psalms and hymns; and they each prayed alone, and contemplated the mysteries of the faith, or the sentences and teachings of Holy Writ, during their work, whether it consisted of the household duties, cooking, baking, washing, and working in the garden, or of separate manual labours. They spun out the yarn of which they wove their garments, and if they had more than was required for their community, they made clothes for the poor and gave them away.

Whosoever resolved to remain in the monastery was kept for three whole years employed in manual labour and in the minor household works, and then for the first time admitted to the spiritual exercises, and to his own place of combat. No one was received who was not free, who was under age, or who had contracted any indissoluble engagements in the world. No money or presents were taken from those who entered, as it might have been a source of vanity to the richer brethren, or of false shame to the poorer ones. Serving the strangers was the first humble occupation of the new-comer. If he could not read, he had to learn to do so, and whilst he was a novice, to learn by heart the whole of the New Testament and the Psalms. This was a good practice for impressing holy doctrines on the memory, and for leading the mind to supernatural things. Besides, owing to the value of books at that time, and the great number of the brethren, it was impossible to provide each one with a copy of the Holy Scriptures, although some of the monks were always employed in copying. A trumpet summoned them to the community prayers. At its sound the monks had immediately to leave their cells, and this they did with such punctuality that they never even finished the letter they had begun; this punctuality is indeed only conscientious obedience, without which no house or community can be kept in order. Every Saturday and Sunday the monks received the most Holy Sacrament. A priest from the nearest church offered the Holy Sacrifice, for there were no priests among the first disciples of Pachomius, and he himself, like Antony, Hilarion, and Ammon, was a layman. No brother was permitted to receive holy orders, and if an ecclesiastic joined the community, he had to submit himself to the same rule of life as all the others, because Pachomius wished to remove every occasion of dissimilarity or ambition.[1]

But while Pachomius is esteemed to have been the first legislator of monastic life, and to have had a special attraction which drew together many hundreds of both sexes to embrace the rule which he gave them, the great model of anchorets first and of cœnobites afterwards was another, who was more than forty years earlier in birth, and survived him eight years. We have the singular felicity to possess of him a life written by one who had been his disciple and friend, and at the time of writing this life was the most renowned confessor and champion of the Catholic faith then existing, besides being the holder of the Church's second See. About the year 365, Athanasius, at the request of some monks—Western, as it is supposed—drew up a life of St. Antony. With these words he began it:—

"It is a good contest in which you have entered with the monks of Egypt, purposing to equal or surpass them in your resolute exercise of virtue; for you also have monasteries, and the name of monks is cultivated among you. This your purpose is worthy of praise, and may God accomplish your prayers for it. But since you have asked of me also concerning the mode of life of blessed Antony, in your wish to learn how he began his ascetic training, and what he was before it, and what was his life's end, and if the things said of him are true, that you may set yourselves after his example, I have most readily accepted your charge. For to me also the sole remembrance of Antony is a great gain. And I know, too, that when you hear me, together with your admiration of the man, you will wish to imitate his purpose. For the life of Antony is a sufficient ascetic standard for monks. Do not, then, disbelieve the things recorded to you of him. Rather think

[1] All the preceding account is taken from different parts of the translation from Hahn-Hahn's "Fathers of the Desert," edited by Father Dalgairns.

that you have heard but little, for certainly they cannot have told you all. For even at your request the things which I send you by letter will be few memorials of him. Do not, then, cease to inquire of those who sail hence. For if each tell you what he knows, the narrative will scarcely reach that one's merits. I wished, then, upon receiving your letter, to send for some of the monks who had been most accustomed to be with him, so that from their information I might tell you more. But the sailing-time was drawing in, and the letter-carrier was urgent. So I made haste to write to your piety what I myself know, for I have often seen him, and what I have been able to learn from him, for I followed him no little time, and poured water over his hands, carefully herein rendering the truth, so that the hearer may neither distrust any things as excessive, nor from defect form an unworthy conception of the man.

"Antony was an Egyptian, born of noble and prosperous Christian parents, and himself brought up a Christian. When a child, he was kept by them in their own house, knowing none beyond. As he grew up, he would not receive a literary education, not desiring intercourse with other children. All his desire was to be a plain man in his own home. Nevertheless he frequented the church with his parents; he knew no idleness, nor as he advanced did he disregard them. He was obedient to them, he attended to his studies, retaining the fruit he derived from them, nor, though brought up in abundance, did he give his parents trouble by costly habits and the pleasures belonging to them. He was simply content with what he found.

"At the death of his parents he was left alone with a very young sister at eighteen or twenty years of age, and managed for himself both house and sister. Before six months were over, going as usual to the church and collecting his own mind, he thought, as he walked, how the Apostles left everything and followed the Saviour, and how those engaged in business brought their possessions and placed them at the feet of the Apostles for distribution to the poor, and how great was the hope laid up for them in heaven. As these thoughts were in his mind he entered the church, and heard the Gospel read in the which the Lord said to the rich man, 'If thou wilt be perfect, go sell what thou hast and give to the poor, and thou shalt have treasure in heaven, and come, follow Me.' But Antony, as if receiving this thought from God, and as if the reading had been for him, going straight out of the church, gave away to the village his ancestral property, three hundred rich and excellent *arouræ*,[1] that he and his sister might be free of all claim from them. All his other goods he likewise, sold, and collecting a considerable sum, gave them to the poor, keeping a little for his sister.

"Entering the church another time, he heard in the Gospel the Lord saying, 'Be not solicitous for the morrow.' Not enduring to wait any longer, he went out and gave the rest away to those who wanted it. But he gave the charge of his sister to faithful well-known virgins, putting her in a house[2] of virgins to be brought up. He devoted himself to the ascetic life, with a strict and careful treatment. For there were not yet many monasteries in Egypt, nor did the monk yet know of the great desert, but every one who wished to keep watch over himself exercised himself alone near his own village. In the neighbouring village there was at that time an old man who from youth had practised the solitary life. Antony saw and followed him, and remained near his own village, and there, if he found any zealous person, would seek him out like a prudent bee, and not leave him till he had got something from him. Thus he so strengthened his mind as never to return to his parents' condition nor to remember his relations, but his whole heart was to the perfection of the ascetic life. He worked with his hands, having heard 'if a man will not work, neither let him eat,' and part he gave to his own support, and part to those in want. He prayed continually, knowing that incessant private prayer is a duty. He was so attentive to reading that he lost nothing, but retained everything, making his memory serve him for books."

---

[1] Measure of 100 square cubits.
[2] εἰς παρθενῶνα ἀνατρέφεσθαι, sec. 3. This is noted as the first recorded instance of such a house; it would date about A.D. 270.

Athanasius now describes the life of Antony during fourteen years, from his twenty-first to his thirty-fifth year, that is, from A.D. 271 to 285, which was at the beginning of Diocletian's reign. This was a time of increasing severity throughout, in which he practised the virtue of all he saw around him, cherishing the continence of one, the kindliness of another, the prayerfulness of a third: he fasted, he lay on the ground; above all, he cherished piety towards Christ and charity towards others. They esteemed him a special friend of God. He underwent every temptation belonging to his age, but without ever failing. The most remarkable incident told of him by his great biographer is, that having shut himself up in a tomb, he remained long alone in it. The friend who brought him at intervals bread for his support, found him once lying as it were dead on the ground, and severely beaten by an attack of demons in the night. The friend rescued him, and having taken him back, Antony suffered another attack from all sorts of beasts and reptiles, who appeared to surround him. At last, he was relieved from these. Light streamed upon him, and he became aware of a presence to whom he cried, 'Where wast Thou? why didst Thou not appear to heal my pains?' And the voice answered, 'Antony, I was here; but I waited to behold thy struggle. Since thou didst endure and wast not conquered, I will ever be thy helper, and give thee a name to be known over the earth.' So he arose refreshed, and felt his bodily strength increased. He was then near thirty-five years old."

The next day he invited the old man above mentioned to go with him and inhabit the desert. When he declined this, both on account of his age and because there was no custom of the kind, Antony at once set off by himself to the mountain. Neither a silver disk which he found in the road lying before him, nor a vast mass of gold afterwards, could induce him to stop. He passed both in haste, and finding on the other side the river a deserted castle full of reptiles, he entered it. He took with him a quantity of bread sufficient for six months, as is a Theban custom, and finding water within, he closed the door and took up his abode there alone for twenty years. Thus he cultivated a solitary ascetic life, receiving bread twice a year for his support from the top of the house.

The years which he thus lived alone were from A.D. 285 to 305, which was the third year in which the persecution of Diocletian was raging. His friends often tried to see him, but he would not open to them. They heard at the door strange noises, as of a multitude fighting within, but looking through the keyhole, they could see nothing. In their terror they would call out for Antony. He would come near the unopened door, and tell them to fear nothing, but sign themselves with the cross and suffer those illusions to proceed. He was unhurt by these diabolic attacks, and celestial visions afterwards refreshed him. They heard him singing, "Let God arise, and let His enemies be scattered, and let those who hate Him flee before Him."

Thus for nearly twenty years, leading apart an ascetic life, he scarcely stirred from his ruined castle, nor was seen by any one. But after this, many desiring to imitate his life, they burst the doors, and Antony came forth as one initiated in a mystery from a shrine and under a divine impulse. Then first he appeared outside his encampment to those who approached. They were astonished to behold him with a body unchanged. An inactive life had not produced obesity, nor had his fastings and diabolic contests made him meagre. He was just as they had known him before his retirement. His mind was pure, neither dissolved by pleasure nor affected by depression: the sight of a multitude did not disturb him, nor their greetings rejoice him. He was as a man altogether even, ruled by reason, standing in his native steadfastness. The Lord healed by him many that appeared before him suffering in their bodies, liberated others from devils, and bestowed grace upon Antony's speech. He consoled many in their sorrow; he restored the friendship of others, enjoining upon all to value nothing in the world more than the charity of Christ. In his conversation he urged to remember the good things prepared for us, and the loving-kindness of God to us, who spared not His own Son, but gave Him up for us all. So he persuaded many to embrace the monastic life. Thus arose monasteries in the mountains also, and the desert became inhabited by monks, who left their homes, and inscribed themselves as citizens of heaven.

It is from this time forth, when Antony had pursued thirty-five years of ascetic life—the first fifteen in or near his own village of Koma, the next twenty in his ruined castle alone—and was now fifty-five years of age, that Athanasius presents him to us as a pattern and leader of men. He was to live fifty years more, the years from 305 to 355, years embracing both the last and greatest of the ten persecutions, the proclamation of the Church's freedom by the victorious Constantine in 313, the holding of the first General Council in 325, the fresh breaking out of the Arian heresy by the scheming of the court-bishop Eusebius, and the gradual alienation of Constantine, and the bitterest persecution of the Catholic faith when the third son of Constantine, by the death of his brothers, had become sole emperor. All these things Antony witnessed in the last fifty years of his life; and, as need required, he came forth from the solitude of his monastery to meet any trial of his brethren. "The need consisted in visiting them."[1] Thus Athanasius mentions that he went for this purpose so far as the canal which passes to Arsenoë (Suez). It was full of crocodiles. He only prayed, and embarked with all his company, and they passed over uninjured. From this time we are to consider him not only as often alone in the ruined castle, or in what is called the inner monastery in the desert, but as meeting those who were leading an ascetic life, guiding them and acting upon them. "When he returned to his solitary life, he pursued the same vigorous labours as before. But by constant intercourse he increased the zeal of those who were already monks; he stirred many others to the love of the ascetic life, and quickly, by the attraction of his word, the monasteries multiplied greatly, and all these he governed as a father."

The sermon which Athanasius here gives at considerable length, translated by him from the Egyptian into Greek, may, I suppose, be esteemed a summary of Antony's doctrine, as to its leading points, made by Athanasius, and

[1] Sec. 15.

comes to us with the double authority of the father of monks and of the man who was the pillar of orthodoxy at the time he published it, in the year 355, that of his fifth banishment by the Arian emperor Valens.

One day, when he was on a progress, and all the monks came to him and asked that they might hear his precepts, he spoke thus to them in the Egyptian tongue: "The Scriptures are indeed sufficient for our standard of teaching, but it is well for us to exhort each other in the faith, and encourage ourselves by mutual converse. Do you then, as children to a father, bring to me what you know, and I, as being your elder in age, share with you my knowledge and my experiences. First of all, let diligence be your common possession. After beginning, not to draw back, not to give way in your labours, not to say, 'It is a long time since we began to be ascetics;' rather, as if every day were the first, increase your willingness, for the whole life of man is very short measured with the ages to come, so that all our time is nothing put beside eternal life. In the world everything is valued at its price, and a fair exchange is made. But the promise of eternal life is made for a small cost. For it is written, the days of our years are threescore and ten years, but if in the strong, they are fourscore years, and what is more of them is labour and sorrow. Well, then, if we continue ascetics all the eighty years, or even a hundred, we shall not reign only a hundred years, but ages upon ages instead of the hundred. And if our conflict be upon the earth, our inheritance will not be there. We have the promises in heaven. We put off a corruptible body, we take it back incorruptible.

"So, my children, let us not faint, nor think we are a long time about it, or are doing something great; for 'the sufferings of this time are not worthy to be compared with the glory to come, that shall be revealed in us.' Nor, looking on the world, should we think that we have renounced something great, for the whole compass of the earth is very small to the whole compass of heaven. If we were lords of the whole earth, and had renounced it all, it would be worth nothing compared with the kingdom of heaven. If one should despise a brass coin to get a hundred gold coins, so the lord of the whole earth who renounces it, gives up little and receives a hundred-fold. But if all the earth is not worthy of heaven, he who gives up a few acres is as one who leaves nothing. If he gives up a house or a lump of gold, let him neither be boastful nor listless; for if we do not give it up for virtue's sake, yet we give it up when we die, and often, as Ecclesiastes reminds, to those whom we do not wish. Why then do we not give it up for virtue's sake to inherit a kingdom? On this account do not take up a desire of possessing. What is the gain of possessing things which we do not even take with us? Why not rather possess those things which we can take with us, such as prudence, justice, temperance, fortitude, understanding, charity, love of the poor, faith in Christ, gentleness, hospitality? If we possess these things, we shall find them ready at our coming to welcome us in the land of the meek.

"By such things every one may persuade himself not to be neglectful, and especially let him consider himself to be the Lord's servant, and one who owes service to his Master. As, then, the servant would not dare to say, 'As I worked yesterday, I will not work to-day,' or measuring past time, refuse the present, but day by day, as is written in the Gospel, shows the same readiness to please his lord and not endanger himself, so we remain ascetics day by day, knowing that if we neglect a single day, allowance will not be made us for the past time, but there will be anger against us for the neglect. So we have heard in Ezekiel. So Judas for one night lost the labour of the past time.

"Let us then, children, cling to our ascetic life, and not be listless. For in this we have our Lord for fellow-worker, as it is written, to every one that chooses the good, God works together unto good. And not to be careless, it is well to meditate on the Apostle's word, 'I die daily; for if we live as dying daily, we shall not sin.' The meaning of which is, that every day as we rise we should think that we last not till the evening, and when we go to rest, expect not to rise, since our life by nature is uncertain and measured every day by Providence. With such a disposition, and so living daily, we shall not sin, nor have a desire for anything, nor be angry with any one, nor lay up treasure on the earth; but, as expecting daily to die, we shall be without possessions, and yield everything to everybody; we shall not hold to desire of woman, or any other unseemly pleasure, but turn away from it as transient, ever waging the conflict, and forecasting the day of judgment. For the greater fear and the conflict with torments ever overcomes the softer pleasure and redresses the yielding soul.

"Having then begun and entered on the way of virtue, let us contend the more to reach the future, and no one turn back, as Lot's wife, especially as the Lord has said, 'No man putting his hand to the plough, and looking back, is fit for the kingdom of heaven.' But to look back is nothing but to change purpose, and again be worldly-minded. But be not afraid when hearing of virtue, nor think it strange because of the name. For it is not far from us, nor exists outside of us. The thing is in ourselves, and the matter is easy, if we have only the will. The Greeks journey and pass the sea to learn literature; but we have no need to journey for the kingdom of heaven, nor to pass the sea for virtue. For the Lord has said already, 'The kingdom of heaven is within you.' Therefore virtue has only need of our will, since it is in us, and is made of us. For virtue consists because the soul is naturally intelligent. And it is in its natural condition when it remains as it was made, and it was made beautiful, and very upright. For this Josue enjoined the people, 'Make straight your heart to the Lord, the God of Israel,' and John, 'Make straight your ways.' For that the soul should be upright, is that its natural intelligence should be as it was created. And again, the soul is said to be vicious when it declines and is perverted from what it is by nature. So then the thing is not difficult, for if we remain as we are made, we are in virtue; but if we turn our mind to corrupt things, we are judged to be vicious. If, then, the thing were to be got from outside us, it would indeed be difficult, but if it is in us, let us guard ourselves from evil thoughts, and as those who have received a deposit, keep the soul for the Lord, that He may recognise His own work, being still as He made it.

"Let it be your effort that anger do not tyrannise over you, nor desire master you; for it is written, 'The anger of man worketh not the justice of God,' and 'When concupiscence hath conceived it bringeth forth sin, but sin, when it is completed, begetteth death.' But living as we do, we must keep constant watch, as is written, 'With all watchfulness keep thy heart, because life issueth out from it.' For we have terrible and crafty enemies, the evil demons, and our wrestling is against these, as the Apostle said, 'Not against flesh and blood, but against principalities and powers, against the rulers of the world of this darkness, against the spirits of wickedness in the high places.' Great then is their multitude in the air about us; they are not far from us. Large also is the difference between them. Much might be said of their nature and their difference, but such a description belongs to greater than to us. What now presses on us and is needful is only to know their insidious designs against ourselves.

"First, then, let us know this, that those who are called demons are not as they were made; for God made nothing evil. They also were made good, but falling away from their heavenly-mindedness, and wallowing in the earth, they deceived the Gentiles with phantasies, but they try everything in their envy against us Christians, wishing to hinder us from entering heaven, that we may not ascend to the place from which they have fallen. Hence the need of much prayer and asceticism, so that receiving through the Spirit the gift of discerning spirits, one may be able to know what concerns them—how some are less bad, and some worse, and with what study each of them employs himself, and how each of them is overcome and cast out. For their deceits are multifold, and the movements of their plotting. Now the blessed Apostle and those about him knew these things when they said, 'We are not ignorant of his devices.' But we ought to be corrected by each other from what we have experienced about them. I, at any rate, having some experience about them, speak to you as my children.

"If, then, they see that all Christians, and monks especially, work hard and advance, their first attempt is to put offences in their way. These offences are bad thoughts. But we are not to fear their suggestions. They are foiled at once by prayers and fastings and faith in our Lord. But when foiled, they do not rest. Again, they make crafty and deceitful approaches. For when they do not succeed in deceiving the heart by openly filthy pleasure, they make a different attack. They try to alarm by various appearances. They assume the shapes of women, wild beasts, reptiles, huge bodies, military troops. But neither have we to dread these their appearances, for they are nothing and quickly disappear, especially if you guard yourself by faith and the sign of the cross. They are venturesome and very shameless. For if they be also conquered in this, they try another way, and pretend to prophesy, and to foretell things about to happen, and to show themselves as tall as the ceiling, and big in proportion, that they may carry away by such appearances those whom they failed to deceive by thoughts. But if they find the soul protected here also by faith and hope, as a last means they bring on their ruler."

And Antony said that they often appeared such as the Lord revealed the devil to Job (xli. 9--11), in the words, "His eyes are like the eyelids of the morning: out of his mouth go forth lamps like torches of lighted fire: out of his nostrils goeth smoke like that of a pot heated and boiling. His breath kindleth coals, and a flame cometh forth out of his mouth." "The ruler of the demons appearing in such guise, the deceiver by his big words, as I have said, inspires terror, as again the Lord convicted him, in his words to Job (xli. 18): 'He shall esteem iron as straw, and brass as rotten wool: the sea he regards as a pot of ointment, and its abyss as his captive: he regards it as a walking-place.' But by the prophet he says (Isaias x. 14): 'I will take all the earth in my hand as a nest, and as eggs are gathered that are left.' Such are the boasts which they made, and such their promises to deceive the worshippers of God. But neither thus are the faithful to be frightened by his appearances or to listen to his words. He is false and says nothing true. With all these big words, and with his confidence, he has been taken as a dragon by the Saviour's hook (Job xl. 19); like a beast of burden his nostrils have received the bridle, as a fugitive slave his lips have been strung. The Lord has bound him as a sparrow to be mocked by us. He and the demons with him, as if they were scorpions and snakes, are put to be trodden under our feet as Christians. A proof of this is our present mode of life defying him. For he who boasted that he would wipe up the sea and gather the earth in his hand, he is not able to prevent your asceticism, nor my words against him. Do not therefore listen to what he says, for he is false, nor fear his appearances, which are also false. It is not really light which appears in them. Rather they bear the prelude and image of the fire in preparation for them, and they try to frighten men by the flames in which they are to be burned themselves. They really appear, but they quickly disappear, injuring no one of the faithful, but carrying in themselves the likeness of the fire which is to receive them. Therefore they are not to be feared, for all their contrivances by the grace of Christ come to nothing.

"They are full of fraud and ready for every change and transformation. Often they pretend to sing psalms in tune, being invisible, and they quote the Scriptures. Sometimes when we are reading, they repeat like an echo the same things. When we are sleeping they awake us to prayer, and this they constantly do, scarcely allowing us to sleep, sometimes transforming themselves into the likeness of monks, they pretend to speak piously, that in the like shape they may lead us into error, and so draw us under deception whither they will. But give no attention to them, though they wake to prayer, though they give counsel to eat nothing, though they feign to accuse and reproach as to matters in which they have had joint knowledge with us. It is not for piety or for truth that they do so, but to lead the simple to despair, and to call the ascetic life unserviceable, and to make men loathe it, as if the monastic life were burdensome and oppressive, and to hamper those who pursue it.

"Now the prophet sent by the Lord (Habakkuk ii. 15)

condemned the misery of such in the words, 'Woe to him that giveth drink to his friend, and presenteth his gall, and maketh him drunk.' For such conduct and purposes subvert the road leading to virtue; and the Lord in His own person silenced the demons though they said the truth, as 'Thou art the Son of God,' and forbade them to speak, lest they should sow their own malice upon the truth, and that He might accustom us never to attend to such like, though they seem to say what is true. For it would be unseemly that we who possess the Holy Scriptures and freedom by gift from the Saviour should be taught by the devil, who kept not his own place and took up another mind. Therefore he forbids him when using words from the Scriptures, saying, 'To the sinner God hath said, Why dost thou declare My justice, and take My covenant in thy mouth?' (Ps. xlix. 10). For thus they do, and talk, and make confusion, and practise hypocrisy, and disturb, to deceive the simple. They make noises, and laugh foolishly, and hiss, and if not attended to, they shed tears and lament as being beaten.

"Now the Lord, as being God, silenced the demons, but we, as being taught by the saints, should do as they did, and imitate their fortitude. For they, when they saw these things, would say, 'I have set a guard to my mouth when the sinner stood against me: I was dumb, and was humbled, and kept silence from good things' (Ps. xxxviii. 2); and again, 'But I as a dead man heard not, and as a dumb man not opening his mouth; and I became as a man that heareth not' (Ps. xxxvii. 14). So we should neither hear them, as if we were foreigners, nor listen to them though they wake us for prayer, though they speak about fasting. Rather, we should follow steadfastly our own ascetic purpose, and not be deceived by them who do everything fraudfully. But we should not fear them, though they seem to assault us, even if they threaten us with death. For they are powerless, and can do nothing except threaten.

"I have hitherto spoken transiently about this, but now I must not hesitate to speak with greater breadth, for the remembrance will be a protection to you. When our

Lord came among us, the enemy fell and his powers were weakened. For this it is that, having no power, yet being a tyrant, though fallen, he is not quiet, but threatens, though he can only use words. Let every one of you consider this, and he can despise the demons. Now if they were confined in such bodies as we are, they might say, We do not find men, because they conceal themselves; if we found them, we should hurt them. And we should be able by concealing ourselves to escape them, shutting the doors against them. But if they are not so, but are able to enter though the doors are shut, and if they and the devil, their chief, are in all the air, and they are of evil will and ready to hurt, as the Saviour said, 'The devil, the father of malice, is a murderer from the beginning,' and now we are alive, and our mode of life is especially against him, it is plain they have no strength. For the place does not prevent their plotting. Nor do they see us to be their friends, that they should spare us; nor are they lovers of the good, that they should correct them. But they are malignant, and are anxious for nothing so much as to hurt those who cherish virtue and worship God. But because they can do nothing, for this they do nothing, or only threaten. For if they had the power, they would not wait, but would do the evil at once, having a purpose ready for this, and most of all against us. See now, we meet together and speak against them, and they know that if we advance they are powerless. If, then, they had the authority, they would leave no one of us Christians alive; for piety is the sinner's abomination. But since they have no power, they rather wound themselves, for they can execute none of their threats. For this also we should consider, in order not to fear them. If the power to act were theirs, they would not come with tumult, nor make appearances nor deceive with transformations. But it would be sufficient for a single one to come and do what he was willing and able to do. And particularly because every one who has authority does not kill with appearances nor frighten with tumults, but uses his authority immediately as he wills. But the demons, having no power, are like actors on a stage, changing their figures, and frightening

B

children by the appearance of a multitude and their dressings up. Whence they should be the more contemptible as being powerless. The real angel sent by the Lord against the Assyrians had no need of tumult, nor of external appearances, nor of noises, nor of applause; but he quietly used his authority, and killed at once a hundred and eighty-five thousand. But demons such as those who have no power try to frighten by appearances.

"But some one may allege the history of Job; why then did the devil go out and do everything against him, and stripped him of his goods, and slew his children, and struck him with a painful sore? Let him reflect that it was not the devil who had the power, but God who delivered Job to be tried by him. The devil being absolutely able to do nothing, asked and received, and did it. So that from this the enemy is even more to be despised, that with all the will he had not the power against a single just man. If he had had the power, he would not have asked for it. But having asked for it not once only, but a second time, he is shown to be weak and powerless. Nor is it to be wondered at that he had no power against Job, since he could not have destroyed even his cattle unless God had permitted. Not even over the swine had he authority, for, as we read in the Gospel, they besought the Lord, 'Send us into the herd of swine.' If they have no authority over swine, how much more have they none over men made after the image of God.

"We must, then, fear God alone, but despise them, and have no dread at all of them. But the more they do these things, let us increase the tenor of our asceticism against them. For an upright life and faith in God is a great defence. They dread in ascetics the fasting, the watching, the prayers, the meekness, the tranquillity, the disregard of wealth and vainglory, the humility, the love of the poor, the almsgiving, the gentleness, and above all, their piety towards Christ. For this they do everything not to meet those who tread them under foot. For they are aware of the grace given to the faithful against them by the Saviour in His words, ' Behold, I give you authority to tread upon serpents and scorpions, and upon all the power of the enemy.

"If, therefore, they also pretend to foretell, let no one heed. For they often foretell the coming of brethren days beforehand, and they really come. But this they do not out of regard for the hearers, but to persuade them to give credit, and so to destroy them when once reduced under their power. Hence do not attend to them, but disregard them, as not needing such things. For what wonder that they, possessing bodies more agile than men, and seeing those beginning their journey, they run before and announce them. A horseman can anticipate a traveller on foot. They deserve no wonder for this, for they know beforehand no future event. For God alone knows all things before they happen. But these like thieves run forward and report what they have first seen. To how many do they signify now what we are about, that we have met, and are engaged about them, before any one of us leaves and reports this. A swift-footed boy can do this, outrunning a slower one. What I say is, if any one begin to walk from the Thebaïs, or any other place, they do not know whether he will walk before he begins; but when they see him walking, they run forward and announce his arrival beforehand. And thus these arrive later; but often, if the walkers turn back, the announcers are proved false.

"So with regard to the waters of the river, sometimes they are deceptive. They have seen that great rains have fallen in Ethiopia, and they know that the river's overflow arises from them, and before the water reaches Egypt they run forward and tell of it. Men also could have done this, had they been able to run as fast. So the watchman of David, by ascending the tower, saw the runner sooner than he who remained below; and the runner himself told before the rest, not things which had not happened, but things already on the way and done. So these demons choose to labour and signify things to others only to deceive. But if in the meantime Providence will so act about the water, or those on the way—for Providence may do so—the demons have spoken falsely, and those who listen to them have been deceived.

"Thus arose the oracles of the Gentiles, and so they were deceived by the demons in old time. But this deception came to an end. For the Lord came, who annulled the demons, together with their craft. For of themselves they know nothing, but like thieves they spread abroad what they have seen in the case of others. They conjecture rather than foretell. For if they sometimes tell the truth, they are not to be admired for this. Physicians experienced in diseases, seeing a recurrence of the same disease in others, often from their experience conjecture the result. Pilots, again, and husbandmen, seeing with their experience the state of the air, foretell storm or fair weather. They could not on this account be said to foretell by a divine inspiration, but from experience and habit. So that if the demons sometimes say likewise by conjecture, let no one wonder at them nor attend to them. What good is it to the hearers to learn from such days beforehand what is coming? What is the worth of knowing such things, even if it be truly known? There is no virtue in this, nor is such knowledge any proof of a good disposition. No one of us is judged because he did not know it; no one is blessed for having learnt it and known it. Every one's judgment consists in this: if he has kept the faith and well fulfilled the commandments.

"We should not therefore think much of this, nor practise for it an ascetic and laborious life, but rather to please God by upright dealing. We should pray, not to have foreknowledge, nor ask this as a reward for asceticism, but that our Lord may be a fellow-worker in our victory over the devil. But if we would care at all to know things beforehand, let us keep the thoughts pure. For I am confident that a soul pure on all sides, and erect according to its nature, is able, becoming transparent, to see more and farther than demons, having the Lord who reveals to it, such as was the soul of Elisæus, seeing what was done by Giezi, and beholding the powers that stood on his side.

"When then they come to you at night, and desire to tell you future things, and say, 'We are angels,' listen not, for they are false. But if they praise your asceticism and bless you, do not hear them, nor seem to notice; rather cross yourself and the house and pray, and you will see them disappear, for they are cowards, and terrified at the sign of the Lord's cross, for by this the Saviour stripped them and made them an example. But if they persist with impudence, dancing with contortions and showing all manner of appearances, do not quiver or crouch, nor attend to them as if they were good, for it is easy and in your power to distinguish the presence of the good and the bad by the gift of God. For the sight of the good brings no disturbance; for 'he shall not strive nor cry, nor shall his voice be heard.' But it happens in quietness and meekness, so as to breathe joy and exultation and confidence in the soul. For the Lord is with them, who is our joy and the power of God the Father. So that the thoughts of the soul remain in undisturbed tranquillity, so that, being irradated, it sees of itself those presented to it. For the desire of divine and future things enters into it, and it will wish to be joined with these, even so as to depart with them. And if some, as being men, fear the sight of the good, these with their appearance take away the fear by love; as Gabriel did to Zachariah, and the angel who appeared at the divine monument to the women, and as He who said to the shepherds in the Gospel, 'Fear not.' For their fear arises not from the soul's cowardice, but from recognising the presence of superior beings. Such like is the vision of the holy.

"But the disturbed phantoms of the evil breaking in is accompanied with noise, echoing, and clamour, like the motion of uneducated young men and robbers. Hence the soul immediately contracts fear, disturbance, disorder of thought, dejection, hatred of the ascetics, listlessness, sorrow, domestic remembrances, and fear of death; and then desire of evil things, disregard for virtue, unsettlement of disposition. When then you feel fear at seeing any one, should the fear be at once removed, and there be substituted an inexpressible joy, good courage, confidence, a recovery and tranquillity of thought, and the other qualities mentioned, and fortitude and love towards God, take good courage and pray. For the joy and settlement of the soul indicate the sanctity of Him present. So Abraham exulted when he saw the Lord; so John when he heard the voice of the mother of God leapt in exultation. But if on the appearance of any disturbance arise external noise, worldly apparatus, threat of death, or the other incidents, be assured that it is an evil incursion.

"And let this too be an indication to you. When the soul remains crouching, it is the presence of enemies, for the demons do not remove the dread of such things, as did the great Archangel Gabriel to Mary and to Zacharias, and he who appeared to the women at the monument. But rather when they see men in fear they increase the appearances, to frighten them the more, and so advance upon them and mock, saying, 'Fall down and worship.' So they deceived the Gentiles, for they were esteemed by them the gods they pretended to be. But the Lord did not leave us to be deceived by the devil when He spoke in rebuke to one presenting Him such appearances, 'Get thee behind Me, Satan; for it is written, Thou shalt adore the Lord thy God, and Him only shalt thou serve.' Let the crafty one then for this be more and more despised by us, for what the Lord said, He did for us, that the demons, hearing also from us such words, may be overthrown by the Lord who so rebuked them.

"As to the casting out of demons, we are not to boast, nor be lifted up by healings, nor to admire him only who casts out demons, and hold as nobody him who does not cast them out; but we are to learn the degree of asceticism in each one, to imitate and emulate or to correct. For to work signs is not ours; that is the Saviour's part. To His disciples He said, 'Rejoice not that the demons are subject to you, but that your names are written in heaven.' For to have our names written in heaven is a witness to our virtue and life, but to cast out demons is a grace of the Saviour's gift. For so He answered those who put their boast not in virtue but in signs, and said, 'Lord, have we not in Thy name cast out devils, and in Thy name done many miracles? Amen, I say unto you, I know you not.' For the Lord does not know the ways of the impious. And we must chiefly pray, as I said before, to receive the gift of discerning spirits, that, as is written, we may not trust every spirit.

"Now I could wish to stop here, and to say nothing about myself; but that you may not think me to speak thus at hazard, but be assured that I say it from experience and reality, even though I become as one unwise; but the Lord who hears me knows the purity of my conscience, and that I do not record this for my own sake, but out of charity and for your instruction. I repeat the practices of the demons which I have seen. How often have they blessed me while I have execrated them in the name of the Lord. How often have they foretold the inundation of the river, and I have said to them, 'What have you to do with this?' At times they have come with threats, and surrounded me as soldiers in all their armour. At other times they have filled the house with horses and wild beasts and reptiles, while I sung, 'Some in chariots, and some on horses, but we will call upon the name of the Lord our God' (Ps. xix. 8), and they were overthrown by the Lord through the prayers. Sometimes they came in darkness, having an appearance of light, and said, 'Antony, we have come to enlighten thee,' and I closed my eyes and prayed, and suddenly the light of the wicked was extinguished. A few months afterwards they came singing psalms and quoting the Scriptures, but I, as a deaf man, did not hear them. Sometimes they shook the monastery, but I remained unmoved and prayed. After this they came again, and clattered and hissed and danced. When I prayed, and, reclining, sung to myself, they began at once to weep and cry, as if all their force was gone; but I gave glory to God, who had pulled down and made a mockery of their boldness and madness.

"Once there appeared with state a demon of very great stature, and he ventured to say, 'I am the power of God; I am Providence. What wilt thou that I give thee?' Then, with the name of Christ, I spat at him with all my power, and attempted to strike him, and I really seemed to have struck him; and instantly that huge one with all his demons disappeared at the name of Christ. As I was fasting, the deceiver once came in the form of a monk, having, as it seemed, a quantity of loaves, and he advised me, saying, 'Come, eat, and cease these great labours; you, too, are a man, and will be ill.' But I perceived his deception and got up to pray. This he could not bear, for he disappeared, and he looked like smoke as he went through the door. How often he put before me the appearance of gold in the desert, only that I might touch it and look at it, but I sung him down, and he wasted away. They often cut me with stripes, and I said, 'Nothing shall separate me from the love of Christ,' and then they laid more vigorously blows on each other. But it was not I who stopped and annulled them, but the Lord, who said, 'I beheld Satan as lightning fall from heaven.' But I, children, remembering the apostolic word, 'I have in a figure transferred to myself,' that you may learn not to faint in your ascetic life, nor to fear the appearances of the devil and his demons.

"But since I have become foolish in what I have said, receive this also for your security, and to be fearless, and believe me, for I am not untrue. Once there was a knock at my door in the monastery, and I went out, and saw one thin and very tall. And I asked, 'Who art thou?' and he said, 'I am Satan.' I asked, 'Why then art thou here?' He answered, 'Why do the monks and all other Christians blame me without cause? Why do they execrate me every hour?' I replied, 'Why dost thou trouble them?' He said, 'It is not I who trouble them; but they disturb themselves, for I have become powerless. Have they not read, "The swords of the enemy have failed unto the end, and their cities thou hast destroyed"? (Ps. xi. 7). No place remains to me, no weapon, no city. They have become Christians everywhere. At last the desert is filled with monks. Let them protect themselves, and not execrate me without reason.' Then, being in wonder at the grace of the Lord, I said to him, 'Thou art always a liar, and never speakest the truth. Yet now, against thy will, thou hast spoken truth. For Christ has come, and has made thee powerless, and has cast thee down and stript thee.' When he heard the name of the Saviour, not bearing the fire kindled by it, he vanished.

"Now if the devil himself confesses that he has no power, we ought utterly to despise him and his demons. Indeed, the enemy, with his dogs, has so many deceitful snares, but we, having learnt his weakness, may despise him. So, then, let us not fail in mind, nor think cowardly thoughts in the soul, nor make up fears for ourselves—such as, lest the devil should come and overthrow me, lest he should lift me up and then cast me down, lest he should suddenly set upon me and confound me. Let us have no such thoughts, nor be sorrowful as if we were perishing. Rather be of good heart and rejoice ever, as being saved, and reason in our minds that the Lord is with us, who routed and broke them up. Let this be always in our mind and thoughts, that, as the Lord is with us, our enemies will do nothing to us. For when they come, they become such to us as they find us, and they adapt their appearances to the thoughts which they find in us. If they find us crouching in fear and disturbed, immediately, like robbers who have found an unguarded spot, they set upon us, and urge with an addition the thoughts with which we ourselves are occupied. If they see us in fear and terror, they increase the terror by their appearances and their threats, and so the miserable soul finds its chastisement in this. But if they find us rejoicing in the Lord, pondering on future blessings, absorbed in the things of the Lord, counting all things to be in the Lord's hand, and that the devil can do nothing against a Christian, and has absolutely no authority against any one; when they see the soul protected by such thoughts, they slink away ashamed. Thus the enemy, seeing Job guarded all round, receded from him; but when he found Judas naked, took him captive. If, then, we would despise the enemy, let thoughts of the Lord be always with us, and the soul ever rejoice in hope, and we shall see the snares of the enemy vanish like smoke. They will fly from us, rather than pursue us; for they are, as I said, very cowardly, always expecting the fire prepared for them.

"And let this be a sure sign to you in yourselves of fearlessness respecting them. When any appearance takes place, do not fall prostrate in fear, but, whatever it be, ask first confidently, 'Who art thou, and whence comest thou?' And if it be a vision of saints, they satisfy you and change your fear into joy. If it be diabolical, it at once becomes weak, seeing a well-established mind; for it is a sure sign of tranquillity simply to ask, 'Who art thou, and whence comest thou?' So Josue asked the question, and received the answer, nor was the enemy concealed from Daniel's inquiry.

"In these words of Antony all took delight. The love of virtue grew in one man, another was aroused from his neglect, others would have a false opinion corrected. All were led to despise the insidious attacks of demons, while they wondered at the grace given by the Lord to Antony for the discerning of spirits. So there came to be monasteries in the mountains, like tents filled with divine choirs; they sung psalms, they studied, they fasted, they prayed, they exulted over the hope of things to come, they gave themselves up to almsgiving, they had charity and agreement with each other. There might you see a country a part of piety and justice. Injustice was neither committed nor suffered, nor was there any complaint against the tax-gatherer; but a multitude of societies, and the mind of all bent upon goodness. A spectator of the monasteries and of such order among the monks would have cried out, 'How beautiful are thy tabernacles, O Jacob, and thy tents, O Israel! As wooded valleys, as watered gardens near the rivers, as tabernacles which the Lord has pitched, as cedars by the water-side.'

"At this time, retiring within his own monastery, he increased the severity of his life, daily sighing over the thought of the heavenly mansions, desiring them, and considering man's daily life. For he was ashamed of eating and sleeping, and the other necessities of the body, when he thought of the soul's intelligence. Often when about to sit down to eat with a number of monks, as he remembered this spiritual nourishment he shrunk away, seeming to blush if he were seen by them eating; still he ate by himself for the body's need, yet often with the brethren also, ashamed indeed, but to benefit them by his words he would say that all thought should be given to the soul rather than the body, while something should be allowed to its necessity.

"After this ensued the persecution of Maximinus, (A.D. 310), when Antony left the monastery and followed the martyrs to Alexandria. He desired to be a martyr himself, but would not give himself up. He attended on the confessors in the mines and prisons. He was zealous in his presence on the judgment in court, encouraging them to persevere, in waiting upon them in their passions and accompanying them till they were consummated. The judge seeing his fearless demeanour and that of those with him, ordered that no monk should appear in the court, nor stay at all in the city. All the rest kept themselves concealed that day. But Antony put on a white dress, and stood the next day on a high spot in view of the judge. While all were wondering, and the commander with his train in arms passed by, Antony stood fearless, showing the Christian ardour, for he wished, as I said, to be himself a martyr. He seemed like one in sorrow at his exclusion from martyrdom, but the Lord was protecting him for our good and that of others, that he might be the teacher of many in the ascetic life which he had learnt from the Scriptures, for at the mere sight of his bearing many were eager to embrace his manner of life. Thus again he followed out his custom of serving the confessors, and as a comrade in their bonds, helped their needs.

"When the persecution ended, and the sainted bishop, Peter, had been martyred, he retired and went back to his monastery, and was there daily bearing witness in his conscience, and taking part in the contests of faith. For he practised a still greater severity; he perpetually fasted; he had an inner-clothing of hair, and an outer one of skin which he kept to the end, never giving himself the refreshment of water, even for the feet, not dipping them in water, but in case of necessity. Nor did any one see him undressed, nor was the body of Antony ever seen naked, but when after his death he was buried.

"While he had thus retired, with the resolution neither to show himself nor to admit any one, a certain Martinian, an officer of high rank, pressed himself upon him, bringing with him a daughter possessed. As he remained a long time knocking at the door, and urging Antony to pray God for his daughter, he refused to open, but leaning down from above, he said, 'Man, why do you cry out after me? I too am a man like yourself. But if you believe in the

Christ whom I serve, go and pray to God according to your belief, and it shall be.' Now the other believed at once, invoked Christ, and went away with his daughter delivered from the devil. By him also many other things the Lord did, who said, 'Ask, and you shall receive.' For a great number of sufferers, when he refused to open the door, only slept outside the monastery, and believing and praying in faith, were delivered.

"But when he found himself disturbed by the number, and not allowed to keep retired as he wished, being anxious lest he should either be puffed up himself through the things which the Lord was doing by him, or that others should think of him for more than he was, he resolved upon reflection to ascend to the Upper Thebäid among those to whom he was unknown. So he took loaves from the brethren, and sat by the banks of the river, waiting for any vessel to go by, that he might embark and go up with them. While he was thus occupied, a voice came to him from above, 'Antony, where art thou going, and why?' Not at all disturbed, but as one accustomed to be so called, he answered, 'Because the crowds will not let me be quiet, I wish to ascend to the Upper Thebäid, because of the many disturbances which happen to me here, and especially because they ask of me things beyond my strength.' The voice answered, 'If thou ascendest to the Thebäid, or, as thou art thinking, descendest to the herds, thou wilt have to undergo double as great a trial. But if thou wouldst be really quiet, go now to the inner desert.' Antony replied, 'And who will show me the way, for I know it not?' The voice at once showed him Saracens who were about to take that road. So Antony approached them and begged that he might go with them to the wilderness. They willingly received him, as if to fulfil a divine injunction. He travelled with them three days and three nights, and came to a very lofty mountain. Under it was a stream of very pure, sweet, and very cold water, and a plain outside it and a few neglected olive-trees.

"Antony loved this place as moved to it by a divine impulse, for it was this which he who spoke to him by the banks of the river pointed out. At the beginning, then, receiving some loaves from his fellow-travellers, he remained alone in the mountain, no one else being with him; for he kept to that place in the future, esteeming it as his own home. The Saracens themselves, seeing his earnestness, went that way on purpose, and with pleasure brought him loaves, and he had also from the palm-trees some slight and cheap succour. Afterwards the brethren, becoming acquainted with the spot, remembering as children their father, took care to send bread to him; but Antony, seeing that through this bread some had trouble and were put out, sparing the monks in this also, took thought for himself, and when some came to him, asked them to bring him a spade and an axe and a little corn. When these were brought him, he inspected the land round the mountain, and finding a very small spot suited for it, he tilled it, and as it was abundantly supplied with water, sowed it. And as he did this every year, he got bread from it, being pleased to trouble nobody for this, and to be a burden to no one. After this, seeing again some that came to him, he also cultivated a few herbs, that any guest might be refreshed after that hard journey. At first the wild creatures in the desert, which came for the water, hurt his seed and its cultivation; but he gently caught hold of one of them, and said to them all, 'Why do ye hurt me who never hurt you? Go away, and, in the Lord's name, never come here any more.' ' And from that time, as if in fear of some command, they never approached the place again.

"He himself remained alone in the inner mountain, given up to praying and the ascetic life. Now the brethren who came to him besought him that in their visits, at intervals of months, they might bring him olives and pulse and oil, for now he was an old man. And we learn from those who approached him in his life there what wrestling he underwent, as it is written, not against flesh and blood, but against the demons who resisted him. For they heard there tumults, and many voices, and blows, as of arms, and they saw the mountain by night becoming full of wild beasts; they also beheld him fighting, as it were, against visible foes, and praying against them. Now he encouraged those that came to him, while he contended himself, bending his knees and praying to the Lord. And it was truly a spectacle of wonder that, being alone in such a desert, he was neither fluttered by the assaulting demons nor feared the savageness of so many quadrupeds and reptiles, but in truth, as it is written, trusted in the Lord as on Mount Sion, unshaken and undisturbed in mind, so that the demons rather fled and savage beasts kept peace with him.

"Now the devil, as David sings, watched Antony, and gnashed his teeth upon him, but Antony was consoled by the Saviour, remaining unhurt by the other's craft and all his many deceits. But while he lay awake in the night, the devil set upon him wild beasts. All the hyenas seemed in that desert to come out of their caverns and encircle him, and he in the midst of them, each of them with open mouth threatening to devour him. But perceiving the enemy's art, he said to them all, 'If you have received power over me, I am ready to be devoured by you; but if you are put here by demons, wait not, but depart, for I am Christ's servant.' At these words of Antony they fled, as pursued by the scourge of the word.

"A few days after, as he was working, for he would not do without work, some one standing at the door pulled the string he was plaiting, for he was making baskets, which he gave to those who came in return for what they brought him. When he rose he saw a wild beast, shaped like a man as far as the thighs, with the legs and feet of an ape. Antony only sealed himself with the cross, and said, 'I am Christ's servant; if thou wast sent against me, here I am.' The beast with his demons fled away so quickly that he dropt down in his speed and expired. The death of that beast was the defeat of the demons. They tried everything to drive him out of the desert, which they could not effect.

"He was once besought by the monks to go down with them, and visit for a time themselves and their habitations. He went with these monks, and a camel carried loaves and water for them, all that desert being without water. There is no drinking-water, except only in that mountain whence they had drawn it, and where his monastery was. So when the water failed, and a burning heat ensued, they were all in danger. They went about and sought water everywhere, and at last they could no longer walk, and lay on the ground. They let the camel go, despairing of themselves. The old man, seeing them all in danger, was in great sorrow and groaning; he went away a little from them, knelt, and stretched out his hands and prayed, and the Lord straightway caused water to spring up where he stood praying, and so they all drank and were restored. They filled their skins, and sought after the camel, and found her, for her cord had got entangled with a stone. They gave her to drink, and charged her with the skins, and so journeyed on in safety. And when they reached the outside monasteries, they all embraced him as their father, and he feasted them with his words, as one who brought them hospitality from the mountain and gave them support. So there was joy in the mountains, advancement and consolation from their mutual faith. Antony himself rejoiced when he saw the zeal of the monks and his own sister, now grown old in her virgin estate, and the superior of other virgins.

"After some days he went back to the mountain, and then many came to him, and other sufferers ventured to come. Now he had constantly repeated one charge to all the monks that came to him. This was, to trust in the Lord, to love Him, and to keep themselves from impure thoughts and fleshly pleasures, according to the proverb, 'Be not deceived by fulness of the stomach.' Also to avoid vainglory, to pray constantly, to sing psalms before and after sleeping, to revolve the commands of Scripture, to bear in mind the actions of holy men, so that the soul reminded of them may be harmonised by them. Specially he advised them continually to meditate on the Apostle's saying, 'Let not the sun go down upon your anger.' And this he extended to every command, so that the sun should not go down, not only upon our anger, but upon any other sin; for that it was good and necessary that neither the sun should condemn us for the day's malice, nor the moon for the night's sin, nor simply for its thought. That this may be kept it would be well to listen to the Apostle, who says, 'Try your own selves, prove yourselves.' Daily, therefore, let each take to himself an account of his actions by day and by night. If he has sinned, let him cease sinning; if he has not sinned, let him not boast, but persevere in the good, and not be negligent, and let him not condemn his neighbour nor justify himself, as St. Paul said, until the Lord come, who will bring to light the hidden things. For the things which we do are often hidden from us: we do not know them, but the Lord knows all things. Leaving, therefore, the judgment to Him, let us sympathise with each other, bearing each other's burdens, but judging ourselves, and endeavouring, to make up that in which we are wanting. Let this, too, be observed for security against sinning. Let us each mark and write down the actions and movements of the soul, as if we were reporting them to each other, and be assured that we shall cease from sinning through shame of being known, and even from thinking the bad. 'For who wishes to be seen when he sins, or who in sinning does not rather practise falsehood to escape notice? As, then, we should not commit impurity in sight of each other, so if we were to write down our thoughts as if reporting them to each other, we shall the better keep ourselves from filthy thoughts, through shame of being known. Let the writing then be instead of the eyes of our fellow-ascetics, so that blushing to write as to be seen, we may not even think the bad. Thus forming ourselves we shall be able to subject the body to please the Lord, and to tread under foot the deceits of the enemy.

"This is what he urged upon those who came to him; with those who suffered he sympathised and prayed. And often, and in the case of many, the Lord heard him; but when he was heard, he uttered no boast, and when he was not heard, he did not murmur. But he always gave thanks himself to the Lord, and invited the suffering to be patient, and to know that cure belonged neither to him nor to men in general, but to God alone, who does when He will and to whom He chooses. So the sufferers received the old man's words as if they were a cure, learning, also, themselves a patient rather than a heedless mind, while those who were healed, learned not to thank Antony, but God alone.

"A certain Fronto, who belonged to the court, and had

a frightful malady, for he was swallowing his own tongue, and was in danger of losing his eyes, came to the mountain and besought Antony to pray for him. Antony having prayed, said to Fronto, 'Go away, and you will be cured.' But he persisted in remaining several days, and Antony continued saying, 'If you stay here you will not be healed. Go away, and as soon as you come to Egypt, you will see the sign which takes place in you.' The other believed and went, and as soon as he beheld Egypt, his malady ceased, and the man became sound according to the word of Antony, which he learned in prayer from the Saviour.

"A certain virgin from Busiris, in the region of Tripolis, had a very terrible and loathsome complaint, for the humours falling from her eyes and nose and ears became instantly worms, and her body was paralytic, and her eyes contorted. Her parents, hearing of the monks who went to Antony, believing in the Lord who had healed the woman with the issue of blood, besought the monks to let them accompany them with their daughter. As they declined, the parents with the child remained outside the mountain with Paphnutius, the confessor and monk. The others went in to make a report only, as they intended, about the maiden. Antony anticipated them, and described the malady of the child and how she had travelled with them. Then, when they asked him to allow the others to come in, this he would not permit, but he said, 'Go, and you will find her cured, if she be not dead. For such a power as this belongs not to me, that she should come to a wretched man such as I am. This cure is for the Saviour, who works in every place His mercy to them who call upon Him. So the Lord granted it to her prayer, and His loving-kindness signified to me that He will heal the child's malady as she is there.' At least the miracle took place, and when they went out, they found the parents rejoicing and the child cured.

"As two brethren were on the way to him, the water failed on the road, and one of them had died; the other, no longer able to journey, was on the point of it; he lay on the ground expecting death. Antony being in the mountain, called two monks who happened to be there, and urged them to take a vessel of water and run upon the road to

Egypt, 'For of two who were coming here, one is already dead, and the other is about to die, if you do not hurry; for this has been shown to me in prayer.' So the monks came, and found one lying dead, and buried him; the second they recovered with the water, and led him to the old man; for it was the distance of a day's journey. If any one should ask why it was not told before the other died, the question is not a right one, for the decision as to death did not belong to Antony, but to God, who judged in the case of the one and revealed in the case of the other. But this alone was the miracle of Antony, that, sitting in the mountain, he had the heart awake, and the Lord showing to him things at a distance.

"Another time, when he was seated in the mountain and looked up to heaven, he saw some one carried up in the air, and the great joy with which he was met. Wrapt in wonder at this blessed company, he prayed to learn what it was, and forthwith a voice came to him that it was the soul of Ammon, the monk of Nitria. Now Ammon had continued an ascetic to his old age, and the distance from Nitria to the mountain where Antony was is a journey of thirteen days. Those with Antony, seeing the old man in a state of amaze, desired to know what it was, and heard that Ammon was just dead. He was well known, because he had often been there, and because of the many signs which had been done by him. This is one of them. He had once to pass the river Lycus in a time of inundation, so he besought Theodorus, who was with him, to be at a distance from him, so that in swimming through the water they might not see each other naked. When Theodorus was gone, he scrupled further at seeing himself naked. While he was thus hesitating, he was suddenly carried to the other side. Theodorus, then himself a devout man, when he drew near and saw that Ammon had come before, and was not even wet, asked to know how he got over. When he saw him not willing to say, he insisted, clinging to his feet, that he would not let him go until he had learnt it from him. Ammon, seeing the persistency of Theodorus, begged in his turn from him that he would not disclose it until his death. And so he revealed that he had been carried over and placed on the other side, and had not even walked on the water, and that this was not possible for men, but for the Lord alone, and for those to whom He gave it, as He did to the great Apostle Peter. So Theodorus, after the death of Ammon, declared this. But the monks to whom Antony told the death of Ammon marked the day, and when, thirty days after, brethren from Nitria came up, they inquired, and learned that Ammon had died on that day and hour in which the old man had seen his soul carried up. And both these and the others wondered at the purity of Antony's soul, how at the distance of thirteen days off he had known it immediately and had seen the soul carried up.

"Also, the Count Archelaus once finding him in the outer mountain, asked him only to pray for Polykratera, the wonderful Christ-bearing virgin in Laodicea.[1] For she suffered dreadful pains in her stomach and side from the excess of her ascetic life, and was altogether weak. So Antony prayed, and the Count marked down the day of his prayer; and when he came to Laodicea, he found the virgin well. Inquiring on what day her sickness had ceased, he brought out the paper on which he had marked the time of the prayer, and finding it agree, showed immediately the writing, and all who read it were astonished that the Lord had made her sufferings cease when Antony was praying and invoking the goodness of the Saviour for her.[2]

"And in the case of those who came to him, he often told it days beforehand, sometimes a month, and the cause for which they were coming, some only to see him, some for sickness, some being vexed by devils, and all these thought nothing of the inconvenience or labour of the road. Every one returned when he had received the help. He

---

[1] This epithet would seem to intimate that Polykratera had received the stigmata.

[2] In seeing things at a distance, in knowing those who were on the way to see him, in sensible combats with the devil, in the continual exercise of miraculous power, in understanding the needs of those who came to him, as well as in the extreme severity of abstinence, traits are recorded of St. Antony by St. Athanasius which have been observed in our own days with respect to the Curé d'Ars.

would let no one who heard and saw such things wonder at him for it, but rather wonder at the Lord who granted to us men the knowledge of Him according to our capacity.

"As once when he came down to the outside monasteries, he was asked to enter a vessel and pray with monks; he was the only one who perceived a grievous and most fetid smell. The sailors said fish were preserved in the vessel, and it was their smell. He said it was of another kind. Even while he was speaking, a young man possessed, who had hidden himself in the boat, suddenly cried out. The demon being rebuked in the name of the Lord Jesus Christ, came out of him. The man was cured, and all recognised that the ill smell had come from the demon.

"Another, a nobleman, came with a singularly horrible possession, who did not know that he was being brought to Antony. They who brought him besought Antony to pray for him. In his compassion for the youth he prayed for him, and kept watch the whole night over him. As the morning came on, the young man suddenly rushed upon Antony and assaulted him. When those who were with him were very indignant, Antony said, 'Be not hard on him; it is not he, but the demon in him, who, being rebuked and ordered to depart into dry places, has fallen into a rage and done this. Glorify therefore the Lord, for to have so attacked me is a sign to you of his being cast out.' At these words of Antony the young man at once became well, and having recovered his right mind, knew where he was, and saluted the old man, giving thanks to God.

"Many other similar things concerning him very many monks have said to have taken place. Yet even these are not so wonderful as other more wonderful things appear. Once as he was sitting down to eat, and rose up to pray about the ninth hour, he felt himself carried away in spirit, and seemed, as it were, out of himself and accompanied into the air. Then certain fierce and terrible ones standing in the air attempted to prevent his passing through. When his guides fought against these, he heard questions asked, whether he was not subject to them. But when they tried to call him to account from his birth, his own guides prevented this with the words, 'As to what has passed since his birth, the Lord has effaced it, but from the time he became monk and gave in his name to God, an account may be asked.' When they made accusations but produced no proofs, his path became open and unimpeded. Then at once he saw himself, as it were, come back, standing complete and all Antony as before. He forgot to eat, and remained all the rest of the day and through the night sighing and praying, for he was amazed when he saw against how many we have to struggle, and through how many labours we must make that transit of the air, and he remembered the Apostle's words, 'According to the prince of the power of the air.' For herein is seated the power of the enemy to fight and endeavour to prevent those who pass through it. Whence it was he urged them 'to take up the whole armour of God, that you may be able to resist in the evil day,' that the enemy, having nothing evil to say against us, may be ashamed; and we, knowing this, should remember the Apostle's words, 'Whether in the body, I know not, or whether out of the body, I know not, God knoweth.' Now Paul was ravished up to the third heaven, and having heard unspeakable words, came down; but Antony saw himself to have reached the air, and to have contended till he gained his freedom.

"And again he had this gift. Sitting by himself in the mountain, if he was doubtful as to any question, that was disclosed to him by Providence in prayer, he was blessed to be, in the words of Scripture, 'taught of God.' For after this he had a disputation with certain who came to him respecting the state of the soul and the place it would be in after death. And on the following night some one called to him from above, 'Antony, rise, come forth, and see.' So he came forth, for he knew to whom he owed obedience, and looking up, he beheld one, huge and frightful, standing and reaching to the clouds, and certain ascending as if winged, and that one stretching out his hands, by which some were stopped, and some flew above him, passing on then, and carried upwards without disquietude. Over these that huge one ground his teeth, in those that fell away he rejoiced. And straightway a voice said to Antony, 'Understand what thou seest.' So his mind was opened, and he understood that it was the passage of souls, and that the huge one standing was the enemy that envies the faithful, who prevails over those subject to him, and prevents their passage, but is unable to prevail over those who do not obey him, as passing beyond him. Seeing this again, and as one reminded of it, he the more contended to advance with what met him day by day. He did not tell these things of his own accord, but remaining long in his prayers and wondering in himself, when those who were with him asked him questions and pressed him, he was compelled to speak, as a 'father cannot conceal from his children, esteeming also that his own conscience was pure, but that the narration would be serviceable to them, by learning that the fruit of ascetic life is good, and visions are often a consolation for labours.

"He was likewise patient in temper and humble in spirit. For being such a one as he was, he most exceedingly honoured the rule of the Church, and considered every cleric to precede him in rank. He was not ashamed to bow his head to bishops and presbyters, and if a deacon ever came to him for assistance, he would talk with him about this, but gave way to him in prayer, not being ashamed to learn himself. He often asked questions, and would listen to those about him, and acknowledged the gain from anything good said. His countenance also possessed a great and singular charm. He had also this gift from our Saviour: if he was among a great number of monks, and some one who did not know him wished to see him as soon as he came, he passed by the rest and hurried to him as if attracted by his looks. Yet he was neither taller nor bigger than others, but the man was struck by the character and purity of his soul. For as his mind was never disturbed, his outward senses were also in repose. His countenance was cheerful because of his soul's joy. You might feel the state of his mind from the motions of his body; as it is written, 'A glad heart maketh a cheerful countenance: but by grief of mind the spirit is cast down' (Prov. xv. 13). So Jacob discerned Laban's plot against him, and said to his wives, 'The face of your father is not as it was to me yesterday and the other day' (Gen. xxxi. 5). So Samuel knew David by his beautiful eyes and his milk-white teeth; for he was never disturbed from the tranquillity of his soul, never gloomy in face by the cheerfulness of his thought.

"In faith and piety he was indeed admirable. With the schismatical Meletians he would hold no communion, seeing from the beginning their malice and transgression. Nor did he practise friendship with the Manichees, or any other heretics, but only spoke with them for their conversion. He esteemed and he avowed friendship and intercourse with them to be injury and destruction to the soul. So he abominated the Arian heresy, and declared to all that he neither associated with them nor shared their evil belief. When some of these Ariomanites came once to him, having examined and found out their impiety, he chased them from the mountain, saying their words were more venomous than the poison of serpents.

"When once the Arians spread the falsehood that he agreed with them, he was indignant against them. Then, at the request of the bishops and all the brethren, he came down from the mountain into Alexandria and publicly condemned them, saying this was the final heresy and the forerunner of Antichrist. And he taught the people that the Son of God was not a creature, nor was generated from the non-existent, but that He is the Eternal Word and Wisdom of the Father's substance. Therefore it is impious to say there was a time when He was not, for He was ever the Word co-existing with the Father. Wherefore, hold no communion with the most impious Arians. For there is no communion between light and darkness. For you are pious Christians, but they, calling the Son and Word of God the Father a creature, differ in nothing from the heathen in that they serve the creature rather than God the Creator. Believe that the whole creature is indignant against them because they number with created things the Creator and God of all, in whom all things have been made.

"Now all the people rejoiced to hear the Christ-opposing heresy anathematised by so great a man. They of this city flocked together to see Antony. Both the heathens and those called their priests came to the church, saying,

'We desire to see the man of God.' For all so called him. There, too, the Lord had delivered through him many from devils, and from mental complaints. Many heathens also wished but to touch the old man, trusting for benefit from it. In those few days as many became Christians as would be seen in a whole year. Then, as some thought he was disturbed by such numbers, and tried to prevent any approaching him, he said, quite undisconcerted, 'These are not more than the demons whom we fight with in the mountains.'"

The time of this visit of Antony to Alexandria is marked as after the accession of the writer to the patriarchate, which occurred in A.D. 328, by the following words: "As we were attending on him at his departure, and had reached the gates, a woman cried out behind, 'Wait, man of God; my daughter is terribly disturbed by a demon. Wait, I beseech you, lest in running after you I perish.' When the old man heard it, at our request he willingly waited. As the woman reached us, the child was thrown on the ground. Antony prayed, and on his naming Christ, the unclean spirit went out of the child and she rose up cured. The mother blessed God, and all gave thanks, and he went away rejoicing, as to his own home.

"He was also very wise, and it was remarkable that, without having had a school education,[1] he was a ready-witted and understanding man. Once two Greek philosophers came to him, thinking they could try Antony. He was in the outer mountain. He knew the men by their look, came out to them, and said by an interpreter, 'Why take you so much trouble, philosophers, for a fool?' They replied that he was not a fool, but an extremely wise man. He rejoined, 'If you came to see a fool, your labour was thrown away. If you think me a wise man, be as I am. Good things should be imitated. If I had come to you, I should have followed your example; but if you have come to me, be as I am. For I am a Christian.' They retired in astonishment, for they saw the demons also fearing Antony.

"Some more like these came to him in the outer moun-

[1] γράμματα μὴ μαθών.

tain, thinking to make a mock of him, as he did not know letters. Antony said to them, 'Which do ye consider the first, mind or letters? or which is the cause of the other—mind of letters, or letters of mind?' They replied, 'Mind was first, and the inventor of letters.' Then Antony said, 'He who has a sound mind has no need of letters.' This struck both the bystanders and the philosophers. They went away wondering to see such understanding in an untaught man, for he had not an uncultivated character as one nurtured in the mountain and grown an old man there, but he was at once graceful and urbane. His language was seasoned with heavenly salt, so that no one felt a grudge towards him, but all that came to see him took pleasure in him.

"Yet besides these, others also came of those who in the repute of the Greeks are wise, and they asked of him an account of our faith in Christ; and as they attempted to reason about the preaching of the divine cross, in the wish to mock at it, Antony, pausing a little, and first pitying them in their ignorance, spoke through an interpreter, who rendered his meaning well. 'Which is better, to confess the cross, or to ascribe adulteries and corruption of the young to those whom you make to be gods? that which we say is a certain proof of fortitude, an avowal of the contempt of death, while yours are passions of impurity. Again, which is superior, to say that the Word of God has not changed, but being the same, has assumed a human body for the salvation and blessing of men, in order that, by partaking of human generation, He may make men to share the divine and intelligent nature, or to assimilate the divine to things without reason, and so to worship four-footed and creeping things and images of men, for these are the things which you wise men adore? Or how do you venture to mock at us when we say that Christ has been manifested as a man? You who, separating the soul from heaven, say it has wandered and fallen from the vault of heaven into a body, and would that it migrated only into a human body, and did not pass into quadrupeds and reptiles; for our faith asserts the presence of Christ for the salvation of men, but you are in error narrating of an ungenerated soul. We dwell upon the power and man-lovingness of Providence, that even this was not impossible to God, while you assert that the soul is an image of the mind, ascribe falls to it, and pretend that it is changeable, and finally, you make the mind itself convertible for the body's sake. For such as was the image, the like it follows that must be whose image it is. But when you suppose such things concerning the mind, consider that you blaspheme the Father himself of the mind.

"'But as to the cross, which is the better thing to say? If the wicked plot against it, to endure the cross, and not to shrink from any death, how terrible soever, or to invent the wanderings of Osiris and Isis, the snares of Typhon, the flight of Saturn, the devouring of children, the slaughter of fathers. These are the points of your wisdom. And when you make mock of the cross, why do you not admire the resurrection? For those who told of the one wrote the other. Or why, when you mention the cross, are you silent about the raising of the dead, the recovery of sight to the blind, the paralytics healed, the lepers cleansed, the walking on the sea, the other signs and prodigies which show Christ not to be man but God? You seem to me to be quite unjust to yourselves, and not to have read our Scriptures with a fair mind. But read them for yourselves, and see that the actions of Christ demonstrate Him for God, who came among us for the salvation of men.

"'Now tell us yourselves what belongs to you. Of things without reason, what? that they are reasonless or savage? If, as I hear, you would like to say that these things are spoken mythically by you, that you turn the rapt of Proserpine into an allegory of the earth, make the lameness of Vulcan to be fire, Heré to signify the air, and Apollo the sun, and Artemis the moon, and Poseidon the sea, not the less you are not worshipping Him as God, but you serve the creature rather than pay God the service of His creation; for if you have put such things together because the creature is beautiful, you should have gone only far enough for admiration, and not turned things made into God, lest you should give the honour of the Maker to what is made. Otherwise you transfer the honour of the architect to the house he has built, or that of the general to the soldier of the line. What do you say to this, that we may know whether there is any ridicule in the cross?'

"As they were disconcerted and twisted themselves about, Antony smiling said again through the interpreter, 'These things are evident at first sight; but since you would rather trust in argument, and as you profess this art, would wish us also not to worship God without argumentative proof, tell us yourselves how are facts, and especially the knowledge of God, accurately distinguished? Is it by proof from words or from the operation of faith? And which is first, faith by operation or demonstration by argument?' They answered that faith by operation is the first, and that this is accurate knowledge. Antony said, 'Well answered; for faith arises from the disposition of the soul, but reasoning is from the art of those who compose it. To those, then, who have the operation of faith, proof by arguments is not necessary, or rather superfluous. For that which we perceive by faith you attempt to establish by argument, and often you are not able to express what we understand, so that operation by faith is better and firmer than your sophistical arguments.

"'Certainly we Christians do not hold the mystery in the wisdom of Greek arguments, but in the power of faith supplied to us through Jesus Christ from God. And that my word is true, see we that have not learnt letters believe in God, knowing by His works His providence over all, and that our faith is operative; see now we rest upon faith in Christ, and you upon sophistical contests of words, and the phantoms of images disappear among you, but faith among us extends itself on every side; and you by syllogisms and sophistry do not change Christians to heathenism, while we, teaching faith in Christ, strip bare your superstition, while all Christians recognise Christ for God and the Son of God. You, with all your eloquence, do not prevent the teaching of Christ, while we with the mere name of Christ crucified chase away all demons whom you dread as gods. And where the sign of the cross takes place, magic is powerless and spells do not work.

"'Say, at least, where now are your oracles? where are

the Egyptian enchantments? where are magical appearances? when have all these stopped or become powerless except when the cross of Christ came? Is it then worthy to be jested on, or are the things annulled and convicted by it of weakness worthy of this? It is strange, again, that of your things nothing has ever been persecuted, but is honoured by men from city to city, while those who are Christ's are persecuted, and yet our affairs flourish and increase beyond yours. Yours, while celebrated and applauded, perish away, but the faith and doctrine of Christ, mocked by you and persecuted often by emperors, has filled the world. For when has the knowledge of God so shone forth, or when has temperance and the virtue of virginity been so bright, or when has death been met with such contempt except since the cross of Christ came? No one doubts of this when he sees the martyrs for Christ's sake despising death, when he sees the virgins in the churches preserving their persons in purity and spotlessness for Christ's sake?

"'And these proofs are sufficient to show that faith in Christ alone is true religion, but you are entirely without faith when you seek out arguments in words. We prove, as our Master said, not in persuasive words of Greek wisdom, but we persuade by faith, which manifestly anticipates any verbal apparatus. See, there are here those suffering possession.' These were some who had come to him disturbed by devils; and leading them into the middle, he said, 'Either do you deliver them by your syllogisms, or, if you will, by art or magic, invoking your own images, or if you are unable, take up the battle against us, and you shall behold the power of the cross of Christ.' With these words he invoked Christ, he sealed the sufferers with the sign of the cross a second and a third time, and immediately the men stood sound in their right mind and thanking the Lord. Those called philosophers were astonished and truly struck dumb by the understanding of the man and by the sign which had taken place. But Antony said, 'Why are you astonished at this? It is not we who have done it, but Christ, who through those that believe does it. Do you then believe, and you will see that it is not art of words which is with us, but faith through love working in Christ, which, if you also were to possess, you will no longer seek verbal arguments, but will deem faith in Christ self-sufficient.' These were Antony's words, and they, admiring him in this also, retired, saluting him and acknowledging their obligations to him.

"The fame of Antony reached even to the emperors, for the Emperor Constantine and his sons, the Emperors Constantius and Constans, hearing what he did, wrote to him as to a father, and desired to receive an answer from him; but he did not make much of writings, nor took pleasure in their letters. He was the same as he was before the emperors wrote to him. But when the letters were brought to him, he called the monks and said, 'Do not be surprised if the emperors write to us; it is a man after all; but rather be surprised that God has written His law for men, and has spoken to us by His own Son.' He wished then not to receive the letters, saying he did not know how to answer such things; but being urged by the monks that the emperors were Christians, and that if disregarded they would be offended, he allowed them to be read and replied, accepting them as adoring Christ, and gave them precepts for their salvation—not to value greatly present things, but rather to remember the judgment to come, and to know that Christ is the only true and eternal king, and invited them to be humane and to be solicitous for justice and the poor. They graciously received what he said. So was he acceptable to all, and all esteemed him as a father."

The Emperor Constantine died in the year 337, nineteen years before Antony ended his long life of 105 years. The visit of Antony to Alexandria, mentioned above, when Athanasius, as archbishop, attended him on leaving to the gate of the city, and witnessed the healing of the poor woman's child by his invocation of Christ, must have taken place before the first banishment of the archbishop by Constantine into Gaul. And Antony's declaration against the Arians, with the invitation received from the bishops to come for that purpose, might well indicate the troubles raised by the faction of Eusebius.

"Being thus well known, and answering those who came

to him in such a manner, he returned back to the inner mountain and continued his accustomed ascetic life. And often as he sat with those who came to him or walked with them, he became dumb, as is written of Daniel. The hour being past he continued to converse with the brethren. Those present were aware that he beheld a vision; for when in the mountain he often saw events which were taking place in Egypt, and told them to Bishop Serapion, who was there, and saw Antony absorbed in the vision. Sometimes when seated at work he became as it were in ecstasy, and broke constantly into groans at what he saw. Then after an hour he turned to those present, groaned, fell into trembling, prayed, and bending his knees, remained so long. Then the old man rose up and wept. Those present fell into trembling, and in great alarm besought him to tell them what it was, and they urged him much until he was compelled to speak. Then, with a deep groaning he cried, 'My children, it were better to die before the things I behold take place.' To their further requests he said, weeping, 'Wrath is about to fall upon the Church, and it is about to be given up to men like to brute beasts. For I beheld the table of the Lord's house, and mules standing in a circle all about it, and so kicking all that was within it as would happen with disorderly beasts lancing out their heels. You must have heard how I groaned, for I heard a voice saying, "My altar shall be profaned."' This is what the old man saw, and two years afterwards the assault of the Arians took place, and the plundering of the churches, when they seized on the sacred vessels by force, and caused them to be carried by heathens, and compelled the heathens from their workshops to attend their meetings, and in their presence committed on the table what deeds they chose. Then we all understood that the kicking of the mules signified before the event to Antony what the Arians are now doing in defiance of reason, as if they were cattle. But after seeing this sight he called those with him and said, 'Children, do not lose courage. For as the Lord has been angry, so will He heal. And quickly again will the Church recover her own order, and shine as usual, and you shall see those who have been cast out restored, and impiety retreating into its own lair, and the holy faith speaking publicly everywhere in full, freedom. Only do not pollute yourselves with the Arians, for their teaching is not that of the apostles, but the teaching of demons and of their father the devil; it is rather without a parent, without reason, and of no sound mind, like the absurdity of mules.'

"Such were the acts of Antony; but we should not disbelieve that so many miracles have been done through a man. For it is the promise of our Saviour in the words, 'If you have faith as a grain of mustard-seed, you shall say to this mountain, Remove from hence, and it shall remove; and nothing shall be impossible to you, and again, Amen, Amen, I say unto you, if you ask the Father anything in My name, He shall give it you. Ask, and you shall receive;' and it is He who says to His disciples and to all that believe on Him, 'Heal the sick, cast out demons; freely you have received, freely give.'

"Antony then did not heal by commanding, but by praying and naming Christ, so that it was plain to all that it was not he who did it, but the Lord, who through Antony was showing His love to man, and healing the sufferers. Antony's was the prayer and the ascetic life, for which he sat in the mountain and rejoiced at the sight of divine things, but was vexed at being often disturbed and drawn into the outer mountain. For all judges claimed to bring him down from the mountain, since it was not possible for them to enter in there, as those who were on their trial followed them. They claimed, however, that he should come, if only they might see him. Now he turned away from this, and tried to evade going to them. But they insisted, and set forward in charge of soldiers those who were under their charge, that he might come down, if only for the excuse of these. Thus enduring constraint and seeing them in lamentation, he came into the outer mountain. Yet the inconvenience he was put to was not without fruit. For his coming was an advantage and a benefaction to many. And the judges he helped by advising them to prefer justice to everything, and to fear God, and to know that with what justice they judge they shall be judged. But he loved his stay in the mountain more than anything.

"Once, then, suffering such compulsion of those who were in need, and the commander having many times urged him to come down, he came and wished to return, after a few words touching on salvation and for those in need. But he who is called Duke begged him to remain awhile; he said he was unable to stay with them, and he used a graceful image to express this. 'As fishes kept long out of water on the dry ground die, so monks lingering with you and loitering lose their strength. So the fish must hasten back to the sea, and we to the mountain. If we stay behind, we may forget what is within.' When the general heard this and many other things from him, he wondered and said, 'Truly this is the servant of God, for how can a private man have so great an understanding unless he were beloved by God?'

"There was a certain commander named Balacius, who bitterly persecuted us Christians through his zeal for those unhappy Arians. And he was so cruel that he beat virgins, and stripped and scourged monastics. Antony sent to him and wrote a letter after this sort: 'I see wrath coming upon thee. Cease then to persecute Christians, lest the wrath seize upon thee, for it is just on the point to reach thee.' Balacius with a laugh threw the letter on the ground and spat on it, and insulted the bearers of it, bidding them to take this answer to Antony, 'Since thou carest about monks, I am just coming after thee.' And before five days were over the wrath came upon him. For Balacius had gone out with Nestorius, the Prefect of Egypt, to the first mansion in Alexandria, and both were mounted on horseback. They both rode private horses of Balacius, the most gentle that he had. But before they had reached the spot, the horses began, according to their wont, to play with each other. And suddenly the gentler of the two, ridden by Nestorius, dismounted Balacius with a bite, and fell upon him, and so tore his thigh with his teeth, that he was immediately carried into the city, and died in three days. And all wondered that what Antony had foretold was rapidly fulfilled.

"Such was his admonition to the cruel, but he so advised

the rest who came to him that, forgetting beside it lawyer's work, they blessed those who retired from the life of the world. But for those who were wronged he so espoused their cause as if not others but himself was their sufferer. And, again, he was sufficient to help all, so that many soldiers and possessors of large means cast aside the burdens of life and became monks. In a word, he was given by God to Egypt for a physician. Who came in sorrow to him and did not leave rejoicing? Who came weeping for his dead and did not at once put aside his mourning? Who came in anger and was not changed to friendship? Who met him in the gloom of poverty, and, when he heard and saw him, did not despise wealth and take consolation of his poverty? What spiritless monk came to him and did not grow strong under his hand? What young man coming to the mountain, and seeing Antony did not at once forsake pleasures and embrace temperance? Who approached him under temptation of a demon and did not find rest? Who came vexed in his thoughts and did not obtain tranquillity?

"For this also was a great force in Antony's ascetic life, that, as I have said, possessing the gift of discerning spirits, he knew their motions, and was not ignorant of the bent and affection in each case. And not only he was not deceived by them, but by addressing those who were perplexed in their thoughts he showed them how they would be able to overthrow insidious attacks. He described the weaknesses and the craft of the workers. Every one came down to the combat, as it were, anointed by him, in confidence against the designs of the devil and his demons. How many girls with suitors, only by seeing Antony at a distance, remained virgins to Christ? Some came, also, from foreign parts to him, and these returned with assistance like the rest, as sped by a parent. Certainly at his death all felt like orphans, and encouraged themselves simply by his memory, bearing in mind his advice and his exhortations.

"What the end of his life was deserves both to be narrated by me and to be heard, as is your desire, by you. For this also was one to be wished for. As was his wont he visited the monks in the outer mountain. He had been informed by the Divine Providence of his coming end, and spoke thus to the brethren: 'This is the last visitation I am making of you, and I shall be surprised if we see each other again in this life. The time is come for me also to be resolved, for I am nigh to a hundred and five years old.' When they heard it they wept, and fell about the old man and embraced him. But he, like one betaking himself from a foreign city to his own, spoke rejoicing, and charged them not to be remiss in their labours, nor to relax in the ascetic life, but to live as if their death was that day, and, as I said before, to be careful to keep the soul from defiling thoughts, and to emulate the saints. But do not approach the schismatic Meletians, for you know their wicked and profane purpose. Nor have any communion with the Arians, for their impiety also is plain to all. And if you see the judges patronising them, do not be disturbed: for their imagination will end; it is mortal and short-lived. The more, therefore, keep yourselves pure from these, and maintain the tradition of your fathers, and especially pious faith in our Lord Jesus Christ, which you have learnt from the Scriptures and often have been reminded of by me.'

"But when the brethren urged him to remain and die with them, he would not hear of it, for many reasons, which he indicated even by his silence, but for this especially. The Egyptians love to bury and wrap in linen the bodies of the good dead, but especially of the holy martyrs, but not to cover them under ground. They place them on low couches and keep them in their houses, meaning by this to honour the departed. Now Antony often urged even bishops to charge their people about this, and in like manner he instructed laymen and reproached women, saying this was not a lawful nor even a holy custom. For even to this time the bodies of patriarchs and of prophets are kept in monuments; nay, our Lord's own body was placed in a sepulchre and a stone was placed upon it, and covered it until He rose again on the third day. And by these words he showed that an unlawful thing was done by any one who did not conceal the bodies of the dead, though they be holy. For what body is greater or more holy than the

Lord's body? Now many, when they heard this, buried for the future in the earth, and gave thanks to the Lord for the good instruction.

"Knowing this himself, and fearing lest they should do the same to his own body, he was careful to take leave of the monks in the outer mountain, and went into the inner mountain, where he was accustomed to remain, and after a few months fell sick. Then he called two who were with him, and also lived within, ascetics for fifteen years, and who ministered to him on account of his age, and said to them, 'I am going, as is written, the way of our fathers, for I see myself called by the Lord; but do you watch, and not lose your long time of exercise, but as if you were now beginning, be zealous to keep your earnestness. You know the demons lie in wait for us; you know how savage they are, and how weak in power. Fear them therefore not, but yearn for Christ and trust Him; live as those who may die daily, watching yourselves, and remembering my precepts to you; and let there be no communication between you and the schismatics, nor at all with the heretical Arians. For you know how I also turned away from them on account of the battle against Christ and the truth shown in their heresy. But take all pains to join yourselves first and chiefly with the Lord, and then with the saints, that after death they may receive you as well-known friends into their eternal habitations. Think of these things, be thus minded, and if you care for me, remember me also as a father. Do not let them carry my body into Egypt, lest they lay it up in their houses. It was for this I entered the mountain and came here. You know, too, how I ever reproved those who did this, and ordered them to stop such a practice. Do you then bury my body and cover it in the earth. And be my word guarded by you so that no one know the spot but you alone; for in the resurrection of the dead I shall receive it back from our Saviour incorrupt. But divide my clothing, and to Athanasius the bishop give one sheepskin and the cloak on which I lie, which he gave to me when new, and which has grown old with me; and to Serapion the bishop give the other sheepskin, and take you the goat's-hair vest.

And now farewell, children, for Antony changes his abode, and is no longer with you.'

"With these words, when they had kissed him, he stretched out his feet, and looking upon those who came after him with joy, and being very joyful because of them, for when he reclined he appeared with a cheerful countenance, he expired and was added to his fathers. And those two burying him, as he had charged, and enfolding his body, covered it in the earth. And no one knew henceforth where he was buried, save only those two. And each of those who received the sheepskin of blessed Antony and his worn vestment preserves it as a great thing; for the sight of them is as beholding Antony still, and the putting them on is as bearing his admonitions with rejoicing.

"This was the end of Antony's life in the body, and such like his beginning as ascetic; and if this be but a brief account beside his merit, yet from this estimate what Antony, the man of God, was, who from youth up to such an age kept with an even tenor his ascetic fervour. Age did not subdue him to the indulgence of more costly food, nor did bodily weakness make him change the manner of his clothing. Nor did he even wash his feet in water. Yet in every respect he remained unhurt. His eyes were perfect and uninjured, with good sight; he had not lost a single tooth: they were only worn under the gums through his great age; in feet and in hands he remained sound, and he appeared brighter and more ready for exertions of strength than all those who used variety of foods, and baths, and change of clothing. This gave him a great name everywhere; all wondered at him; those even who had not seen him longed for the sight—an assurance of his virtue, and of a soul dear to God. For Antony became known not for his writings, not for Gentile wisdom, not for any art, but solely for his piety. No one can deny that this is a gift of God. For how was a man hidden in a mountain, and dwelling there, to be heard of in Spain, in Gaul, in Rome, and Africa, unless it were God, who everywhere makes known His own, and who had promised this in the beginning to Antony? For though they work in concealment, though they wish to be hid, yet the Lord shows them as lights to all; that thus also those who hear of them may recognise that the commandments are sufficient for success, and may be encouraged to embrace the way of virtue.

"Read, then, this to the other brethren, that they may learn what the life of monks ought to be, and be persuaded that our Lord and Saviour Jesus Christ glorifies them who glorify Him, and not only leads those who serve Him to the end up to the kingdom of heaven, but likewise here makes those who conceal themselves and earnestly seek retirement to be conspicuous and celebrated both for their own virtue and for the advantage of others. Should there be need, read this also to the heathen, that even by such means also they may learn that our Lord Jesus Christ is not only God and the Son of God, but that likewise those who serve Him lawfully and believe in Him piously as Christians, convict the demons whom the heathen themselves esteem to be gods not only to be no gods, but trample upon them and chase them away as deceivers and corrupters of men. In Jesus Christ our Lord, to whom be glory for ever and ever, Amen."

CHAPTER II

MONASTIC LIFE IN THE FOURTH CENTURY

The fifty years during which St. Antony, in the narrative given to the Church by St. Athanasius, appears as the standard of the monastic life, as it was to spring from his example, and to be the leader and former of men, were most critical years in the history of the Church. His death occurred January 17, 356, that is, a few days before the 9th February 356, when the Duke Syrianus, by express command of the Emperor Constantius, surrounded the great church at Alexandria, in which St. Athanasius as Patriarch was occupied in worship, with the intention of seizing him. He escaped through a scene of sacrilegious outrage and massacre, no man knew how; a price was set upon his head, and he remained banished and hunted for his life during six years, until the Emperor Constantius had died prematurely, and his successor, Julian the Apostate, allowed by decree the banished bishops to return to their sees. This was in 362. Julian had ordered this in the hope that the returning bishops would increase the troubles of the Church by their disagreement. On the contrary, Athanasius immediately summoned a great Council at Alexandria, in which he showed a wisdom so consummate, and a charity so compassionate, that he was regarded by all with the greatest veneration. Julian in wrath banished him that same year, 362, to the Thebaïs; and Athanasius on his way thither answered the regrets of those who mourned over his banishment with the words, "Be not afraid; this is but a passing cloud." In the following June a Parthian lance ended the misdeeds of Julian, and frustrated the persecution which would have followed his victory. Athanasius returned to his see in 363, was highly honoured and specially consulted by the succeeding emperor, Jovian. That emperor, who was bent on undoing the injuries done to the Church, was suddenly cut off, and his successor, Valentinian, nominated his brother Valens to the Eastern Roman empire, which contained the sees of Alexandria, Antioch, and Constantinople. Valens, under the guidance of Eudoxius, bishop of Constantinople, became an Arian more bitter and persecuting than Constantius; he renewed in 365 the decree of banishment against those bishops who had been expelled by Constantius. This was the fifth and last banishment of Athanasius, and owing to the great respect in which he was held, Valens in a short time allowed him to return.

Thus when, in the year 365, Athanasius published his life of St. Antony as one whom he had personally known, nay, whose disciple he had been, and of whom he was proud to record that he "had poured out water for his hands," he was the most renowned confessor of his time, while he was likewise the holder of the Church's second see. He had been for thirty-seven years Patriarch of Alexandria, and before that the chief defender of the Godhead of his Lord, though not a bishop, in the first great Council of the Church, held at Nicea in 325. He had been banished to Treves in 335 by the first Christian emperor, Constantine, but brought back after his death in 337 by the decree of the three emperors, his sons, who were said to be fulfilling in this the intention of their father. Thus welcomed back to his see with the warmest expressions of respect in 338, he had in 340 been obliged to leave it again, and fled for refuge to Pope Julius, who heard his cause and reinstated him, though the ill-will of the Arian Constantius did not allow him to return to his see until 346. After ten years he was banished again by Constantius; then again by the apostate emperor Julian, and again by the Arian emperor Valens. In these thirty-seven years his defence of his Lord's Godhead had never faltered, the vigour with which he maintained the true doctrine had never lessened, while in conduct not one act of weakness could be alleged against him; he had been valiantly supported by Popes Julius and Liberius; he had in his turn acknowledged and maintained their government, and their defence of the doctrine he had preached; he was equally esteemed and honoured by the great Pope Damasus, their successor. All men looked upon him, as St. Basil a few years later addressed him, as the pillar of the Church. I suppose that among the writings of fathers of the fourth and fifth centuries, which are priceless, there is no one more valuable than this authentic history of the Father of Monks by one whose own position in his day was unique, who knew and loved and imitated the man whom he has described, and who heralded with his own glorious name, for the instruction of his own day, and for the generations which followed, the sort of life inaugurated and pursued by St. Antony. It is one of those biographies through which the grace of God has thought fit to work a number of conversions and raised up troops of imitators. One of these may be mentioned, for by this writing the greatest of confessors and the greatest of doctors touch each other, and less than twenty years after it was written the conversion of St. Augustine was wrought by hearing the effect which this life had produced upon two young courtiers in the imperial service, and the life of St. Antony by the former may be said to be the parent of the Confessions of the latter, " et quasi cursores vitai lampada tradunt."

In the review of the life, character, and actions of Athanasius given by St. Gregory Nazianzene in his twenty-first sermon, he calls this biography "a code of the monastic life in the form of a narrative." We have here not only an attestation of the biography as authentic, but the warmest praise of its intrinsic value as an exhibition of one of the Church's greatest institutions, a praise given by the man whose special title among the fathers is to be called the Theologian. St. Chrysostom is quite of the same mind when he says, "If any one has not visited those tents, let him bear in mind the man who up to this time is in everybody's mouth, that great and blessed Antony, whom, since the apostles, Egypt has produced. Born as he was in the land of Pharaoh, he was not injured, but was even granted the Divine vision, and exhibited the kind of life which the laws of Christ demand. This may be accurately learnt by any one who falls on the book containing the history of his life, in which he will see a great deal of prophecy. For he told beforehand of those who had the sickness of Arius, the injury that would spring from it, and saw spread out before his eyes the miseries which were to come."[1] In our own time Möhler has written an admirable life of St. Athanasius himself, as well as a treatise on the rise of the monastic life, which shows his great knowledge of the centuries in which it rose, as well as his esteem for it and his sympathy with it. He says, "The scope of this life is to show what is the really important thing in the monastic life to which every attention must be directed—namely, to use its loneliness and its privations for the attainment of something higher; for inward sanctification; to describe more accurately the means leading to this; to guard against being led away to any bypath; in fine, to show how the monk, though not living in the companionship of society, yet may be its benefactor."[2]

It is very instructive to trace the bearings on each other of the events in the life of Athanasius and the first appearance of the monks. It is in his early youth that he acquires a personal knowledge of St. Antony, becomes his disciple, and as such pours out water for his hands in attendance on him. In the year 328 Athanasius was chosen Patriarch of Alexandria, and describing in the life one of the visits made by St. Antony, records his zeal against the Arians, conducts him to the gate of the city at his departure, and witnesses the remarkable effect of his invoking the name of Christ. When Constantine is induced by the deceit of Eusebius to distrust the loyalty of Athanasius and to banish him to Treves in the year 335, Athanasius makes his first visit to the West, and carries with him full knowledge of the life which the Fathers of the Desert, Antony, Pachomius, Ammon, and many others were leading. By the judgment of the three emperors, who had succeeded their father, Constantine, he returns to his see in 338. In 340 the Eusebian party are able to drive him out of Alexandria, as they had succeeded some years before in driving St. Eustathius out of Antioch, using in both cases the imperial

[1] Ἀντωνίου τοῦ θείου βίον συνέγραψε. τοῦ μοναδικοῦ βίου νομοθεσία νέν πλάσματι διηγήσεως. Orat. 21, 5. Chrysostom, tom. vii. 128.
[2] *Athanasius der Grosse, und die Kirche seiner Zeit*, 2nd edit., p. 381.

power to work out their own designs. This time Athanasius flees to Rome, and brings his cause before Pope Julius, whose own letter has been preserved by him, and attests that the Pope of Rome, as sole superior of the Pope of Alexandria, was the only person before whom in such a case the conduct of the second bishop in the Church could be brought, according to the discipline of that day. On this occasion Athanasius took with him two monks very highly esteemed, Ammon and Isidorus. Ammon, after long practice of the monastic life, had become superior of a great number of monks in the desert of Nitria, not far from Alexandria. In early life Ammon was married, and on the day of his marriage he set before his bride the doctrine of St. Paul upon the married and the virginal life as compared with each other; and, as St. Cecilia had done at Rome with her bridegroom, so he persuaded his bride of the superior beauty of the virginal life. They lived together as brother and sister during eighteen years, and finally, while he became the head of a large number of monks, she became abbess to a house of nuns. It was this Ammon, the vision of whose carrying to heaven, as seen by Antony at a distance of thirteen days' journey, we have found recorded by Athanasius. His stay at Rome, accompanied by these two monks, first kindled in the Roman Church the love of the monastic institute. Ammon cared so little for grandeur that the only places which he would visit at Rome were the basilicas of St. Peter and St. Paul. That of St. Mary Major was not yet built. Isidorus was no less austere in his life.[1] Their example told upon the Romans, who then first learnt to cultivate the monastic discipline. Athanasius, with his companions, was kept some time at Rome, while Pope Julius sent two priests to the bishops at Antioch, inviting them to come to Rome to answer the charges brought against them by Athanasius as to their conduct towards him and other bishops. In this considerable time Athanasius had the opportunity of setting forth the life of St. Antony as the father of monks. Thus the long sojourn of Athanasius with his two Fathers of the Desert at Rome, brought about by the violence of the

[1] See Life of Athanasius, by the editor, prefixed to his works, p. 36.

Eusebian party at Antioch, had the result of making this new life pursued by the Fathers in the deserts of Egypt more widely known. It was carried to the knowledge of the West, and to Rome itself, by the very champion of the truth which the West, with Rome in chief, most vigorously held. And all the persuasiveness which belonged to Athanasius by virtue of his actions, his writings, his rank, and his sufferings, served to recommend this new discipline of the monastic life which he set forth at this time by word of mouth, and by the presence of Ammon and Isidorus attending on him.

This visit to Rome was fifteen years before the death of Antony, and twenty-five years before the publication of the biography which afterwards spread so widely the knowledge of that life, and caused the construction of so many monasteries in the West, while it was followed by the conversion of so many of the Roman nobility of both sexes. This visit was about the time of St. Jerome's birth. There is an interval of thirty years between the first visit of Athanasius to Rome in 335, on his way to his exile at Treves, and the publication of his life of St. Antony nine years after the death of its subject in 365. In that interval Rome had undergone the fiercest persecution of Constantius, who in 350 had become sole emperor. He had sent Pope Liberius, simply by his imperial fiat, into banishment from his see to the custody of an Arian bishop in Thrace. St. Jerome speaks in his letter to the noble lady Principia, then a nun, of St. Marcella, the first Roman lady of high rank who had embraced the religious life, and made, at least in some degree, a convent of her palace. In the year 358 Cerealis was a consul at Rome, and he had entreated Marcella, when a very young widow, after a marriage which had only lasted seven months, to become his wife, drawn by the antiquity and dignity of her family and her own distinguished beauty. She refused him out of love for the religious life, and by refusing so eminent a suitor kept at a distance all others. She lived to see the capture of Rome by the Goths in 410, and by her intrepid bravery to protect and save a young lady living under her care. During a long life her example was an attraction to many others of the Roman nobility. When she began her own religious life, St. Jerome notes that "there was not at Rome a noble lady who was acquainted with the monastic mode of life or who ventured on account of the novelty of the thing to assume a name ignominious, as it was then thought, and vulgar in popular estimation. It was from Alexandrian priests, from Athanasius, and from Peter, who succeeded him at his death, when, avoiding the persecution of the Arian heresy, they had fled to Rome as the safest harbour their communion could find, Marcella had learnt the life of St. Antony while he was still living, and the discipline of the monasteries in the Thebaïs, of Pachomius, and of the virgins and widows there. Nor was she ashamed to profess what she knew was pleasing to Christ." The Patriarch Peter may have been in Rome about 374. When St. Augustine wrote on the morals of the Church a few years later, in 388, he offered this remarkable testimony to lives of which he had been an eye-witness. This testimony is the more valuable because in it he speaks of anchorets, of cœnobites, of those who are now called secular clergy, and of religious houses which he had seen in Italian cities. "Who does not know that a multitude of Christian men of the highest continence is daily more widely spread over the whole world, and specially in the East and Egypt?—a thing which you Manicheans cannot be ignorant of. I will not speak of those who, severed altogether from all sight of men, are contented with bread alone, brought to them at certain intervals, and water, who inhabit utterly deserted places, enjoying intercourse with God, to whom they cleave with pure minds, most blessed with the contemplation of His beauty, the perception of which is only possible to the intellect of the holy. Of these I will say nothing, because to some they seem to have given up human things more than they ought. That is, it seems so to such who do not understand what a help to us in prayer their mind is, and their life in example, though we are not permitted to see their bodies. It would be tedious and superfluous to dwell on this, for whoever of himself does not think this extreme height of sanctity marvellous and honourable, how could he be brought to see it by my words? Only those deserve a warning who boast of themselves without any reason, that the temperance and continence of the most holy Christians of the Catholic faith have reached such a degree that some think that a check should be put upon it, recalling it, as it were, to human limits. And this judgment is formed by those who, though they do not approve of it, feel that these minds have exceeded human capacity.

"But if anchorets go beyond our power of toleration, who would not admire and proclaim those who despise and relinquish the charms of this world, who pursue together a common life of the utmost purity and holiness, who live in prayer, in study, in mutual discussion, not lifted up by pride, not disturbed by obstinacy, not deranged by jealousy. Full of modest and quiet consideration for others, they lead a life of the utmost concord, intensely fixed on God, an offering most acceptable to Him from whom they have received qualities so precious. No one has anything of his own; no one is a burden to another. They work with their hands what can maintain the body and not impede the mind's approach to God. They give their work to officers called deans, because they are set over ten in number. So no one of them is troubled about his own person as to food, or clothing, or for any other such thing, the need of the day, or indisposition, as it happens. But these deans, who dispose everything with scrupulous care, and have ready whatever that life demands for the body's weakness, give also an account of themselves to one whom they call Father. These Fathers are not only most holy in their conduct, but likewise very excellent in divine doctrine, in everything very high; they consider the good of those whom they call sons without any touch of pride. The authority with which they enjoin is only equalled by the willingness with which they are obeyed. At the last time of day, still fasting, they all come from their dwellings to hear the Father, each of whom has at the least three thousand, for there are instances of much greater numbers. They listen with incredible attention in the utmost silence. As the speaker's words affect them they give expression to their feelings, whether groaning, or weeping, or not disclosing a moderate secret joy. Then they take bodily refreshment so far as sufficient for support and health, each putting a check on his own desire lest he fall with too great readiness on that sparely-given cheap food. Whatever they earn more than the necessary food, and this is very much, arising from their manual labour, and their great moderation in eating, is distributed to those in need with much greater care than they have spent in getting it. For they take no pains to have an abundance, but they do take great pains to keep by them nothing of that abundance, so that they send vessels freighted with it to places which the poor inhabit. In a matter so well known this is enough.

"There is also the life of women serving God carefully in chastity. These, as is fitting, live in separate dwellings removed as far as possible from the other sex, with whom their only union is one of charity and imitation of virtue. Young men have no access to them, nor even the gravest and most approved of old men, who go no farther than the entrance, to supply them with what is absolutely needed. Their exercise and maintenance is by woollen work; they make clothing for the brethren, receiving back from them what is required for food. If I desire to extol such conduct, such a life, such regularity, such an institute, I am not worthy to do it, and moreover fear lest I should seem to think a plain mention of it would fail to please, if over and above simply narrating, I should assume the air of an orator.

"But the goodness of Catholic life is not so restricted that I should confine my praise to the lives of those whom I have mentioned. For how many bishops have I known, most excellent men and most holy, how many presbyters, and how many deacons, and such-like ministers of the divine sacraments, whose virtue appears to me the more admirable, and worthy of greater extolment, because it is more difficult to be preserved in intercourse with a great number, and in a life subject to so much disturbance. They preside over flocks who may be said rather to need healing than to have received it. The vices of the multitude must be suffered in order to be cured, and the pestilence borne before it can be stopped. In such a state it is most difficult to maintain the best mode of life, and a settled and tranquil mind. To explain my meaning shortly, the sphere of the one is laid where life is being taught, of the other where it is attained.

"Nor would I derogate from that laudable race of Christians who live in cities yet most remote from an ordinary life. I have seen a community of saints at Milan composed of a large number. Its superior was an excellent and most learned presbyter; at Rome also I have known several, each having a superior of special gravity, prudence, and divine knowledge. He rules the rest who dwell with him in a life of Christian charity, holiness, and liberty. They are a burden to no one, but maintain themselves by their own handiwork, after the Oriental custom, and by the authority of the Apostle Paul. It came to my knowledge that many exercised quite incredible fastings, not taking refreshment once a day at the approach of night, which is the universal custom, but very often passing three or more days without food or drink. And this was the case not only with men, but also women, where many widows and virgins dwelt together, maintaining themselves by woollen work and spinning. Each house has a Superior of recognised gravity and experience, not only in directing and maintaining good conduct, but of ready skill in the cultivation of mind."[1]

From these words of St. Augustine we learn that the institute of which the first knowledge was brought to Rome by St. Athanasius in 340, which St. Jerome asserts to have been unknown and ignominious in popular opinion when Marcella introduced it among the Roman aristocracy, had become in 388 a well-known practised thing. And St. Augustine's own life shows how powerfully it had affected his own mind. It entered into his conversion with decisive effect. The idea of monastic life formed an inseparable portion of his spiritual being. His first act as a convert was to retire with a few friends into the most hidden privacy. As soon as he became a priest at Hippo, he set up a complete monastic house. When he became bishop, he formed another house of which his own clergy collectively were members. Hardly any one can be found who exerted so great an influence upon his own and subsequent

[1] *De Moribus Ecclesiæ Catholicæ*, lib. i. chap. 31-3.

ages. But not only his dogmatic writings had this effect, he also enriched the Church's life with an institution which, after all the changes through which it has passed, remains to the present day active and efficient. His introduction of monastic life into Hippo decided for Africa, his combination of the clerical and the monastic life for Africa and for Europe. St. Jerome has left us many valuable letters describing how those whose palaces were full of images of consuls, their ancestors, and whose wealth in many lands was princely, had in both sexes embraced lives of poverty and self-denial. A few years after the mention of anchorites and cœnobites given by St. Augustine, that is, in the year 397, Jerome writes with great admiration to his friend Pammachius. Upon the death of his wife, Paulina, herself the daughter of St. Paula, he says, "The Church bore to us Pammachius, instead of a widower a monk, a patrician by the nobility both of his father and his wife, in his almsgivings rich, in his humility sublime. The Apostle writes to the Corinthians, 'You see, brethren, your vocation, how not many are rich, not many noble.' The beginnings of the infant Church required this, that the grain of mustard might grow by degrees into a tree, that the ferment of the gospel might gradually raise the whole mass of the Church. Rome in our times possesses what the world before knew not. Then wise, powerful, noble Christians were few; now there are many monks wise, powerful, noble. My dear Pammachius is more wise, more powerful, more noble, than all of these. He is great among the great, first among the first, commander-in-chief of the monks. Paulina by her death has given us such children as when living she desired to possess. Who would believe this that the descendant of proconsuls, the lustre of the Furian race, should walk among the people of senators in a sorry black cloak, and not be ashamed at the looks his equals cast upon him, but meet their mockery with contempt. 'There is a confusion leading to death, and a confusion leading to life.' It is a monk's first virtue to despise the judgments of men and ever to remember the Apostle's words, 'If I still please men, I should not be the servant of Christ.' Something like this is what the Lord says to the prophets, 'I have made thee this day a fortified city and a pillar of iron, and a wall of brass' (Jer. i. 18), that they might not hear the insults of the people, but subdue the insolence of mockery with the hardness of their faces. A sense of shame is more powerful with cultivated minds than fear, and human respect prevails sometimes where tortures fail. It is not a little thing that one noble, one eloquent, one rich, should turn aside in the streets from the company of the powerful, should mix himself up with a crowd, should be hail-fellow-well-met with the poor, join himself with rustics, and from a prince become a workman. The greater his humility, the greater his grandeur."[1]

At the end of this letter he notes that, as they had built a monastery at Bethlehem in order that, if Joseph and Mary came there again, they might find hospitality, they were flooded with such a multitude of monks coming from all parts of the world, that while they could not desert their work, they knew not how to support it.

We have seen how Athanasius, first by his personal intercourse at Rome, when attended by the monks Ammon and Isidorus, had carried to the West information of the monastic life pursued by so many in Egypt, and then at a later period, when crowned with the authority of a long confessorship, published the biography of St. Antony, and made his manner of life famous through the world. I have given next the attestation of St. Augustine as an eye-witness of this life in the cities of Rome and Milan, and one reference out of very many which St. Jerome affords to its astonishing effect on the Roman nobility in his time. I give now a passage singularly interesting because it narrates the effect of this life on the personal history of one the equal of these three great saints. St. Basil, when Archbishop of Cæsarea in the year 375, that is, two years after the death of St. Athanasius, eleven years before the conversion of St. Augustine, and some years before St. Jerome had yet come into notice, gives in a letter this account of himself: "Having wasted much time in vanity, and lost nearly all my youth in the fruitless labour with which I toiled in the attainment of the acquisitions possessed by the wisdom which God has

[1] St. Jerome, Ep. 66 to Pammachius.

turned to folly, when at length, like one waking out of a deep sleep, I looked upon the marvellous light of truth in the Gospel, I perceived the uselessness of the wisdom which the rulers of this world, who come to nought, have got, and greatly did I lament my miserable life. But I begged for guidance to be given me into the doctrines of piety. Above all, I longed for an improvement in the moral habit so long perverted by intercourse with those whose standard (φαυλους) was false. When, then, I read the Gospel, and found there that the selling of one's goods helped very greatly to perfection, and the giving to brethren who were in want, and generally absence of solicitude for this life, and the soul's exemption from affection for temporal things, I tried to find some brother who had chosen this course of life, to pass together with him the brief tossing of its unquiet waves. Now, many such I found in Alexandria, many in the rest of Egypt, others in Palestine, in Coelé-Syria, and Mesopotamia. I admired their abstinence in food, their endurance in labour. I was amazed at their perseverance in prayer; how, yielding to no physical necessity, they overmastered sleep; how they preserved the spirit in its height and freedom during hunger and thirst, cold and nakedness, not regarding the body, not spending on it any care, but as living in a flesh which was not their own. They showed what it is in reality to be pilgrims here, what to have your conversation in heaven. Admiring these things, and esteeming the life of such men blessed, who show in reality that they carry about in the body the mortification of Jesus, I wished myself, as far as I could, to be the imitator of those men."[1]

Basil himself was every way as real as those whom he thus praises, and whose manner of life so attracted him. Twenty years before he wrote these words, when he was about twenty-five himself, he had left Athens, after mastering Greek literature, which he calls the wisdom of those who were perverted in their standard of right and wrong. Then it was that he travelled and saw in the countries which he mentions so many religious houses set up after the pattern of those in Egypt. His friend Gregory writes of that time: "We had even been advanced by the science

[1] Ep. 223.

of the heathen in the fear of God, since through the knowledge of the less good we reached the better, and made out of their impotence a support of our own belief." Basil gave up his profession as a teacher of literature, and followed the example of his mother and his sister Macrina. He resigned most of his fortune to the poor, and lived in a monastery near his relations with Gregory. They pursued the strictest ascetic life, after the pattern of the Fathers of the Desert. He founded several monasteries, in which he united the anchoretic with the cœnobitic discipline. Thus he introduced the monastic life in Pontus and Cappadocia, and from him dates the Basilian order still followed in the Greek Church. In this work a period of seven years passed, in which the friends were given up to study as well as to the ascetic life, and both became great defenders of the Church's doctrine against the Arian heresy. When Valens used for fourteen years, from 364 to 378, the imperial power in the East to persecute the Catholics, he found no more intrepid opponents than Basil and Gregory, and none more devoted to the monastic life.

The character of St. Basil's own life, and of that monastic life which he did his utmost to foster, and of which he stands out through all the centuries as one of the chief supporters, is conveyed most perfectly in his own words, which he terms a picture of the ascetic discipline:[1]—

"There is honour in the edicts of a king to his subjects; greater and more royal his commands to his soldiers. Listen, then, as to military commands, whoever desires a great supernal dignity, to be for ever by the side of Christ, to hear that great voice, 'If any one will be My disciple, let him follow Me, and where I am there let My disciple be.' Where is Christ the King? In heaven. Thither, O soldier, it is thine to direct thy course. Forget all rest upon earth. No soldier builds him a house, nor acquires lands, nor involves himself in various traffics producing money. 'No man being a soldier entangleth himself with secular businesses, that he may please him to whom he has engaged himself.' The soldier has provision from the king; he needs not to provide provision for himself. His time is

[1] S. Basilii, ἀσκητικὴ προδιατύπωσις, tom. ii. 199-202.

not to be given to this. Everywhere by the king's command the subjects find him a house. He has not to labour for a house. His place of acting is in the street: his food is taken at need, his drink is water, his sleep what nature requires. He has to travel, to watch perpetually. He has to endure heat and frost. He has to fight the enemy. His dangers have no end; the risks of death are many. But death is glorious; his honours, the gifts made him, royal. The life is laborious in war-time, splendid in peace. The honour of his rank, the crown of his successes, is to be intrusted with rule, to be called the king's friend, to be at his side, to receive welcome, to be honoured by the king's hand, to be pre-eminent among his subjects, to gain for friends their requests.

"Well, then, soldier of Christ, take some small example from human things. Consider everlasting goods. Set before thee a life houseless, cityless, landless; be free, delivered from all worldly cares. Let not desire of woman captivate thee, nor thought of child; in the divine army that is impossible, for 'the weapons of our warfare are not carnal, but mighty to God' (2 Cor. x. 4). A bodily nature does not conquer thee, nor strangle thee against thy will, makes thee not a prisoner for a freeman, seeks not to leave children on earth, but to carry them up to heaven; not to cling to corporeal embraces, but to desire spiritual, to rule souls and have spiritual offspring. Imitate the Heavenly Bridegroom; sweep away the assaults of invisible foes; fight 'with principalities and powers;' drive them out first from thine own soul, that they may have no portion in thee, then from those who fly to thee, who hold thee as the leader and champion of those whom thy words protect. Pull down reasonings that rise up against the faith of Christ; battle through the true doctrine against the impious and wicked argument, destroying, he saith, 'counsels and every height that exalteth itself against the knowledge of God' (2 Cor. x. 5). And trust most of all in the King's strong hand, which by its sole appearance routs opponents. And when it is His will that thou become through dangers valiant, and that His own army should engage the army of the adversary, then be thou invincible in thy preparation against every labour, immovable in spirit against danger. Go readily from land to land, from sea to sea; for He says, 'When they pursue you, fly from city to city, and when called before the tribunal and to stand before rulers, and to bear the attacks of multitudes, and to meet the fierce look of the headsman, and to hear the harsh voice, and to stand the hard sight of instruments of torture, and to be tried by torments, and to contend unto death, turn not away from all these, having before your eyes Christ, who was in these things for you, knowing that for Christ's sake you are to be in these things and conquer in them. For you follow a conquering King, who wills you to be partaker of His conquest; for in death you were not overcome, but then most completely conquered, preserving the truth for yourself unchangeable to the end, and holding unshaken the freedom which belongs to the truth.

"And from death you will go to eternal life, from dishonour before men to glory before God, from tribulation and suffering in the world to everlasting rest with the angels. Earth would not have you for a citizen, heaven welcomes you; the world rejected you, the angels bear you in their arms to present you to Christ. You shall be called His friend, and hear the praise so longed after: 'Good and faithful servant, noble soldier and imitator of thy Lord, companion of the King, I will reward thee with My gifts, I will listen to thy words as thou hast listened to Mine.' You will ask for the salvation of afflicted brethren, and will receive from the King for the sharers of your faith and the fellow-disciples of holy charity the joint possession of blessings. You will be one in those unending choirs; you will share the crown of angels, reigning over creation under the King, and passing a blessed eternity together with the blessed host. But if it please Him to leave thee upon earth after thy conflicts, to engage in still more conflicts, various in their kind, and to save many out of visible and invisible battles, great will be thy glory even upon earth, and amongst thy friends thou wilt be honoured, who have found thee a defender, a helper, a good intercessor; they will cherish thee as a valiant soldier, honour thee as a noble chief, grasp hold of thee, and welcome thee with joy as an angel of God—in Paul's words, as Jesus Christ: such-like are the examples of divine warfare. Nor do these words belong only to men; the female sex also is marshalled by Christ for spiritual valour in His army. It is not rejected for bodily weakness. Many women have excelled not less than men; some have surpassed them: of such are those who fill the choir of virgins; of such those who shine in the conflicts of confession and in the victories of martyrdom. Not men only, but women also, followed the Lord when 'He appeared, and the service of both was performed to the Saviour. Such being the rewards laid up for Christian warfare, let fathers think of them for sons and mothers for daughters. Let them bring their offspring, rejoicing over the eternal hopes which their children will share with them, desiring to have them for patrons and intercessors. Let us not be faint-hearted about our children, nor fear labours for them, but rejoice for their being glorified. Let us present to the Lord His own gifts, that we may share the good report of our children, offering and presenting ourselves with them. To combatants thus zealous the words of the Psalmist might be applied, 'Blessed are you of the Lord who made heaven and earth,' and as Moses prays, 'Bless, O Lord, their works, and strike the backs of their enemies.' Be men, fight nobly, run fairly the course for the eternal crowns in Christ Jesus our Lord, to whom be glory for ever."

We will add here what he says concerning the demeanour which becomes a monk:[1]—

"First and chiefest of all a monk must possess nothing. His body must be in solitude, his dress seemly, his voice measured, his word well ordered. He must be untroubled as to meat and drink, and eat in quiet; silent before elders; a listener to men wiser than himself; he must feel charity towards equals; be of kindly instruction to inferiors; avoid the evil, the carnal, and busybodies. Let him think much and speak little; not be confident in assertion, nor abundant in discourse, nor ready for laughing. Let modesty be his adornment, his eye cast down, his soul raised up, not engaging in contradictions. In temper compliant; labouring

[1] πῶς δεῖ κοσμεῖσθαι τὸν μοναχόν, tom. ii. 211.

with the hands; ever to bear in mind the last things. Rejoicing in hope; patient in affliction; praying without ceasing. Giving thanks for everything; humble towards all; hateful of arrogance. Watching and guarding the heart from bad thoughts. Laying up treasure in heaven by fulfilling commandments. Examining self in daily thoughts and actions; not to be involved in businesses and vain talkings; not to be curious about the lives of the negligent, but zealous about the lives of the holy fathers. To rejoice with the upright, and not envy; to sympathise and mourn with the suffering; to grieve greatly with them, but not to condemn them. Not to reproach one who turns away from sin. Never to justify himself; to confess himself a sinner before all men, in the sight of God and man. To admonish the disordered; to encourage the low-spirited; to serve the helpless; to wash the feet of the saints; to practise hospitality and brotherly kindness. To be at peace with the household of faith; to turn away from a heretic. To read the canonical books; not to touch the apocryphal. Not to question of the Father, the Son, and the Holy Ghost, but freely to profess and hold the uncreated and consubstantial Trinity, and to say to those who ask, 'We should be baptized as we have received, and believe as we have been baptized, and glorify as we have believed.' To be well employed in word and deed. To make oath not at all; not to lend money at usury; not to make profit by dealing in corn, wine, and oil. To abstain from inordinate food and drink and worldly cares. To have no part with deceit, nor to speak against any one. Not to detract, nor listen with pleasure to detraction. Not easily to believe against any one. Not to be ruled by anger. Not to be governed by desire. Not rashly to be angry with your neighbour; not to hold wrath against any one. Not to return evil for evil. To be spoken ill of rather than to speak ill; to be beaten rather than to beat; to be wronged rather than to wrong; to suffer rather than to inflict loss.

"Especially a monk must avoid contact with women and with wine, since wine and women will lead even those who understand to apostasy. And one that, to the best of his power, is fulfilling the commandments of the Lord must not despond, but expect reward and praise from Him, and long for the enjoyment of eternal life, and keep ever before his eyes the saying of David, 'I set the Lord always in my sight, for He is at my right hand that I be not moved.' And as a son, with all his heart and strength and mind and might, should love God; and as a servant should reverence, and fear, and obey Him, and with fear and trembling work out his own salvation. To be burning in spirit, clothed with all the armour of the Holy Spirit; to run not uncertainly; to fight not as one beating the air; to overcome the enemy with the body's infirmity and the soul's poverty. To fulfil all the commandments, and call himself unprofitable. To give thanks to the holy, glorious, and terrible God, and to do nothing out of strife and vainglory, but for God and to please Him. For 'God hath scattered the bones of them that please men.' Altogether not to boast, nor speak praises of one's self, nor be pleased when others praise. But to do all services in secret, and not for the sight of men, but only to seek the praise of God, and to bear in mind His fearful and glorious advent, the transposition hence, the goods that are laid up for the just, and equally the fire that is prepared for the devil and his angels. And in all this to remember the apostle's word, that 'the sufferings of this time are not worthy to be compared with the glory to come, which shall be revealed in us.' And to say with David, 'In keeping His commandments there is great reward,' a vast retribution, crowns of justice, eternal habitations, endless life, joy unspeakable, an indissoluble dwelling with the Father, and the Son, and the Holy Ghost, the true God in heaven. The manifestation of face to face. To join the choirs of angels, of fathers, of patriarchs, of prophets, of apostles, of martyrs, of confessors, of those eternally pleasing to God. With these be it our care to be found, by the grace of our Lord Jesus Christ, to whom be glory and power for ever and ever."

St. Basil in all his ways had followed the example of his Lord. He began "to do and to teach." The character which he has thus drawn out in words he had first accomplished in deed. The woods and streams of Pontus had beheld him for years pursuing, with his bosom friend Gregory, the labours of the monastic life, with the study of the divine science. Borne in spite of himself to the bishop's office in a great city, he had shown himself the ruler of men; a quarter of his episcopal city, filled with the great structures which he was able to draw from the love of his people, bore in remembrance of its author the name Basilias. The chief minister of the Arian tyrant sought to overcome him with threats, but was forced to admit to his master that he had utterly failed. On the death of St. Athanasius, Basil became the chief leader of the Eastern bishops. We possess from his hand the most startling narrative[1] of their sufferings and their weaknesses. His short pontificate was closed before he was fifty, but he lived long enough to gain imperishable glory by his actions and his writings, and not the least as the standard at once of episcopal life and monastic asceticism.

When Basil and Gregory were students together at Athens, they came in contact with Julian, then a prince of the imperial family. A few years afterwards, when Julian had become first Cæsar and then Augustus, had thrown off the profession of the Christian faith, and bitterly persecuted it, and then, after a short rule of twenty months, had come to an untimely end, Gregory in a sermon recording his deeds contrasted the heathen greatness which Julian had admired with the monastic life which he had scorned.[2] "See you these men who are without the enjoyments of life, who have no hearth, who are almost without flesh and blood, and in virtue of this near to God. These men who wash not their feet and sleep on the ground, as your Homer says, to honour some demon by his figment.[3] These men, low in position, high in thought, human yet above human things, in fetters and yet free; who suffer mastery, yet are unmastered; who have nothing in the world, yet all things above the world; whose life is double, the one life despised, the other sedulously pursued. They who by mortification become immortal, by dissolution are united with God. They who are void of desire, but full of divine and passionless love. With whom

---

[1] In his ninety-second letter, quoted vol. v. p. 231.
[2] St. Greg. Naz. Orat. 4, tom. i. 110.
[3] Referring to Iliad 16, 236: Σοὶ ναίουσ' ὑποφῆται ἀνιπτόποδες, χαμαιεῦναι.

is the fountain of light, and they irradiated with its beams. Who have the angelic psalmistries, the all-night watching, the mind already ravished in ecstasy to God, who purify themselves and are pure, and know not any measure of the mind's ascent and deification. Who dwell among rocks, and have the heavens for their portion. Who are rejected, and sit on thrones. Who are in nakedness, and wear the raiment of incorruption. Who have the desert and the angelic company which springs from it; who subdue their pleasures, and have the indissoluble 'unspeakable enjoyment; whose tears dissolve sin and purify the world. The stretching forth of whose hands quenches fire, pacifies wild beasts, blunts the sword, puts to flight armies, and will even rebuke, be assured of it, thine impiety though for a moment thou art exalted, and playest out thy fable of wickedness with thy demons."

Gregory also was a man of deeds as well as words, who spent his early manhood with Basil in Pontus in monastic severity; who by his eloquence raised up the sinking Catholics in his little Church of the Resurrection in Constantinople; who, unable to overcome the party spirit of the bishops around him, descended from the throne to which he had been elected by them, and spent his last years in private solitude.

The third glory of Cappadocia, St. Gregory, Bishop of Nyssa, brother of St. Basil, and friend of St. Gregory of Nazianzum, the equal of both in rank as author, among his many writings composed about the year 370 in solitude a treatise on Virginity, or the state of perfection. I transcribe one of the twenty-four chapters as a passage revealing the whole mind of a great Father. The title of this chapter runs, "Virginity the special beauty of the divine and incorporeal nature."[1] "Need have we of great understanding to know this superlative grace, which enters into the praise of the incorruptible Father. Strange indeed it is that virginity should be found in a Father who has a Son, and who begets without passion. It is comprehended in conjunction with the only-begotten God, the bestower of incorruption, since it shines forth as a part of His pure and passionless genera-

[1] St. Greg. Orat. 4, tom. i. 110.

tion. Again, a Son conceived through virginity is equally
strange. It is beheld alike in the physical and incorruptible
purity of the Holy Spirit. For if you name purity and incorruption, it is another name for virginity. It dwells with
the whole celestial nature being present with the superemi-
nent powers through their passionlessness. It is not severed
from any one of the divine powers, nor does it belong to
any one of the opposite powers. For all which by nature
or by purpose tend to virtue exult in the purity of incorruption; and all which converge to the opposing rank are such,
and are so called, by their lapse from purity. What power
of words, then, will be sufficient to equal such a grace? Or
how should one not fear lest through zeal of praising, injury
should be done to the height of dignity by imprinting on
the hearers an opinion lower than their previous conception.
It were well then to avoid encomiums here, since there is
no means of raising language to the height of such a subject.
But it is possible ever to bear in mind the gift of God, and
to have on the tongue the blessing which is the choice
peculiarity of the incorporeal nature.[1] But it has been
given by the loving-kindness of God to those who have
received life through flesh and blood; so that virginity,
when human nature was cast down through a constitution
subject to passion, stretching forth as it were a hand which
partook of purity, should raise it again and guide it to look
upwards. For this reason I conceive the fountain of incorruption, our Lord Jesus Christ Himself, did not through
marriage enter into the world, that He might manifest this
great mystery by the manner of His incarnation, that purity
alone is able to receive the approach and presence of God.
For this purity cannot be reached in absolute perfection
unless one sever himself entirely from affections of the
flesh. For that which took place bodily in the spotless Mary,
when the fulness of the Godhead in Christ shone through
the Virgin in its radiance, this takes place in every soul
which, by the direction of reason, maintains virginity: the
Lord no more makes a bodily presence, for He says we no
longer 'know Christ according to the flesh;' but He enters
in spirit, and brings together with Him His Father, as the

[1] τῇ τοῦ θεοῦ λατρεία σοξῆν.

Gospel says. Since, then, so great is the power of virginity as to remain in heaven with the Father of spirits, and to exult among the celestial powers, and to take a part in human salvation, bringing down God through it to the communion of human life, and by it giving man wings for the desire of heavenly things, and clasping, as it were, God and man together, who in virtue are so far apart, by its mediation making harmony between them, what power of words can be found to reach this marvel? But since it would be absurd to appear altogether voiceless and insensible, and one of two things must happen, either to seem not conscious of the beauty of virginity, or to show oneself without touch or motion to the perception of beauty, I have been minded to speak briefly about it, because it is my duty in all things to obey the authority of Him who commands us. Let no one seek from me boastful words. Perhaps if I wished to give them it would be beyond my power, being inexperienced in such speaking. But, had I the power to boast, I should not prefer reputation among a few to that which would be of general use; for one of any sense should, I think, seek most of all not the things at which the few will wonder, but the things which may benefit both himself and others."

St. Basil, his brother, and his friend, the triple passion-flower of their province in the company of Fathers, are entirely of one mind in their praise and esteem of the monastic life. They have not only the common gift of genius, but they lived the life which they praised, and suffered for the faith which they upheld.

Another name there is in the Eastern episcopate before the end of the same fourth century fit to range with St. Athanasius, St. Basil, St. Gregory of Nazianzan, and St. Gregory of Nyssa, one whose youth had been passed during several years in monastic severity, who then became the chosen preacher of a great capital, surpassing all men in his eloquence, and who was at last carried away by the court of the East through the admiration which he had inspired, and against his will placed on that dangerous throne of the East, where he had to exercise spiritual rule in a city the very centre of social corruption, as it was the seat of absolute power. It remains to add the judgment of St. Chrysostom concerning the life to which he was no stranger. He thus enters on a comparison of royal power with the life of Christian philosophy:[1]—

"Beholding that the mass of men love and admire what seems to be good rather than what is really serviceable and truly good, I think it needful to say a few words on both, and to put side by side that which the many neglect, and that which they zealously pursue. So, by seeing the difference between them, we may value the things worthy of our zeal and learn to despise the other as worthless. Wealth and power, and rule and glory, are loved. Most men felicitate the governors of nations, who ride in splendid chariots, are proclaimed by heralds, and encompassed with guards, but despise the life of those who pursue wisdom, and have chosen the monastic life. When these appear, they turn the eyes of the people on them; when the others show themselves, they draw the eyes of none or of very few. No one wishes to be like the one; all to be like the other. Yet it is hard, and for most men impossible, to acquire dominion and the government of nations. The lovers of empire would require vast wealth, while it is ready and easy for all to choose the monastic discipline, and to live in and by the adoration of God.[2] And the acquisition of empire perishes with this life, or rather deserts its lovers while they still live, and has already carried many into great danger or disgrace. But the monastic life, while it fills the just with many blessings at present, leads them after the end of this life, bright and rejoicing, to the tribunal of our God and Father, whereas the majority of rulers will be found suffering great penalties for their deeds in life. Place, then, side by side the goods which the pursuit of wisdom brings, and the seeming goods of rule and glory in this present life. Let us examine the difference of both. When they stand side by side that will be more plain; or, if you will, put royalty, the height of blessings, by the side of the lover of wisdom; look at the fruits of each possession, and accurately distinguish what things the king

[1] St. Chrysostom, i. 116–121.
[2] τῇ τοῦ θεοῦ λατρείᾳ συζῆν.

rules over, and what the lover of wisdom. The king has authority over cities and countries, and many races; at his bidding stand generals and prefects, armies, assemblies, and senates. He who has given himself to God and chosen the monastic life has subdued anger, and envy, and avarice, and pleasure, and the other ills. He is ever watching and studying not to yield his soul to the dominion of disgraceful passions, nor his reason to the slavery of a bitter subjection, but to keep his mind ever superior, imposing the fear of God on his passions. This, then, is the domain and empire possessed respectively by the king and by the monk. It would, then, be more just to call the latter the king rather than the one shining in purple, crowned and seated on a golden throne.

"For he is most truly a king who is master of anger, and envy, and pleasure, who brings all his actions under the law of God, who keeps his mind in freedom, and does not permit the despotism of pleasure to enthral his soul. Such a one I would willingly see ruling over peoples, and land, and sea, and cities, and assembled crowds, and armies. For he who has set reason over the passions of the soul can easily use the divine laws to rule men, so that those he governs should esteem him as a father, when, with gentle sway, he appears in their cities. But he who seems to rule men while he is the slave of anger, love of rule and pleasure, appears ridiculous to his subjects, as wearing, indeed, an inlaid crown of gold, but not crowned with temperance; his body shining with purple, his soul devoid of beauty. Moreover, he will not know how to manage government, for since he cannot govern himself, how can he make others obedient to law? And if you would see the battle which each has, you will find the one encountering demons, showing strength, gaining victory, crowned by Christ; for with divine aid he advances to the conflict, clothed with celestial armour, so that he must prevail; whereas the king fights with barbarians; and as demons are more terrible than men, he who conquers them is the greater victor. If you look at the cause of the conflicts, great is the difference. The one fights with demons for piety and the adoration of God, or to rescue villages and cities from the dominion of error; the other fights barbarians for the loss of fortresses, for territory, for money. Covetousness or attachment to an unjust rule is the incentive. Many kings have many a time, through a desire to become greater, lost what they had. Their government, then, and their wars, show the king and the man bent on making the adoration of God his life to be thus widely different from each other. This would be seen in detail by observing the life of each and their daily actions. One would be found conversing with prophets, making the wisdom of Paul the beauty of his soul, passing perpetually from Moses to Isaias, from Isaias to John, from John to another. The king would be found in constant intercourse with commanders, and prefects, and guards. But the character is fashioned by those with whom we have daily intercourse. The solitary, then, is already forming his mind after apostles and prophets; the king, after generals, officers, and attendants, men given to drink, ministers of pleasure, passing the greater part of the day at the banquet, which prevents them from knowing anything good or opportune. For this also, then, the monastic life is to be esteemed, rather than one spent in sovereignty and dominion.

"If we were to examine how the night is spent, we should see the monk devoting himself to prayer and adoration earlier than the birds in song, with angels for his companions, with God in converse, enjoying heavenly goods. We should find the ruler of nations, assemblies, and armies, whose sway extends over land and sea, stretched in stertorous sleep. The monk feeds on food which does not require deep slumber. The king is put to sleep in luxury, with potions which keep him in bed to full day. The monk is moderate, both in clothing and at table, and his comrades emulate his virtue in this. The king must be set off with gold and jewels, must have a splendid table; and for guests, if he be foolish, men worthy of his own badness; if a man of sense and temperance, perhaps they will be good and just, but far behind the excellence of those others. If the king practise the love of wisdom, he cannot approach near the high standard of the monk. In his journeys he is oppressive to his subjects; in his city life in peace, in his wars he is an exacter of taxes, a levyer of armies; he makes captives; he is a conqueror; he is defeated. When defeated, he fills those whom he rules with his own evils; when a conqueror, he becomes unbearable, boasting his trophies, high-minded, giving his soldiers permission to seize, to plunder, to wrong travellers, to besiege cities, to sack the poor man's home, to exact from those who receive them every day what no law sanctions, on pretext of some ancient custom contrary to law and justice. It is not the rich man whom the king hurts by these evils; it is poverty which he makes suffer, as if he reverenced in truth the wealthy. Not so the monk. At once, on his appearance, he has something good for both equally. He has one garment in the year; he drinks water more readily than others the finest wine. For himself he asks nothing, great or small; from the rich, for those in want he asks much and often, in which he benefits both those who give and those who receive. Thus he is a physician equally for rich and poor, healing the sins of the one by his good advice, and delivering the other from their wants. But when the king lessens the taxes, he helps the rich rather than the poor; when he increases them, he hurts the small possessors. The hardness of the taxes affects the rich man slightly, but like a torrent he sweeps away the houses of the poor, filling the villages with wailing. Tax-gatherers have no pity on old age, nor widowhood, nor orphanage. Their revel is continual; common enemies of the country, they take from the cultivators of the land what it never produced.

"But what advantage respectively are the king and the monk to their several subjects? The one gives worldly goods, the other spiritual grace. The one, if he be good, releases from poverty; the other by his prayers delivers souls from demoniacal tyranny. If any one be tossed by storms of this kind, he passes by the king as he would lifeless objects, and flies for refuge to the monk's dwelling, as a man pursued by a wolf takes refuge with a hunter though he be sword in hand. What the sword is to the hunter, prayer is to the monk. Wolves do not fear the sword so much as demons fear the prayers of the just. And it is not only we who in our needs fly to the holy monks, but kings themselves in moments of alarm fly to them, as in a famine the poor beset the houses of the rich. Did not the Jewish king Ahab, in a time of famine and dearth, place his hope of preservation in the prayers of Elias? Did not Hezekias, who held the same sovereign power, ill and at the point of death, seeing decease imminent, fly to the prophet, as more powerful than death, and having the gift of life? Even when war had broken out, and Palestine was in danger of being torn up by the roots, the kings of the Jews, disregarding the army, footmen, and bowmen and horsemen, commanders and captains, take refuge in the prayers of Elisæus? For they thought that the servant of God would count to them for many thousands. Hezekias also, when the Persian war had broken out, and the city was shaken to its very foundations, and those on the ramparts were trembling and shaking, as expecting a storm or the overthrow of an earthquake, the king set the prayers of Isaias against the many thousands of Persians, and was not deceived in his hope. The prophet raised his hands to heaven, and God at once scattered the Persian host by bolts from heaven, teaching kings to account His servants the common saviours of the land, that they might learn, when invited by the just, to reverence their advice for every good and merciful action and to yield to their admonition. By this we may see the difference of the two. And further, even should both fail, and the one lose his virtue and the other his kingdom, in this case the former will recover himself, and speedily wipe away his sins by prayer and tears and sorrow and tending the poor, and so before long mount again to his former height. But if the king be cast out, he will require many allies, infantry and cavalry, horses and wealth, and hazardous chances; and, in a word, his hope of safety lies in others. But the monk has a speedy hope of safety which follows upon counsel and diligence and change of mind; for, He says, the kingdom of heaven is within you. Moreover, death to the king is fearful, to the lover of wisdom is painless. For he who despises wealth and pleasure and luxury, for which most men desire life, must easily bear the removal hence. And if the one and the other were killed, the monk will embrace danger for the sake of piety, reaching through death an everlasting heavenly life; but the king will have in his slaughterer one in love with his rule, and be, when he is dead, a sad and sorry sight, whereas the sight of a monk who has died for his piety is sweet and salutary. The monk will have many lovers and imitators of his good things, many disciples praying to be like him; the king will spend many words in praying to God that no one may arise in love with his kingdom. No one would wish to kill the one, deeming it an impiety against God if he were to kill such a man, but many destroyers beset the other, in love with unbounded power. The one has a guard of soldiers; the other, fearing no man, fortifies cities with prayer. The king has fear and dread of murder for the companion of his life, for he bears about with him danger in the coveting of others, as the monk bears a fearless security. This is sufficient for their state in this life. If we would look farther into the future conflict, we shall see the one carried bright and conspicuous into the clouds to meet the Lord in the air, after the pattern of the leader and institutor of this life, which bears salvation and all virtue; but the king, should he have administered his rule with justice and loving-kindness, which is a great rarity, will have salvation with a lower rank of honour. For it is not equal to be a good king, and to be a monk living with the highest adoration of God. But if he should appear to have been wicked and malevolent, one who has filled his land with many evils, who can express the miseries which he will be seen to have met, burning, scourged and tortured, suffering things unspeakable, unendurable. When we think over and know all this, we should not admire the rich, for he that has been the lord of these cannot the least approach the virtue of the monk. When, then, you see a rich man in magnificent clothing, arrayed in gold, borne in a chariot in stately procession, do not think him happy. The wealth is transitory, the seeming splendour perishes with this life. When you see the monk walking alone, humble, meek, quiet, and gentle, strive to be like him, imitate his practice of loving wisdom, pray to be near him in justice. For the words are, "Ask, and it shall be given you." For these things are really beautiful; they bring salvation and they endure through the loving-kindness and providence of Christ, to whom be glory and might for ever and ever."

Equal in dignity to Chrysostom as bishop of the great city Milan, and one of the four Western doctors, as he was one of the four Eastern, St. Ambrose was in front of those who cherished the monastic institute at its first introduction into Italy. In his treatise on virginity, he records for us how he was wont to dwell with his sister Marcellina on the day of her profession. "It is time," he says, "sister, to consider those precepts of Liberius of blessed memory, often repeated by you to me; for the holier the speaker, the dearer his words. For when on Christmas day, at the Apostle Peter's, you marked your profession of the virginal life by also changing your dress, in the presence of a large number of girls dedicated to God, who would be rivals to each other in your society, 'My daughter,' he said, 'it is a happier marriage which you have desired. You see how many have assembled for the birthday of your Bridegroom,[1] and no one goes away without his share of the feast. He it is who, when invited to the marriage feast, turned the water into wine. On you also He will confer the unblemished sacrament of virginity: on you, who before were exposed to the vile elements of material nature. He it is who fed four thousand people in the desert with five loaves and two fishes. More He could have fed had there been more present to feed. Moreover, He has invited many to your marriage; but it is not now wheaten bread, but His Body from heaven which is dispensed.

"'On this day He was, according to human nature, a man born of a virgin, but begotten before all things of the Father. In His body He represented His mother; in his power the Father. The only-begotten on earth, the only-begotten in heaven, God of God, and offspring of the Virgin; Justice from the Father, Power from the Powerful, Light of Light; not unequal to the Begetter, not separate in power, not suffering confusion by an extension or production of the Word, as if mixed up with the Father, but distinct from the Father by his generation. He, without whom neither things in heaven, nor in the seas, nor on

[1] Ambrosius de Virginibus, lib. iii. c. 1, tom. II, p. 174.

earth consist, is thine in brotherhood. The good Word of the Father, "which was," he says, "in the beginning;" here you have His eternity: and was, he says, "with the Father;" here you have His power unsevered and inseparable from the Father: "and the Word was God;" here you have His unbegotten Godhead. Take this short summary of the faith.

"'This is He whom thou must love, my daughter, for He is good. "None is good but God alone" (Luke xviii. 19); for if there is no doubt that He is God the Son, and God is good, certainly there is no doubt that God is a good Son. Him, I say, do thou love. He it is whom the Father begot "before the daystar," as being eternal; begot from his womb as the Son; brought forth from his heart as the Word. It is He in whom the Father "is well pleased." He is the Father's arm, because He is the Creator of all things; He is the Father's wisdom, because He proceeds from the mouth of God; He is the Father's power, because the fulness of the Godhead dwells in Him bodily. Whom the Father so loves that He carries Him in His bosom, that He places Him at His right hand, in order that you may learn wisdom, may know power.

"'If, then, Christ be the power of God, is God ever without power? Is the Father ever without the Son? If certainly He is ever Father, certainly ever is the Son. Therefore He is perfect Son of perfect Father; for whoever takes from His power takes from Him whose power He is. Perfect Godhead does not admit inequality, therefore love thou Him whom the Father loves; honour Him whom the Father honours, for "he who honoureth not the Son honoureth not the Father; and he who denieth the Son, neither hath the Father" (John v. 23).'" There follow abundant directions to Marcellina respecting her life as a nun; to practise great moderation in food, taking wine only for the sake of her health; to see very few persons; to keep silence; "for if women are commanded to be silent in the church even as to divine things, and to be informed by their husbands in the privacy of home, what caution do we think should be used in the case of virgins, in whom modesty is the ornament of their time of life, while silence is a safeguard of modesty."

Then St. Ambrose, addressing his sister, says, "These words Liberius of holy memory used to you; in the case of others such words were not borne out by facts, but in you they were surpassed by them, for your virtue not only reached the utmost extent of discipline, but even surpassed it." His treatise bears the date of A.D. 377, and so he speaks of Pope Liberius eleven years after his death as a holy pontiff. In the same year his great colleague, St. Basil, in his 264th letter,[1] speaks of the injunctions laid upon Eustathius, Bishop of Sebaste in Armenia, "by the most blessed Bishop Liberius" (tom. ii. 406). St. Epiphanius speaks of him in the like terms, and Pope Siricius, his next successor after Pope Damasus, writing to a Spanish bishop, speaks of "the general decrees sent to the provinces by Liberius, my predecessor of venerable memory, after annulling the Council of Rimini." It is a special providence of God to have preserved to us by St. Ambrose the words of a Pope solemnly receiving a nun's profession in St. Peter's about the year 362. They show that twenty years after the visit of St. Athanasius, a point of time at which the monastic life at Rome was yet a novelty, it had become an established institution, embraced by a daughter of one who had lately died pretorian prefect of the Gauls and Spain. At the time of her embracing it she had already many companions in it, while general rules concerning it were laid down by the Pope, and she as a nun recognised by him as the bride of Christ; to which we may add, that four bishops of the highest character for orthodoxy in the fourth century, all contemporaries and one a successor of Pope Liberius, attest after his death the unblemished character which he bore in the See of Rome, for what is attested by Basil, Ambrose, Epiphanius, and Siricius is surely an unimpeachable fact.

I would here add the testimony of one who, from the time of his death to the present day, has had a name of singular authority and attraction in the Gallic episcopate, St. Martin, Bishop of Tours.[2] The first monasteries founded

---

[1] St. Basil, Ep. 264; St. Epiphanius, Hæresi., 25, c. 7; St. Siricius, Ep. 1 ad Himerium: "post cassatum Ariminense Concilium missa ad provincias a venerandæ memoriæ prædecessore meo Liberio generalia decreta."

[2] Translated from Möhler, *Mönchthum*, pp. 191-192.

upon strict rules, so far as history can show, are those set up by him at Ligugé, near Poitiers, and then near Tours, which became the famous house of Marmoutier. This he raised shortly after he came to the episcopal chair in Tours, A.D. 371–372. The history of St. Martin especially shows how strong the inclination to the monastic life burst out in all classes of society, even where no germ of it appeared to have been dropped beforehand. He was the son of a tribune in the imperial army, and, moreover, of a father devoted to the heathen gods, who died in their service, though the Christian faith had come near him in most attractive guise. Yet Martin, in spite of every hindrance, opened for himself a way to the lofty purpose which he had set before him. In his tenth year he withdrew from his father's house to offer himself to the priests as a Christian nursling. Life then, as is the case in all transition times, was full of contradictions, which appeared in strongest form exactly where the bonds of nature touch most nearly, and divine and human laws concur in maintaining the most perfect union. The first violent solution of a painful contradiction was quickly followed by another. An uncontrollable eagerness for the monastic life awoke in him, while the laws compelled him, as the son of a veteran, to military service. The father's interest could easily have procured a remission of what the law required, but the father, who was unwilling to see his son a Christian, could much less endure to have a son who was a monk. So Martin found himself compelled in his fifteenth year to take service in the cavalry, and we see the most perfect opposition in one who is monk in heart and soldier in outward guise; yet it was only the monk and the soldier who were in opposition, not the soldier and the Christian. The virtues of the Christian he exercised incomparably in the soldier, and far from becoming an object of derision among his comrades, he obtained the esteem and love of them all. Especially noted was his sympathy with suffering. He once in a great frost met a half-clothed man; many that were well off passed him by unregarded. Martin's heart was touched at the sight of him, and as he could help him in no other way, he divided his cloak with him.

In 356, when he obtained release from the army, he showed a most praiseworthy though a fruitless courage in the spiritual contest called forth by the Arian troubles. Then he withdrew into ascetic quiet at Milan. There also he was persecuted, and retired to the island of Capraria. Then he attached himself to St. Hilary of Poitiers, and with his help founded Ligugé and then Marmoutier. He was, in truth, a man of mind, one of the most distinguished, the most amiable, and powerful bishops whom Gaul has ever produced, equally honoured by the great and powerful of the land and by the people. If a man so esteemed recommended the monastic life, it obtained an immovable basis, since no man doubted that he was a chosen instrument of the Lord. His funeral was celebrated by two thousand monks, though before him no monastery had been founded in Gaul. Sulpicius Severus was his devoted pupil, and described his ascetic life.[1] In a few years this Life became known in every province of the Christian Church. Sulpicius completely shared the feelings of Martin as to the monastic life; he developed them with great descriptive art and power of thought. So this Life contributed not less than its hero to its further advancement.

At the time when the first General Council was sitting at Nicæa, the monk Pachomius was gathering together the first monastery at Tabennæ, on the Nile, and placing the first convent of women under his sister. His own devoted life had kindled the like flame in that sister. She is said to have had four hundred virgins in her monastery. The sister also of St. Antony and the virgin wife of St. Ammon presided over large numbers of the female sex, which showed equal ardour with the male in embracing this life. In the year 340 the patriarch Athanasius was driven by the scheming of Eusebian bishops at Antioch, supported by imperial power, to fly for protection to Pope Julius at Rome, and carried with him full knowledge of the life thus set up in the desert, together with the presence of two monks, who personally witnessed and had long practised it; and these three introduced the knowledge and the esteem of this life at Rome. About twenty years later, probably in 362, the

[1] See this Life in Gallandi's Collection, tom. viii.

Pope who succeeded Julius was receiving the solemn profession of a Roman lady of high rank in St. Peter's, amid a great company of nuns, her friends and partners of her life. And in 377 her brother, then become Archbishop of Milan, records in his treatise on the virginal life the words which the Pope addressed to his sister as the bride of Christ. Ten years after this, in 387, St. Augustine, then a young convert, attests having seen monasteries of men and women at Rome and Milan; and at the same time the noblest of Roman patricians, both men and women, were dedicating their lives to the monastic discipline, and their revenues to its promulgation. Of these we may mention by name Fabiola. In penance for having divorced a worthless husband, as the civil Roman law enabled her to do, she, having learnt after her conversion that the law of Christ did not allow of such divorce, was lining the coasts of Italy with convents, for building which her great possessions supplied ample funds. St. Ambrose, speaking of the sea as a beautiful work of its Creator, alludes to this when he says, " Why should I enumerate the islands which the sea wears as a necklace? Here they who fly from the snares of secular indulgence make their choice by a faithful purpose of continence to lie hidden from the world. Thus the sea becomes a harbour of security, an incentive of devotion; chanted psalms blend with the gentle murmur of waves, and the islands utter their voice of joy like a tranquil chorus to the hymns of saints."

These various instances point out to us how the seventy years which followed the first monastery of Pachomius on the Nile found the monastic institute received throughout the provinces of the Church from Palestine to Gaul, and how the life of a monk who fled from sight into the deserts of Egypt had drawn after it a multitude of imitators in Egypt itself, while it had been proclaimed both to East and West by the great champion who had suffered five times banishment from his patriarchal See, and was maintaining, at the risk of his life, the Godhead of his Lord. St. Antony and St. Athanasius met and rebuked from the beginning the Arian insurrection against the Christian faith, and the monastic life which the one founded and the other proclaimed showed throughout its whole course the steadfastness which they had shown at first. The emphatic assertion of Antony, that Arius was the forerunner of Antichrist, received in subsequent history a wonderful accomplishment, since the desertion of the true Christian faith by the Monophysites of Egypt led them to help to the possession of Egypt the followers of one who put himself in the place of Christ; and so Mohammed crowned the work of Arius, and the impostor found his chosen seat in the land where the heretic had sprung up.

We have the most precise statements from St. Jerome, one of the chief propagators of this life, that it was a new thing—that is, new as to the public, avowed, and authorised living together of men and of women under monastic rule. There had been from the beginning, as a direct following of the Apostles and of the Apostolic Church at Jerusalem, those who pursued in their own persons many, at least, of the practices contained in the monastic discipline. St. Cyprian termed the virgins brides of Christ a hundred years before Pope Liberius in St. Peter's dwelt upon that dignity in the sister of St. Ambrose. But until the freedom of the Church, granted by Constantine, it was not feasible to have houses openly acknowledged for their leading together "the common life." But it was precisely in this practice of "the common life" that the strength of the monastic institute consisted; that one, who was termed a father, ruled with paternal authority a number of men, and in like manner an abbess, that is a mother, a number of women, who in their natural and civil condition were no ways related, and that the house so ruled constituted as distinct and stable a unity as the domestic home had done. This novelty added the two forces of obedience and the nonpossession of private property to the unmarried condition, with which, previous to Constantine's enfranchisement, those stricter members of the Church had to content themselves; and it is the junction of these three things which makes up "the common life." The construction of the rule, in accordance with which "the common life" was to be carried out, formed the chief difficulty of establishing the institution. Those who best succeeded in this drew the rule which they recommended to others from their own practice, as we see in St. Basil, St. Augustine, and afterwards St. Benedict. And they who have set up this rule, and, by its wisdom and tempered strength, caused it to be accepted by generations who succeeded them, have been the greatest legislators of the human race and its greatest benefactors.

The time when this new force was developed out of the Church's bosom was a most critical time. Constantine's act in setting the Church free from censure of the law had made it possible, and at the same time had rendered it necessary. The very act which we so praised had exposed the Church to a host of fresh difficulties. Freedom from persecution had developed her worst enemies, for Diocletian's tortures were not so dangerous as the contagion of a bishop who migrated first from the small See of Berytus, in Palestine, to Nicomedia, when the court of Constantine was there, and then from Nicomedia to Constantinople, when the first Christian emperor had made it New Rome. For the first time in Christian history it might be profitable to temporal interests to become a Christian. The whole Christian people was visibly affected by this possibility. The calamities which Basil had traced[1] with the hand of a master and the compunction of a saint sprang up in this way among the Eastern episcopate. Bishops had temporal greatness thrust upon them, and many lost therein episcopal independence. Not all of them, like Basil himself, laughed to scorn the threats of an imperial satrap and prime minister. Julian was tempted to apostasy by the corruption of the time-serving Christians whom he saw around him. It is said positively that he thought the most effective way to divide the Church which he hated was by suffering bishops who had been deposed under Constantius to return to their Sees. In that fourth century civil society in the unconverted heathen population of the Roman empire was in a state of the utmost corruption. From the deserts of Egypt was brought the power to wage conflict with it. The life which Antony, and Pachomius, and Ammon, with a host of disciples, both male and female, there nurtured in solitude and privation was the most absolute contradiction of the criminal luxury to be found

---

[1] See his ninety-second letter, quoted vol. v. p. 231.

at Rome, at Carthage, at Antioch,[1] at Alexandria, at Constantinople. And so contemporaneous with the action of the first Christian Council, the assembling of which was Constantine's gift to the Church, came the introduction of a new force into the Church's life, which was to show itself at the moment the last surviving son of Constantine had sent a Pope into exile, and all but substituted the deadly error which his father proscribed for the Church's faith. And it is to be noted here again that the monastic discipline which brought with it "the common life" was from the beginning, and has been throughout its course, the most strenuous defender of the Christian faith. Through age after age it has saved the faith from overthrow, has beaten back the conquering power of the unchristian life, and shown that those who surrender their will as one of the three sacrifices carry the faith in their hearts, and proclaim it by doing and by suffering with imperturbable constancy. The few instances which I have given above, and which might be multiplied to any extent, show that the greatest men in the Christian hierarchy and literature embraced this offspring of the desert Fathers with unanimous assent, with even the cordial homage of their example. As not a saint in the calendar can be found who does not, like St. Elizabeth, when filled with the Holy Ghost, cry out to our Blessed Lady with heart and voice, "Blessed art thou among women, and blessed is the fruit of thy womb. And whence is this to me that the Mother of my Lord should come to me?" so not one is to be found who does not accept the heroic Christian institute as the flower of Christian life, as the most perfect following of the crucified Lord.

We shall not, therefore, be wrong in considering that in the history of the Church the necessitated counterpart to her delivery from the violence of heathen persecution is the liberty for her children to profess together and maintain "the common life." In it is preserved a faithful seed which will sustain for ever the purity of conduct with the strength of belief, and is free to devote the energy which springs from this double force to meet the various needs which attend upon civilisation in its perpetual development.

[1] For what it was at Antioch, see the testimony of an eye-witness, its great preacher, St. Chrysostom, vol. i. p. 88.

CHAPTER III

THE FORCE OF THE MONASTIC LIFE

HAVING heard what the chief fathers of the fourth century said in their own words of the monastic life upon its public introduction among them, we can turn to consider in its general bearings the result of that fact upon the whole Christian society. Why was it sent, and why especially at such a time, the time, namely, when Constantine's decree of toleration had opened a new epoch to the Church? Fifteen centuries have gone by, and many things lie open now to us which were hidden from the actors in the hundred years following on that decree of toleration. We see, for instance, that the century opened what was to be the final trial of the great Roman empire. When St. Antony had finished his fifty years' noviciate, and came forth from his life in solitude to be the guide and director of other men like himself, about A.D. 305, a great heathen persecution was waging against the Church; the empire was standing under four emperors; the barbarians were on the other side the Danube, heaving their tumultuous billows against the great Roman wall which kept the frontier of civilisation from the Euxine to the Northern Sea. For a hundred and fifty years from Decius onwards, a succession of emperors, some of them at least military commanders of great eminence, were to hold the Teuton and the Scythian at bay. Constantine, the greatest of them all, was just coming to the birth of his power, and would use the choicest and the bravest of the Northern invaders to replenish and to strengthen his newly arranged legions. The glory of old Rome was still dazzling the eyes of men. No one foresaw that before the first century of the Church's freedom was fully worn out, a Gothic chief who had faithfully served a Roman emperor and helped him to save that empire, would have claimed from his son the supreme command of his armies, and being refused, would take the imperial city herself, and close the predestined years of her dominion. Just at the time Constantine arose, Egypt, in the remotest corner of Rome's empire, and there, not in the magnificent city which bore the name and exhibited the conquests of the great Alexander, but in her deserts, gave birth to a new race of men, who turned their backs upon cities, and the life generated in them, on all the luxury and the vices which defiled them, who treated their bodies with bread and water, and supported their souls upon God alone. All the tissue of their lives was an utterance of that one word which the Spanish saint has consecrated, *Solo Dios basta*.

This race appeared in the deserts of Egypt, but it was from its chief city that the most renowned champion of the Christian faith, driven by a religious persecution, took refuge with the Pope in Rome; and in doing so proclaimed to the West the mode of life pursued by the Fathers of the Desert, and by Antony himself, their leader, then ninety years old, and destined still to lead them for another fifteen years. The most dangerous of heresies had emerged simultaneously with the Church's civil freedom. For fifty years that heresy, sheltered and fostered under the wing of despotic emperors, one of them the son and sole successor of Constantine, disturbed, and in the eastern part of the empire dislocated, her episcopate, and especially ravaged the city which Constantine had crowned for the Christian capital of his chosen dominion. Nova Roma housed Arianism, and her bishop, Eudoxius, perverted the Emperor Valens, and through him infected the chiefest Gothic tribe with the same perversion. Old Rome under Julius, Liberius, and Damasus, preserved the faith. The evil which Constantius and Valens laboured to effect, a Spanish emperor, Theodosius, strove to undo. In the meantime the saints whom we have recorded from Athanasius to Chrysostom hailed the life which the Fathers of the Desert had introduced. All the provinces of the east rapidly received monasteries and convents founded after their example.

The greatest and strongest men in the Church, from Athanasius forward, took an active part in the ordered establishment of the cœnobitic life.¹ In the quotations which I have made from them we see a difference of touch, betokening the individual character in each, but they are all agreed as to one point. They term the life itself "a living with God," or, "a running to meet the life which bears the cross," a "living together with the adoration of God," a "dwelling in solitude with Christ," as many hundred years later, St. Bernard said, "Living in a cell is living in heaven. What means this? It means to give your thoughts to God is to enjoy God." One who had seen apostles perhaps gathered up all these words in his own, "My love is crucified," showing thereby that the life thus introduced was indeed a renewal of that earliest Christian life. One and all looked upon this life as supernatural. In it they place the contrast between the mundane and the religious life. All around them the Greek and the Roman heathenism was breaking up from intrinsic corruption. Herein they found something which defied that corruption.

But contemplate somewhat nearer the coming of such a force to the Church at such a time out of such a country as Egypt.

The conduct of St. Antony through that long noviciate of self-imposed and internal discipline, which Athanasius has described, is ruled entirely by one desire, to follow his Lord, to be like Him, to enjoy communion with Him. All-thought of the world is absent from his mind. When his course was far advanced, and he had gone to Alexandria at the bidding of the authority which he revered, he laid it down as a maxim that monks must live in the mountains as fish live in the sea. The watchword of the Desert Fathers was piety towards Christ.²

All the facts which we know concerning Antony, Puchomius, Ammon, and the multitude of disciples which followed them, point to one conclusion as to their utter unconsciousness that they were doing anything except

---

¹ συζῆν τῷ θεῷ—Athanasius. προσδραμεῖν τῷ σταυροφόρῳ βίῳ—Basil. τῇ τοῦ θεοῦ λατρείᾳ συζῆν—Chrysostom. εἰ δὲ καὶ οἷος ναετδειν ἐθέλοις χριστῷ ξυνούμενος οἴω—Gregory Naz. Quod geritur in cellis, hoc est in cœlis, quidnam est hoc? Vacare Deo, frui Deo—Bernard. ὁ ἐμὸς ἔρως ἐσταύρωται—Ignatius of Antioch.

² εὐσέβεια εἰς Χριστόν.

pursuing the cultivation of the inner life; and that is the fact concerning them recognised by the Fathers who examined and approved their work.[1]

As an instance of the power with which the character and example of Antony laid hold of others, we may take Hilarion. He was born in Gaza, and was sent in earliest youth by his parents, who were idolaters, to Alexandria to learn the liberal arts in the far-famed schools of the Egyptian capital. As he joined innocence and purity of life with great diligence, he pleased his teachers and made considerable progress in learning. Thus he appeared a fit subject for the Christian religion into which he entered. The fame of St. Antony reached also to him: a journey to visit the much-talked of hermit took place. This decided the course of his life. For the youth felt himself so impressed with the wisdom and virtues of Antony, that after a few months he left him with the resolution to live in his own country after Antony's pattern. This resolution was not the result of a passing enthusiasm, but followed upon the deepest spiritual affinity. When he looked on Antony he saw in him his own idea. And so he became the image of Antony, not merely in external ascetic appearance, but in his inmost being, as well as in the blessed influence which he exercised upon the world around him. No one doubted that Hilarion was a friend of God, and therefore that through him a check to every oppression might be found. His great art consisted in drawing to himself men of all classes from the remotest distance, in winning hearts, in changing even masses of heathen into Christians. Thus a Teuton, in the person of a noble Frank who served at Constantine's court in the guard among those called candidates, came to him to gain help. Julian the Apostate issued special orders to persecute him, which he escaped by flight. After many wanderings he died in the island of Cyprus, more than eighty years old, about 370, after having founded many monasteries in Palestine.

From Palestine the monastic institution went farther east, and so quickly that St. Basil in 357, only a year after the death of its patriarch, Antony, found well-arranged

[1] *Mönchthum*, p. 148, trans.

and flourishing monasteries already from thirty to forty years old in Cœle-Syria and Mesopotamia. Basil delighted himself to find in the Syrian and Egyptian monks a life devoted both to labour and to piety. In his own practice of it he joined to these qualities great learning. When Archbishop of Cæsarea he counted his monks the fairest portion of his diocese.[1] He composed for them his longer and his shorter Rule, works which show the greatness of his mind no less than his dogmatic writings and his letters, while they have had a great effect both in East and West on the formation of the higher mind. From St. Basil's death in 379 no province of the Eastern Church was deprived of the possession of living monks in its borders. From these issued a continually new progeny.[2]

The great character of Basil in union with his high rank in the hierarchy was of much advantage to the spread of the monastic institution. He was largely occupied in forming a rule for it. This touches upon the first difficulty which arises in that state. Of the monks in general it is said that they carried on that form of apostolic conduct which had first been shown in the infant Church at Jerusalem; and that in a not untrue sense it may be said that the disciples of the Lord in the first three hundred years were all of them monks. Cast out of the world, the Christian lived in it like a pilgrim, as much severed from it by his manners as by his belief; for his manners were the image of his belief. The fact that the Son of God had become man for the salvation of men, and died upon the Cross, laid hold of the heart in all its force, and the word of the Apostle that baptism into Christ was baptism into His death, had its full meaning for every believer. Such a conviction might of itself draw a young and fervent spirit, such as that of Antony, into the desert; but there is a great step between an individual mind actuated with such feelings, and a community living a joint life together in the exercise of them. While Antony was thought to be the most perfect example of the ascetic life in itself, Pachomius rather bore the title of its legislator. The first community-life at Tabenna was formed by him. The power by which

---

[1] *Mönchthum*, pp. 187, 188. [2] *Ibid.*, p. 166.

such a community became a house, having its own corporate life; a father, who was the mainspring of its action; members, whose office was as distinct as the office of the eye, the hand, and the foot of the human body, yet who grew together from day to day, from month to month, from year to year, this power added to the individual ascetic an impact of numbers which betokened another creation. Herein lay the vast importance of the new life which sprung from the action of the Fathers of the Desert.

Basil entered very much into this new life. He had seen it in his visits to Egypt, Palestine, and Mesopotamia. He carried it out personally in his own life with St. Gregory on the banks of the Iris in Pontus. He furthered its attainment in his capital city, Cæsarea. The formation, growth, and consolidation of the monastic *family* is the crown of the ascetic life; the persistence of such a family to endure not merely for single lives but for generations, preserving one spirit, is the crown of perfect success—a success incomparably more difficult than an individual life, however high its purpose and perfect its accomplishment. Since the Church herself in all her grandeur, as in all her tenderness, is one family of Christ, it may well be that a monastic family, as a crystal of like quality, however small, may be the most perfect specimen of the one Church.

History shows that the attainment of a *rule* was the greatest difficulty which the monastic life encountered.

As Antony, the patriarch of monks, had been preceded by Paul the first hermit, so the long noviciate of fifty years passed by Antony as a hermit was matured at length by his example, forming as it were the kernel of many monasteries. The greater severity of penance, which seemed to mark the hermit's loneliness, was balanced by the greater opportunity of exercising charity which would be required to maintain a household, by virtue of that supernatural power of the living together under rule. In all ages of the Church there have been solitaries whose lives showed every degree of self-denial, and all practice of the presence of God, and all exercise of the power of prayer. Nevertheless those who had fled to solitude from persecution, or through disgust at the luxury which prevailed around them, would become aware by personal experience of many defects in their own character which the living under in the society of others would help them to amend. And this was a powerful cause for the prevailing of the cœnobitic over the solitary life, which was the result before long among those who inhabited the desert, and in those who through the East propagated their institution.[1] And so the great effect of the monastic life in building up the fabric of the Church, in maintaining the one faith, by learning, by acting, by suffering, is seen in the creation of "the common life" from its first manifestation in the deserts of Egypt. Upon this Basil spent much time and thought,[2] and the monks of the Eastern Church have largely lived upon his rule. But it would seem that the reception of the same rule by different religious houses, who were at a distance from each other, and whose government was independent, being complete in the house itself, was a matter of long time and no little difficulty.

Thus at the end of the fourth century we find in the East St. Athanasius, St. Basil, St. Chrysostom, St. Gregory Nazianzen, and St. Gregory of Nyssa have done their utmost to encourage, promote, and extol the monastic life. No less in the West St. Ambrose, St. Jerome, and St. Augustine, of whom the first praised it in the example of his sister, and by the solemn approval of the Pope; the second exulted in its reception by the noblest Roman families in both sexes, spending the last part of his life in the construction and government of religious houses at Bethlehem; while the third not only made it the first thought of his life as a convert, but attached it to the hierarchy of the Church by making his episcopal house a monastery. And it must be noted that when he did this, not only was the life itself, as to its second condition of obedience, and its third condition of poverty, new in the Church, but that religious were in their first state of the laity, and not reckoned among the clergy. So that if the doctrine of St. Augustine told most powerfully on

---

[1] *Mönchthum*, p. 176.
[2] S. Greg. Nanz.: μέσην τιν' ἦλθον ἀζύγων καὶ μιγάδων τῶν μὲν τὸ συννοῦν τῶν δὲ τὸ χρηστὸν φέρων.—*Life of Basil*, p. xlviii.

the growth of theology in the after centuries of the Church over wide regions, no less did his example bear fruit in her practice.

In the same year, 410, in which Rome was taken by Alaric, a monastery arose upon an island at the southern extremity of France, which was to be a home of learning and piety and zeal in that terrible fifth century when the whole land of France became the prey of the Northern invaders. Honoratus, a man of Gallic blood and consular race, highly educated by his father, wished to embrace the religious life. His father opposed this wish, and tried to turn him from it by the society of his elder brother; but, on the contrary, Honoratus was able to gain over his brother. After many wanderings, he landed on the desert isle of Lerin, where once had been a city, long destroyed, but which was then only known for the multitude of its snakes. He was accompanied by many friends, who soon formed a community of austere monks and most laborious workers. The snakes retired, and that monastic house arose in a country plentifully watered, well shaded with lofty trees, rich in verdure, enamelled with flowers. Honoratus, whose paternal love invited all who loved Christ to share his new home, found disciples arrive from every region. He was speedily enabled to renew on the coast of Provence the wonders of the Thebaïde. That monastery became a school of theology and Christian philosophy. Its insular position placed it beyond the reach of barbarian invasion. It continued to be an asylum for literature and knowledge, a nursery also of bishops and saints when the mainland of Italy and Gaul was suffering the horrors of a conquest unequalled for its cruelty and the desolation inflicted.[1]

The churches of Arles, Avignon, Lyons, Troyes, Frejus, Valence, Nice, Venu, Apt, Venasque, Antibes, Saintes, received from what was called "the blessed island" their most illustrious bishops. Honoratus was taken from the monastery he had founded to occupy the primatial see of Arles, but at least once a year he came to visit the community which he had built up with all a father's affection. One of his disciples has left us his last words to those

[1] Montalembert on Lerin, i. 232.

who surrounded his bed: "Live, my children, in such sort that you may not fear your last hour. This is the inheritance your father leaves you with his last breath, an invitation to the heavenly kingdom." He was succeeded at Arles by a disciple of Lerin, the well-known St. Hilary of Arles, who continued during his episcopate the penitent and laborious life of the cloister. He traversed his diocese on foot and with naked feet, even in the snow. To help the poor he sold his sacred vessels, and used paten and chalice of glass. He worked with his own hands to cultivate the fields of his church, or to make nets to help his ruined people and redeem captives dragged into slavery during the wars between the Romans and the Goths and Burgundians, who ravaged Southern Gaul. He had the misfortune to fall under the censure of the great St. Leo, who deprived him of his rank of metropolitan, but after his death entitled him, "Hilary of holy memory."

A monk of this monastery also was that St. Vincent who has left but one short writing, written in 434, three years after the Council of Ephesus, and containing the most precise and detailed statement as to the doctrine of development which is to be found in patristic writing, and which has been quoted with approbation by the last Ecumenical Council at the Vatican.

Salvian also, who wrote upon the corruption which drew down that terrible chastisement on the Roman world, passed five years in the place and solitude of Lerin.

St. Eucher was a monk of Lerin when two deputies of the Church of Lyons went to invite him to be their bishop. They could not prevail on him to leave his solitude, upon which they broke down the stones which closed his cavern, and carried him off by force to the metropolitan See, which received him with acclamations, and where he sat nearly twenty years. It is an instance among many of the eagerness with which bishops were sought from the monastic life.

Another disciple of Lerin, St. Loup, was Bishop of Troyes, where he encountered Attila, and ventured to ask the king of the Huns, "Who art thou?" receiving the reply, "I am Attila, the scourge of God." But Attila did St. Loup and his city no harm. He was also joined with St. Germain of Auxerre in a journey to England to combat the Pelagian heresy. During fifty-two years of pontificate, he faithfully practised the observances of the monastic life learnt at Lerin, as well as a great study of learning.

Another of the most famous bishops of Gaul spent his youth at Lerin. Cæsarius was the third Archbishop of Arles taken from that house. He was bishop more than forty years, from 501 to 542, presiding over four Councils, and directing the chief controversies of his age. He nobly maintained the episcopal independence in the face of the barbarous sovereigns who one after the other occupied Provence. He was exiled by Alaric, king of the Visigoths, and imprisoned by Theodoric, king of the Ostrogoths, but they afterwards did him justice. Passionately loved by his own flock, he left a hundred and thirty sermons, which bear the stamp of his charity, and long formed the basis of instruction in the Gallic Church.[1] He was also devoted throughout to the monastic life, and drew up for different communities of men a sort of rule in twenty-six articles. But still more known was that which he gave to the great monastery of women in his metropolitan city. The Franks and Burgundians, in their siege of Arles in 508, ruined this building. When they were gone, Cæsarius resumed his work and rebuilt it; and to protect this refuge against the flood of invasion, he had its foundation confirmed by Pope Hormisdas. The Pope also, at his express request, exempted it from episcopal jurisdiction. The bishop's sister, Cæsaria, was for thirty years abbess, and had two hundred religious. When Cæsarius was dying he addressed the nuns, speaking of "the blessed and happy isle of Lerin; those whom she receives as children she makes fathers; she takes them as recruits, she gives them up as kings."[2]

The Abbey of St. Victor at Marseilles was another monastic metropolis of Southern Gaul. It was founded by John Cassian, by some said to have been a Scythian, by others an Athenian or Gaul. He was at first a monk at Bethlehem, then in Egypt, where he lived seven years among the solitaries of Nitria and the Thebaïde. He has left us an exact and touching picture of their life. Afterwards he went to

[1] Ozanam, *Etud. Ger.*, ii. p. 87.   [2] Montalembert, i. 242.

Constantinople to find St. John Chrysostom, who ordained him deacon, and sent him to Rome to set forth his cause to Pope Innocent I. At Rome he became the friend of St. Leo the Great, before his elevation to the papacy, and wrote at his request a refutation of the Nestorian heresy.[1]

Thus Cassian had studied the monastic life in many places before he came to rest at Lerin. Thence he went to Marseilles to found that great monastery of St. Victor. Before long it counted five thousand monks, including not only those which it contained itself, but those who dwelt in houses created by its influence. Cassian wrote the four books of his Institutions and his four and twenty conferences, works which have taken a place among the codes of monastic life. He records in them the manner of life, the prayer and mortification which he had witnessed in the Thebaïde and in Palestine, their interior life, their spirit, and their supernatural wisdom.

Most of the great chiefs of the cœnobitic institute had, since St. Pachomius, drawn up instructions or constitutions for the use of their own disciples, which they termed a rule, but none of these had been permanently and generally accepted. The rule of St. Basil had been largely used in the East, yet Cassian, when he visited Egypt, Palestine, and Mesopotamia, found almost as many rules as there were monasteries.[2]

Cassian did not desire that his monastery should become what Lerin was, a sort of seminary of bishops and priests around it. He had himself been ordained deacon by St. Chrysostom, and priest by Pope Innocent I. Yet he would have liked to maintain the old barrier which separated the monks from the clergy. But the feelings of the times broke down this barrier. The populations sought eagerly for bishops and priests formed in the monastic sanctuaries. Lerin and St. Victor gave bishops and priests to the Churches of Gaul in the fifth century who had both theological knowledge and moral standing, which often failed in prelates

---

[1] Montalembert, i. 245.
[2] Montalembert, i. 286, who quotes the words of Cassian: "Tot propemodum typos ac regulas usurpatas vidimus, quot monasteria cellasque conspeximus."—Instit., lib. ii. c. 2.

taken from the Gallo-Roman aristocracy who had not passed through the religious life.

The East and the West had embraced the monastic life with wonderful rapidity. Not that it did not meet with great opposition. Of these, the heathen opponents would regard the doctrine of the crucified Son of God, of the necessity to die to themselves and to the world, as utter antagonism to the Hellenic view of life. So Libanius, defending the heathen temples, mocked the monks as men who considered it virtue to pass their lives in mourning. The title of "the men clothed in black" embraces everything which the heathen Greek would feel against them. The Arians also pursued them with the keenest dislike, for which their own worldliness was a quite sufficient reason. The still and quiet life, given up to prayer and contemplation, with hard manual labour, would meet indeed with acknowledgment as to its visible fruits, but as to the invisible communion with God would only be treated by the worldly as idleness and uselessness.[1]

It is here, however, that we have to place one of the greatest benefits conferred by the monks on the whole Christian society. Antony could pass a whole night in prayer to God, and complain when the rays of the rising sun came to intervene with his contemplation, "O sun, why comest thou to draw me away from the royal sight of the true light?" This fixing of the soul on God gave the monk an insight into the mind and heart not before reached. Thus he came to have the tenderest sympathy with the brethren around him. As a matter of fact, the service which the monks rendered to the advance of science in the Church was very great.[2] From the first formation of the monastic life, we find very few important ecclesiastical writers in proportion who had not been either ascetics or monks, or at least had spent a long time among them and gained in their circle the theological culture which they reached. Athanasius, Basil, Gregory the theologian, Chrysostom, Theodoret, Maximus, among the Greeks; Jerome, Rufinus, Augustine, Sulpicius Severus, Cassian, Salvian,

[1] Montalembert, i. 247-248.
[2] *Mönchthum*, p. 211, trans.

Gregory the Great, Fulgentius, Vincent of Lerin, Cæsarius of Arles, among the Latins, are sufficient witness of this. Ancient literature has no greater names to show. The most important periods in the development of dogma and the scientific perception of the faith are attached to those named. To the present day their writings are storehouses of theology. Nor is such a result casual. The thorough solution of every difficult problem in any department of science requires withdrawal of the mind from dissipation and irregular emotions. How much more does the science of what is holy and divine require this? But especially the science of a faith given by God has something peculiar to itself. That which we call philosophy first inquires whether there is anything holy and divine, and presents itself to the inquiry without much reverence and humility. But the Christian theologian possesses these qualities beforehand, and knows that he cannot set himself to any inquiry without a strict moral purification, without persistent prayer, and without the guiding help of the Holy Spirit. But contact with the spirit of the world, and contamination through the spirit of the world, which prevents the soaring above by prayer and the reception of the higher light, are nearly the same thing. And so it comes that the ascetic cell of the monks is pointed out by a divine disposition as the fittest place for meditation to the Christian theologian. Nor is this open to the historical objection that many of the above-named Fathers of the Church issued their most important and influential writings when they were already such fathers; for when they had once received the consecration of the monastic life they maintained its habits during the remainder of their course.[1]

This brings us to a merit of the monastic life at this time which cannot be too highly prized, that of having educated and given to the Church her worthiest bishops. It must be remembered that at this time no special places for the formation of the clergy had been provided. During the persecutions, when the opposition between the world's domain and the kingdom of God was openly manifested, when Christians and heathen were sharply severed, and the

[1] *Mönchthum*, p. 212, translated.

first dwelt in a great separation by themselves; the future priest did not require a special education. All social intercourse presented him with new elements of spiritual life. But now the world had forcibly pressed itself into the limits of the Church, and the results soon showed themselves in the moral relation of the higher and the lower clergy. The priest would have to come out of the community. So the need became urgent to hold apart from the community the head who was forming for it, to obtain for him a separate education, which might detach him from the all-prevailing corruption, keep before him as high a standard as possible, and lend him the strength to raise up again members who in so many things had sunk below the level. It was a manifest leading of the Divine Providence that, at the very time when these circumstances began to be developed, and this double need came forth, the ascetics went into the deserts, and there formed their own communities, well protected against the spirit of the world. The life which ruled among them of itself invited not a few to devote themselves to those studies which were indispensable to a spiritual pastor. From these, therefore, many priests and bishops were chosen; and, by Augustine making his episcopal house a monastery, they became themselves patterns of the places which bishops devoted to the education of the clergy. As little, and never exclusively, was the fourth century in the possession of schools intended to communicate theoretical instruction for the increase of the priesthood. The public addresses of the bishop or of his representatives sufficed for all without distinction; whoever was conspicuous for spotless virtue, unswerving faith, prudence and thoughtfulness, a higher mind, natural or acquired eloquence, might be chosen for a priest by the bishop's confidence. Observation of the manner in which every one discharged his office took the place of trial, and the bishop conferred a higher function or a larger trust as he saw how lower services had been performed. The whole special formation of the priest was gained merely by practice. But the position of the Church changed also as to this. The old simplicity required to be given up. It conveyed daily less assurance against attacks of heretics, pointed with great skill and knowledge, the refutation of which required, nay, absolutely demanded, special preparation.

In the time of the patriarch Timotheus of Alexandria, A.D. 381–385,[1] the people of a suffering city besought him to give them Abbot Ammon for bishop. He assented, only adding that they should bring the abbot to him. But as soon as the abbot heard of their desire he took to flight. When caught, he told them he would not leave his cell. As they continued to press him, he cut off his right ear, crying out that he could not now be consecrated a bishop. The patriarch was told the incident, and replied, "It is true that in the Old Testament such a loss would incapacitate for the priesthood, but in the New Testament it was the Spirit which decided." Still Ammon did not yield. A few examples from the Latin Church may instruct us as to the benefits which the monasteries brought to the Church. Sulpicius Severus, after describing the extreme difficulty with which Martin was induced to accept the bishopric of Tours, goes on to say [2] "that he continued the monastic life there as before. He showed the same humility, the same poverty in his dress, and exerted the episcopal dignity without surrendering the purpose of the monk. At first he lived in a cell close to the church, but found himself incommoded by the number of visitors; so he constructed a monastery in a very retired spot about two miles from the city. It was as lonely as the desert, having on one side the precipitous rock of a lofty mountain, on the other the river Loire, and approached only by one very narrow road. He himself occupied a wooden cell, as did many of his companions, while the rest hollowed out their cells in the rock. Here he had eighty disciples, who were formed after the model of their master. None had any private property; they might not buy or sell; they followed no art except writing, which was kept for the more youthful, while the elder were devoted to prayer. The cell was seldom left, except when they met in common prayer. All took their food together after fast-time:

---

[1] *Mönchthum*, p. 214.
[2] *Vita Beati Martini*, sec. 10, freely translated.

they had no wine, except in case of illness. Most of them were dressed in camel's hair. A softer vestment was looked upon as criminal, a thing the more remarkable because many of them were noble, and, having been brought up in a very different life, had compelled themselves to this humility and patience. Very many of them we afterwards saw as bishops, for what city or church was there which did not seek to have its prelate from Martin's monastery?"[1] Such was the beginning of Marmoutier, and of the fourteen hundred years during which it glorified the name and kept alive the spirit of St. Martin.

At the other side of France, a certain Romanus, brought up at the monastery of Ainay near Lyons, set out at the age of thirty-five, with the "Life of the Fathers in the Desert," a few herbs, and some tools, plunged into the lofty mountains and uninhabited forests which crowned his native land, and at last found a spot shut in between three steep hills at the junction of two streams. There he began, under the name of Condat, a monastery which was to become one of the most celebrated in the West. There he found his first shelter under a great pine, planted his pulse, and felt secure from interruption by the difficulty of access. In due time he was joined by his brother Lupicinus, and then by others in such numbers that they had to form new settlements in the neighbourhood. The two brothers governed in common these monasteries; and the women were not behind them, for on a neighbouring rock, perched like a nest on a precipice, the sister of the two abbots governed 105 nuns, so severely cloistered that after they had once entered no one could see them till their bodies passed from the sickbed to the cemetery.

The monks had each a separate cell and a refectory in common; in summer they took their siesta under the great pines, which in winter protected their dwelling from the snow and cutting wind. They sought to imitate the Eastern anchorites, whose various rules they studied, tempering their severity with such relaxations as the climate, daily labour, and the Gallic constitution required. They wore wooden shoes and the skins of beasts rudely stitched together. So

[1] *Mönchthum*, p. 215.

fruitful were they in colonies, which swarmed from their hive and filled the neighbouring provinces, that of them the word was first used, "They made of this Burgundian country, on which the Jura and the Alps look down, a new Thebaïde." The monastery of Condat, founded in 425, lived through long ages of barbarism. It long bore the name of its fourth abbot, Eugende, becoming one of the most celebrated schools in Gaul. In the end it took the name of Saint Claude, and was the seat of a bishop, and only ended its thirteen hundred years of life at the great Revolution.

Thus, from the middle of the fifth century, the cœnobitic institute coming out of the Thebaïde occupied one after another all the provinces of the Roman empire. We find it encamped on every frontier, waiting for the coming of the barbarians, and prepared to convert them.[1] Those who lived such a life, followed with the utmost freedom of choice, pondered unceasingly on the divine Word and imbibed its spirit. Who was fitter than they to give expression to its force, to diffuse its consoling and vivifying power among others? They did not think that it lessened the episcopal dignity to live so still and noiseless, so self-denying a life as they had been accustomed to lead when monks. Hence it was that as bishops they did not squander Church property, and could found such stately works as Constantinople, Cæsarea, and many other cities received from the hands of their great bishops, Chrysostom and Basil. Rufinus says of the Nitrian monks, "Never have we seen charity so flourish, never the work of mercy and the study of hospitality so fulfilled, never such proficiency in the study of the Holy Scriptures, in the understanding of them, and in sacred knowledge, so that you might take almost every one as an eloquent theologian." No doubt at times a bishop chosen from the monks would show a certain inaptitude to deal with difficult circumstances, but, as a general rule, they showed that they possessed a far greater knowledge of the world, as needed by a bishop, than those who had never been out of the world. The supplying of the episcopate from the ranks of the monks worked beneficially, not only upon the city in which the See lay and its immediate circle, but likewise on

[1] Drawn from Montalembert, i. 257-267.

the bishops of the whole province, and even yet farther. Their apostolical life and action served as a tacit reproach to many of their colleagues. The meetings of synods or their high rank in the hierarchy gave occasion to exercise a most happy influence on the spirit, discipline, and good order of the widest circles.

The nature of the monastic life itself caused it to act as an example to the whole secular clergy. Those who live in the world are easily affected by its spirit.

The intrinsic force of the monastic life, as well as its aptitude for the time in which it appeared, will be further shown by comparing together the secular history of the Roman state and the spiritual history of the Christian Church, in the time which follows Constantine to the extinction of the Western Empire.

Constantine in 323, by the defeat and subsequent death of Licinius, became sole master of the Roman empire; it is from that time the development of his mind towards the Christian Church becomes more visible. The one emperor recognised the one Church; the victorious general had no sympathy with insurgent sects. Donatism did not prevail with him by its adulation of imperial authority in spiritual things. He is true to this recognition of the Church at the Nicene Council in 325. In 330 he proclaimed the foundation of a new capital, situated on the most commanding site in the eastern part of his empire, and he bestowed on it the title of New Rome, which from the beginning was not only a title, but a great power. His single rule lasted fourteen years, from 323 to 337. His intention was to make his new capital Christian from the beginning in its buildings, in its inhabitants, in its worship, and above all, in its influence upon his whole empire. But from the time that he was seated in an Oriental capital he became himself, at least he began to be, an Oriental sovereign. The primary and all-important relation between the two great powers which he had recognised at the first General Council of the Church, began to be impaired; but his death in 337 brought with it great alteration. Instead of his firm if somewhat despotic grasp, the empire was divided between his three sons; instead of the one man who was above other men by the head and shoulders, three men, all of them incompetent for the secular government of vast regions, inherited only what he could leave—the bodily structure of his realm. The West was divided between Constans and Constantine II.; the former took Illyria, Italy, and Africa, the latter Gaul, Spain, and Britain. Both these princes were faithful to the Church, but lived at enmity with each other. The third brother, Constantius, who received as his portion the whole East, was from the beginning doubtful in his faith, and speedily fell into the hands of the faction among the Eastern bishops who strove to make the emperor their own by yielding to him in the Church a power like that which he possessed in the State. Constantine II. died three years after his father, in 340, and the territory of his rule accrued to his brother Constans; but by the death of Constans in 350 Constantius became sole emperor, and then during eleven years he used the vast imperial power both in East and West to subdue the bishops to that Arian doctrine which he chose to patronise. Thus the time from 350 to 361 is one of the darkest in the history of the Church. At his death, at the age of forty-four, after receiving baptism on his death-bed from an Arian bishop, the peril which he had created was so great that the accession of an apostate, who preferred heathenism to the Christian faith, seemed a relief to the suffering Church. The apostate ruled less than two years, and was succeeded in 363 by Jovian, whose death in 364 gave place to Valentinian.

The accession of Valentinian fully revealed the permanent weakness of the empire. The new sovereign found himself compelled to appoint a colleague for the eastern part, and selected his brother, Valens. From this time forth the empire, of which the seat was in Constantinople, became practically, in its administration, a distinct empire from that whose ruler resided no longer at Rome but at Milan, or Treves, or Ravenna, some city, in fact, where he could hold a camp or maintain a fortress against the threatening Northern barbarians.

The division of the empire at Constantine's death was in itself a great blow, but his sons were likewise disunited, and also of marked incapacity for government. The third son, who during eleven years ruled the whole empire, was unsound in his own belief, and a flagrant persecutor of the faith which his father had received at the great Council, and so thoroughly tyrannical that he strove to make his own will a law for the bishops, whom his father had recognised as speaking with the authority of Christ in their conciliar decrees. At his death, his cousin, the apostate to heathenism, succeeded to the throne, which he held only for twenty months. When Jovian was elected by a defeated army in the enemy's country, at a moment of the utmost danger, to take his place, a Catholic, with the best intentions to heal the wounds which the last and favourite son of Constantine had inflicted both on Church and State, he was carried off by a sudden illness in a few months. Thus when Valentinian succeeded in the year 364, only twenty-seven years after the death of the great Constantine, a Pope had been banished from Rome, and the episcopate, even in the West, but much more in the East, been oppressed and dislocated. The empire which Constantine had held in his hand was far from being in the hands of his successors. It required the utmost exertions of Valentinian to maintain peace in the West. As for the East, he felt it necessary to surrender that throne to another. He chose a brother. Valens, at the time of his choice, was supposed to be a Catholic, but he speedily fell under the influence of Eudoxius, the Arian Bishop of Constantinople, and during fourteen years, until he lost his life in battle with the Goths, to whom he had given the Arian instead of the Catholic doctrine, he used the power of an absolute ruler against the Eastern Catholics.

Valentinian I., a man of energy and fairness, had not allowed the tyranny which afflicted the Eastern Catholics to be practised in the West, but he died suddenly and prematurely, after a reign of eleven years, in 375, leaving two young sons, Gratian and Valentinian II. When, three years later, in 378, Valens had been overthrown by the Goths in a defeat which, for completeness, the Romans likened to that of Cannæ, the young Gratian sought succour to his own inability to save the Eastern empire by summoning Theodosius, the son of a general lately executed through a court intrigue, to take the Eastern throne. A short reprieve for the shaken empire was found in the fifteen years granted to Theodosius; yet in this time he witnessed the murder of the young Gratian, and was obliged to tolerate the contriver of that murder, the usurper Maximus, as emperor in Gaul for five years, from 383 to 388. After this he had to witness the murder of a second brother of his wife, Valentinian II., in 392, and to overthrow a second usurper in Rome, Eugenius, in the same year. He had been emperor in the East for thirteen years from 379 to 392, and then became, during three years, from 392 to 395, sole ruler, and was taken away before the age of fifty, having done the utmost which valour in the field, and wisdom in the cabinet, and fidelity to the Catholic faith could do to stem the advance of evils and maintain a Roman empire.

In the fifty-eight years which elapsed from the death of Constantine in 337 to the death of Theodosius in 395, the power of the Roman empire had been greatly shaken. Both these great men had known how to use the valour and vigour of the Northern barbarians to recruit their legions and to supply themselves with officers and office-holders whom they could trust. Alaric was a faithful Roman general when he served Theodosius, and Theodosius chose Stilicho for the husband of his niece Serena, whom he loved as a daughter, besides making him his chief counsellor and minister in the West. But the empire depended on a continuance of such men to rule it as Constantine and Theodosius. Even under them the settled countries of the vast realm heaved with insurrections, while the Northern tribes pressed nearer and nearer in their efforts to reach the great sea, all whose shores smiled upon Roman lands. Great as was the weakness introduced by the division of the empire, which we may say became definitive at the election of Valentinian in 364, Theodosius left it standing. But he was compelled to leave it in a condition which entailed a rapid fall. He could only give to the East for ruler his son Arcadius, who had scarcely reached manhood, and to the West his son Honorius, a child of eleven, both of them born in the purple, nursed in Oriental luxury, and all their lives utterly devoid of capacity to maintain the empire whose fall had been delayed by the valour and conduct of their father. From the time that Arcadius was enthroned the East became a government of eunuchs and favourites, presently to become the court of an empress proud of her beauty and influence. In the West Honorius preserved an appearance of power so long as he depended on the counsels of Stilicho, and was saved by the wonderful victories which repulsed for a time the advancing barbarian hosts. It is indeed still a problem of history whether Stilicho was as faithful as he was valiant and skilful, but it is undoubted that his sacrifice by Honorius left Rome a prey to Alaric. The Gothic chief, who had obeyed an emperor at once feared and respected, scorned obedience to the incapable son who had put to death not only his own friend and comrade, but likewise the defender given by his father, and closely allied to him. And so the great city, whose name alone expressed the strength and fortune of the empire, fell, because its rival in the East preferred the ruin of Rome to the occupation of Constantinople by a barbarian conqueror. Thus, even under the sons of Theodosius, the calamity of a divided empire reached its full height. Constantine's new Rome gave the Goths possession of the old. Nor was even this all, for ninety-eight years only after his decree of toleration, his empire in the West fell a prize to the barbarian, and the Emperor Valens, his own successor, seated in the new capital, by him intended to be Christian, had led the greatest and noblest of those barbarian peoples unconsciously to take the Arian perversion for the real Christian faith.

It is enough to sum up the result of the fifth century, and needless to tell again the details of its disasters. When, in 476, Odoacer the Herule deposed the last of the eight phantoms who had been styled at Rome emperors, and required the Senate to send back to the emperor at Constantinople the symbols of sovereignty, and to declare at the same time that no emperor was needed for the West, Gaul and Spain, and Africa and Britain had ceased to belong to the empire, and had become a prey to a multitude of Northern invaders. Rome had been taken and plundered by Alaric the Goth in 410, had been threatened with utter destruction by Attila in 451, and only saved by the unarmed presence of St. Leo, in whom "the scourge of God" recognised the pastor of his people, defended by St. Peter and St. Paul. A few years later, in 455, Rome had been plundered afresh by the Arian Vandal Genseric, and yet again by the Arian Visigoth Ricimer, even more severely, in 472; and, thereupon, the fate coming on Italy was to be ruled for fifty years by two Arians, Odoacer the Herule from 476 to 493, and Theodoric the Ostrogoth from 493 to 526. Both these ruled by a pretended title from the Byzantine emperor, but in reality by their own strength.

The course of the empire, from the single rule of Constantine in 323 to the death of Theodoric in 526, is thus marked out as a train of perpetual calamities. Constantine's dominion in the West had ended in complete dissolution, but the Eastern half had saved itself for a further time by the surrender of Italy, and of the countries belonging to Italy, not only to the Northern invaders, but to the Arian misbelief.

When we turn to the history of the Church in the same two hundred years dating from the single monarchy of Constantine, we find the conversion of that emperor stand likewise at the head of a new era in the Church's spiritual work.[1] With the co-operation of the Church's three great Sees of Rome, Alexandria, and Antioch, Constantine caused the first General Council to be held in the year 325. But the holding of such a Council, under the sanction and protection of the Roman emperor, was a public proclamation of union between the two great powers which conduct between them the undivided life of man, that one life on earth which procures for him all natural goods, and gains for him the goods of another, better, permanent existence. This one imperishable glory belongs to Constantine, that he expunged the enmity which had inspired three centuries of Pagan persecution, and for this the Fathers, even after they had witnessed the calamities which had sprung from his later despotism and his breaking away from his first generosity,

---

[1] A reference here to vol. v. pp. 384-386, in which the four things here noted are mentioned: 1. beginning of union between the two powers; 2. of freedom to the Church in her action as one body; 3. of Papal deliverance from Pagan oppression; 4. of freedom to proclaim doctrine, hence the impulse to theology.

still pronounced him blessed. And this his first action at the Council, at which he did not sit or vote among the bishops, but acknowledged their freedom to form a spiritual judgment, and the authority of that judgment when formed by them, was indeed the beginning of a new time, which neither his own listening to the flatteries of unfaithful bishops, nor the extravagant despotism of his son Constantius, could abrogate, but only reduce to a temporary perplexity. And again that same action of his delivered the successor of St. Peter from the superincumbent weight of Pagan oppression, and enabled him to act as chief bishop among all the bishops of the world, and by this public action to be no longer a latent but an avowed power. The gift of an imperial palace and a cathedral in the most stately part of Rome, great as it was, was yet surpassed by the congregation of the whole body of the episcopate, wherein an absent Pope was recognised by his legates, representing in their persons the whole West, and further presiding over those whose conciliar decrees in the estimation of a Roman emperor conveyed the doctrine of Christ. Again, the holding of such a Council proclaimed to all that the doctrine of the Church was not that of a suspected and proscribed malefactor, but of a power free to show, exhibit, and expand itself. It contained in itself the promise of a theology which was to spring with a force hitherto unexperienced out of its very bosom. And to reach the value of these four things we must consider not only each by itself, but all of them together, working simultaneously, and accumulating their power by co-operation. And from the time of Constantine to the present day, a period of more than fifteen hundred years, these four results of his conduct have not ceased to exist.

Let us take the Nicene Council as standing the first among a number of subsequent Councils. From 325 to the Council of Chalcedon in 451 is a period of 126 years. This period witnesses the dissolution of the Roman empire in the West; it is spent by the Church in establishing the full doctrine of the Incarnation. That Godhead of Christ which was impeached by Arius is asserted, not only by the 318 Fathers at Nicæa, but, after forming the battlefield for a number of Councils between 325 and 380, prevails in spite of the tyranny of the Emperors Constantius and Valens, and is accepted as the test of Christian faith, by Pope Damasus confirming the decrees of the Eastern bishops whom Theodosius had assembled, and by the imperial law which recognised Damasus at Rome and Peter at Alexandria as teaching what was the standard of Catholic truth upon the highest of all subjects, the being of God, while those who denied it were to suffer "the infamy of heresy."

Fifty years later, twenty years after Rome had been taken by the Goths, when all secular power was lodged in Constantinople, the Archbishop of that city, renowned for his eloquence, and the favourite of the emperor, assaulted the dignity of the Blessed Virgin, which was part of the mystery of the Incarnation, and thereby caused her to be solemnly proclaimed as the mother of God in the first General Council at Ephesus. And yet again, in 451, another attempt, springing also from Constantinople, this time not in her bishop, but in the person of an aged abbot, which touched in an opposite direction, but with equally fatal effect, the Person of Christ, led to the discomfiture of the Eutychean heresy.

One character belongs to this conciliar action, that of elucidating and building up doctrine to its full consistency, of maintaining what has been handed down, of resisting incoherence and ambiguity.

Exactly contemporaneous with this action of Councils is the efflorescence of Christian literature, beginning with Athanasius and ending with Leo. No other like period was granted to the ancient Church, nor can any reason be assigned why it commenced with Athanasius, or why it ended with Leo; but in it all that concerned the Person of Christ, the nature and prerogatives of His Church and kingdom, was considered on every side by many minds. The advance of Christian doctrine by its fuller comprehension was thus carried on during this whole period, so that the description of development which occurs in the work of Vincent of Lerins in 434 seems rather a transcript of the Church's history from the beginning down to that time, than anything devised by the writer.

When St. Leo, by his great letter, set his seal upon the

perfect doctrine of the Incarnation, at the same time annulling by his single voice the legitimately called General Council of Ephesus in 449, which had attempted to support the heresy of Eutyches, we must bear in mind the immense growth of the Christian mind and thought which, since the Nicene Council had sprung up in the Fathers, elsewhere commemorated.[1] The works of three among them, Chrysostom, Cyril of Alexandria, and Augustine, are themselves like worlds. In time it would require a long life, and in ability no slight powers of mind, to embrace the whole doctrine of the last one alone. In the 130 years which produced these Fathers, the Church had been fighting for her life against the most destructive of heresies, since it was levelled at the Person of her Lord and Maker, and the most ruinous of schisms, since it was able to fatally divide the African episcopate. Exactly that time of the empire which surrendered to barbarian occupation all the countries of the West, the fruit of Roman fortitude and wisdom during 800 years, showed how "all Christian ideas are magnified in the Church." There is conciliar action, there is mental power in the multiplication and range of authors; there is a third thing no less in progress all the time—the Church becomes more definite in all the parts of her government. The majesty of the Roman peace, that one great result of the imperial rule which fixed itself in the mind and affections of so many nations, was broken at last by an indefinite number of Northern raiders or pirates, who, becoming chiefs for the time absolute among their people by the necessity of warfare, seized what parcels of territory they could lay hold of in Gaul, and Spain, and Britain, as a wild beast seizes so much flesh of his victim. Gepids, and Herules, and Sueves, Burgundians and Vandals, were continually occupying territory, in perpetual conflict with each other, as the Saxons most of all divided one small island, wasting their conquests and each other for generations. But at this moment, while the Western empire was breaking up, the Pope with increasing power dealt with four successive heresies. As Silvester condemned Arius, so Innocent preserved the doctrine of grace against

[1] For which see vol. v. pp. 383-491.

Pelagius, Celestine guarded the Person of our Lord against Nestorius, and Leo completed the victory against Eutyches. The growth of government kept pace with the expansion of learning and the consolidation of doctrine. There was one and the same idea in the Nicene decree which condemned Arius and the letter of St. Leo which unmasked the dangerous exaggeration of Eutyches. Arius and Eutyches seemed at the opposite poles from each other; both ended in the cession of Egypt by the faithless Monophysite to Mohammed, the complete Arius.

At the time when the great wisdom and firm character of St. Leo was protecting and establishing the doctrine of the Incarnation, Attila was threatening Rome itself with destruction. Leo himself averted that danger. But hardly had he confirmed the fourth Council, at the request of the Council itself, and at the earnest entreaty of the Emperor Marcian, when the Vandal Genseric got possession of Rome, carried into captivity the widowed empress with her daughters, the eldest of whom he made to marry his son. Then succeeded that agony of twenty years on which followed the abolition of the Western emperor. The great enemy of the Christian faith in our times wrote the truth that "the warlike barbarians of Scythia and Germany had subverted the empire of the Romans." How was the Pope left? Under hostile domination, that of an Arian Herule, captain of free lances, who held all Italy in his grip. An insurgent emperor, possessing for a few months the Byzantine throne, was trying to force upon Eastern bishops another doctrine than that of St. Leo, which was followed by the lawful emperor pursuing a like course in a document drawn up by the Archbishop of the Eastern capital himself. Acacius thought the time propitious to make the primacy of the Church follow the Western empire to Byzantium. The Pope was left nothing but his apostolic power. No temporal sovereign supported the Catholic faith. For thirty-four years, from 484 to 518, a succession of Popes defended St. Leo's doctrine and government solely by the apostolic power against which Acacius had risen, and at the end of that time, the East, the bishops, the abbots, the senate, the emperor, the archbishop who had taken the place of Acacius, acknowledged together that "the solidity of the Christian religion rested entire and perfect in the Apostolic See.[1]

Thus the Apostolic See traversed the first fifty years since the Western empire had been extinguished with an acknowledgment of all that it claimed from its Eastern rival—an acknowledgment surpassing in force and definiteness everything which had occurred to that time. It would be difficult to construct in words a more stringent statement that its doctrinal decision was infallible than that given by the Eastern patriarch at the head of the whole people who constituted what remained of the Roman empire. At the time the sole emperor was seated at Byzantium. An Arian king had ruled not Italy only, but a large surrounding territory with moderation and great renown for twenty-five years, and had enlaced with Arian connections of his family all the Western governments except that portion of Gaul which was held by Clovis. The eldest daughter of the Church had indeed been born when Clovis was converted to the Catholic faith in 496, but it would have required the foresight of a prophet to discern those acts of God which were to be done by the Franks.[2] It was the only gleam of light presented by the temporal governments in the West.

Thus at the very time during which the Western empire was hastening to irreparable dissolution, the Church of God was showing a perpetual development in doctrine, in government, in defence of those great mysteries which encompass and attend upon the Incarnation of her Lord. Of these developments no one was more fruitful than that which dates also from the assembling of the first General Council, the public introduction of the monastic life. If its origin amid the deserts of Egypt, in the person of Antony, two hundred years before, when the empire of Constantine was at its height, was wonderful, no less wonderful was the new growth it was to take, in the midst of universal calamity, from the person of a Roman noble, who, in his search after the perfection of Christian life, fled for refuge into the Samnite mountains.

At the birth of St. Benedict in 480, the state of Europe

[1] See vol. vi. p. 168.   [2] Acta Dei per Francos.

was miserable. Italy was groaning under Odoacer the Herule, Spain and Aquitaine under Alaric the Visigoth, and the north of Spain under the Sueves. All of these were Arians; the Burgundians, also Arians, occupied a large part of Gaul; Childeric, king of the Franks, was an idolater; the Saxons, likewise idolaters, were in possession of England. When, before the age of sixteen, Benedict withdrew from Rome in 493, Theodoric the Ostrogoth had, after a long contest, inflicting the most cruel sufferings on Italy, conquered Odoacer and put him to death at a banquet. Pope Gelasius during his five years' pontificate was fighting an heroic battle in defence of the Council of Chalcedon and of the intrinsic liberty of the Church against the sole Roman emperor, Anastasius. Clovis, with his chief Franks, had not yet been baptized. Neither Italy, nor Spain, nor Gaul, nor Germany, nor Britain offered any hope to the Pope, who courageously proclaimed the principate of the Holy See, the second rank belonging to Alexandria, and the third to Antioch, and the acknowledged three Councils of Nicæa, Ephesus, and Chalcedon, while he pronounced in synod of Constantinople that "it holds no rank among bishops."[1] We may say that the full misery which the Northern barbarians had brought upon Europe was at its height; for it was not a stable conquest, but a perpetually changing succession of invaders, whose boundaries fluctuated; an ever-new interference with the possession of the land; a multitude of diverse tribes, destitute of cohesion with each other, and the Arian yoke besides imposed on Catholics. At that moment a Roman youth of high birth deserted his father's palace and occupied a cave in the mountains above Subiaco. There, by the sole force of his character and the renown of his sanctity, he set up twelve monasteries, and founded a mode of life which provided the safest resource against human miseries. And indeed almost all Europe in that century of Benedict received the true religion through the labours of monks."[2] The words in which, sixty years after him, St.

---

[1] See vol. vi. pp. 115, 116.

[2] "Quasi funestissima illa ætate comparatum fuisset hoc vivendi institutum tutissimum adversus humanas miserias refugium. Et quedem Europa fere tota Benedicti sæculo monachis adlaborantibus veram religionem suscepit."—*Acta Sanctorum Ordinis St. Benedicte*, Mabillon, vol. i. Præfatio, p. xii.

Gregory the Great recorded his life are these: "As God's servant daily increased in virtue, and became continually more famous for miracles, many were by him in the same place drawn to the service of Almighty God, so that, by Christ's assistance, he built there twelve abbeys, over which he appointed governors, and in each of them he placed twelve monks, and a few he kept with himself, namely, such as he thought would more profit and be better instructed by his own presence. At that time also many noble and religious men of Rome came unto him and committed their children to be brought up under him for the service of God. Then also Æquitius delivered him Maurus, and Tertullus the senator brought Placidus, being their sons, of great hope and towardness; of which two, Maurus, growing to great virtue, began to be his master's coadjutor, but Placidus as yet was but a boy of tender years."[1]

After a stay of thirty-five years in the mountain above Subiaco, Benedict withdrew from his twelve monasteries in the year 529. Three years before his farther retreat the settled government of Theodoric had ceased, and the attempt to rule Italy with Gothic valour and Roman counsel had broken down. Benedict founded his new monastery at Monte Cassino. He ruled it during fourteen years until his death in 543. He was there when Rome was captured by Belisarius in December 536, the first of its five captures which marked the extreme miseries of the Gothic war. One of these preceded the death of Benedict: four more were to follow. He witnessed the victories of Totila, and by the sole majesty of his presence subdued him and made him human. It was during the thirty-five years he spent at Subiaco and the fourteen at Monte Cassino that, from the experience he had of his disciples, he drew up that rule which was to be embraced by so many generations and to change the face of Europe. Of this rule St. Gregory wrote: "I would not have you ignorant but that the man of God, among so many miracles for which he was so famous in the world, was also sufficiently learned in the teaching of doctrine, for he wrote a rule for his monks both excellent for discretion and also eloquent for style. Of whose life

[1] St. Gregory, Dialogues, Book ii. ch. 3, old translation.

and conversation if any be curious to know further, he may in the institution of that rule understand all his manner of life and discipline, for the holy man could not otherwise teach than himself lived."[1]

Another incident recorded by St. Gregory will be sufficient to give a picture of the state of Italy and of the character of Benedict. "There was a certain Goth called Zalla, an Arian heretic, who in the time of King Totila persecuted with such monstrous cruelty religious men of the Catholic Church, that what priest soever came into his presence, he never departed alive. This man on a certain day, set upon rapine and pillage, pitifully tormented a peasant, who, overcome with the extremity of pain, said that he had committed his goods to the custody of Benedict the servant of God. This he did that his tormentor, giving credit to his words, might at least for a while cease from his horrible cruelty. Zalla hearing this, tormented him no longer, but binding his arms with strong cords, drove him before his horse to bring him to this Benedict, whom he said to have his goods in keeping. The peasant thus pinioned, and running before Zalla, carried him to the holy man's monastery, where he found him sitting before the gate reading a book. Then turning back to Zalla, who came after him furious, he said, 'This is Father Benedict of whom I told you.' Zalla, looking upon him in a great fury, and thinking to deal as terribly with him as he did with others, screamed out, 'Rise up, rise up, and deliver to me quickly what thou hast in keeping of this peasant.' The man of God, hearing such a noise, lifted up his eyes from reading, looked upon him, and then on the peasant who was in bonds. Turning his eyes upon these bonds, they fell from the man's arms so rapidly, that no one could have undone them so quickly. When the man who had been bound stood by him suddenly free, at such an act of power Zalla fell trembling to the ground, and bowing that rigid and cruel neck to Benedict's feet, begged for his prayers. The venerable man did not rise, but calling for some of his brethren, bid them to take him in and give him some refreshment. When he was brought back, he told him to refrain from such mad cruelty.

[1] Dialogues, ii. 36.

Zalla, thus overcome, retreated, and attempted to take no more from the peasant since the man of God had set him free, not by a touch, but by a look. This is what I told you, that they who more intimately serve God sometimes work miracles by the power bestowed on them. For he who, while he was sitting, repressed the ferocity of the terrible Goth, and unloosed with his eyes the knots and cords which pinioned the innocent man's arms, plainly showed by the quickness of the miracle that he had received power to work what he did."[1]

In the year 543 St. Benedict died and was buried at Monte Cassino. Twelve years afterwards the Ostrogothic reign in Italy was finally overthrown, and Italy became a province of Byzantium under the Greek exarch, whose dominion was limited in three years by the incursion of a fresh invading host, that of the savage Lombards, which, like Odoacer and Theodoric, was under Alboin, an Arian. Rome sunk to its lowest point, a garrisoned city in a conquered province, but not its capital. The exarch had his seat in Ravenna.

How far had the monastic life gone before it was taken up by Benedict? First, it had lasted full two hundred years from its commencement in Antony. From Egypt it had spread throughout the East. The greatest Eastern saints had encouraged it by their example, and that Eastern bishop distinguished among all for his five banishments and his hairbreadth escapes in defence of the Catholic faith from the fraud or the force of two tyrants, who propagated the Arian heresy with all the power first of the whole empire, then of its eastern part, had himself carried it into the West, and written a life of its first patriarch which had become a household word. Next to him, the most famous of the Western Fathers had made it an institution of his diocese, pointing it out to his brethren in the episcopate as the form of an episcopal home. It may be said that the three vows on which it rested, the unmarried life as its primary basis, the life renouncing private property, a renunciation which was incompatible with marriage, and the life of obedience, which alone could supply a living bond equivalent in the spiritual home to the bond of marriage in the secular home, had been

[1] Dialogues, iii. 32.

universally accepted and acted upon. So far the *common life* which the union of these three conditions expressed had been reached. And it was the establishment of this common life which so entirely separated the cœnobitic institution from every form of life which has its root in the union of the sexes. But the common life had not been accepted generally under one rule. It is true that the rule drawn up with great pains by St. Basil had been received in many monasteries. But when Cassian visited the East at the beginning of the fifth century, he found almost as many rules followed in them as there were monasteries. But what may seem more strange is, that not every part of a monastery followed the same rule. Rules were often mixed, and different rules followed by those who dwelt in one house. Many practices were derived from the Fathers of the Desert, from whom the first impulse to this life as a public institution had originally come. Thus there had been a vast number leading the cœnobitic life, among them great and illustrious saints,[1] but yet to the days of St. Benedict there had been no religious order. In places great irregularities had happened; false brethren wandered from city to city, from house to house, escaping from discipline, and sullying the dignity of their profession. Thus we find at the General Council of Chalcedon the Emperor Marcian obtaining a decree that henceforth no monastery should be built without the consent of the diocesan bishop, and that monks both in city and country should be subjected to the local bishop's authority under pain of excommunication. He forbade expressly their leaving the monastery in which they had been first received, or meddling with any business, ecclesiastical or secular.

St. Benedict began his rule in these words:[2]—

"It is well known that there are four kinds of monks. The first are the Cœnobites, that is, those in monasteries, who live under a rule or an abbot. The second are the Anchorites or Hermits, that is, those who, not in the first fervour of religious life, but after long probation in the

---

[1] Montalembert, i. 187; i. 136-137.
[2] "The Rule of Our Most Holy Father Saint Benedict," translated by Dom Hunter Blair. Burns & Oates, 1886.

monastery, have learnt, by the help and experience of others, to fight against the devil; and going forth well armed from the ranks of their brethren to the single-handed combat of the desert, are able, without the support of others, to fight by the strength of their own arm and the help of God against the vices of the flesh and their evil thoughts. A third and most baneful kind of monks are the Sarabites, who have been tried by no rule nor by the experience of a master, as gold in the furnace, but being soft as lead, and still serving the world in their works, are known by their tonsure to lie to God.[1] These, in twos or threes, or even singly, without a shepherd, shut up, not in the Lord's sheepfields, but in their own, make a law to themselves in their own pleasures and desires; whatever they think fit or choose to do, that they call holy; and what they like not, that they consider unlawful.

"The fourth kind of monks are those called Girovagi, who spend all their lives long wandering about divers provinces, staying in different cells for three or four days at a time, ever roaming, with no stability, given up to their own pleasures and the snares of gluttony, and worse in all things than the Sarabites. Of the most wretched life of these it is better to say nothing than to speak. Leaving them alone, therefore, let us set to work, by the help of God, to lay down a rule for the Cœnobites, that is, the most stable kind of monks."

Thus the maker of this rule does not seek to found an institute, but, finding it in operation, seeks to regulate it.

He proceeds to lay down what should be the character of the man in whom it is maintained:[2]—

"An abbot who is worthy to rule over the monastery ought always to remember what he is called, and correspond to his name by his works; for he is considered to hold the place of Christ in the monastery, since he is called by His name, as the Apostle says, 'Ye have received the spirit of the adoption of children, in whom we cry, Abba, Father.' And therefore the abbot ought not (God forbid) to teach or ordain or command anything contrary to the law of the Lord; but let his bidding and his doctrine be infused into the minds of his disciples like the leaven of divine justice.

[1] "Mentiri Deo per tonsuram noscuntur."   [2] Chap. ii.

"Let the abbot be ever mindful that at the dreadful judgment of God an account will have to be given both of his own teaching and of the obedience of his disciples; and let him know that to the fault of the shepherd shall be imputed any lack of profit which the father of the household may find in his sheep. Only then shall he be acquitted if he shall have bestowed all pastoral diligence on his unquiet and disobedient flock, and employed all his care to amend their corrupt manner of life: then shall he be absolved by the judgment of the Lord, and may say to the Lord with the prophet, 'I have not hid Thy justice in my heart; I have declared Thy truth and Thy salvation, but they despised and condemned me.' And then at length the punishment of death shall be inflicted on the disobedient. Therefore, when any one receiveth the name of abbot, he ought to govern his disciples by a twofold teaching—that is, he should show forth all goodness and holiness by his deeds rather than his works, declaring to the intelligent among his disciples the commandments of the Lord by words, but to the hard-hearted and the simple-minded setting forth the divine precepts by the example of his deeds. Let him make no distinction of persons in the monastery. Let not one be loved more than another, unless he be found to excel in good works or in obedience. Let no one of noble birth be put before him who was formerly a slave, unless some other reasonable cause exist for it. But if, upon just consideration, it should so seem good to the abbot, let him arrange as he please concerning the place of any one whomsoever, but otherwise let them keep their own places, because, whether bond or free, we are all one in Christ, and bear an equal rank in the service of one Lord; for with God there is no respecting of persons. Only for one reason are we preferred in His sight: if we be found to surpass others in good works and in humility. Let the abbot, then, show equal love to all, and let the same discipline be imposed upon all according to their deserts.

"The abbot ought always to remember what he is and what he is called, and to know that to whom more is committed, from him more is required; and he must consider how difficult and arduous a task he hath undertaken, of ruling souls, and adapting himself to many dispositions. Let him so accommodate and suit himself to the character and intelligence of each, winning some by kindness, others by reproof, others by persuasion, that he may not only suffer no loss in the flock committed to him, but may even rejoice in their virtuous increase.[1]

"The abbot is to be chosen by all the brethren, with one consent, in the fear of God, for the merit of his life and the wisdom of his doctrine, even though he should be the last of the community. He that has been appointed abbot must ever bear in mind what a burden he has received, and to Whom he will have to give an account of his stewardship; and let him know that it beseemeth him more to profit his brethren than to preside over them. He must therefore be learned in the law of God, that he may know whence to bring forth new things and old; he must be chaste, sober, and merciful, ever preferring mercy to justice, that he himself may obtain mercy. Let him hate sin and love the brethren; and even in his corrections let him act with prudence, and not go too far, lest while he seeketh too eager to scrape off the rust the vessel be broken. Let him keep his own frailty ever before his eyes, and remember that the bruised reed must not be broken.[2]

"The office of abbot is thus supreme, but it is the supremacy of a father.[3] As often as any important matters have to be transacted in the monastery, let the abbot call together the whole community, and himself declare what is to be settled; and having heard the counsel of the brethren, let him weigh it within himself, and then do what he shall judge most expedient. We have said that all should be called to council, because it is often to the younger that the Lord revealeth what is best; but let the brethren give their advice with all subjection and humility, and not presume stubbornly to defend their own opinion, but rather let the matter rest with the abbot's discretion, that all may submit to whatever he shall consider best. Yet, even as it becometh disciples to obey their master, so doth it behove him to order all things prudently and with

[1] Chap. ii. [2] Chap. lxiv. [3] Chap. iii.

justice. Let all therefore follow the rule in all things as their guide, and from it let no man rashly turn aside. Let no one in the monastery follow the will of his own heart, nor let any one presume insolently to contend with his abbot either within or without the monastery. If it happen that less important matters have to be transacted for the good of the monastery, let the abbot take counsel with the seniors only, as it is written, 'Do all things with counsel, and thou shalt not afterwards repent it.'"

In all this the rule of St. Benedict is carrying out what St. Augustine[1] had observed a hundred and fifty years before in the monasteries of his own time, directed, as he expressly says, by one called the father, who was the mainspring of the house. This combination of an authority at once absolute,[2] permanent, and elective, with the obligation to take counsel of the whole community, and to act with a single regard to its interest, is a principle in which the religious life was far in advance of the civil. It may be remarked that this rule was issued from St. Benedict's monastery at Monte Cassino about the year 535, when Justinian was publishing his consolidation of the Roman law; when also his general, Belisarius, was taking possession of Rome, deposing Pope Silverius by arbitrary force, and commencing that war of the Ostrogothic reign which ended in the imposition of a despotism from Byzantium more regardless of the good of the subject than any government exercised by persons called Christians down to that time.

But the monastery of St. Benedict's rule was, if possible, "to be so constituted that all things necessary, such as water, a mill, and a garden, and the various crafts may be contained within it, so that there may be no need for the monks to go abroad; for this is by no means expedient for their souls. And we wish this rule to be frequently read in the community, that none of the brethren may excuse himself on the plea of ignorance."[3]

The whole monastic life was built upon obedience.[4]

"The first degree of humility is obedience without delay.

---

[1] See above, chap. ii. p. 6. [2] Montalembert, ii. 56, quoted.
[3] Chap. lxvi. [4] Chap. v.

This becometh those who hold nothing dearer to them than Christ, and who, on account of the holy servitude which they have taken upon them, either for fear of hell or for the glory of life everlasting, as soon as anything is ordered by the superior, suffer no more delay in doing it than if it had been commanded by God Himself. It is of these that the Lord saith, 'At the hearing of the ear he hath obeyed Me.' And again to teachers He saith, 'He that heareth you heareth Me.' Such as these, therefore, leaving immediately their own occupations and forsaking their own will, with their hands disengaged, and leaving unfinished what they were about, with the speedy step of obedience follow by their deeds the voice of him who commands; and so as it were at the same instant the bidding of the master and the perfect fulfilment of the disciple are joined together in the swiftness of the fear of God by those who are moved with the desire of attaining eternal life. These, therefore, choose the narrow way, of which the Lord saith, 'Narrow is the way which leadeth unto life;' so that, living not by their own will, nor obeying their own desires and pleasures, but walking according to the direction and command of another, they desire to live in community, and to have an abbot over them. Such as these without doubt fulfil that saying of the Lord, 'I came not to do Mine own will, but the will of Him who sent Me.'

"But this very obedience will then only be acceptable to God and sweet to men if what is commanded be done not fearfully, tardily, nor coldly, nor with murmuring, nor with an answer showing unwillingness; for the obedience which is given to superiors is given to God, since He Himself hath said, 'He that heareth you heareth Me.' And it ought to be given by disciples with a good will, because God loveth a cheerful giver. For if the disciple obey with ill-will, and not merely murmur with his lips, but even in his heart, although he fulfil the command, yet it will not be accepted by God, who regardeth the heart of the murmurer. And for such an action he shall gain no reward; nay, rather he shall incur the punishment due to murmurers, unless he amend and make satisfaction."

But this famous sacrifice carries in its hand another.

I

"The vice of private ownership is above all to be cut off from the monastery by the roots.[1] Let none presume to give or receive anything without leave of the abbot, nor to keep anything as their own, either book, or writing tablet, or pen, or anything whatever, since they are permitted to have neither body nor will in their own power. But all that is necessary they may hope to receive from the father of the monastery; nor are they allowed to keep anything which the Abbot has not given, or at least permitted them to have. Let all things be common to all, as it is written, 'Neither did any one say that ought which he possessed was his own.' But if any one shall be found to indulge in this most baneful vice, and after one or two admonitions do not amend, let him be subjected to correction."

The rule especially provided that none should enter on this life without an exact knowledge of its conditions.[2] "To him that newly cometh to change his life, let not an easy entrance be granted, but, as the Apostle saith, 'Try the spirits, if they be of God.' If, therefore, he that cometh persevere in knocking, and after four or five days seem patiently to endure the wrongs done to him, and the difficulty made about his coming in, and to persist in his petition, let entrance be granted him, and let him be in the guest-house for a few days. Afterwards let him go into the noviciate, where he is to meditate and study, to take his meals and to sleep. Let a senior, one who is skilled in gaining souls, be appointed over him, to watch him with the utmost care, and to see whether he is truly seeking God, and is fervent in the work of God, in obedience, and in humiliations. Let all the hard and rugged paths by which we walk towards God be set before him. And if he promise steadfastly to persevere, after the lapse of two months let this rule be read through to him, with these words, 'Behold the law under which thou desirest to fight. If thou canst observe it, enter in; if thou canst not, freely depart.' If he still stand firm, let him be taken back to the aforesaid cell of the novices, and again tried with all patience. And after a space of six months, let the rule be again read to him, that he may know unto

[1] Chap. xxxiii. [2] Chap. lviii.

what he cometh. Should he still persevere, after four months let the same rule be read to him once more. And if, having well considered within himself, he promise to keep it in all things, and to observe everything that is commanded him, let him be received into the community, knowing that he is now bound by the law of the rule, so that from that day forward he cannot depart from the monastery, nor shake from off his neck the yoke of the rule, which after such prolonged deliberation he was free either to refuse or to accept.

"Let him who is to be received make, before all, in the oratory, a promise of *stability*, conversion of life, and obedience, in the presence of God and of His saints, so that if he should ever act otherwise, he may know that he will be condemned by Him whom he mocketh. Let him draw up this promise in writing, in the name of the saints whose relics are in the altar, and of the abbot there present; and let him write it with his own hand, or at least, if he knoweth not how, let another write it at his request, and let the novice put his mark to it, and place it with his own hand upon the altar. When he hath done this, let the novice himself immediately begin this verse: 'Uphold me, O Lord, according to Thy word, and I shall live, and let me not be confounded in my expectation.' And this verse let the whole community thrice repeat, adding thereto Gloria Patri. Then let the newly-received brother cast himself at the feet of all, that they may pray for him; and from that day let him be counted as one of the community. Whatever property he hath, let him first bestow upon the poor, or by a solemn deed of gift make over to the monastery, keeping nothing of it all for himself, as knowing from that day forward he will have no power even over his own body. Forthwith, therefore, in the oratory let him be stripped of his own garments, wherewith he is clad, and be clothed in those of the monastery. And let the garments that are taken from him be laid by and kept in the wardrobe; so that if ever, by persuasion of the devil, he consent (which God forbid) to leave the monastery, he may be stripped of the monastic habit and cast forth. But the form of his profession, which the abbot took from the altar, shall not be given back to him, but be kept in the monastery."

One chapter of this rule contains what St. Benedict calls "the instruments of good works," in seventy-five precepts, of which the first is to love the Lord God with all the heart, with all the soul, and with all the strength, and the last never to despair of God's mercy. Of the rule as a whole the master of Christian eloquence[1] has used words which dispense with all other words: "This rule is a summing up of Christianity, a learned and mysterious abridgment of the whole doctrine of the Gospels, of all the institutions of the fathers, of all the counsels of perfection. Therein appear conspicuous prudence and simplicity, humility and courage, severity and mildness, liberty and dependence. Correction shows its utmost firmness; condescendence all its attraction, command all its vigour, submission its repose, silence its gravity, and speech its grace, strength shows its exercise and weakness its support; and yet he calls it a beginning to nourish you ever in fear."

But these words are surpassed by a fact which goes beyond all words. When the rule went out from Monte Cassino, Europe was prostrated in desolation; the Goths were being cast out of Italy, and rent it as they went. Rome was five times taken, and fell into the hands of a Roman emperor whose delegate exceeded in treachery, according to the judgment of St. Gregory the Great, even the savage Arianism of the Lombard who was to come after the Goth. Spain and Gaul were trampled down by moving hordes of invaders, till the order of civil life was all but extinguished, and Gaul alone witnessed seven great deserts where cities had been flourishing under the Roman peace. Hengist and Horsa had cast Christ out of England, and substituted the altar of blood for the unbloody sacrifice. It was then that a succession of twenty generations accepted voluntarily and with full knowledge the life delineated in this rule, that the very flower of the Teutonic race in all these countries embraced that life of triple sacrifice, of virginity or continence, renouncing private property, and practising obedience.

[1] Bossuet, *Panégyrique de Saint Benoit.*

The rule of St. Benedict has gone beyond the words of Bossuet, being recorded as the parent of 37,000 religious houses; and to their 600 years of continuous work we owe it that "the warlike barbarians of Scythia and Germany," after subverting the empire, "embraced the religion of the Romans."[1]

[1] Gibbon, chap. xxxvii.

CHAPTER IV

THE BLESSING OF ST. BENEDICT

IN the year 542, the year preceding his death, the patriarch Benedict saw arrive at Monte Cassino two messengers from Innocent, Bishop of Mans, who wished to found in his diocese a colony of the new Italian cœnobites. This Bishop, during his pontificate, had already witnessed the foundation of forty monasteries. Benedict listened to the request, and intrusted the mission to a young deacon named Maurus, sprung, like himself, of patrician blood at Rome, and a most strict observer of his rule. He gave Maurus four companions, with a copy of his rule written by his own hand, as well as the weight of bread and the measure of wine which each religious was to consume in a day. These would serve as the invariable standard of that abstinence on which the new institution largely rested.

With this handful of missionaries Maurus left Monte Cassino, passed through Italy and the Alps, stopped a moment at the Burgundian sanctuary of St. Maurice, and visited in the Jura the colonies formed from the great monastery of Condat, where he would show his master's rule. When he reached the Loire, the successor of the bishop who had invited him would not receive him, but he was welcomed by Florus, a vicomte governing the country under the authority of Theodebert, king of Austrasia, grandson of Clovis. Florus offered him one of his estates for settling a colony, and one of his sons of whom to make a religious, announcing his own intention to devote himself to God. This donation Maurus accepted, provided it was made legally before witnesses. "For," he said to the Frank lord, "our rule requires especially peace and security." The estate was on the banks of the Loire, and there he founded the monastery of Glanfeuil, which took afterwards his own name, and was called St. Maur-sur-Loire, the first of the host of Benedictine monasteries which are so inwoven with the history of France.

That dear son of St. Benedict passed forty years presiding over his French colony, and saw in it 140 brethren. When he died, after retiring during two years to a solitary cell, "alone under the eyes of his Heavenly Witness," he had dropped a germ into the soil of France which was not to perish, and which, a thousand years afterwards, produced in the congregation of St. Maur, named after him, a renowned model of monastic learning.

The great cœnobitic centres in France of Marmoutier, Lerins, and Condat had preceded St. Benedict; but one of that very congregation of St. Maur, the most learned Mabillon, has recorded the foundation, in that sixth century, of eighty new monasteries in the valleys of the Saône and the Rhone; of ninety-four in the country from the Pyrenees to the Loire; of fifty-four between the Loire and the Vosges; of ten from the Vosges to the Rhine. The establishment, during one century, of 238 monasteries in this great region points to a movement of cœnobitic life which would seem to mean a fresh conversion of the country. By degrees every province received monks for apostles, who were usually bishops also, and founded dioceses as well as monasteries, which would be at the same time citadels and seminaries for a diocesan clergy.[1]

A succession of Gallic Councils in this century, following the lead of the General Council of Chalcedon, forbad to found new monasteries except with cognisance of the bishop, and subjected them completely to the bishop's authority. The abbots could not absent themselves, nor part with any property of the community, without the bishop's permission, and once a year were bound to go to receive his advice, or, if need be, his correction. By the great number of different rules and successive reforms, and also the acts of violence and the scandals recorded by Gregory of Tours, we learn the great resistance experienced by the Christian ideal of the common life.

The reception of the one Benedictine rule by all these

[1] The above is drawn from Montalembert, sect. vii. 2.

monasteries was only accomplished gradually and insensibly. The rule of St. Columba was a formidable rival. But we have the strong testimony of St. Odilo, Abbot of Cluny, that after St. Benedict's departure from this life, almost the whole of Gaul accepted his rule and institutions, and through his disciple, St. Maur, and those whom he taught, that rule, through long intervals of time, grew up to its perfection, and at length embraced all the monasteries in Gallic territory.[1]

The mission of Maurus marks the first meeting of the Benedictine rule and the French monarchy. This had shortly before made its appearance in the person of Clovis, but was to become, during many hundred years, the faithful ally of the religious institution. Florus addressed himself to King Theodebert, for a double authorisation: the first, to settle in his territory religious from abroad; the second, to be allowed himself to join them. The king sanctioned one of his chief officers in thus quitting him. He even attended in royal state on the occasion, and the Frank sovereign meeting Maurus, prostrated himself before the Roman monk, as Totila the Goth had prostrated himself before Benedict, asked for his prayers, and to have his name inscribed among the brethren. Theodebert presented his young son to the community, had marked out to him the monks who had accompanied Maurus, asked for their names, and embraced them with the rest as brethren. He examined their home, ate with the monks in the refectory, and ordered his chief secretary to draw out and seal with his ring a donation of land to the monastery. Florus obtained the king's presence when he took the habit. He added to his former gifts, enfranchised twenty slaves, and laid upon the altar his belt; while the king, at the abbot's request, cut off the first lock of his hair, and the other lords present completed his tonsure. The king, before quitting the monastery, saw his friend in his new habit, which he charged him to wear with honour, as he had his secular dress.

Thus the two powers which were to found France, direct it, and represent it during so many centuries, met for the first time. It may serve at least for a picture of the life that was beginning between the princes of Teuton race and

[1] Montalembert, ii. 279.

the monks, a life repeated in countless instances of their twofold history.[1]

The three Teutonic peoples who occupied Gaul are the Burgundians, the Visigoths, and the Franks.[2] Many other peoples, many particular bands, Vandals, Alains, Sueves, Saxons, made raids on its territory; but some only passed through it, others were promptly absorbed, and these small partial incursions have no historical importance. The Burgundians, the Visigoths, and the Franks alone deserve to be counted as ancestors of the actual race. The Burgundians settled themselves definitively in Gaul from the year 406 to 413. They occupied the country between the Jura, the Saône, and the Durance. Lyons was the centre of their dominion. The Visigoths, from the year 412 to the year 450, spread in the provinces comprised between the Rhone (including even its left bank south of the Durance), the Loire, and the Pyrenees. Their king was seated at Toulouse. The Franks, from the year 481 to the year 500, advanced in the north of France, and settled themselves between the Rhine, the Scheldt, and the Loire, not including Brittany and the western portion of Normandy. The capitals of Clovis were Soissons and Paris. Thus at the end of the fifth century the definitive occupation of Gallic territory by the three great Teutonic peoples was accomplished.

About the year 534 the Burgundian country fell under the yoke of the Franks. From the year 507 to 542 that of the Visigoths met with nearly the same lot. At the middle of the sixth century the Frank race had spread and prevailed through the whole of Gaul. The Visigoths still preserved a portion of Languedoc, and claimed some cities at the foot of the Pyrenees, but in fact, with the exception of Brittany, all Gaul was, if not ruled, at least invaded by the Franks.

These barbaric invasions, taken each by itself, were partial, local, momentary; a band arrived, usually not at all numerous; the most powerful, those which have founded kingdoms —the band of Clovis, for example—were only about from

---

[1] The three pages hitherto are all drawn from Montalembert, sect. ii. 273-282, *Arrivée des Bénédictins en Gaule*.

[2] From Guizot, *Civilisation en France*, 8th leçon.

5000 to 6000 men: the whole Burgundian nation did not exceed 60,000 men. It passed rapidly over a narrow territory, ravaged a district, attacked a city, sometimes withdrew, carrying off its booty, sometimes settled itself somewhere, taking care not to disperse too much; houses were burnt, fields laid waste, crops carried off, men killed or taken captive: with this damage done, after a few days the flood closed, the mark it made was effaced, the sufferings of individuals were forgotten, society reappeared, or seemed at least to resume its former state. This is what happened in Gaul in the fourth century.

But human society, what we call a people, is not a simple juxtaposition of isolated transitory existences. Had it been nothing more, the barbaric invasions would not have produced the impression which documents of the time describe. During a long time the number of places and of men who suffered from them was much less than the number of those who escaped; but the social life of each man is not concentrated in the material space where it takes place, nor in its fleeting moment of action. It spreads over all the relations which he has contracted with different points of his country, and not only over those which he has contracted, but likewise over those which he may contract or only conceive; it embraces not merely the present, but the future. Man lives at a thousand points which he does not inhabit, at a thousand moments which are yet to come. If such a growth of his life is cut off, if he is found to shut himself up in the narrow limits of his material and actual existence, to make himself a point in space and time, social life is mutilated, society exists no longer.

This was the effect produced by those invasions, by the starting up of barbarian bands, short, indeed, and limited, but for ever recurring, everywhere possible, always threatening. They destroyed, first, all regular, habitual, easy correspondence between different parts of the country; secondly, all security and prospect of the future; they broke the ties which unite together the inhabitants of the same country, the moments of the same life; they isolated men, and the days for each man. In many spots and for many years the aspect of a country might remain the same, but the social organisation was attacked, and the members had no longer any hold on each other. The play of the muscles was lost, the blood no longer circulated freely or surely in the veins. Evil broke out now on this point, now on that. A city was pillaged, a road made impassable, a bridge broken down, such or such communication stopped, cultivation of the land became impossible in this or that district: in a word, the organic harmony, the general activity of the social body became daily impeded, disturbed; dissolution and paralysis made day by day some fresh progress.

In this manner the Roman society in Gaul was destroyed, in very deed destroyed, not in the way that a valley is ravaged by a torrent, but as the most solid body is disorganised by a continual infiltration of a foreign substance. The barbarians threw themselves unceasingly in the midst of all the members of the State, at all the moments of each man's life. Such was the dismemberment of the Roman empire, the impossibility in which its masters found themselves to hold together its different parts. Thus the imperial administration was compelled to retire of its own accord from Great Britain, from Gaul, incapable of struggling against the dissolution of this vast body. What had taken place in the empire was equally taking place in each province; as the empire had been broken up, so each province was breaking up; the districts and the cities became unattached to each other, to go back into a local and isolated existence. The invasion operated everywhere in the same manner. All those bonds by which Rome had succeeded after so many efforts to unite with each other the different parts of the world, that grand system of administration, of taxes, of military service, of public works, of roads, could not be maintained. There only remained what could subsist isolated and locally, that is to say, fragments of the municipal government.

Even in the cities the old society was far from maintaining itself in its completeness and strength. Amid the invasive movement the cities were specially fortresses. The people were shut up in them to escape the bands which ravaged the country. When the barbarian immigration had been in some degree arrested and the new settlers planted on the land, still the cities remained fortresses. Instead of having to defend themselves against wandering bands, they had to defend themselves against neighbours, against greedy and turbulent possessors of the country surrounding them. Thus behind these feeble ramparts there was little security. Cities, indeed, are centres of population and of labour, but on certain conditions: on the one hand, that the country population shall labour for itself; on the other, that an extended and active trade shall be there to consume the products of the citizens' labour. If agriculture and trade are perishing, the cities will perish; their prosperity and strength do not exist apart. Such was the state into which the lands of Gaul were falling in the sixth century. The cities might escape for a time, but day by day the evil would gain on them. It did in fact so gain, and soon this last relic of the empire seemed struck with the same feebleness, a prey to the same dissolution. Such in the sixth century were the general effects upon the Roman society of the barbarian invasion and settlement, and these effects apply to the whole vast range of country from the Straits of Gibraltar on the south to the Eyder on the north, and to the whole of Britain, once christianised and civilised under the dominion of Rome, now dissevered by bands of Saxons.[1]

We have seen Theodebert, king of Austrasia, grandson of Clovis, welcome the foundation of a monastery on the Loire in his territory, take part in the reception of a high officer in his army, and present it with a donation of land, besides prostrating himself before the monk who was founding it by mission of St. Benedict; and these acts fairly represent the conduct of the Merovingian race from the time that Clovis, in the year 496, with 3000 chief Franks, received baptism. The moment was hailed with joy by the chief bishops who witnessed it, and undoubtedly the Franks had two great merits. They prevented the further occupation of France by fresh inundations of barbarian tribes, and moreover, as they had never been soiled by the Arian heresy, they kept throughout their Christian faith, and subdued both the Visigoths, who from the beginning were Arians, and the Burgundians, who had fallen for the time a prey to that

---

[1] Guizot, 8th leçon, translated to " settlement."

heresy;[1] but the Christian faith which had mastered their convictions found a long resistance in their morals. It became, indeed, the well or ill understood principle of their public right. They placed bishops among their councillors, and the name of the Blessed Trinity at the head of their capitulars. Wars with them took a new character and became religious wars. When Clovis, at the head of his soldiers, declared that he could not endure an Arian Aquitaine, when he fell on the Visigoths and reduced their provinces under his power, certainly we need not hesitate to doubt that his zeal was disinterested. The whole conquest of Aquitaine is pronounced to be a holy war.[2] The king's messengers came to the tomb of St. Martin at Tours to gather a prestige of victory, and as they enter the basilica hear the psalm chanted, "Lord, Thou hast girt me with courage for battle, Thou hast put mine enemies under my feet." Later, the invasion of Burgundy has the same religious colouring put upon it. It was to establish the only Catholic kingdom, to humiliate unbelievers, to increase the inheritance of Christ. The same language was used afterwards against the Saxons, against the Slavs, against all the Northern heathens. Nevertheless, when the Franks put the secular power to the service of the Christian religion, they laid down the principle on which the whole policy of the Middle Ages is based.

St. Gregory[3] of Tours records that Clovis, when he conquered the Visigoths, in the midst of his warriors and the priests, received from the Emperor Anastasius the title of consul, put on the purple robes and wore the crown, and mounting his horse, gave largess of gold and silver to those around him, and was called from that time consul and emperor.

These were results of the conversion of the Franks. They placed secular power under the law of the gospel, checked the advance of barbarism, and so far established one Christian kingdom. It must be added that the whole Merovingian race generally made munificent gifts of land to found monas-

---

[1] Ozanam, Ger. ii. 60-61.
[2] Montalembert, ii. 269.
[3] Hist. ii. 38, quoted by Ozanam, p. 64.

teries. Their lives were passed in the twofold enjoyment of war and the chase. In both they came from time to time across monks founding as missionaries scattered dwellings often in the midst of forests, with the companionship of wild beasts. The king, whether hunting or fighting, was often indignant at this invasion of his solitude, but ended by giving with a lavish hand the territory in which the future monastery was placed—a territory at the time of the royal gift almost worthless, but which, submitted to the careful culture of monastic life during many generations, became in time the head of a great lordship, when the spiritual descendant of a solitary pilgrim found himself after hundreds of years a prince of the great Christian empire.

Therefore Saint Remy[1] said to the detractors of Clovis, "We must pardon much to him who is become the propagator of the faith and the saviour of provinces." Thus kind words came to be used by Christian authorities to those whose public and private life lay under the charge of abominable crimes. Again, the Byzantine emperors all thought themselves superior theologians to their bishops; the race of Clovis mixed little with sacred dogmas, and except too often interfering with episcopal elections in behalf of their servants or their favourites, left the Church full independence in matters of faith and discipline.

One who has well studied their history says,[2] "It must be admitted that the Franks on coming out of the cathedral of Reims were not transformed by magic into other men. The gentle Sicander did not give up either murdering the chiefs of his family or sacking the cities of Aquitaine. He left behind him two hundred years of fratricides and of impious wars. Gaul saw with fright princes who cut their nephews' throats. One such was that Theodebert whom we have seen active and present, even a devout worshipper, at the foundation of Glanfeuil. Kings and sons of kings perished by the dagger of a crowned concubine; while in another case, her own trusted but ungrateful nobles tied their aged queen, herself of royal Spanish blood, to their horse-tails. Their armed bands came down on Burgundy

---

[1] Montalembert, ii. 269. [2] Ozanam, ii. 57.

and Auvergne, burning cities and destroying monuments and churches, leaving nothing behind but the earth which they could not carry away, and going back with long files of prisoners in fetters, to be sold in the markets of the North."

We cannot deny the barbarity of the sixth, seventh, and eighth centuries. We are obliged to believe all that historians report of that age of violence, of the crimes which stained it with blood, of the disorders which threatened the world with eternal night. We must even add to what they say. Their accounts will never reach the full number of unknown tyrannies, of unavenged ruins, from one end to the other of those rich imperial provinces given over to peoples who made force their right.[1]

Another great writer[2] speaks of the wonderful munificence of the Merovingian race, their gifts to bishops and monks, their not only restoring what they had taken away from churches, but giving immense possessions which had come by conquest to their royal domain, and how the vast farms, in which they lived in royal pomp and as great cultivators, sometimes became religious establishments. But he adds: "And yet they were miserable Christians. While they respected the liberty of the Catholic faith, while they outwardly professed, they broke without scruple all its precepts, and with them the most sacred laws of humanity. They fell prostrate before the tomb of a martyr or confessor, or having made choice of a bishop without reproach, or listened with respect to the voice of pontiff or monk, they were seen sometimes in an excess of passion, sometimes with cold-blooded cruelty, to give full course to all the evil instincts of their savage nature. Their incredible perverseness showed itself in those domestic tragedies, in fratricidal executions and assassinations, of which Clovis gave the first example, which stain ineffaceably the history of his sons and grandsons. Polygamy and perjury mixed in their life with a semi-pagan superstition; and where we read their biographies sodden in blood, scarcely traversed by some passing gleams of faith and humility, we are tempted to believe that in embracing Christianity, they

[1] Ozanam, ii. 506.   [2] Montalembert, ii. 269.

had not given up a single pagan vice nor adopted a single Christian virtue."[1]

Let us here speak of one who in her life represents adequately the whole state of Gaul in the middle of the sixth century. A captive princess, forced to marry her captor, and so dwelling for six years by the side of the most cruel and voluptuous of Merovingian kings, and escaping at last from him through the murder of her brother, Radegonda, is the first queen to submit to the monastic discipline.

In the year 529 she had fallen into the hands of the Frank king, Clotaire I., when, with his brother Thierry I., he had conquered Thuringia. Even in extreme youth her beauty was so great that the brothers quarrelled for her possession. When she fell to Clotaire, he caused a careful education to be given to her with the intention of marrying her. And here she received from her captivity itself one great blessing. Her family had been pagan before the capture of Thuringia, but Clotaire caused her to be carefully instructed in the Christian religion, and from the time of her baptism she showed how deeply she had received into her heart the mysteries of the faith. She grew up not only with a most distinguished beauty, but with a most uncommon piety and cultivated mind. At the age of eighteen Clotaire carried out his resolution to marry her, and she tried in vain to escape the crown which he imposed on her. He made her against her will a queen, and after his fashion was greatly attached to her. He could only complain that she was more desirous to be a nun than a wife. But at the end of six years he put to death, for some unexplained reason, her young brother, and she obtained permission from Clotaire to leave him. She quitted his palace at Soissons, and with great difficulty induced Medard, Bishop of Noyon, to receive her as a deaconess. Then, using the liberty she had thus obtained, she passed from one sanctuary to another, offering at them her royal jewels and vestments. She rested for a time at Tours by St. Martin's tomb, a place of pilgrimage where all who were in trouble flocked. Then she seated herself

[1] Drawn from Montalembert, ii. 334-356.

on a domain in Poitou, which her husband had granted her, and there the young queen of twenty-four practised the most rigorous austerities of the monastic life, and was especially devoted in discharging to the poor and sick the most repulsive services.

A rumour came that the king wished her to return to him. "I had rather die," she said, "than be delivered again to an earthly king." She took refuge by the tomb of St. Hilary at Poitiers, and Clotaire, ruled again by a religious fear, granted her permission to build a monastery there and to enclose herself. When it was finished, she entered it in triumph through a host of spectators, who crowded not only the streets, but the roofs of the houses to see her pass.

Again she was alarmed by the report that Clotaire had come to Tours, under pretext of devotion, but with the intention to come on to Poitiers and claim again one whom he called his dear queen. In that distress she betook herself to St. Germain, then Bishop of Paris. He came to the king at the shrine of St. Martin, and besought him on his knees, with tears, not to go on to Poitiers. Clotaire recognised the voice of Radegonda in the words of St. Germain, but he recognised also that he did not deserve to have for queen a woman who had always preferred the will of God to his own. Clotaire, in his turn, threw himself at the bishop's feet, and asked him to obtain Radegonda's pardon for what bad counsel had led him to intend against her. And from that time he left her in peace.

Thus Radegonda passed the last forty years of her life in the monastery of the Holy Cross at Poitiers, which the king from whose side she had fled enabled her to found. She erected close to her monastery a college of monks, whose duty it was to serve it. The two houses formed the first example in Gaul of those double monasteries which are found so frequently in history. The female community was very numerous. The queen drew round her as many as two hundred of diverse race and condition, among whom were members of senatorial Gallo-Roman families, and five Frank princesses of Merovingian blood. But she would

K

not be herself superior; she selected for abbess a young pupil of her own, named Agnes. She restricted herself to the rank and duties of a simple religious; in her turn she cooked, drew water from the well, carried heavy burdens of wood, washed the dishes, cleansed the houses, cleaned the shoes of the nuns while they slept. Nevertheless she continued her patristic readings; she studied St. Gregory and St. Basil, St. Athanasius, St. Hilary, St. Ambrose, St. Jerome, St. Augustine, Sedulius, and Paul Orosius. She continued her care of the poor, and shrunk not from kissing the wounds of leprous women. But all this humility did not prevent her being considered, not only by the nuns, but by the whole Church, as the real superior of the monastery she had founded. At her request the bishops of the second Council of Tours sanctioned the irrevocable cloistering of consecrated virgins, according to the rule of St. Cæsarius, which she went to Arles to study, and brought back in all its severity as that great bishop had established it in the previous generation for the house governed by his sister. She sent to the Emperor Justin at Constantinople to ask of him a particle of the true cross, which he granted her, and which she received with great joy. And on the reception Venantius Lius Fortunatus, then her secretary, who became twelve years after her death Bishop of Poitiers, composed the two hymns "Vexilla regis" and "Pange lingua," which the Church for more than twelve hundred years has made her own.

But this cloistered queen, whose life was the most severe of all her two hundred nuns, kept her eyes also upon the Merovingian princes of her time. She did all that was possible to lessen the enmity of two wives of her husband's sons, which was the source of crimes innumerable in the royal family. She wrote to the kings one after another, and to the chief Frankish lords, entreating them to watch over the interests of their people.

To the day of her death she carried next to her skin an iron chain, the gift of a nobleman of Poitou named Junian, who supported a large house of monks under the Benedictine rule, lately introduced in Gaul. He maintained numerous herds and flocks in order to supply the peasants with their greatest needs in clothing, eggs, and food. He wore no other dress than what the queen spun for him. They had agreed to pray for each other after their death, and they died on the same day and hour—the messengers who left Saint Cross at Poitiers and the monastery of Junian met midway, bearing news of the death both of queen and abbot.

At last, in the year 587, St. Gregory, Bishop of Tours, has recorded for us what he saw at her death. As she lay in her coffin, her beauty was still dazzling. Around it the two hundred nuns whom she had drawn out of the world chanted sorrowfully, with passionate interruptions of grief, as he accompanied her body to the cemetery, to which the severe enclosure prescribed by Radegonda, according to the rule of St. Cæsarius, forbade the nuns to follow; he saw them crowding the windows, the walls, and the battlements of the monastery, beseeching with loud cries that her body might rest a moment under a tower within the circuit, whilst their sobs and lamentations subdued the voice of the chanters, and offered a last homage to the royal foundress. Before her death she had drawn up a sort of will, in which she called herself nothing but Radegonda the Sinner, and placed her dear monastery under the protection of St. Martin and St. Hilary, entreating bishops and kings to treat as despoilers and persecutors of the poor those who should attempt to trouble the community or depose the abbess.

This picture of the contrasts afforded by the sixth century would not be complete without adding that the two princesses who formed part of the community at Radegonda's death were stirred up by their own furious passions, and raised such a storm against the abbess, that the monastery fell into the utmost disorder, and after a series of the most shocking scandals it required all the authority of the neighbouring bishops, as well as that of the kings, Gontran of Burgundy and Childebert of Austrasia, uncle and cousin of the two chief criminals, to restore the abbess and recover the monastery.[1] Thus we have together nuns whose charity to others is only exceeded by their severity to themselves, and nuns in league with bandits and lost to all moral sense. Daughters

[1] Montalembert, ii. 362.

of Frank and German kings, one a queen reaching the height of sanctity, others inflicting or submitting to horrible outrages; kings by turns fiercely brutal or kind and considerate; murders and sacrileges, together with passionate devotion to the most venerable relics; a mixture of saints and monsters, of whom the former subdue barbaric violence into Christian dignity, and the latter surpass in turpitude the most corrupted victims of a worn-out despotism.

The time at which this scandal broke out and troubled all Gaul from the Loire southwards was the year 590, the year in which, at the farther end of Gaul, arose the most famous monastery of Luxeuil, founded by the Celtic missionary St. Columban, and destined to be for a time the most fruitful mother of monasteries, a monastic metropolis of the Frank realm; the year also in which St. Gregory the Great, who has been called the Father of monks, began his fourteen years of suffering and of triumph on the throne of St. Peter.

We may sum up as representing in the main the same condition of things the whole Merovingian period, from the conversion of Clovis in the year 496, to the deposition of his last descendant in the year 752, when St. Boniface acted on the decision of Pope Zacharias, and sanctioned the election of the great assembly, half lay and half ecclesiastical, held at Soissons by consecrating, as Archbishop of Mainz, Pepin to be king of the Franks. The mayor of the palace, who had possessed the power, entered then into possession of the right; the Merovingian race was deposed; the Carlovingian was established, and a great revolution was effected without effort or resistance.

What had been the political and social state of France during this long period of two hundred and fifty years. Even at its conclusion nothing had been solidly founded. Franco-Gallic society had not clothed itself in any stable and general form: a Frank State did not yet exist, and Gaul had no State; for a State means a certain extent of territory, with an established centre, fixed limits, inhabited by men who bear a common name and are bound together in a common destiny. In the middle of the eighth century no such thing existed in what we now call France.

First, as to the perpetual shifting of boundaries and change of kingdoms. There had been kingdoms of Metz, of Soissons, of Orleans, of Paris. These had given place to kingdoms of Neustria, of Austrasia, of Burgundy, of Aquitaine, with an incessant change of masters, of frontiers, of extent, of importance. At length being merged in two, Austrasia and Neustria, it even then had no stability or regularity. Provinces were interchanged, sovereigns perpetually varied. The frontiers themselves were undetermined on the north and east, the invading movement of the Teutonic tribes continued. Thuringians, Allemans, Bavarians, made incessant efforts to cross the Rhine and take their share of land occupied by Franks which the Franks met by attacking these tribes on their own side of the Rhine, with the intention of reducing them to a subordinate condition, however precarious and undefinable that might be. With the Frisons and the Saxons to the north the Franks had to keep up a perpetual conflict, so that on this side the frontiers were absolutely irregular; while the Bretons on the side of Armorica kept the Neustria territories in the like uncertainty.

In the south, in Provence and Aquitaine, the old Roman population was trying incessantly to recover its independence. The Franks had conquered, but were not in full possession. When their great incursions paused, cities and country strove to rise together and shake off the yoke. The Mohammedan dominion, born in 622, towards the end of the seventh century, or at least the beginning of the eighth, was inundating the south of Italy and the south of Gaul, and almost all Spain, with a vehemence of effort even exceeding that of the Teutonic tribes on the Rhine. So north and east, west and south, Frank territory was in perpetual assault. No doubt, through this great territory the force of the Franks prevailed, but without territorial security and political unity. There was no one State, ruling by an acknowledged right of nations, and commanding its subjects to look up to such a right, to trust in it, and to practise it.[1]

The state of things thus described in Gaul began in Britain from the time that Stilicho was reduced to the necessity of withdrawing the Roman armies and the pro-

[1] Guizot, 12th leçon, translated.

tection of civilised life which the empire conferred. A detailed history of the hundred and fifty years preceding the mission of St. Augustine from the Cœlian Hill does not exist. We may be sure that the terrible sufferings which accompanied the Teutonic invasions of Gaul from the middle of the fifth century were at least equalled in Britain during the Saxon invasions, which parcelled England into seven or eight minute kingdoms, if we may dignify with such a name the several camping-grounds of pirates who had fleshed themselves with the inhabitants of what had been one province of the great empire. That one province was now subjected to perpetual subdivisions. Here, as in Gaul, there was no longer one State, nor one law, nor security of possession, nor sense of one government. Gradually the Britons were driven into the western mountain district of their former country, and were styled *foreigners* by the invaders. The Teuton called the Briton Welshman, and earned imperishable hatred from those whom he had dispossessed or subjugated, a hatred which not even Christian charity in subsequent times was able to overcome, for the monks of Bangor hated those whom they should have converted.

The overthrow of Roman rule in Spain by Vandals and Sueves would not seem to have differed in character from that which took place in Gaul and Britain until the emergence of a Visigothic kingdom, which became Catholic in the time of St. Gregory, showed the earliest and most complete union of bishops and nobles in a common government by a king with a real and yet a limited authority. In Italy, also, during the thirty-three years of Theodoric, from 493 to 526, there would seem to have been one State, in which the great Ostrogoth managed to use the best Roman intellects for the maintenance of the old constitution of law and order. But that State perished in the Gothic war, and was succeeded by a Lombard invasion and the selfish despotism of exarchs representing a Byzantine master; so that the two centuries which followed the conquest of Narses to the coronation of Pepin were times of exceeding sorrow and desolation for Italy, and the fifty years which began with the eighth century saw the Visigothic kingdom in Spain overflowed by a Mohammedan inundation which threatened at once extinction of Roman law and Christian civilisation.[1]

Thus in these three centuries, from 480 to 750, the political unity of the Roman empire has perished in a vast convulsion through the immense territory, which includes Gaul, with its undefined frontiers up to the Baltic, the whole Spanish peninsula, and Italy, with its northern frontiers to the Danube, and also Britain, from its southern sea to the Roman wall protecting it on the north. "At the moment when the Roman empire breaks up and disappears," a great writer, not a Catholic, exclaims, "the Christian Church collects herself into a definitive form. Political unity perishes, religious unity springs to full stature. I know not how many peoples, diverse in origin, in manners, in language, in destiny, force themselves upon the scene. Everything becomes local and partial; every large idea, every general institution, every great social combination disappears. This is the very moment at which the Christian Church proclaims louder than ever the unity of her doctrines, the universality of her right.

"A glorious and powerful fact, which from the fifth to the thirteenth century has rendered immense services to humanity. The unity of the Church has alone maintained some bond between countries and peoples which everything else tended to separate. By her influence, some general notions, some feelings of a vast sympathy, have continued their development. And from the bosom of the most frightful political confusion which the world has ever known has sprung an idea of the widest extent and of the greatest purity which perhaps has ever gathered men together—the idea of a spiritual society, for that is the Church's philosophical name, the type which she has aimed at realising.

"A common conviction, that is, the same idea recognised and accepted as true, is the fundamental basis, the secret bond of human society. We may stop at the most limited, the simplest associations, or rise to the widest and most complicated. We may examine what passes between three or four barbarians joined in a hunting expedition, or in a

---

[1] These four paragraphs, from "We may sum up," drawn from Guizot's 19th leçon.

chamber convoked to treat of a great people's affairs. In every case it is in the adhesion of individuals to the same thought that the fact of association consists. So long as they have not understood and agreed together, they are but isolated beings side by side, who are not in touch nor hold together. The same feeling, the same belief, whatever its nature or object, is the first condition of the social state. Only in the bosom of the truth, or of what they take for truth, men are united and society springs up. There is no society but between minds, society only subsists on the points and within the limits wherein union of minds is accomplished. Where minds have nothing in common, there is no society. The society of minds is the only society, an element necessary, as it were, the basis of all outward associations perceived by the senses.

"Now the essential character of truth, precisely that which specially makes the social bond, is unity. Truth is one, which is the reason why those who have recognised and accepted it are united. This is a union which has nothing accidental or arbitrary, for truth does not depend either on the accidents of things or on the incertitude of men. It has nothing transitory, being eternal; nothing limited, being itself complete and infinite. Unity, then, being the essential character of truth, will be the same of the society which has only truth for its object—that is, of the society which is purely spiritual. There are not, and there cannot be, two spiritual societies. It is of its nature unique and universal.

"Herein is the birth of the Church; herein the unity proclaimed by her as her principle, the universality at which she has always aimed. This is the idea which, more or less evident, more or less rigorously drawn, lies at the bottom of all her doctrines, hovers over all her labours. Long before the sixth century, from the very cradle of Christianity, it appears in the writings and in the acts of her most illustrious interpreters.

"At this time the practical consequences already produced by that unity of the Church of which we have set forth the rational characteristics, were such as these. It shines especially in ecclesiastical legislation, and with the more brilliance because in contradiction with all which passes otherwise. In treating of civil legislation from the fifth to the eighth century, a diversity ever more and more increasing seemed its most striking feature. But the tendency of the religious society is quite different. It aspires to unity in its laws, and to unity it attains. Nor does it always draw its laws from the primitive monuments of religion in the sacred books, always and everywhere the same. As the religion grows new needs appear, new laws are required, a new legislator. Who shall he be? East has separated from West. The West every day parcels itself out in distinct and independent states. Will there be plurality of legislators for a dispersed Church? Will Gallic, Spanish, Italian councils give them religious laws? No; above the diversity of national churches, of national councils, above all the differences of necessity introduced in discipline, worship, customs, the whole Church will have a general legislation, and that unique. From the fourth to the eighth century there were six Ecumenical or General Councils: the first at Nicæa in 325; the second at Constantinople in 381; the third at Ephesus in 431; the fourth at Chalcedon in 451; the fifth at Constantinople in 553; the sixth at Constantinople in 680. In spite of all causes for misunderstanding and separation, in spite of diversity of language, of government, of manners, and what went much further, in spite of the rival position of the Patriarchs in Rome, Alexandria, and Constantinople, the legislation of the General Councils was everywhere accepted, by the West as well as by the East. Scarcely some decrees of the fifth Council were for the moment contested, so powerful was the idea of unity already in the Church, and to such a degree the spiritual bond overmastered all."

The same writer notes that all these six Councils were held in the East under the influence of the Eastern emperors; scarcely a few bishops of the West attended them. A more detailed notice of them might have shown that in the first Council the legates of the Pope, not himself present, but authorising its convocation, assured its being counted as ecumenical when the Pope had accepted it, though of the 318 bishops, scarcely five Western bishops were present.

In the case of the second, it was not even summoned from the West; it was held by Eastern bishops only, at a moment of great peril arising from the long struggle engendered by the Arian heresy, and only became ecumenical when Pope Damasus accepted its doctrinal decrees, and only so far as these decrees, its alterations of discipline never being accepted. In the case of the third, presided over by St. Cyril, Archbishop of Alexandria, with the authority of the Pope, the Eastern bishops expressly welcomed the judgment of the Pope, acknowledging the Pope to have been seated up to that time in the See of Peter. In the fourth, the Eastern bishops composing it, and the Eastern emperor supporting it, solicited and obtained the confirmation of St. Leo, by which only it became ecumenical. In the case of the fifth, held most abnormally by the despotic power of Justinian, not convoked by the Pope, and not attended by him nor by the Western bishops, it only became general by subsequent acceptance of the Pope. And in the case of the sixth, Pope St. Agatho presided over its convocation, and Pope St. Leo II. confirmed its decrees, and this alone made it ecumenical, for scarcely any Western bishops save the Papal legates attended it. The great predominance as to numbers of the Eastern bishops in all these six Councils, and yet the acceptance of the Councils themselves by the West as by the East, is one of the strongest proofs offered by history of the power exerted from the beginning by the See of St. Peter in the government of the Church and the preservation of unity with truth. The power thus shown is entirely without a parallel in the case of any other bishop, or any other patriarch.

The beneficent rule of the Roman empire in making so many nations one, giving them a law which they all respected, and, with an army so moderate in numbers, keeping peace over the vast region guarded on the north by the Danube and the Rhine, with their line of military fortresses, and reaching on the south to the great deserts of Africa, that majestic peace which we find so dwelt upon by different writers at the beginning of the fifth century, had thus been completely broken up by the succession of Northern invaders throughout its western half. This overthrow may be considered as complete in the time of St. Leo, when Gaul and Italy narrowly escaped even a Mongol desolation under Attila. When the first Benedictine colony was settled at Glanfeuil in 543, nearly a hundred years had passed over the country which possessed no State. Many writers have dwelt upon the extortions of the imperial tax-gatherers, and on the sufferings everywhere endured by the inhabitants of town and country from the incidence of the rates for which Roman citizens were answerable. It has even been supposed that the invasion of barbarian tribes was often welcomed as preferable to the exactions used to fill the imperial treasury. But long before the time when Glanfeuil was settled, we may be sure that Gaul had felt in all its parts how great was the loss of one rule under a settled government. To take one particular, the cultivated land had passed into forest.[1] Merely in the northern part of the country occupied by the Burgundians to the north of the Rhône, there were counted at the beginning of the sixth century six great deserts—the desert of Reôme, between Tonnerre and Montbard; the desert of Morvan, the desert of the Jura, the desert of the Vosges, wherein Luxeuil and Lure were soon to rise; the Swiss desert, between Brienne and Lucerne; lastly, the desert of La Gruyere, between the Saône and the Aar. Savoy and Switzerland were then scarcely more than a vast forest. The primitive cantons, Lucerne, Schwitz, Uri, and Unterwald still bear the name of the Forest cantons,[2] whose impenetrable woods then surrounded their beautiful lake. We must then picture to ourselves the whole of Gaul, and all the neighbouring countries, all actual France, Switzerland, Belgium, the two banks of the Rhine—that is to say, the richest and most populous countries of modern Europe —covered with such forests as we scarcely see still even in America, while not a trace of them remains in the ancient world. Imagine these massive woods, dark, impenetrable, covering mountain and valley, including both high table-lands, and low marshes. They come down to the great rivers, or even to the sea, intersected here and there by torrents bursting their way through upheaved trunks and roots. Thus they make that mixture of mountain and forest which the one German word expresses wherein roam wild

---

[1] See Montalembert, ii. 372.   [2] Die Waldstätten.

beasts whose ferocity has not yet crouched before the advance of man, and many of whose species have completely disappeared from our country.[1]

Can we in the present day, by any effort of imagination, reach the courage of the solitary monk and missionary who, without the guardianship of peace or respected right, made his way into these forests, erected a precarious shelter of branches for the night, besought the divine protection, and lay down in his solitude? Let us cite one of these. The noble Imier, returning from a pilgrimage to Jerusalem to seek an inaccessible retreat in the mountains of his native country, hears in the silence of the night the sound of the bells of the monastery which shall one day replace his hermitage. "Brother," said he to his only companion, "do you hear that distant bell which has thrice awakened me?" "I do not," replied his servant; but Imier rose and let himself be guided by that mysterious sound through the heights and narrow gorges of the valley of the Doubs to the fountain springing up before him. There he fixed himself, and it has kept his name to this day, when the town of St. Imier is the centre of a large watchmaking industry in the Bernese Jura. Thus it was that the woods which had displaced ancient cities over the broad fields of Gaul became in their turn penetrated by monasteries of men and women, each sustained by their own life, as citadels of Christian culture in the midst of barbarism. In numberless cases outside of cities, the parish priest had sunk under the unequal battle with an invading horde; but there St. Benedict's hemire of wine and measure of bread, nourishing a company of valiant hearts, wherein Teutonic vigour was joined with Christian charity and soldierly courage, won its way, maintained itself in poverty at first, and finally restored the wilderness to cultivated life. Twenty generations of men in succession, we are told by the historian, found their happiness in buildings which had thus arisen.[2] In the midst of that life which they

---

[1] Montalembert, ii. 378.

[2] Montalembert, i., Introduction, p. lxxvii. There are names of Benedictine, Cistercian, Charterhouse, Premonstratensian abbeys in France, Belgium, England, Norway, Spain, Switzerland, Germany.

had disregarded, which they had offered in sacrifice to God, that God by a permanent miracle of His mercy caused them ever to find a joy and a happiness unknown to the rest of men. Happiness, the gift so rare, so yearned after in our lower world, reigned unbroken in the monasteries faithful to their founder's rules, to the law of their existence. It is pictured in the very names given by the monks to the places of their retreat and their penitence: the "fair place," the "good place," the "beautiful place," the "joyous place," the "dear place," the "dear isle," the "sweet valley," the "delight," the "good harbour," the "sweet rest," the "good mountain," the "holy valley," the "blessed valley," the "valley of peace," the "valley of hope," the "valley of grace," the "good valley," the "valley of salvation," the "bird's nest," the "sweet fountain," the "way of Heaven," the "gate of Heaven," the "crown of Heaven," the "yoke of God," "God's portion," "God's peace," "God's brightness," "God's knowledge," the "field of God," the "place of God," the "harbour of sweetness," the "happy meadow," the "blessed meadow," the "blessed wood," the "rule," the "rest," the "comfort," the "abundance," the "joy." In France it would appear that three-eighths of the cities and towns owe their existence to the monastic order.[1]

In the year of St. Benedict's death was born the man who seemed for a time as if his example would exceed in energy, and his rule compete in success. Two generations after St. Patrick's mission to Ireland arose among his children St. Columban. The monastic germ planted by Patrick in the land which he converted sprung up with prodigious fecundity. We are told that in the three following centuries Ireland became like a vast monastery; no valley so secluded, no forest so dense along the Atlantic shore, which did not serve for a retreat. Concerning one man, Luan, St. Bernard records, six centuries after him, that he had founded a hundred religious houses. He was himself a shepherd, educated by the monks in the vast Abbey of Bangor, which, as well as Clonfort, is said to have contained 3000 cœnobites. This must not be confused with another great Celtic monastery of the same name,

[1] P. lxx., as calculated by Longueval, *Histoire de l'Eglise Gallicane.*

the Welsh Bangor. The Irish Bangor was also a great place of education, which in that day of destruction, the fifth century, flourished with greatest brightness there. The distinguishing mark of the Irish monks at this time was to carry their faith everywhere into foreign lands. The intensity of apostolic zeal kindled by Patrick in Ireland, together with a proportionate love of knowledge, can only be estimated by the fact of the vast spread of Irish propagation during six centuries; while Ireland was sought by others to learn religion, they covered the lands and seas of the West with their missionaries. Let us pass to the action of one in Gaul.

Columban from his first youth was brought up in liberal studies. He learnt Greek as well as Latin; he was given up to grammar, rhetoric, geometry, the study of Holy Scripture. His personal beauty was so great, that a recluse warned him that if he would escape the seduction under which Adam and Samson, David and Solomon had yielded, he must fly. He passed accordingly several years under the discipline of Abbot Comgall, amid the thousands of monks who studied for knowledge and strove for holiness at Bangor.

But he had ever ringing in his ears the word, "Go forth out of thy country, and from thy kindred, and out of thy father's house, and come into the land which I shall show thee." At thirty years of age, in the year 573, he left Bangor with twelve other monks, traversed Great Britain, and landed in Gaul. He found the country terribly disturbed by intestine wars, and ecclesiastical discipline much interrupted. In the course of his preaching he reached Burgundy, where Gontran was then reigning, the least reprehensible, as it would seem, of the grandsons of Clovis. His eloquence enchanted Gontran and the great of his court. He would only receive, from the king's earnest desire to keep him, an old Roman castle at Annegray, where with his companions he practised for years the rudest of lives. He carried in the woods his Bible suspended by a satchel from his shoulder, and was one day surrounded by wolves. He remained quiet, only reciting "Deus in adjutorium;" the wolves smelt his raiment and passed on, and presently he heard a multitude of voices, Teuton brigands of the Sueve tribe, who were then ravaging the country. He did not see them, but only heard: wolves and brigands indicate the two dangers which continually surrounded the monks in their pioneering labours —from savage nature and more savage men.

After some years, the number of his disciples increased so much that he was constrained to move. Agnoald, one of the king's chief ministers, who had married a Burgundian lady of very high rank, procured for him, from the king Gontran, another strong castle named Luxeuil, where magnificent baths had been built by the Romans. In the neighbouring forests were still to be seen idols which the Gaulish idolaters had worshipped. Here Columban planted what became the great monastic metropolis of Austrasia and Burgundy.

The spot was between these two kingdoms. The whole country on the side of the Vosges mountains and the Jura, 150 miles in length, and in breadth from 25 to 35, then consisted of parallel chains of inaccessible defiles, separated by impenetrable forests, which were clothed with huge pines descending from the loftiest heights to the rapid waters of three rivers. Barbarian invasions from the time of Attila had destroyed the Roman cities, and done away with husbandry and population. It was reserved for the disciples of Columban and Benedict to reduce the forests to cultivation, and change the wild beasts into peasants.

Before long the Irish colonist was encompassed with Frank and Burgundian nobles, who brought him their sons to educate. They deposited their gifts, and even requested him at times to shear the long locks of their children, the mark of their nobility, and admit them into the ranks of his army. Labour and prayer had won upon them, and so great was the crowd of poor serfs and of rich lords, that Columban was able to institute that perpetual office called the "Laus perennis," which was already heard in the monastery of St. Maurice, on the other side the Jura. But the sound of perpetual praise, maintained by one detachment of monks after another, was intermixed with incessant labours of tilling, harvesting, felling trees, and cleaving wood. An article of his rule prescribed that the monk should go to bed so weary that he fell asleep in going, while he was to wake before he had slept out his sleep. Such is the labour out of which Europe sprung.

After twenty years thus spent, wherein his example spread wide, while his rigid adherence to certain Irish practices, and a temper of no little resolution, met with much opposition, an end came which brought out the characteristic boldness of the 'missionary. Gontran had died, and likewise his nephew Childebert II., son of the famous Queen Brunehaut. Her two young grandchildren Theodibert II. and Thierry II. reigned, the former over Austrasia, the latter over Burgundy, while the grandmother Brunehaut administered both their kingdoms. But the nobles succeeded in expelling her from Austrasia: she ruled her grandson Thierry II. and his nobles in Burgundy. It is said that Brunehaut in her old age encouraged her grandson to live an illicit life, rather than she would see a lawful queen who might limit her own authority. Columban had often rebuked the king for his disorders, and often received his promise of amendment. He had come to visit the Queen Brunehaut at the manor of Bourcheresse.[1] She presented to him the four sons whom Thierry had had by his concubines. "What do these children want of me?" said the monk. "They are the king's sons," said the queen; "give them thy blessing." Columban replied, "No; they shall not reign: they come out of a bad place." From that moment Brunehaut made him a mortal quarrel. First she forbade the monks to go out of any monasteries governed by Columban, or any one to receive them or give them any succour. Columban tried to recover Thierry, and went to visit him at a royal villa. The king heard that he was at the door, but refused to enter. He had a sumptuous repast provided for him, which Columban refused to accept from one who forbade the servants of God to approach the houses of others. Under his malediction the dishes burst asunder. The king started at this prodigy, and his grandmother came to beg his pardon, and promised correction. Columban was appeased, and returned

---

[1] Jonas, Vita, 32.

to his monastery, where he soon learnt that Thierry had fallen back into his old evil practices. Thereupon he wrote the king a letter of vehement reproaches, and threatened him with excommunication.

Thierry, urged on by Brunehaut, presented himself at Luxeuil, and demanded of Columban why he disregarded the usage of the country, why he prevented visits being made inside the monastery, and that even by women; for it was one of Brunehaut's grievances that she, queen as she was, could not pass the threshold. The king got himself as far as the refectory, requiring that Columban must either admit every one everywhere, or forfeit every royal gift. Columban replied, "If you attempt to break what has hitherto been bound by regular discipline, be assured I will neither take your gifts, nor be supported by you in anything, and if you have come to this place in order to destroy the common dwelling of God's servants, and put a stain upon regular discipline, know that your kingdom will be soon utterly ruined, together with the whole royal race." The king retreated in alarm, and was afterwards pressed by strong reproaches. He retorted saying, "You think that I shall give you the crown of martyrdom. I am not so foolish as to commit the crime; but you had better take other advice, and if you will have nothing to do with secular intercourse, depart by the way by which you came." The courtiers then exclaimed together, "We will have none here who do not associate with all." Columban said that he would not leave his monastery unless he were taken away by force.

In the end he was carried away first to Besançon, and then across France to Nantes. He was placed on board a vessel to return to Ireland, but it was driven back by stormy weather, and Columban returned by way of Paris, and received a kind reception of the King Clothaire, who sent him on to Theodebert, king of Austrasia. That king offered him the most pleasant sites to settle on, but allowed him free choice. His choice was the conversion of unbelievers, which led him to Bregenz, where dwelt at the time idolatrous Sueves and Alamans. But this was not to be the end of his course. In three years his two enemies Theodobert and Thierry had yielded up their kingdoms to Clothaire II. Brunehaut had been put to death with great cruelty and ignominy, tied to the tails of wild horses. Columban crossed the Alps with a single companion, was received by the Lombard king, Agilulf, and given a choice spot in the mountains, on which he set up the great monastery of Bobbio, near the banks of the Trebbia, where Hannibal had won a great victory. Here Columban in his old age constructed a citadel of orthodoxy against the Arians, kindling a home of learning which for a long time was the light of Northern Italy. In a palimpsest manuscript of the library belonging to this monastery, Cardinal Mai in our days recovered a great part of Cicero's lost book on the Commonwealth, the parchment of which still bears the inscription, "Book of St. Columban of Bobbio."

In the last year of his life, the year 615, in which he founded Bobbio, he wrote at the request of the Lombard king, Agilulf, and his queen, the illustrious Theodelinda, a letter to Pope Boniface IV. Amid several pages of straggling and incoherent matter, there is yet a distinct recognition of the Pope's singular rank.[1] He addresses him in the title as the most dear Pope, the exalted prelate, the pastor of pastors. "We," he says, "are bound to the chair of St. Peter, for though Rome is great and widely known, it is only through that chair that it is for us great and renowned. It is since God and the Son of God condescended to be here, and by those two most fervid coursers of God's Spirit, the Apostles Peter and Paul, whose dear pledges are your felicity, has stirred many waters, and multiplied His chariots among innumerable peoples, the supreme Charioteer, who is Christ, the true Father, who moves Israel, has come even to us. From that time you are great and illustrious, and Rome her self more noble and brilliant, and if it may be said, on account of the two Apostles of Christ, you are well-nigh heavenly, and Rome is the head of the Churches of the whole world, reserving the singular prerogative of the spot of the Lord's resurrection."

Clothaire II. having become sole king of Austrasia and Burgundy as well as Neustria, taking the kingdoms of the

---

[1] See Gallandi, vol. xii. p. 351-355 for the whole letter. The section quoted is x. p. 354.

former persecutors of Columban, sent Eustasius, who had become Abbot of Luxeuil, to bring Columban back, but he utterly refused to leave his new-founded Bobbio, and died there in a wild cavern adjoining, which he had made a chapel of the Blessed Virgin. It was long frequented by sufferers, and three centuries after his time the annals of the monastery recorded that those who entered it sorrowing left it rejoiced and consoled by the peace of mind which its two patrons had obtained for them.

The second successor of Columban as Abbot of Bobbio, Bertulfé, a noble Austrasian and near relative of Arnoul, Bishop of Metz, first known progenitor of the Carlovingian race, had to struggle with the Bishop of Tortona, who sought to reduce the abbey under his jurisdiction, by the help of Ariowald, then king of the Lombards. Bertulfe betook himself to Pope Honorius and made known his rule, for which he obtained the Pope's approbation, and came back with a privilege which exempted from all episcopal jurisdiction the monastery in which Columban had finished his career.

The great Irish missionary, in the pre-eminence of his dauntless courage, shrunk, where need was, from no contest with the Merovingian centaurs who ruled divided Gaul. They could indeed be munificent patrons, sometimes even Christian, so far as the waist, while from the waist downwards they were monsters. Upon their land Columban planted Luxeuil, from which many other monasteries were drawn in successive swarms. He carried to them the rule under which he had lived himself at Bangor, the rule which St. Patrick had everywhere spread in Ireland, more severe and peremptory than that which St. Benedict had sent to Glanfeuil. One of Columban's disciples, Sigisbert, had followed him on his way across the Alps, but leaving him at the St. Gothard, betook himself to the source of the Rhine, and there built himself a cell with branches. The few people round were still idolaters; they reverenced him and listened to him, but when he sought to make them cut down their sacred oak, one of the pagans lifted his axe against him. A sign of the cross disarmed him. A long struggle of conversion ensued, but he was helped by a neighbouring lord, who became a Christian on the word of the

Irish missionary, and then a monk, and dowered the rising monastery with all his goods. It still exists under the name of Dissentis; and so the Rhine, whose waters were to wash the walls of so many monasteries, was blessed at its birth.

Another disciple, St. Gall, upon the Lake of Constance, in the midst of rocks and thorns, hung the reliques which he wore round his neck on a wooden cross, which he made of a branch, and passed the night in prayer. This too was the beginning of a monastery famous in after time, which helped to convert the people of the Alamans into a Christian province, and was a chief centre of intellectual life in the German world.

But it was at Luxeuil,[1] from which King Thierry and Queen Brunehaut had expelled by force Columban, that his work was carried on most successfully. It became the centre of monastic colonisation in Frankish Gaul during all the seventh century. Its second abbot was Eustasius, sprung from a noble Burgundian family, who had borne arms before he became a monk at Luxeuil. Eustasius had followed Columban to Bregenz; he then returned to Luxeuil, and Clotaire II. had sent him to induce Columban to return to the government of his old monastery. This he failed to do, but governed the monastery himself during ten years; he enjoyed the support of the Frankish nobility, as well as the favour of the king, Clotaire, and it became under him the recognised monastic capital of all the Frank dominion. It restored the discipline of other drooping monasteries, becoming a nursery-ground of bishops and abbots, of preachers and reformers, especially for the two kingdoms of Austrasia and Burgundy. The flourishing school which Columban had created, and which he had intrusted to Eustasius, helped on this result. The clergy and the monks from other monasteries, and the children of the noblest Frank and Burgundian families, frequented it. The most famous cities of Gaul, Lyons, Autun, Langres, Strasbourg, sent their lay children to it. From the banks of the Lake of Geneva to the coasts of the Northern Sea, every year saw some monastery founded and peopled by the sons

---

[1] Drawn from Montalembert, ii. pp. 539-554.

of Luxeuil. Episcopal cities sought for rulers in the men trained there to the government of souls.

The successor of Eustasius was Walbert, a pupil likewise and companion of Columban. Of Sicambrian race, a noble and very wealthy family, he had obtained a great name as a soldier. But the attraction of the cloister overmastered the warlike spirit of the Frank. He came to Luxeuil, and brought it in donation, not his vast domains only, but the military habits which he did not quit in the monastery. He suspended to the vault of the church the arms in which he had won renown. Three hundred years after his time they are mentioned as being still there. He was living by himself in a hollow rock near a spring, three miles from the abbey, when the monks came to bring him home as their third abbot. He governed them well and happily during forty years, A.D. 625–665. His name has remained in the adjoining country the most popular of those who governed the great Sequanese abbey. He maintained discipline and great study, and increased the domains of the community, first by his own great donations, and then by those which the renown of his house drew from all parts.

Not only was temporal independence thus secured, but a sort of spiritual independence was likewise sought. The great monasteries tried to gain this from provincial councils or from popes. Their effort was to be sheltered by a solemn privilege from the abuse of authority and the vexations which the diocesan bishop, under cover of his spiritual jurisdiction, might inflict upon them. He might impose his presence on them with a great surrounding, or make them pay exorbitantly for holy oils and ordination of the brethren, or especially he might hamper the liberty of their internal elections. Lerins had obtained this privilege from the Council of Arles in 451; St. Maurice from the Council of Châlons in 579. As Pope Honorius had given it to the Abbey of Bobbio, so his next successor, John IV., gave it under the abbacy of Walbert, and at the request of Clovis II., then a minor, to Luxeuil.

Six hundred monks made under Walbert's crosier the permanent garrison of this monastic citadel. Missionaries, single or in bands, went thence perpetually to found new religious colonies. Under him more than under his predecessors the fertility of Luxeuil became prodigious. An old Life of the Abbess of Salaberga [1] of the seventh century says, "In his time troops of monks and swarms of sacred virgins began to spring up through the provinces of Gaul, not only in fields, villages, and castles, but through the waste places of the desert, from the rule of Benedict and Columban, whereas before that time but few had been found in those regions."

The forty years during which Walbert was abbot mark exactly the rise of Mohammed's attack upon Christian life. The Saracenic rule was the exact contradictory of the monastic discipline; wherever Saracen armies came, they had a special instruction to destroy the monk; and instead of the nun, their mission was to convert the life which had its beginning at Nazareth into the foulness of the conqueror's harem, as devised and executed in Mohammed's own life. The outburst of the monastic institute in the first half of the seventh century, as noted in the mediæval Life just quoted, is therefore a fact of the utmost relevance. What had been in past times, as it were, a specimen of rare devotion, became by its multiplication the opening of a new epoch in Christian history. We have recorded for us numberless examples of the noblest men and women, often of Gallo-Roman, but specially of Teutonic race, bestowing first their own persons on the hardest and most self-denying of lives, and then adding the endowment of large landed properties to the monastery, which had become a Christian citadel in the wilderness produced originally by the conquest of the Northern invaders. The completeness of the conquest had alone made possible the greatness of the reparation. Whence did Walbert, the noble Sicambrian, obtain possession of the vast lands with which he dowered Luxeuil? If there had not been seven deserts in that Burgundy, there would not have been the means to turn cells made in the caverns of rocks, or formed of branches crossed together from the overhanging woods, into stately dwellings, where hundreds of monks never ceased to echo the *Laus perennis:* the nuns of such places as Remiremont could not have existed. A

---

[1] Mabillon, ii. p. 407, Vita Sanctæ Salabergæ.

disciple of St. Patrick could not have stirred a whole country with his heroic example, nor foiled the ambition of such a queen as Brunehaut, nor rebuked the Merovingian impurities which defiled the land.

For the unsettled political state of Gaul enhances the effect of the monastic multiplication. The historian of civilisation is careful to urge upon his pupils of the nineteeth century that during all this period of 250 years Gaul possessed no State, but only rival competitors of the longhaired race of Clovis, who partitioned the great Gaul of Roman times into ever-changing districts, liable to endless convulsions. Such cities as remained still had bishops, who defended them as well as the remains of their old authority still subsisting allowed; but what portion of their dioceses outside of the city still enjoyed Christian government we know not. We know only enough to see that a solitary priest, in an open unguarded mission, had but a small chance of carrying on his priestly functions, and that a monastery, founded in strict poverty, and in its completeness containing men who were willing to carry their life in their hands, and divided the days into hours of worship and hours of manual labour, the praise of God being in both the work aimed at, were able to carry the Christian faith through every part of the great country which had yet no State, and was subject to the most arbitrary interruptions on all sides.

Among the progeny of Luxeuil we find close to it a great foundation due to one of the Irish monks, a companion to him who, four hundred years after his death, was still called the "king of monks, and the driver of God's chariot." When he was expelled from Luxeuil, only Irish religious were allowed to follow him. One of these, advanced in age, is supposed to have been a brother of St. Gall. His Celtic name has been hidden under its Latin translation, Deicola, shortened into Desle. When he reached with Columban, on his way to Besançon, a spot full of briers, he felt his strength fail. He threw himself at the feet of his abbot, and begged his blessing to finish his pilgrimage on the spot. Then looking about in the forest for a place of retreat, he met a herd of swine, whose herdsman was startled at the sight of a tall stranger in an unknown costume. "Who are you?" he asked; "whence do you come, and what are you seeking? What are you doing in this savage spot without guide or companion?" "Be not alarmed, brother," said the old Irishman; "I am a traveller and a monk. I beg you, for charity, to show me some place here where a man can dwell." The swineherd replied that he only knew in that neighbourhood one spot, marshy enough, but habitable from the abundance of water, and belonging to a powerful vassal named Werfaire. But he refused to conduct the stranger thither, lest his herd in the meantime should stray. Desle insisted, saying, "If you will do me this little service, I answer for it that you shall not lose the least of your pigs. My staff will take your place, and serve for herdsman in your absence." He stuck thereupon his staff in the soil, which all the pigs gathered round. So the two went through the woods together—the Irish monk and the Burgundian swineherd. Thus the situation of the actual city of Lure was discovered, and of its celebrated monastery, whose abbot, eleven hundred years after this, was still one of the princes of the Holy Roman Empire.

But Desle was not at the end of his difficulties. Near his new retreat was a small church frequented by shepherds and peasants, and served by a secular priest, who by no means liked the arrival near him of a disciple of Columban. "That monk," he said, "will prevent me making my livelihood." And he told his flock that the stranger was a magician, hiding himself in the woods to follow his incantations. "He comes at midnight on pretence of praying in my chapel. It is useless my shutting the doors. He can open them with a word." And then he denounced him to the local lord, Werfaire, asking him if he thought fit to allow a certain strange monk to take possession of his chapel, so that no one could turn him out. To which Werfaire made the brutal reply of ordering his people to seize Desle if they could and mutilate him. But before they could do this a mortal malady, of the nature which he had wished to inflict, took away his life. His widow, in the hope of winning the divine justice on behalf of her husband's soul, made a donation to him who was called Christ's traveller of all the territory surrounding the site of Lure. Soon many disciples came to seek with him a life of peace and prayer. One day their solitude was broken by King Clotaire II., whose name constantly recurs in the history of Columban and his disciples. As he came to hunt in a royal domain near Lure, a wild boar, which the lords in his train were pursuing, came for refuge to Deicola's own cell. The saint laid his hand upon him, saying, "You have come asking for charity, and you shall save your life." The king, informed by the huntsmen, who had followed the beast's track, came himself to see the wonder. When he found the old recluse was a disciple of the Columban whom he had always honoured and protected, he inquired affectionately after the means of subsistence which the abbot and his comrades could find in that solitude. "It is written," replied the Irishman, "that those who fear God want nothing. We lead a poor life, but it is sufficient for us with the fear of God." Clotaire bestowed on the new community all the forests, pastures, fisheries which the royal treasury possessed in the neighbourhood of Lure. From that moment it became and remained one of most richly endowed monasteries in Christendom.[1]

Another of Columban's companions, probably Irish, since he was one of those who left Luxeuil with him, founded a small monastery in the neighbourhood, which was afterwards conducted by a young inhabitant of Treves, of very noble birth, named Germain. At seventeen years of age, in spite both of king and bishop, he had left everything to fly into solitude. He was one of that number who, in coming to Luxeuil, had alarmed Abbot Walbert. Afterwards the abbot sent him into a rich well-watered valley, part of the gift of the Alsatian Duke Goudoin. The valley was shut in by a defile, which Germain had to find the means of opening. Walbert, with the consent of his brethren, had released from their obedience to him all the monks whom he put under Germain's authority to found this house of Moustier-Grandval. A new Alsatian duke, Adalric, chose to treat them as rebels. He led against

---

[1] See the mediæval Life of St. Deicola, by an anonymous monk in the tenth century, given by Mabillon in the second volume of his Acta, pp. 95-99, which I have drawn from Montalembert's compressed mention of it, vol. ii. 556-560.

them a company of Alamans, ready for fighting and pillage. Germain, when he saw the cottages round burning, and their inhabitants slaughtered, broke out into reproaches. As Germain returned to Grandval he met other soldiers, whom he attempted to stop. They turned upon him, stripped and slew him. The martyr's body was taken to the church which he had built at St. Ursanne, and thus arose another saint, who, without passing through Luxeuil, had felt the ascendancy of Columban's genius.

Vandregisile was born near Verdun, of rich and noble parents, connected with two Mayors of the Palace, Erchinoald and Pepin of Sandens, one of whom governed Neustria and the other Austrasia, under King Dagobert I., son and successor of Clotaire II., who had so favoured Columban and his disciples. Thus he became Count of the Palace—that is, judge of causes brought before the king, and at the head of the royal revenues. But the great examples furnished by the Frank noblesse had raised his heart above the desire of power and the sway of ambition. He renounced a marriage arranged by relatives and took refuge with a solitary on the banks of the Meuse. Now the Merovingian kings had already imposed on all Frank nobles a prohibition to take the clerical or monastic habit without their leave. This was grounded on the obligation of military service to the prince, which was the soul of social organisation among Teutonic peoples. Dagobert, therefore, looked with very evil eye upon a Frank brought up in the royal court and holding a public charge, who thus withdrew himself without sovereign permission from the duties of his rank. He sent Vandregisile an order to return. As, much against his will, he was entering the palace, he saw a poor man whose cart had turned over in the mud before the very gate of the king. All the passers-by left him there, and some even trod on him. The Count of the Palace dismounted, held his hand out to the poor labourer, and the two together righted the cart. He then went in to Dagobert, amid shouts of derision, his clothes soiled with mud. But in the king's eyes they shone with the fire of charity. He was touched with that humble devotion, allowed him to follow his vocation, and forbade any one to interfere with him.

Vandregisile,[1] delivered from this anxiety, took refuge at the tomb of St. Ursanne, which was situated on one of his domains. He set himself to subdue the flesh by great austerities; to struggle against the temptations of youth by plunging during the winter in the snow, or in the frozen waters of the Doubs, while he chanted psalms. There, too, he was to catch traces of the teaching and the example of Columban. So he was led from the sides of the Jura across the Alps to Bobbio. There he admired the fervour of those whom the great Irish missionary had left behind him. There, too, no doubt, he was so struck with the remembrance and rule of Columban, that he determined to go to Ireland to seek in the country of the founder of Bobbio and Luxeuil the secret of the penitential life and the narrow way. But on the way he passed through Rouen, then the See of a celebrated bishop, Ouen, who had known him at Dagobert's court, and had been himself touched by Columban's example. The metropolitan of Rouen would not lose a man marked out doubly by approved virtue and high birth. The Abbot of Luxeuil, in seeking a superior for his colony, had long to search for a monk at once learned, holy, and noble. We see that birth was esteemed a quality most precious for the founders of religious institutions at that time, doubtless because it gave support to the chiefs of communities to maintain them even materially against the usurpations and violences of the lords whose possessions surrounded the new monasteries. Thus Archbishop Ouen constrained his old friend and companion to receive sacred orders, but without being able to prevent him from a further search after monastic life. But he succeeded in fixing him to his own diocese through the munificence of the Mayor of the Palace, Erchinoald, who bestowed on his cousin a great domain not far from the Seine. It was not under cultivation, and among the rocks and briars were seen the ruins of an old city utterly destroyed at the Frank invasion.

On this desert spot Vandregisile constructed the Abbey of Fontenelle, which, under his own name of St. Vandrille,

[1] See the Life in Mabillon, vol. ii. pp. 503-511, by an anonymous monk of the same time.

was to hold so important a place in the history of Normandy and of France. The holy Queen Bathilde, her son King Clovis II., and many noble Neustrians, added rich donations to that of Erchinoald, whilst others in great number came to lead the cœnobitic life under his authority. He had to build four churches in the midst of their cells to meet the needs of their devotion. He was specially careful in the observance of his rule to impose on them, together with the exercise of manual labour, an absolute renouncement of private property. That is precisely the point which would offer the hardest rub to the feelings of the rich and warlike. The writer of the Life remarks how admirable it was to teach those the art of sacrificing their own goods who had been accustomed to seize the goods of others. By their art he planted on a neighbouring slope in a good aspect the first vine known in Normandy.

Fontenelle was situated in the country of Caux, the whole of which was then only in name Christian; its inhabitants had fallen back into a complete and brutal barbarism. The abbot preached through the whole country, with such effect, that the people no longer met a priest or a monk without prostrating themselves before him as an image of Christ. When he died, Vandregisile left three hundred monks in his monastery, and a memory so popular that, four hundred years after it, Latin hymns were translated into the vulgar tongue. Fontenelle, close to Caudebec, became, with Jumièges, one of the greatest ornaments of the banks of the Seine. Travellers were long shown the rude seats on which the founder, with his two friends, the Archbishop Ouen and Philibert, the founder of Jumièges, united their counsels for the triumph of justice and peace in France. The glorious church of the thirteenth century lasted till it was destroyed in the fury of the anti-Christian revolution. Of its splendour very little remains, but the ruined towers of Jumièges still bear witness to the magnificence of that other abbey, the fairest ornament of that part of Neustria, connected also by its founder with the work and lineage of Columban. Philibert also had been recommended by his father to King Dagobert, and at twenty years had quitted the court and military life for the life of the cloister. He had been monk and then abbot at the monastery of Rebais, immediate daughter of Luxeuil; had made his pilgrimage to Bobbio and the other communities which followed the Irish rule, and had been a friend in youth of Archbishop Ouen.

Philibert often visited his neighbour Vandregisile, and with his monks laboured like him in clearing the lands granted to him by Queen Bathilde and Clovis II. They made out of them meadows of marvellous fertility, and had to brave the enmity of the royal foresters, who stole their horses. Jumièges, like Fontenelle, had been built on the site of an ancient Gallo-Roman castle, which was to be replaced by what those of that age called "the noble castle of God." Being on the very edge of the Seine, in a peninsula formed by the windings of the stream, Philibert's abbey was more accessible by water, and became speedily the centre of a great trade. Breton and Irish sailors touched there, who brought the monks stuff for their clothing in exchange for their wheat and cattle. The monks also equipped vessels, in which they went to ransom captives and slaves from a distance.

Some of these captives no doubt contributed to swell the number of monks at Jumièges, which rose to nine hundred, without counting the fifteen hundred servants who filled there the office of lay-brothers. It followed a rule composed by Philibert, after carefully considering the numerous monasteries of France, Italy, and Burgundy, which he had visited for this purpose. This rule was followed by the greater part of the communities which were then formed in Neustria, to whom Jumièges was a fostering power to which abbots and monks came to be formed or refreshed. Philibert had combined the teaching of the Eastern Fathers, such as St. Basil and St. Macarius, with the precepts of the two chief Western, St. Benedict and St. Columban. But Columban's influence would naturally be the greatest, on account of Philibert's earliest monastic education, and his long stay at Luxeuil and Bobbio. In his magnificent church, which astonished his contemporaries, he had raised an altar to Columban alone, of all the saints whose rules he had studied and practised.[1]

[1] See the authorities quoted by Montalembert, ii. 584.

CHAPTER V

ST. PATRICK AND ST. AUGUSTINE

> "From Canterbury's towers,
> 'Rome of the North' long named, from them alone
> Above sea-surge still rose that vestal fire,
> By tempest fanned, not quenched; and at her breast
> For centuries six were nursed that Cœlian race,
> The Benedictine Primates of the land."
> AUBREY DE VERE—*The Penance of St. Laurence*, p. 64.

WHAT is that *vita communis*, the advance of which by a divine impulse from the deserts of Egypt over all the provinces of the Roman empire I have attempted in the four preceding chapters to trace? What is it which moved the greatest of confessors and champions of the faith to delineate its first patriarch at length, and commend his life for a pattern to the monks of the West? What is it which stirred with one voice St. Basil and his companion St. Gregory, St. Ambrose, St. Jerome, St. Augustine, St. Martin, St. Gregory the Great, to praise it, and not merely in words, but in that highest praise, the imitation of their lives? What is it which St. Benedict sent with the dearest of his disciples to prosper on the banks of the Loire, in the middle of the sixth century, endowing it with the measure of bread and wine which his long experience had found sufficient for the material sustenance of the life established by him at Monte Cassino.

Perhaps a comparison with another great work of the Church will illustrate what it is. The basis of human society had been laid by establishing, on the express authority of Christ, marriage as one and indissoluble. The original marriage, as founded by God Himself in Adam and Eve, had been touched by the Passion of Christ, and made an image of His espousal of human nature, and so created a sacrament. The Church had made the civil

Roman law give up its divorce. The practice of fornication, which had polluted to the utmost Greek and Roman and heathen society, had been stamped with reprobation. No conquest of the Christian faith over the heathen mind had cost the Church more persevering efforts than this establishment of Christian marriage, this purification of married life.

The Church had thus effected the sanctity of the Christian home. In the *vita communis* another home was created, of altogether supernatural character. Another father appeared, the head of the house, whose members were not connected by any natural relationship. This father, in the name and with the character of Christ, was to rule a community which rested on three things, each of them a great sacrifice of the natural man. This home, instead of being founded on marriage, was to profess in each of its members the unmarried life of virginity or continence; instead of the possession of property, which the whole world seeks after as the condition of its progress, was to profess an absolute renouncement of all property in the individual. And thirdly, instead of that exercise of the will which is the crown of natural life, was to add the continual sacrifice of private will to the rule of the father, who was the mainspring of the house so founded. Such a house, then, contradicted by its very existence the three strongest motive powers of the natural man. The first sacrifice, that of the unmarried life, alone made it possible to carry out the second, the surrender of individual property; and again, both of these exercised together alone made it possible to exercise that surrender of the individual will in which monastic obedience consisted.

On what spiritual resources did a life rest the essential basis of which consists in a total defiance of the principles whereon the ordinary life of man rests? The prologue of St. Benedict's rule gives this answer to the question: "We are about to establish a school of the Lord's service, in the setting forth of which we hope to order nothing that is harsh or rigorous. But if anything be somewhat strictly laid down, according to the dictates of sound reason, for the amendment of vices or the preservation of charity, do not therefore fly in dismay from the way of salvation, whose beginning cannot but be strait and difficult. But as we go forward in our life and in faith, we shall with hearts enlarged and unspeakable sweetness of love run the way of God's commandments; so that never departing from His guidance, but persevering in His teaching in the monastery until death, we may by patience share in the sufferings of Christ, that we may deserve to be partakers of His kingdom." [1]

St. Benedict calls his institution a "school of the Lord's service." Bossuet calls his rule " a summing up of Christianity; a learned and mysterious abridgment of the whole doctrine of the Gospel, of all the institutions of the Fathers, of all the councils of perfection." As an explanation of praise so ample and so emphatic by one who weighs his words and speaks with all the authority of vast learning and acknowledged genius, we may remark that the triple sacrifice which belongs to the monastic life in all the various Orders in which it has been exercised is in fact the construction of a life which realises the eight beatitudes. To acknowledge these in words is much; but every religious house which actually lived under St. Benedict's rule acknowledged them in fact, subsisted by realising them. This and no less is the life of which St. Athanasius described the patriarch; of which St. Basil and St. Augustine witnessed the execution; for which St. Benedict, the Roman nobleman, in the last decade of the fifth century, at a moment when civil life seemed all failing, fled from his city to the Samnite mountains, and there in solitude drew round him his twelve monasteries.

The establishment of such a life in a living monastery we point to as the creation of a supernatural home equal in importance for the spiritual life to the establishment of Christian marriage for society in general. Specimens of such a life had already been given during more than two hundred years from the time of St. Antony in many countries of the East and West. It had exercised the most admirable Christian minds. We must now speak of its more extended development in regions which had largely lost the benefit of

---

[1] Prologue of the Rule, translated by a monk of St. Benedict's Abbey, Fort Augustus, p. 11.

fixed civil government, and of the attainment of one rule, which had hitherto been wanting, and had been found the most difficult of attainment in the many countries wherein specimens of the life itself had been shown. The setting up of such a house by St. Maurus in one of those deserts which the overthrow of civilised life by the Teutonic invasion had produced in France did not in itself differ in character from the many instances in the same country of which mention has already been made. Like them, it consisted in an imitation of the life of Christ, not by separate individuals, but in a house which was ruled by one idea, under the government of a father, in which each one contributed his own defined work as member of a body. This was in itself the instrument more potent for the propagation of the faith than any which had been found before its institution. This is that which I have likened to the institution of Christian marriage. The special work of St. Benedict was that from the experience of his own life at Subiaco and at Monte Cassino he had drawn out a rule of such practical wisdom, carrying out to perfection the idea of such a house, yet not too severe for human weakness, and that this rule was embraced by a vast number of monasteries. The very houses formed by the great Irish missionary Columban modified the rule after which he had built them by amalgamation, first with the rule of St. Benedict, and in no long time by its full reception. It was the instrument predestined by Providence for overcoming barbarism, for spreading the faith, and for creating, instead of a society which had been dissolved in moral corruption, a society more deeply christianised than that which had been reached in Constantine's empire. This is the significance of the *vita communis*. This is what St. Augustine saw when he made his episcopal house a monastery. If the establishment of one such house is a marvel far surpassing any other example of human government, what are we to say when it is continued on from generation to generation, when the home, in its beginning and in all its principles supernatural, propagates itself, and, amidst the perpetual instability of human things, the fortress of Christian life shows a continuance of the same spirit, and through a line of centuries

M

twenty fathers succeed each other, formed in the same mould, an inheritance of nobility far exceeding that of the noblest earthly families?

We are, then, contemplating a country which has passed from the settled civil government of the Roman empire into the hands of a new race. The Frank race, in its chief Clovis, had accepted the Catholic faith. In the preceding chapter we have sufficiently considered the quality of its acceptance and the character of its rulers. We have quoted the conclusion of a most competent historian, that during this Merovingian rule there was no State in the proper sense throughout the country which would constitute one France. Now taking the death of St. Benedict as an epoch, one which marks a moment of great disaster, when the Gothic war was inflicting upon Rome calamities terrible enough to have destroyed any city possessing only a civil life, when France was a scene of confusion and perpetual warfare, we have to note during 150 years the acceptance of this supernatural life by a vast multitude of men and women, both of Teutonic and of Gallo-Roman race. Amongst these a captive Thuringian princess, the spoil of war, becomes a Christian, and is forced to be a queen. After a marriage as to which she had no choice, and living with a husband utterly unworthy of her, upon the occasion of an act of cruelty perpetrated on her brother, she obtains leave to quit him and to found a monastery, over which she presides for forty years, drawing round her two hundred companions. The royal race in her time is full of scandals and cruelties, which she tries in vain to overcome, which break out after her death even in her own monastery; but her own example shines with the purest light of heroic faith and charity. It would take volumes to recite the history of those who gave up the wealth which they enjoyed as part of the conquering nobility, and by their own example founded houses which exhibited lives instinct with that triple sacrifice, and in virtue of it producing every fruit of charity. As a rule, these monasteries began in great poverty, from the preaching of such men as St. Maurus and St. Columban. Then the vast gifts of land made to them by kings and rich men and women, both of the conquering and the subject race, form an endowment which at the time the land is given is of little present value. But the continual labour exercised on the cultivation of the land, as part of their rule, gradually raises the religious house to the highest secular rank and influence. The landless and houseless stranger missionary develops through ages of continual benefaction towards the Christian neighbourhood, growing around his house into the abbot who ranks with princes, and is the counsellor of kings.

But there is a third very important element running through the two just mentioned. This is the good-will of secular sovereigns to the monastic order and life. It is shown in Merovingian kings, not only when themselves good, if such there were, but even when dissolute in their private conduct. It is shown by Saxon kings in England, by Gothic in Spain. It runs through the nobility in all the countries wherein the invasion from the North takes effect. This whole temper of the two Powers to each other is a most marked feature during hundreds of years, and as part of this the spontaneous preference for the coenobitic life shown by both the sexes. The monks who began as laymen devoted to a strict Christian life and to manual labour, speedily became, by the choice of those among whom they lived, men most prized for the episcopal office. The monastery of St. Martin became the nursery of bishops. There ensued a very close union between bishops and monks. The Benedictine rule, beginning in France with the settlement of St. Maurus on the Loire, gradually became the rule of the monasteries planted by St. Columban, or derived by descent from those which he had planted. It was the rule of a Roman nobleman accepted and supported by St. Gregory and the Popes who followed him. By no compulsion, but by the well-felt experience of its superior moderation and practical wisdom, this rule became that of the vast number of monasteries founded throughout France.[1] The impulse given to the monastic state in the seventh century is said to have been greater than any which existed before in the West. We may contrast the permanency of these great monasteries with the fleeting character of the Fathers of the

[1] Montalembert, ii. 526.

Desert in Egypt. And there is a contrast no less striking between the natural qualities of the Franco-German race, whose noblest in such multitudes embraced the monastic state, and those choice specimens of the Eastern Christians who originally embraced that state. No sources exist for giving a real history of the 150 years following the advent of St. Maurus in 543. There is a perpetual civil war, a successive partition of territory, in the midst of which monastic sanctity emerges amid Merovingian barbarism. We can just trace five causes helping together to convert the shapeless mass of Teutonic violence into stable communities possessing the one Catholic faith, clear of the Arian distemper. Five things were all necessary together; no one of them could have been dispensed with. The vast number of monasteries, both of men and women, founded; the vast gifts of land out of the desert into which France had then fallen, land at first of no value, but made precious by the cultivation which the energetic labour of the monks bestowed on it; the favour with which both sovereigns and nobles regarded the spiritual work, as well as the civilising labour of the religious orders. The union of the episcopate and the monks, and the guiding hand of the Papacy, fostering the reception of one rule. The union of the Papacy and the episcopate had existed from the beginning, but the destruction of civilised life had been so great that it would not have sufficed alone to recover desolated wastes and overcome Gallo-Roman corruption.

It is time that we should turn from the monastic life springing up in the foundation of numberless monasteries for men and for women throughout Gaul during the sixth and seventh centuries to the part which it took among other Northern races in the fifth century. In the year 410 Alaric the Goth had taken Rome; in 451 the Mongol Attila had threatened both France and Italy with utter destruction; in 455 the Vandal Genseric had plundered Rome again. In the generation which intervened between these events we may place the definitive overthrow of the Roman empire in Gaul, and the possession taken of it by successive hordes of Teutonic invaders. In the midst of it occurs that third General Council, the Council of Ephesus, which established for ever the dignity of the Blessed Virgin, by solemnly assigning to her the title of Mother of God. That Council was ratified by Pope Cœlestine when it had in its clearest terms recognised him as successor of St. Peter, and the whole line of pontiffs from St. Peter to him as the channel of that succession. The same Pope in the same year, 432, sent forth a missionary to Ireland, and bestowed upon him episcopal dignity for that work. In the year 409 the Roman armies had been withdrawn from Britain for the defence of Italy. Britain ceased to be part of the empire, and entered a period of internal convulsions by submitting to Saxon invaders. Thus at the time that Gaul and Britain ceased to belong to the empire, the Pope sent forth one to extend the kingdom of Christ over an island which had never known the Roman rule, and had long been held by a noble but barbaric race of heathens.

Patrick, the missionary so sent, was the son of Calphurnius, a provincial colonist. His mother, a relation of St. Martin of Tours, had fallen into captivity in Gaul, and been sold as a slave. In that condition the son of her master had married her, and they were living in the Roman service on the Clyde, near Glasgow, where Patrick first appears. In the year 373, at the age of sixteen, it fell to him to lose his parents, Calphurnius and Conchessa, and to be carried as a slave into Ireland, where during six years he tended his master's sheep. After a hard service in these six years, he took flight to the coast, and finally escaped into France.

The old biographers unite in bringing him to St. Martin in the last years of that saint's life, when he was living at Marmoutier, and had become, by his eminent virtues and the number he attracted to him, the father of the monastic life in France. His death is placed in 397. Before that St. Patrick had been taught by him the rules of a severe and mortified life. He witnessed the government of his house and the death of that great saint, and must have been one of the two thousand monks who waited on his funeral. From Tours St. Patrick went to the island of Lerins, then under its founder, St. Honoratus. It was at the time that learning had taken refuge there from the assaults to which it was exposed in the wandering of the nations. And after

Lerins the great renown of St. Germanus, Bishop of Auxerre, drew him to that place. Many years he spent there "in patience, obedience, brotherly love, chastity, and purity."[1] Ancient lives attest this completion of Patrick's ecclesiastical education under St. Germanus, with whom he spent as many as fourteen years. When Pope Cœlestine sent as his legate Germanus, Bishop of Auxerre, to whom the Gallic bishops added St. Lupus, Bishop of Troyes, to help the British bishops to overcome the error of Pelagius, A.D. 429, St. Patrick accompanied them. It is recorded that on one occasion, when the preaching of St. Germanus had not met with due effect, he took counsel with his companions. And Patrick said, "Let us keep a strict fast three days at the gate of the city, and leave the issue in God's hands." This met with success. At this time the same Pope had sent the deacon Palladius as bishop to convert Ireland. But he was not cordially received, resigned his task, and was returning back to Italy, when he died on his way in Britain. This death led to the commission given to St. Patrick to take his place. After long training in the school of St. Martin and St. Germanus, after visiting Rome and other parts of Italy, at the age of sixty, when the death of Palladius came to be known, Patrick received from Pope Cœlestine the charge to go as missionary to a heathen island, where he could only expect to find martyrdom.

St. Patrick was occupied sixty years in Ireland, from 433 to 493, dying at the age of 120 years. He had planted the Christian faith throughout the whole island. He went fully instructed in that faith, and strengthened by observing the practice of the greatest masters of the spiritual life in Gaul, St. Martin, St. Honoratus, St. Germanus, St. Lupus. In 403, at the age of thirty, he had received the diaconate. The Church which he founded in Ireland learnt from him the monastic life which he had witnessed in Gaul, and the celibacy of the clergy which he himself had ever practised. Every future generation bore in steadfast memory his teaching and his wonderful deeds. The island to which he had come as a stranger with a mission from Pope Cœlestine identified itself with him as its apostle with a fervour which has

[1] Bellesheim, p. 30, from Hogan.

lasted to the present day. I restrict myself here to one particular part of his teaching. He strove to propagate the ascetic zeal and love of knowledge which he had seen and shared at Marmoutier and Lerins in similar institutions. His last years, after he had laid down his active work as bishop, he spent in the monastery he had founded at Saul in Downshire. The like he founded at Downpatrick; another at Armagh, to which pupils came from across the sea. Many others sprung from his personal foundation.

In the sixth and seventh centuries great monasteries in Ireland made the golden age of the Irish Church; her princes laid their crowns on the altar and became monks in them; her noblest daughters became nuns. While the Continent trembled with the march of barbarian hordes, while Eastern lands, long in the possession of Christ, became the prey of Islam, which exterminated with special hatred the inmates of monasteries, Clonard, Clonmacnoise, Clonfert, Bangor became great centres of spiritual life. In study they ranked as universities; in holy zeal as fosterparents of missionaries and martyrs. At Clonard St. Columba was formed for his future work. The study of Scripture and the Fathers especially flourished here. At Clonfert on the Shannon there are said to have been at times about three thousand monks. On the north-eastern coast arose Bangor, the renown of which went everywhere, one of whose sons was the famous Columban. St. Comball founded it in 559, and governed it for more than forty years, while his spirit long continued in it. Its rule was very severe, as one of the hymns says, "Excellent the rule of Bangor, correct and divine, exact, holy, constant, exalted, just, and admirable. Blessed the family of Bangor, founded on unerring faith, graced with the hope of salvation, perfect in charity."[1]

We are not to suppose that these vast monasteries consisted of great buildings, as in the later Middle Ages. They were a collection of poor cells, not of stone, but of wood or wicker-work; up to the eighth century they were so constructed.[2]

The monastic life in Ireland becomes, as everywhere else,

[1] Bellesheim, p. 85.   [2] Bellesheim, p. 93.

a perpetual spring of missionary zeal. In the interval between St. Patrick and the Danish invasions of Ireland went forth from her monasteries that stream of inspired men who helped to convert the neighbouring islands, and showed the fruits of their labours in Britain, Caledonia, Gaul, Germany, Switzerland, and Italy. Columban was one of these. His fearless spirit, his disregard of the most threatening dangers, his endurance of poverty, show in what manner these missionaries fought the hard battle with heathendom. Thus it was that they impressed the Christian life upon those who, in so many instances, surrendered that turbulent independence in which they were born, and the wealth which conquest had given them, to imitate themselves that severe and self-denying life which they saw the stranger practise. Columban, the pupil of the Irish Bangor, became for some time the rival of St. Benedict. Through him Luxeuil, and so many other great houses in France, derived from Bangor their parentage. "It was at the end of the sixth century that the action of Ireland on the region directly under Frank domination became decisive. Then Ireland paid off generously her debt to Gaul. She had received Patrick from Gaul; she gave back Columban."[1] Let this, the greatest of them, represent that vast host of missionaries who came forth to make the Teutonic race Christian from the monasteries of an island which, when Cœlestine sent out his missionary from a Rome deprived of temporal power, was itself only known as the abode of barbarous hordes wasted by perpetual intestine wars, and worshipping through long ages Druidic gods in its mountains, streams, and forests.

It is in this sixth century and the seventh, when barbarous ignorance had taken the place of learning in Gaul and Italy, that the learning sedulously practised and encouraged by association of large numbers together, is praised in the Irish monasteries. The country was as yet undisturbed by foreign aggression. The dwellers in monasteries enjoyed special privileges. In them the slave became free; and, moreover, the natural clannish spirit powerfully contributed to maintain union in the monastery within, while

---

[1] Montalembert, ii. 468, quoted.

protecting it from outward aggression. We find the study of the Scriptures, and the cultivation of the Latin and Greek, and even Hebrew languages, specially noted in a century towards the end of which Pope Agatho publicly deplores that the disturbance of civil life was so great as to prevent in Italy even the most necessary learning. This is the time when the peace, which was refused to the countries of the old Roman rule under Gothic war and Frankish confusion, was enjoyed at least in the monasteries of the Western island before the cruel desecration of the Dane prevailed.

Especially on the west coast of Britain, in Cornwall and in Wales, Irish missionaries were active. The monastery of St. David's, in the beginning of the sixth century, was one of their most remarkable settlements. It had a great attraction for Irish pilgrims. From a spot near to the monastery, Patrick is said to have begun his mission to the land, having heard the call to him, "That is the land which is to be thy inheritance for ever." St. David was attached to Ireland. Irish blood was in his mother's veins. An Irish bishop baptized him. Irish monks came to St. David's to strengthen themselves in monastic discipline. Glastonbury was a famous monastery when St. Patrick went to Ireland. It was so beloved and frequented by the Irish as to be called "Glastonbury of the Irish in the land of the Saxons." Four hundred monks dwelt there, who in perpetual worship served God night and day, a hundred at a time.[1]

When Wales became the refuge of the Britons, who sought in its mountains the preservation of their independence and their faith from the Saxons, we find monks associated with the princes who fought, as well as with the bards who daily with music and song encouraged them, and monks were the chief maintainers and propagators of Christian doctrine. King Arthur, according to the Celtic tradition, was crowned by Bishop Dubricius, whose history says that he was contemporary of St. Patrick as well as of King Arthur, was ordained by St. Germain of Auxerre Bishop of Llandaff, and that he lived very long, and finished

---

[1] See Bellesheim, pp. 96-98.

his life in the north of Wales as an anchoret. He had educated more than a thousand monks. One of these, St. Iltud, founded the great monastery of the Welsh Bangor, which became a centre of religious propagation, as well as of political resistance to the Saxon conquerors. Bangor was said to have seven divisions, each of three hundred monks, who lived by manual labour. Iltud, says the legend of his life, was born in Armorica, but was drawn into Wales by the renown of his cousin, King Arthur. He began as a warrior, but was converted at a falcon chase by seeing his companions, who were plundering St. Cadoc, the founder of Llanarvan, when they were swallowed up suddenly by the earth. Iltud listened to St. Cadoc, and consecrated himself to the service of God, though he was married to a young and beautiful wife. He resigned his wife, his horses, and his servants, and dwelt in a forest, where the number of disciples coming to him speedily raised a monastery.

Kentigern was one of the chief monastic personages in Wales, and founded there at St. Asaph, by the confluence of the rivers Clyde and Elwy, an immense monastery of 969 monks, of whom three hundred cultivated the ground, a like number worked in the monastery, and another three hundred celebrated without ceasing the Divine Office. The monastery became the seat of a bishop, for, as in Saxon England, every bishopric had a monastery for its cradle.

More celebrated than all was St. David, who, as monk and bishop, became the patron of Wales. The son of a prince, nephew of King Arthur, though most irregularly born, he was brought up with great care, became a priest and a monk, who travelled much and exercised great influence. Of the same date as St. Benedict, he likewise founded twelve monasteries, enjoining both manual labour and the labour of the mind. They were employed not only to fell the forest and dig the earth, but even to drag the plough themselves, and then retired to their cells to read or write, and to rise without finishing the half-written word at the sound of the bell for worship.

He went on a pilgrimage to Jerusalem, where he was consecrated a bishop by the patriarch, and on his return he was recognised as metropolitan by all that part of the country which the Saxons had not yet invaded, presiding in two numerously attended councils.

This great bishop and Breton chief was buried at St. David's, where his tomb became a noted place of pilgrimage. Not only Welsh Bretons, and Irish, and others of Celtic race frequented it; three English kings, William the Conqueror, Henry II., and Edward I., went there. It remains from his day to ours a spot of striking solemnity.[1]

One other must be named, the legend of whose story gives a picture of the time and the people. St. Kadoc was the son of a prince in Southern Wales surnamed the Warrior, who with three hundred vassals had broken into a neighbouring chief's house and carried off on horseback his beautiful daughter. He not only stole a wife, but likewise the cow of an Irish monk, to whom it served for sole support and that of his twelve disciples. The monk came to rescue his cow from the father of Kadoc, who used the opportunity to get him to baptize his new-born son, and afterwards to conduct his education. At the age of seven the young Kadoc was sent to the Irish monk, who for twelve years taught him grammar, and likewise taught him to prefer a solitary life to his father's domain. The young Prince Kadoc passed twelve years lighting the fire and dressing the food of the Irish monk, and then went to perfect himself in the Abbey of Lismore, at that time a celebrated school. Kadoc resolved to embrace the monastic life. He plunged into a forest, where he was nearly killed by the swineherd of a neighbouring chieftain. He came also by a deserted fountain upon an enormous wild boar, white with age, who made three bounds towards him, stopping at each to regard with fury the stranger who was intruding on his lair. Kadoc marked with three branches the springs of the wild boar. He chose them for the site of the church, the dormitory, and the refectory of the great Abbey of Llanarvon, which he founded. Llanarvon—"the church of the stags," because two of them had come to take the place of two idle and rebellious monks who had refused to be harnessed for drawing the beams wanted in the building—Llanarvon was a great religious house with a most

[1] Montalembert, iii. 55-72.

severe rule. They cleared the forest, and cultivated what they had cleared. It was also a great school of religion and learning, for the study of Scripture and ancient authors. Among many thoughts attributed to the teaching of St. Kadoc is this: "Truth is the eldest daughter of God; without light is no good; without light is no piety; without light is no religion; without light there is no faith; without seeing God there can be no light;" and the ardour with which they pursued divine knowledge is well expressed in a similar triad: "Without knowledge there is no power; without knowledge there is no wisdom; without knowledge there is no liberty; without knowledge there is no beauty; without knowledge there is no nobility; without knowledge there is no victory; without knowledge there is no honour; without knowledge there is no God." Kadoc was possessed after the death of his father and mother of large domains, and was a prince as well as a monk. Finally, the Saxons advanced to the banks of the Severn and the Usk. He saw his monastery profaned and wasted. He took refuge, as so many other victims of that terrible war took refuge, and founded another monastery in Armorica, which, in consequence of the British settling there, took its new name of Brittany. After many years he returned to Britain, and finished his course at Weedon, where a band of Saxons rode into the chuch and slew him as he was saying mass.

The monastic life plays almost as great a part in the history of Wales as in that of Ireland. The Sees of Llandaff and St. David's, of Bangor and St. Asaph, were cradled in it.

We possess no detailed account of the destruction which the Saxon invaders wrought of the British Church, but one proof of that Church's power has survived, not only in the memory of man, but in its effect even to the present day.[1] Armorica had remained up to 450 a heathen country, in which Druidical memorials abounded and Druidical superstition prevailed. It became Catholic by a singular conversion. A host of British monks flying from Saxon savagery, at the head of a large male and female population, both of freemen and of slaves, flung themselves into boats,

[1] Montalembert, ii. 299-316.

not of wood, but of skins sewn together,[1] and in these succeeded in passing the sea to the coast of Armorica. This Celtic emigration lasted a century, from 450 to 550; they came upon another Celtic people speaking their own language. The monks who led them gave their name, and the faith which they carried with them, to the land which hospitably received them. A Breton, himself a religious, apostrophising in the seventeenth century these apostles from across the sea, cried out to them, "The sun has never shone upon ground of more constant and unchangeable fidelity to the true faith, from which you banished idolatry. Thirteen hundred years have passed in which infidelity has never polluted the language which served you to preach Jesus Christ. The man has yet to be born who has heard a Breton of Brittany preach any other religion than the Catholic."[2]

The monks who came over the sea in the barks made of skin had a hard struggle, but they conquered at last. Fifty years after their coming, the peninsula had embraced in the main the faith which they brought over from Britain: the Church expiring in blood, whose three Archbishops of London, York, and Caerleon represented her in the Council of Arles, and besought Pope Silvester to carry out their decrees, has left an undying witness on Gallic soil. The monks, whether coenobite or solitary, formed the clergy for several centuries, and laid hold of the popular spirit, fixing in it that veneration for the priest which still continues. A vast number of monasteries sprang up on different points of the province, especially the coast. Such, on the farthest promontory, was St. Matthew's Abbey at the World's End, looking down upon a coast full of terror for the mariner.

The principal communities created by these monks soon became bishoprics. Samson of Dol and his six suffragans,

---

[1] This is attested by a contemporary, Sidonius Apollinaris, who became Bishop of Clermont in 472; and before he was bishop, in his panegyric to his kinsman the Emperor Avitus (369), he writes:—

"Quin et Aremoricus piratam Saxona tractus
Sperabat, cui pelle salum sulcare Britannum
Ludus, et assuto glaucum mare findere lembo."
GALLANDI, x. p. 586.

[2] Montalembert, iii. 297, 312-313, 316.

all like himself monks, missionaries, and bishops, have been called the Seven Saints of Brittany; and an Englishman of the nineteenth century may exult that the province of France most faithful to the one true religion is the dying legacy of the original British Church.

The Celtic organisation, both in Ireland and in Scotland, rested from the beginning on the monastic life. In the vast number of monasteries preachers and teachers formed themselves in the strictest religious life and in persistent studies, both of the Latin and Greek languages, and of doctrine. They showed the most prodigious activity in their missionary work through various countries of Europe. An ancient writer has given the number of monasteries which Irish monks founded outside of Ireland. The list is probably imperfect, but he gives thirteen in Scotland, twelve in England, seven in France, twelve in Brittany, seven in Lorraine, ten in Alsatia, fifteen in Rhetia, Switzerland, and Allemania, besides several more in Thuringia and on the left bank of the Lower Rhine, and six in Italy. Those who have been canonised as patrons and founders of the churches for which they often shed their blood are a hundred and fifty in Germany, of whom thirty-six were martyrs; forty-five in Gaul, of whom six were martyrs; thirty in Belgium; forty-four in England; thirteen in Italy; eight, all of them martyrs, in Norway and Iceland.

While Ireland was sending out her sons into all regions of the then known world, a vast number of foreigners came to her to gather lore in that great treasure-house of faith and knowledge, which her insular situation enabled her to preserve at the time of barbarous invasions elsewhere.

From the seventh to the eleventh century English students abounded in Ireland. The monks welcomed all comers, without stint and without payment, to all which they had to give, their instruction and their books. The Anglo-Saxons were those who most availed themselves of this free gift. During four hundred years they frequented Irish schools, and before a Norman host was seen on Irish land, they had contracted the most precious debt towards those whom their descendants were to repay by a persecution of their faith during an equal period. Nor must it be forgotten that while the monasteries continued this their work, their annals bear witness that the secular life around them was disturbed by endless quarrels and contentions. The single words war, desolation, plunder, slaughter, and the like, show that the zeal and charity of the religious life in monasteries left in full sway outside the natural passions to run their savage course. Ireland received the Christian faith, but continued still in respect of war that life which had not gone beyond the perpetual disunion of a tribal clanship.

While the monastic life was spreading itself with great effect in France, and gathering under a discipline of obedience, labour, and self-denial the most vigorous men and women of the Teuton race, it had, as we have just seen, taken a large part in that conversion of Ireland which St. Patrick accomplished. Let us place ourselves now at those fourteen years from 590 to 604 which mark the great pontificate of St. Gregory. The century at the close of which he rose was one of terrible disaster and suffering to Rome and Italy. His birth, about 540, was very nearly contemporaneous with the death of St. Benedict; he has given the best account which we possess of the person and conduct of that saint. He witnessed the great extension of his rule in Gaul from the founding of its first house by St. Maurus. He is believed by the best authorities to have embraced that rule himself, and to have given up the palace which he inherited from his father to the observance of it before he became Pope, and when Pope, to have encouraged and supported it by his authority. His name is to be added to the greatest of those great names which, from St. Athanasius and St. Augustine onwards, recommended to the Church the life itself. World-famous is the renown of his visit to the Roman Forum, when his compassion was drawn forth to the captive Angles, and when he made a resolution to deliver them from the double slavery of the flesh and of the spirit. Eight years would seem to have elapsed before he was able to carry out his purpose. He was willing to go himself as a missionary, and leave Rome for that lost and barbarous Isle of the West. He was destined, after defending Rome for thirty years from the invasion of barbarous Lombards, to send a monastic band from that palace in which he had lived as monk, and by them to convert a land which, having been Christian, had fallen a prey to a savage heathenism.

It would seem that in the course of the 150 years[1] in which the Saxons had come into possession of the whole country, "the Christian religion had been so entirely extinguished, that amongst all the Saxons there was not a single person professing it" on the coming of St. Augustine. Such had been the oppression, that the small number of Christian Britons who continued to live in Roman cities had left, and in 586 Theon, Bishop of London, and Thadioc, Bishop of York, abandoned their churches and took refuge, with the relics of their saints, in the Welsh mountains. So great were the wrongs and cruelties which the British had suffered in this long invasion of the land, that they who had carried the Christian religion with them in their retreat to Wales could never be prevailed on to join in preaching that religion to the Saxon conquerors. The Saxon language also obtained complete dominion over the British, and that portion of the Britons who still continued to subsist in subjection, gave up not only their religion, but their native tongue. The heathenism which had taken possession of Italy, France, and Spain, neither destroyed the Christian faith, nor substituted its own language for that of the invaded land. So much more terrible had the Saxon invasion of Britain been than the Frank, Burgundian, Gothic, or Lombardian invasion on the Continent. When St. Gregory cast his eyes of compassion on Britain, the subjection in which it lay, both as to the British people, the British language, and the Christian religion, was complete.

In the six years during which he had been Pope he had struggled against the pestilence within Rome itself, against famines, against inundations of the Tiber, against continual suspicion and enmity on the part of the Byzantine emperor, against the ever-menacing encroachments of the Lombard invaders. His own words describe the extent to which his mind was assaulted by these trials, so that in the impending fall of Rome he expected the end of all

---

[1] Burke, 2nd Book of History, i. 253; and Ozanam, ii. 148.

things. The great island which, two hundred years before, had been part of the empire, had submitted instead to successive attacks of Saxon invaders. These were accounted to be the least civilised of any among the multitude of tribes which Germany had sent forth, and none so well as he knew the misery and confusion which their coming had wrought in what had been the empire. What act of greater faith, of more heroic courage, could there be than to direct the prior of a Roman monastery, at the head of forty monks, to attempt the conversion of those who had made the whole island heathen, except that mountainous part wherein their victims had taken refuge?

Of Augustine[1] we are told that it was in obedience to the call of the Pope, who had before been his abbot, that he undertook this work, and in the same obedience his companions followed. They had gone so far on their way as to be close to the island of Lerins, when the reports which they met of the barbarous, savage, and unbelieving nations to whom they were sent, not knowing a word of their languages, induced them, after taking counsel together, to send Augustine back to the Pope, with an earnest application that they might not attempt so dangerous, toilsome, and hazardous a pilgrimage. St. Gregory delivered to Augustine the following answer to their entreaty:—"Gregory, servant of the servants of God, to the servants of our Lord. Since it would be better not to begin good things than to withdraw in thought from them when begun, fulfil, beloved sons, with the utmost zeal, the good work on which, by the help of the Lord, you have entered. Let not the labour of the journey, nor the tongue of ill-speaking men, deter you, but carry through, with all urgency and fervour, what, by God's prompting, you have begun, knowing that great labour is followed by a greater glory of eternal reward. When Augustine, your superior, rejoins you, whom we also appoint your abbot, yield him in all things humble obedience, knowing that whatever at his injunction you complete will in all things profit your souls. Almighty God protect you with His grace, and grant me to behold the fruit of your work in the eternal country, so that, though I cannot

[1] Bede, Hist., i. 23, 24, 25.

work with you, I may be found together with you in the joy of reward, because it is my will to work. Beloved sons, God keep you in safety.".

Gregory likewise recommended the missionaries to the Archbishop of Arles, whose ancient See then held the primacy of Gaul; also to the bishops of Tours, Marseilles, Vienne, and Autun, and to Queen Brunehaut, then in her greatness. So they traversed France, where sometimes forty men, travelling as pilgrims and passing the night under a lofty tree, met with mockery and derision. So at length they arrived at the same spot in the Isle of Thanet to which Julius Cæsar carried the Roman conquests and Hengist the Saxon.

Augustine found Ethelbert reigning in Kent,[1] and sent to him Frank interpreters by command of Pope Gregory, who were to announce that he had come from Rome with tidings of high import, promising to those who obeyed him eternal joys in heaven, and an endless kingdom with the living and true God. Ethelbert, hearing this, bade them remain in the island where they were, and be supplied with what they needed until he could see what to do; for the report of the Christian religion had already reached him, inasmuch as he had for wife Bertha, a daughter of the royal Frank race, and of its king at Paris, whom he had taken on condition of her being allowed freely to practise her religion under safeguard of a bishop who attended on her.

After some days the king came to them in the island, meeting them in the open air, that he might not be subject to any imagined magical power. But they came to him not with a demoniacal, but with a divine power, bearing as their banner a silver cross and a picture of the Lord our Saviour, singing a litany in which they besought their own salvation and that of those for whose sake they had come. And they stopped at the king's command and preached the word of life to him and all that were with him. And he replied, "Your words and promises are fair; but since they are new and uncertain, I cannot so assent to them as to give up what I have kept for so long a time with

[1] Bede, i. 25.

the whole English people. But since you have come as pilgrims hither from so far, and as I seem to see that you wish to communicate to us what you think true and very good, we will not molest you, but rather receive you with kind hospitality and provide you with needful food, nor do we forbid you to associate by your preaching all whom you can gain to your faith." So he gave them a dwelling in the city which was the metropolis of his whole kingdom. And as, according to their custom, they drew near the city with the holy cross and the picture of the great King, our Lord Jesus Christ, they sung in harmony the litany, "We beseech thee, Lord, in all Thy mercy, that Thy wrath and anger be removed from this city, and from Thy holy house, for we have sinned. Alleluia."

When they had entered in the dwelling given to them,[1] they began to imitate the apostolic life of the early Church. They maintained perpetual prayer, watching, and fasting; they preached the word of life to whom they could; they despised everything of this world as not belonging to them; they received only the necessary food from those whom they taught; they lived in accordance with all that they taught; they showed the will to suffer every adversity, even to die for the truth which they proclaimed. Some believed and were baptized, admiring the simplicity of their innocent life and the sweetness of their heavenly doctrine. Near the city, to the east, there was a church dedicated to St. Martin, built in old times when the Romans possessed Britain, in which the queen, Bertha, who, as we said, was Christian, used to pray. This they used to frequent, to sing, pray, and say mass, until, after the king's conversion, they received a larger permission to preach and to build or restore churches.

But after that the king, among others, deeply touched with their extreme purity of life and the charm of their promises, the truth of which they had established by working many miracles, believed and was baptized, those who came to hear them increased in numbers, relinquished their heathen worship, and joined in belief the unity of the holy Church of Christ. The king is said to have shown great

[1] Bede, i. 26.

pleasure at their faith and conversion, while he compelled no one to be Christian, but only embraced those who believed with warmer affection as his fellow-citizens in the heavenly kingdom; for he had learnt from the teachers and authors of his own salvation that the service of Christ must be accepted out of free-will, not upon compulsion. And the king at once bestowed upon his teachers a suitable residence in his metropolis, and other possessions of various kinds which they needed.

The first Christian king of the Saxons was baptized at the Pentecost of the year 597, the next following the advent of Augustine; he was accompanied by many of his people. The beginning of the church of Canterbury took place in the voluntary acceptance of the Christian faith received from the teaching of monks specially sent by the Pope. No possession did they bring with them but a silver cross and a picture of their Saviour borne in procession. The Pope's recommendation to the Frank bishops and to Brunehaut, then in the height of her power as queen, carried them through Gaul. The king of Kent permitted them to deliver their message, weighed it with deliberation, was moved by the sanctity of their life, and by the miracles which attested their truth. After his baptism he bestowed his own palace in Canterbury upon them, as Constantine had bestowed on Pope Silvester the palace in which the cathedral of Rome was built.

Augustine, so far crowned with success, returned at once through Gaul to Arles, to receive consecration from its archbishop, who held the pallium over all the bishops of the Frank kingdom, and had received from the Pope the commission to consecrate him as archbishop of the English. He returned at once as bishop to Canterbury, and sent two of his company to bear to St. Gregory the joyful news of his own consecration and of the converted people. One of these was Laurentius, at that time a priest, who was to be his successor, and one Peter, a monk, who was to be the first abbot of the new monastery of St. Peter and St. Paul, then about to be founded; and they bore from the Archbishop a number of questions concerning the spiritual government of this new people, which he proposed to Pope Gregory for answer. The Pope sent back these messengers with careful answers to the questions, showing the great interest which he took in the conversion, and the care which he took in forming them aright when converted. It had indeed followed from the mission originated by himself; and as St. Augustine had suggested that the harvest was abundant but the labourers few, the Pope sent back with the two messengers several fresh missionaries, monks like the others, Mellitus, Justus, Paulinus, and Rufinianus,[1] and everything required for the worship and ministry of the Church—sacred vessels, altar clothings, vestments for the priests and clergy, relics likewise of apostles and martyrs, and many books. He also wrote that he had sent the pallium to Augustine, and marked in what manner he should appoint bishops in Britain. His words are:[2] " Since this new Church of the Angles has been brought about by the gift of the Lord and by your labour, we grant you the use of the pallium, only at the solemnity of mass, so that you may ordain twelve bishops, each in his place, to be subject to your rule; and that the Bishop of London may in future always be consecrated by his own synod, and receive the honour of the pallium from this holy and apostolic See, which by God's gift I serve. To York it is our will that you send such a bishop as you shall ordain; so that, if it receive, together with the neighbouring region, the Word of God, he also shall ordain twelve bishops, and be a metropolitan, because it is our intention, if life continue, to grant him the pallium, whom, however, during your life, it is our will to submit to you; but after your death he will preside over the bishops whom he has ordained, so as not to be subject to the Bishop of London. But your fraternity shall have subject to you, not only the bishops whom you have yourself ordained, nor those only ordained by the Bishop of York, but all the bishops of Britain, by authority of God our Lord Jesus Christ, so that they may learn the rule of right belief and good life from the lips and the life of your holiness." The intention herein noted of making the Bishop of London primate was not carried out, but Canterbury, as the capital of Ethelbert, was chosen.

---

[1] Bede, Hist., i. 29.   [2] Greg. Ep. xi. 65.

Among the questions[1] proposed by Augustine, one was how he should act with the bishops of Gaul and of Britain. To this the Pope's answer ran, "We give you no authority over the bishops of Gaul, because, from the old time of my predecessors, the Bishop of Arles has received the pallium, whom we should by no means deprive of the authority enjoyed by him. But all the bishops of Britain we commit to your fraternity, that, if unlearned, they may be instructed; if weak, they may be strengthened by persuasion; if perverted, they may be corrected by authority."

What took place at the first Christmas on the return of the new Archbishop in the year 597, Pope St. Gregory thus records to his friend Eulogius, Patriarch of Alexandria: "The nation of the Angles, seated in the extreme point of the world, would still be dwelling without faith in the worship of trees and stones, but, encouraged by your prayers, I sent to them, by impulse from God, a monk of my monastery to preach to them. With my permission he had been made a bishop by the German bishops, and, supported by them also, he has reached this nation at the end of the world, and now tidings have come to us of his welfare and work, that either he or those sent with him are so distinguished in that nation as to seem to imitate the great deeds of the apostles in the miracles which they exhibit. At the feast of the Lord's Nativity, more than ten thousand Angles are announced to us as having been baptized by this our brother and colleague."[2]

We do not possess a contemporary history of Ireland's conversion by one man.[3] We have from St. Patrick himself that account of his life called his Confession, bequeathed

---

[1] These questions and answers to them are contained in St. Gregory's Ep. xi. 64, col. 1150-1163, inserted by Bede in his History.

[2] Ep. lib. viii. 30.

[3] A good substitute for such a history may be found in that volume of eloquent genius named the "Legend of St. Patrick," by Aubrey de Vere. Those who master this series of poems will be able to comprehend the majesty of Patrick as a teacher, the skill with which he treated a race barbarous indeed, but living largely on patriarchal inherited traditions, capable in both its sexes of sacrifice and self-denial, whose men embraced martyrdom, whose women embraced virginity, whose kings embraced Christian law when the life-giving stream of baptism was poured on them by him who bore the crosier-staff given by the hand of Christ Himself, and kept as the most sacred of relics by the See of Armagh until it was destroyed by the agents of Queen Elizabeth.

to us shortly before its close, and one letter to a chieftain denouncing his cruelty. We know that the marvellous conversion wrought in those sixty years amongst a people of such a character is a fact, for the continuous faith of fourteen hundred years bears witness to it, the life of innumerable confessors, the labours of a missionary host, the death of unsurpassed martyrs. We know that the monastic spirit which Patrick had found at Rome, at Marmoutier, at Lerins, at Auxerre, he planted deep in the hearts of his people. But the one thing which we do not possess in the case of Patrick we have given to us in the case of Augustine: a mission from Rome attested by him who sent it, as he says himself, "Auctore Deo," by an impulse derived from God; the first arrival, the immediate result, the announcement of miracles with which it was accomplished. We have the primacy of England bestowed by the Pope, and recorded by the Pope himself who bestowed it; the tender nursing of the infant Church in the arms of him whose labour and danger gained it, directed by that spirit from whose love, superior to all fear, to all impossibility, to all hazard, it sprung. It rose to the astonishment of all beholders. Forty monks, coming straight from the palace on the Cœlian Hill, which had been made a monastery by its possessor, won back a realm to Christ which had once been His, but had become the lair of internecine war and nature-worship.

Trace the nine centuries which unfold themselves, having their root in the silver cross, the picture of the Lord, the chanted litany of the bearers, as they approach the Saxon king, "We beseech thee, O Lord, by all Thy mercy, that Thy wrath and anger be turned away from this city, for we have sinned. Alleluia." The king first listens, then reflects, afterwards he returns their visit in the isle where he has left them. Later he believes them and trusts them. The fifth from Hengist in a race of pirates and freebooters, he becomes the first of a race of kings[1] and queens and princesses, who will lay their crowns on the altar of St. Peter's, who will yield their bodies to be buried under the shadow of his church, who will dwell in the silence of

---

[1] Ozanam, ii., 169. Lingard gives them: Cædwalla, Ine, Offa, Cœred, Offa, Siric, Ethelwulf, and Canute, i. 105.

monasteries rather than in the bridal chambers of monarchs. Ethelbert, the first son of Odin who becomes a Christian, is distant but two generations from that daughter of a Saxon king who, in spite of being forced into two marriages, kept her original vow of continence, left a throne after twelve years' possession of it, and founded a double monastery on the ground which her first husband had given her as a dowry, so that the love of succeeding generations melted down her name of Etheldreda into that of Audrey, to be a household word of veneration during eight hundred years. And again, Ethelbert's own grand-daughter was that Queen Eanfleda who fostered and educated St. Wilfrid, the counsellor and supporter of Etheldreda's resolution, as the first to carry his appeal against every wrong to the throne of St. Peter. Ethelbert had seen the last two Christian bishops of London and of York leave their churches and fly for refuge into Wales. From his conversion dates that belief among the Saxons in the presence of Christ in the sacrifice of the mass which filled the whole land with churches, and from those forty monks came that monastic spirit in both sexes which prevailed with unheard of power throughout the land.

"To the Saxons, in whom, during the tide of conquest, the opportunity of gratification had strengthened the impulse of the passions, a life of chastity appeared the most arduous effort of human nature; they revered its professors as beings of a nature, in this respect, superior to their own, and learned to esteem a religion which could elevate a man so much above the influence of his inclinations. As they became acquainted with the maxims of the gospel, their veneration for this virtue increased, and whoever compares the dissolute manners of the pagan Saxons with the severe celibacy of the monastic orders, will be astonished at the number of male and female recluses who, within a century after the arrival of St. Augustine, had voluntarily embraced a life of perpetual continency."[1]

In another of these documents which I have termed contemporaneous, a letter from St. Gregory to that Mellitus whom he was sending to replenish the mission of St. Augus-

[1] Lingard, "Anglo-Saxon Church," i. 201.

tine, and who became Augustine's second successor, the Pope shows how the spirit that guided him repeated the manner of teaching which St. Patrick had shown.[1] "Gregory to Mellitus, Abbot in France: After the departure of our troop which accompanies you, we were kept in great suspense by having no good tidings of your journey. But when Almighty God has brought you to our most reverend brother, the Bishop Augustine, tell him what, after long thought upon the English matter, I have considered. It is that the temples of idols should be by no means destroyed among that people, but only the idols which are in them. Have holy water and sprinkle them therewith, build altars, and put in them relics; because if the same temples are well built they must be changed from the worship of demons into obedience to the true God; so that the nation, seeing that the temples themselves are not destroyed, may banish error from the heart, and, learning and adoring the true God, may more readily meet at the accustomed spots. And because they are wont to kill many oxen in sacrifice, in their case also there should be a change in the solemnity practised. On the day of dedication, or the birthdays of the holy martyrs whose relics are placed there, let them make themselves tents of boughs round about those churches which have been changed from temples, and celebrate the worship with religious entertainments. Nor are they to immolate animals to the devil, but kill them for their own food to the honour of God, and return thanks to the Giver of all for their satisfied appetite. So, by reserving for them some external pleasures, they may be able to consent more easily to inward joys. For it is clearly impossible to sever hard minds at one stroke from everything; just as the man who tries to mount a lofty spot must get up by stairs or steps, not by leaping. So also the Lord made Himself known to the people of Israel in Egypt, but kept for them in His own worship the use of sacrifices, which it had been their custom to offer to devils, commanding in His own worship the immolation of animals. Thus, with a change of heart, they would lose one thing but keep another in the sacrifice. There would be the same animals which they

[1] Ep. xi.; 6, p. 1176.

were accustomed to offer, but immolating them to God and not to idols, they would not be the same sacrifices. This your dilection must say to your brother that he, being on the spot, may estimate how to dispense in every case. My very dear son, God keep you in all things."

A comment[1] made on this passage is that the Roman Church made it a rule to distinguish two things in heathenism: one, error in adoring the creature; another, truth, which forms the essence of religion, as conceived and willed by human nature, with temples, priesthoods, and sacrifices. Far dearer than the land which bears them, or the children brought up on their knees, are the traditions which consecrate their land and the festivals which for a moment break off the monotony of life.

The Church founded in England by St. Augustine's mission from St. Gregory, was not only begun by monks, but was to be continued in monks. St. Augustine's first message to the Pope was, "How are bishops to live with their clergy, how to divide the oblations made for their support?" The Pope's reply is, "The custom of the Apostolic See is to hand over a rule to bishops, when ordained, to divide all their income into four portions—one for the bishop and his household for hospitality and reception, a second for the clergy, a third for the poor, a fourth for the repair of churches. But since your fraternity, learned in the rules of the monastery, ought not to live separate from the clergy in the English Church, which, by inspiration of God, has lately been brought to the faith, you should institute that mode of life which at the beginning of the Church was the life of our fathers, amongst whom no one said that anything which he possessed was his own, but all things were common to them."[2]

In these words the monastic life is prescribed for the bishop and his clergy, and in accordance with them, Augustine, the first Archbishop of Canterbury, lived as a monk, and his four next successors, Laurentius, Mellitus, Justus, and Honorius, were monks like himself, of the band who accompanied him, or were added to it afterwards.

These two conversions, of Ireland under St. Patrick in the fifth century, from A.D. 432–492, and of England in the

---

[1] By Ozanam, ii. 159.   [2] Ep. xi. 64; Ozanam, ii. 160.

seventh century under St. Augustine, in 596–607, and his successors, down to the end of St. Theodore in 690, for a period of ninety-four years, are events not only of so great importance in the history of the monastic life and its effects, but in the whole establishment of the Christian religion, that it will be well to draw out some of the lessons which they jointly teach us. They are conversions like none which preceded them in the history of the Church.

First, as to Ireland: The sixty years during which, under the instruction of one man, a missionary sent from Rome, it passed from a heathen country, divided among a number of tribal chiefs, whose worship consisted in a certain veneration for forests, streams, and mountains, "a race barbaric, but far indeed from savage,"[1] "preserving in a large measure the patriarchal system of the East," into a race accepting the Christian faith in its completeness, was precisely the time at which that Christian faith in three great countries, Italy, France, and Spain, was undergoing fearful losses by invasion from Teuton tribes, also barbarous, and living on their own wild traditions. While Attila was devastating Gaul and Italy, and aiming to reduce Rome itself from the capital of the world to Mongol annihilation, that Patrick, whom Rome's Bishop had sent out twenty years before to convert an unknown island, had brought it to accept the faith imperilled in Italy, had taught its sons and daughters to surrender themselves to the monastic life. That monastic life which, starting from the deserts of Egypt in the third century, had won for itself homes scattered through all the provinces of the Roman empire, now, when that empire was falling a prey to heathen invasion, appeared for the first time as a chief instrument of national conversion in the case of tribes very much in the condition of the Teuton conquerors in lands long Christian and Catholic. That saint, without his equal as a converter, had power given to him to draw to the Christian faith the nobler part of a Celtic race distinguished for its natural gifts. In Erin "her clans were families, and her chiefs were patriarchs, who led their household to battle, and seized or recovered the spoil. To such a people the Christian

[1] "Legends of St. Patrick."

Church announced herself 'by the voice of Patrick' as a great family—the family of man."[1] And this he did when at Rome a Roman emperor was proclaimed to be needless, and a barbarian, who had become an Arian misbeliever, ruled over a trampled Italy in his stead. And with such effect had Patrick turned clans into monasteries, that not only had they become seats of learning when France and Italy had lost the learning which they had once possessed, but the monks whom they nurtured went forth into those lands at their utmost need, and the houses founded by a Columban, and others whom he represents, in the end wrought out a new and more Christian France, which grew up under the rule of St. Benedict, and gained the final victory for the Catholic faith in a Catholic realm.

As to the conversion of Britain, it is well to consider what Burke has recorded, that "whatever was the condition of the other parts of Europe, it is generally agreed that the state of Britain was the worst of all."[2] And he notes that "on the Continent the Christian religion after the Northern irruptions not only remained but flourished. In England it was so entirely extinguished that when Augustine undertook his mission, it does not appear that among all the Saxons there was a single person professing Christianity." But Lingard, in his most careful study, enlarges this picture. "By the ancient writers the Saxons are unanimously classed with the most barbarous of the nations that invaded and dismembered the Roman empire. Their valour was disgraced by its brutality. To the services they generally preferred the blood of their captives; and the man whose life they condescended to spare was taught to consider perpetual servitude a gratuitous favour. Among themselves a rude and imperfect system of legislation intrusted to private revenge the punishment of private injuries, and the ferocity of their passions continually multiplied these deadly and hereditary feuds. Avarice and the lust of sensual enjoyment had extinguished in their breasts some of the first feelings of nature. The savages of Africa may traffic with Europeans for the negroes whom they have

---

[1] "Legends of St. Patrick," preface, p. 19.
[2] Burke, "Abridgment of English History," Book ii. ch. i. p. 254.

seized by treachery or captured in open war, but the more savage conquerors of Britain sold without scruple to the merchants of the Continent their countrymen, and even their own children. Their religion was accommodated to their manners, and their manners were perpetuated by their religion. In their theology they acknowledged no sin but cowardice, and revered no virtue but courage. Their gods they appeased with the blood of human victims. Of a future life their notions were faint and wavering; and if the soul were fated to survive the body, to quaff ale out of the skulls of their enemies was to be the great reward of the virtuous; to lead a life of hunger and inactivity the endless punishment of the wicked."[1]

Now taking the 150 years from the coming of Augustine to the Council at Cloveshoe in 747, let us review some points of the religion which he and his successors had firmly planted in Saxon soil.

In about eighty years the conversion of the Anglo-Saxons was successfully completed.[2] The Archbishop of Canterbury, as named by St. Gregory the Great to be the chief bishop of the English, had taken his place at their head. The four immediate successors of St. Augustine were monks like himself, and of the same band who brought the Christian religion from the monastery on the Cœlian Hill by Gregory's command. To Honorius, the fifth archbishop, Pope Honorius writing,[3] specially noted that the archbishop "followed the rule of his teacher and head, St. Gregory," which he begs that God may confirm with perpetual stability; that what he and his predecessors had gained from the beginning made by Gregory might be blessed with increase. The Pope added that, in accordance with his own petition, as well as that of the kings, his sons, he granted him authority, in the name of St. Peter, Prince of the Apostles, that when one see of an archbishop should be vacant, the other archbishop might consecrate the successor, and that he had for this sent the pallium to each. This was granted on account of the distance intervening between Rome and Canterbury, and of the inconvenience which delay might cause. This

[1] Lingard, "Anglo-Saxons," i. 41. [2] Ibid., i. 36.
[3] Bede, ii. 18, 110; Mansi, x. 583.

letter was dated in the year 633, that which succeeded the death of Mohammed. It reminds us that the whole conversion of England, which followed during the remainder of that seventh century, and being itself the work of monks, ensued on the establishment of so many monasteries for both sexes throughout England, was exactly coeval with the outburst of the Mohammedan religion in the East. That outburst showed itself in special animosity against the monastic life. Its whole religion and mode of life was in direct antagonism to the religion and mode of life which St. Gregory had sent to England, and he was called to his reward before the faintest appearance of the new religion had come into the world.

To a letter [1] of Archbishop Honorius asking Pope Honorius that the authority of his See might be confirmed by the privilege of Papal authority, the Pope replied, "Without any delay, assenting of our own accord, because it is right that what has once been decreed and disposed by our predecessors be confirmed by us; following their footsteps, according to old custom, which your Church has held to the present from the time of Augustine of holy memory, your predecessor, we grant, Honorius, to you and your successors for ever, by authority of blessed Peter, Prince of the Apostles, the primacy over all the churches of Britain. We command, therefore, all the churches and regions of England to be subject to your jurisdiction. And that the metropolitan place and honour of the archiepiscopate and the head of all the churches of the English peoples be ever for the future kept in the city of Canterbury, and be changed by no man through any evil persuasion to another place. But if any one do to the contrary, through instinct of pride and in disobedience to our authority, and contend for resistance to the terms of dignity granted to that Church, let him know that he is separated from partaking of the body and blood of Jesus Christ our Lord and Redeemer."

Thus in the fifth archbishop we find the original authority given by St. Gregory confirmed, and at the same time his intention to place a second archbishop at York, and each of them to have the pallium; and the direction that on the

---

[1] Mansi, x. 583; Wilkins, i. 35.

death of one the other should consecrate his successor, carried out in the case of Paulinus, who consecrated Honorius at Lincoln. But Paulinus was driven away from York, became Bishop of Rochester, and dying, left his pallium there, which was not bestowed on York again until Archbishop Egbert's time in 734.

But the grant to Canterbury continued. "The successors of Augustine often exercised the metropolitan authority beyond the limits of their own province, perhaps in virtue of their office of apostolic vicar, which seems to have been constantly granted to them together with the pallium.[1]

"By Archbishop Theodore the discipline of the Anglo-Saxon Church was reduced to a more perfect form." But from the beginning "the national church of the Anglo-Saxons was not an isolated body unconnected with and independent of the rest of Christendom. It formed from its establishment an integral part of the Catholic or universal Church, governed by the same laws, and acknowledging the same gradation of rank and authority from the parish priest to the prelate who sat in the chair of St. Peter." "Twice in the year, on the calends of May and November, the bishops were to summon their clergy to meet them in the diocesan synod. Above these the convoking of national councils was vested in the Archbishop of Canterbury, in which he would be directed sometimes by his own prudence, but sometimes by the commands of the Popes. More frequently by the decrees of preceding councils." "The metropolitan selected the subjects of discussion, and composed a competent number of canons, which he submitted to the judgment of his brethren. Their approbation imparted to them the sanction of laws which bound the whole Saxon Church, and were enforced with the accustomed threat of excommunication against the transgressors."

"But there was still another authority acknowledged in the Anglo-Saxon Church, higher than even that of the national council, the authority of the Bishop of Rome as successor of St. Peter." "When," says Bede,[2] "St. Gregory

---

[1] Lingard, "Anglo-Saxon Church," i. 77, 83, 96, 99, 100, 103, 104, 105, 106.
[2] Bede, ii. 1, 69, 70.

was holding the first pontificate in the whole world, and already presided over the churches which had received faith in the truth, he made our nation, up to that time enslaved to idols, to be the Church of Christ, so that we may well hold concerning him that apostolic language, if he is not an apostle to others, at least he is to us; for we are the seal of his apostolate in the Lord." From Gregory's time, without a break, they counted his benediction as the choicest of blessings. To obtain it was one of the principal motives which drew so many pilgrims to Rome, eight Saxon kings being among them. The clergy of each church, the monks of each convent, sought to shelter themselves under his protection. Monarchs, sensible that their authority was confined to the narrow limits of their own lives, besought in favour of their religious foundations the interference of a power whose influence would always last. Papal charters, said to have been issued at the prayer of kings, bishops, and abbots, in confirmation of grants and concessions made by the civil power, are to be found in the collections of Anglo-Saxon councils. There cannot be a doubt of the actual existence of such instruments as early as the middle of the seventh century. When St. Bennet Biscop had built the monastery of St. Peter at Wearmouth on the land given him by King Egfrid, he proceeded to Rome with the permission, consent, desire, and exhortation of that monarch, to procure a letter of privilege from Pope Agatho, which might protect the monastery from all external violation of its rights. St. Wilfrid about the same time obtained a similar charter of confirmation for his monasteries at Ripon and Hexham.

But the confirmation of royal grants and monastic privileges was the least important part in the exercise of the Papal prerogative. By his authority the Pontiff, 1st, established, extended, or restricted the jurisdiction of the archiepiscopal sees; 2nd, confirmed the election of the metropolitans; 3rd, enforced the observance of canonical discipline; and 4thly, revised the decisions of the national councils.

While the division of old or the erection of new bishoprics was intrusted to the metropolitan in his provincial council, with the consent of the king and the Witan, no establishment or alteration of metropolitan sees could take place without the authority of the Pontiff. Gregory the Great divided the Anglo-Saxon territory into two provinces. Pope Vitalian placed all the Anglo-Saxon churches under the jurisdiction of Theodore, and sanctioned the twelve bishops which arose under his organisation. Bede before his death had the satisfaction to greet Archbishop Egbert[1] at York as receiving once more the gift of the pallium in that see after its discontinuance when St. Paulinus was driven away. Pope Adrian I. was induced to put a third metropolitan at Lichfield, but his successor, Leo III., revoked that disposition and confirmed its former jurisdiction to Canterbury, which so continued until the change of religion in the sixteenth century.

We must not forget one important point in the discipline of that age. The archbishop formed the connecting link between the bishops of his province and the Bishop of Rome. Their election was confirmed by him, his by the Pope. The new metropolitan might, by Papal grant, receive episcopal consecration from the bishops of the province or some neighbouring archbishop, according to precedent or necessity, but he could not enter on the exercise of his office as metropolitan—that is, claim the ordination of the bishops of his province, or call them to his synod, or sit upon the archiepiscopal throne—till he had obtained the Papal confirmation, which was granted at his petition by the delivery to him of the pallium, the badge of the metropolitan dignity, to be worn by him only during the celebration of mass and in the discharge of his duties as metropolitan.[2] Thus by the reception of the pallium when he first entered on the office of metropolitan, and the obligation of wearing it as often as he exercised that office, he was constantly reminded of his subordination in dignity and authority to him from whom he had received it.

For more than two centuries it would appear that the archbishops were spared the fatigue of the journey to Rome for the pallium, which was forwarded to them by their own messengers, but then it began to be required that the metropolitan should receive it in person from the Pope.

[1] See Montalambert, v. 108, for the action of Egbert with St. Gregory II.
[2] Lingard, i. 107.

Canute the Great, in his pilgrimage to Rome, had to plead earnestly with the Pope that his metropolitans, coming with personal attendance for the pallium, might be dispensed with costly gifts for its attainment.

The preservation of worship and the observance of discipline were always considered by the Popes as the most important of their duties. Thus as early as 680 Pope Agatho had summoned Archbishop Theodore and his suffragans to attend a Council at Rome for the condemnation of the Monothelite heresy. As they pleaded for absence, the Pope consented to accept a public profession of their faith. John, the Abbot of St. Martin's at Rome, was selected as deputy. Theodore and his suffragans assembled at Hatfield, and declared their adhesion to the decrees of the five first General Councils, and to the condemnation of the heresy by Pope Martin I., and the Abbot John forwarded the copy of their acts to Rome.

As the first conversion of England was brought about by a band of monks coming from Rome by commission of the Pope, so the part in the winning of the country to the Christian faith during the succeeding century very largely belongs to the monastic institute. A great change had passed over this institute in the interval which had taken place between the time of St. Antony and that of St. Augustine bringing the gospel to the Anglo-Saxons. "The solitary of the desert had become the inmate of a numerous establishment, and the lay recluse, earning a scanty subsistence with the labour of his hands, had been transformed into a cleric actually discharging, or preparing himself to discharge, the duties of the priesthood. He was still withdrawn from secular pursuits, but he was made serviceable to others. He was become an active minister of religion, and was able not only to edify the world by his example, but also to instruct the ignorant by his preaching, and to labour with the zeal of an apostle in the conversion of pagan nations."[1]

[1] Lingard, i. 181.

CHAPTER VI

THE MONKS MAKE ENGLAND

THESE are the words in which Bede concludes his History:[1] —"Thus have I, by God's help, drawn out what I could learn either from records of the ancients, or the tradition of those before us, or from my own personal knowledge, concerning the history of the British provinces, especially of the English people, being Bede, the servant of Christ, and presbyter of the monastery of the blessed Apostles Peter and Paul at Wearmouth and Yarrow.

"I was born on the land of that monastery, and when I was seven years old was, by the care of relations, given for education to the right reverend Abbot Benedict, and then to Ceolfrid. I spent the whole time of my life dwelling in that monastery, and gave all my thoughts to the meditation of the Scriptures, and in the observance of regular discipline and the daily charge of singing in the church. It was my delight ever to be either learning, or teaching, or writing.

"In the nineteenth year of my life I received the diaconate; in the thirtieth the rank of the presbyterate, both by the ministry of the right reverend Bishop John, at the request of Abbot Ceolfrid.

"From the time of my receiving the presbyterate to the fifty-ninth year of my life, it has been my care to make short annotations upon Holy Scripture for my own need and that of my people from the treatises of the venerable Fathers, or to make additions to their meaning and to their interpretation."

He then gives a list of the works he has thus compiled, and closes it with these words: "And I beseech Thee, good Jesus, who hast so kindly given me to imbibe with delight the words of Thy wisdom, to bestow on me also one day

[1] Hist., p. 311.

to reach Thee, who art the fountain of all wisdom, and to appear for ever before Thy face."

Four years afterwards, being aged sixty-three, he knew that he was dying, and having almost finished the portion of St. John's Gospel which he was translating into the Anglo-Saxon tongue, "at the hour of none he sent to the priests of the monastery and distributed to them the incense, the spices, the fine linen, which he was keeping as objects of value in his chest. Then he made his farewell to them, and besought each of them to say masses for him. So he passed his last day until evening. Then the disciple attending on him said, 'Dear master beloved, there is one verse not written.' He answered, 'Write it then quickly.' The young man having done as he bade, in a few minutes said, 'Now, it is finished.' And he said, 'It is true; it is finished. Take my head in thy hands and turn me, for I have much comfort to look to the spot where I have so often prayed.' And so, lying on the pavement of his cell, he began to sing for the last time, 'Glory be to the Father, and to the Son, and to the Holy Spirit;' and with these words he expired."

Bede was born in the year 672, that is, seventy-five years after St. Augustine's arrival in England. He died in the year 735. He became acquainted with all that passed in that first and most important period of the Anglo-Saxon conversion, which may be called its heroic age. He was near enough to St. Augustine to learn about him from those to whom the tradition of his presence and his teaching was quite fresh. With St. Theodore, who became Archbishop of Canterbury in 668 and died in 690, he was contemporary. He bestows upon that prelate very high praise, noting how much he did for the multiplication of the episcopate in the several kingdoms of the Heptarchy; how the learning of the Greek and Latin tongues flourished under his encouragement and his example, and the schools which he established; how all ecclesiastical learning progressed during his primacy, and England learnt practically to accept the leading of Canterbury as St. Gregory had intended; so that, while the various kingdoms still subsisted, the unification of the whole country was greatly helped by St. Theodore's mission, which itself sprung from Pope Vitalian's careful choice of him to meet the wants of the time and land to which he was sent. Bede began his labours as a historian when, at thirty years of age, he was ordained priest by St. John of Beverley, that is, in the year 702. During the thirty years which followed, he enjoyed personal intercourse with many whose information he has quoted in his narrative. Bishops of the South as well as of the North placed their knowledge at his disposal. He specifies Daniel, Bishop of Venta, that is, Winchester. Egbert had been promoted to the See of York, and received as its archbishop from the Holy See the pallium, which had been discontinued from the time that St. Paulinus had retired from Northumbria on the death of King Edwin. Egbert had also been Bede's pupil, from whom we have in the year 734, the last before his death, a most valuable letter to the archbishop concerning the state of things at that time. Egbert, who was brother of the King of Northumbria, the Ceolwulf to whom Bede has dedicated his History, would come to visit him at Yarrow, and Bede would pass some days at the episcopal monastery at York. Here he would find remembrances of St. Paulinus, and the whole history of St. Wilfrid and of Northumbria, for which we are indebted to him.

Bede's own life made him the very type of the Anglo-Saxon monk. In the thirty-three years of his priesthood, passed in the double monastery of Wearmouth and Yarrow, he became the most learned man of his time, the most intellectual person of his age and country. An Anglo-Saxon at the extremity of the world, this "father of the English learning—when we reflect upon the time in which he lived, the place in which he spent his whole life, within the walls of a monastery, in so remote and wild a country, it is impossible to refuse him the praise of an incredible industry and a generous thirst of knowledge. That a nation who, not fifty years before, had but just begun to emerge from a barbarism so perfect that they were unfurnished even with an alphabet, should, in so short a time, have established so flourishing a seminary of learning, and have produced so eminent a teacher, is a circumstance which, I imagine, no other nation besides England can boast."[1]

[1] Burke's "Abridgment of English History," p. 281.

In his erudition he grasped all that was then known in the world. This encyclopedic character was what most astonished his contemporaries. He wrote either in prose or verse, in Anglo-Saxon or Latin. His works prove that he also knew Greek. Theology was his favourite study. He has enumerated for us forty-five works, dwelling especially upon his commentaries and homilies on Scripture. St. Boniface said of him, " The monk Beda, that most sagacious interpreter of Scripture."[1] But so far was he from restricting himself to this his favourite study, that he wrote upon astronomy and meteorology, on physics, and on music, on philosophy and geography, on arithmetic and rhetoric, on grammar and on versification, on medicine also, and even orthography. Whatever could interest or benefit his monastic disciples he set before them in a catechetical form. But the master-thought of his heart was God, and in God the soul of man and his eternal salvation. He dedicated his History to Ceolwulf, king of Northumbria, saying that among all who had helped him, the greatest support of his " small work " was the very reverend and most learned Abbot Albin, who had been brought up in the church of Canterbury by Theodore, Archbishop, of blessed memory, and by the Abbot Adrian. Albin had been instructed either from written records, or from the tradition of those older than himself, in everything which had been done in the province of Canterbury, or even in the neighbouring regions, by the disciples of Blessed Pope Gregory, and had transmitted to him whatever he thought worthy of note. He had obtained instruction about the various provinces from those who had acted in them; but as to Northumbria, from the time it had received the faith of Christ to his own time, he had learnt all which had passed, not from one person, but from the faithful asseveration of innumerable witnesses, besides what he knew himself. He particularly notes what he had said of St. Cuthbert, and he ends by entreating all to whom his History might come of his own nation, whether by hearing it or reading it, to beseech the divine clemency for his infirmities of mind or body, so that each in his own province might remunerate him for his care

---

[1] Quoted by Montalembert, v. 62.

in what he had said of them by frequent acts of intercession.[1]

Bede died in the year 735. St. Boniface, born eight years after him, in 680, was long his contemporary, and was martyred in 755, twenty years after his death. That glory of the Saxon race has left in one of his letters this testimony: "It seems to me right that the whole nation of the English in all their provinces, wheresoever they are, should return thanks to God for bestowing on their nation a man so admirable."[2]

The History thus composed by a man of the most scrupulous exactitude, having at command the best information, and pursued as a religious task during thirty years, was received with universal assent. "Succeeding generations preserved it piously as a memorial of the virtue of their ancestors; and about a hundred and fifty years after him, Alfred the Great translated it into the Anglo-Saxon tongue, for the instruction of those who could not read it in the original. To us it is an invaluable work; for without it we should know nothing of the missionaries who brought to our pagan ancestors the light of the gospel, or of the manners of the clergy, or the worship and rites of the infant Church."[3]

Bede had stored his mind with the records of the Universal Church. He was a teacher in a monastery which possessed, in his time, six hundred monks. His own position as a teacher, with the character of his own mind, had led him to acquire a systematic knowledge of Christian doctrine up to his own time. Thus he may be reckoned a father of the Church as to what had taken place before him. The bounteousness of St. Bennet Biscop had bestowed on his house a library most precious in those days of disturbance on the Continent. At the very moment when Pope St. Agatho, in 680, deplored to the sixth General Council how the misery of the times made it scarcely possible to pursue Christian learning in Italy, Bede enjoyed profound peace in his Northumbrian monastery, fortress alike of knowledge

---

[1] Drawn from his Preface.
[2] Letter 134, ed. Jaffé, quoted by Montalembert, v. 99.
[3] Lingard, "Anglo-Saxon Church," ii. 176.

and of religion. No half-taught beginner, but a practised theologian, he knew exactly what it was important to say of the Church of which he describes the beginning from the preaching of St. Augustine during the 138 years which passed to his own death. We have it drawn out for us in such detail that a very learned historian and theologian of our own days could from its pages "describe the Anglo-Saxon Church, its constitution, laws, and polity; its doctrines, sacraments, and daily services; the sources from which it derived its revenues, and the duties which it required from its prelates and working clergy; the discipline and literature of its clerical and monastic bodies, and the events which chiefly contributed to establish and confirm its influence with the people." [1]

Thus the picture which Bede has left us of the English Church in the seventh century enables us to compare it with the Catholic Church elsewhere at that time, from the direct mission of whose head it sprung, while it was counselled and supported by his advice and that of his successors, ever fostering it and guiding it during that seventh century. Not only was the whole conception of the Roman mission to England by St. Augustine the special work of St. Gregory's tenderness for the Saxon captives, whose mental slavery in the kingdom of Deira was contrasted to him by their personal beauty; not only did he answer its every need in solving the questions set before him by the archbishop whom he had sent, but his successors referred back to his statutes with their own repeated confirmation, and watched every pulse of the nascent Church.

Bede has given us particulars of this continued guardianship by the Holy See of the conquest over paganism which Gregory had obtained. Some of these I shall draw from him either as a contemporary or an eyewitness. His History is one great boon for which all generations of the English race are bound to thank the saint of Benedictine piety.

Another is that his book gives us the assurance that the Church of the present day, both in England and throughout the world, is in exact accordance, both as to doctrine, to

---

[1] Lingard, Preface, p. vi.

practice, and to government, after the lapse of more than 1100 years, with the Church which his book sets before us. There is perhaps no extant writing from any other author which could give us this assurance in an equal degree. Nor indeed does any other nation possess a document so faithfully delineating the beginning of its Christian conversion. A beginning in truth it was in the fullest sense of the word, for in the 150 years from Hengist and Horsa to Ethelbert, the pagan Saxon had extinguished that previous Christian Church whose three metropolitans, by their appearance at the Council of Arles in 314, bore witness to their hierarchical union with Pope Silvester before the time of Constantine.

How remarkable is the gift which Bede has bestowed upon the Anglo-Saxon Church by his History is further shown by a comparison with the historical deficiency of the Catholic Church as to its earliest records. A history written in A.D. 135, that is, towards the close of the reign of the Emperor Adrian, with the like detail and accuracy as that of Bede, by one equally learned and equally informed from the first hands, which should give the chief events from the Incarnation of our Lord to that time, would, if it existed, be of incalculable value. It would have told us the acts of the several Apostles and their first successors, the doctrines which they preached, the government which they established, authentic statements of the several countries which they evangelised, and so satisfy the most legitimate desire for knowledge on those heads which the Christian student feels. It would also determine numberless points which the absence of adequate records allows either ignorance or ill-will to misrepresent. But the providence of God has not permitted such a history to come down to us. It is true that two hundred years later than Bede's distance from St. Augustine, the learned Eusebius has given what is called a history of the 330 years before him from the birth of Christ. But this is far from reaching the accuracy of detail shown by Bede in his work. It also leaves on the mind rather a regret for the subjects omitted than a satisfaction with the treatment of the subjects which it contains.

Bede has specially dwelt upon the train of events which drew the North of England into the Church.[1] As a presage of the heavenly kingdom, a king of the Angles had obtained such a dominion as no Anglo-Saxon before him had reached. In the year 616, after a long time of exile and persecution, Edwin had succeeded Ethelfrid the Ravager. In the year 625 he and all his people were alike pagans. The occasion of this race receiving the faith was that King Edwin sought an alliance with the king of Kent. This was Eadbald, son of Ethelbert, who had become a Christian. To him King Edwin sent an embassy, asking the hand of his sister, Ethelburga, daughter of Ethelbert and Bertha. He received for answer that a Christian maiden could not be given in marriage to a pagan, lest the faith and the sacrament of the Celestial King should be profaned by the alliance of a king utterly alien from the worship of the true God. When King Edwin's messengers bore back to him these words, he promised that he would do nothing contrary to the Christian faith held by the virgin he sought; that rather he would sanction her observing as a Christian the faith and the worship of her own religion, with all the men and women, priests, or attendants, who should come in her train; nor did he fail to say that he would accept himself the same religion, if, on examination with his Witan, he found it the more holy and worthy of God. Thereupon, Ethelburga was promised to him, and Justus, Archbishop of Canterbury, in the year 625, consecrated Paulinus, one of those added to the original band of monks, to accompany the princess with his companions, and "to support her by his daily advice and the celebration of the heavenly sacraments, that they might not suffer pollution from the society of pagans."

On Easter Day the next year, 625, an assassin sent by the king of Wessex attempted to stab King Edwin while listening to him as a royal messenger. An officer, who saw the intention, interposed with his body, which was pierced through by the poisoned dagger, and the king wounded. That same night Queen Ethelburga bore him a daughter. King Edwin, in the presence of Paulinus, returned thanks

[1] Bede, ii. 9, p. 91.

to his gods for her birth; the bishop returned thanks to
Christ for having at his prayer given the queen an easy
delivery. The king, delighted with his words, promised
that he would renounce his idols and serve Christ if he was
given life and victory over the king who had sent that
murderer; and as a pledge he gave that new-born daughter,
Eanfleda to Paulinus to consecrate to Christ, and she was
baptized on the day of Pentecost with eleven of the royal
household. She was the first Christian of the Northumbrian
nation.

But the Pope of that day, Boniface V., took a personal
interest in this alliance of King Edwin with the Kentish
princess, the daughter of King Ethelbert, which, says Bede,
was the occasion of England north of the Humber receiving the faith.[1] In that year, 625, he wrote to King Edwin
a letter,[2] pointing out to him the admirable order preserved
in the creation of heaven and earth by God, with the
counsel of His co-eternal Word and in the unity of His
Spirit, and the race of man, formed by Him after His own
image and likeness, worship this indivisible Trinity from
the rising to the setting sun, as his own Maker, to whom
all kingdoms and powers are subject. "And your illustrious
wife, that portion of your own body, we acknowledge as
illuminated by the regeneration of holy baptism for the
eternal reward." Then he conjures the king to reject the
abomination of idols, quoting to him the words of the
Psalmist, "All the gods of the heathen are demons, but the
Lord made the heavens;" and after marking the impotence
of the images of these idols, he entreated him to accept the
God who created him and who sent for his redemption His
only Son.

But Pope Boniface wrote also another letter[1] to the
queen. "Boniface the bishop, servant of the servants of
God, to our illustrious daughter the Queen Ethelburga."
In this he congratulates her that the mystical cleansing of
baptism had made known to her the creation and the
redemption of man and the manifold providence of God.
He states his joy that the like had happened to her brother,

---

[1] Bede, ii. 9, p. 91. [2] *Ibid.* ii. 10. pp. 94-96.
[3] *Ibid.* ii. 10-11, pp. 94, 96.

King Eadbald, but that his charity as a father inquiring after her illustrious husband, found that he was still in the servitude of idols. Then he entreats her to work in time and out of time by the divine assistance that her husband may be joined to the number of Christians; for how can the unity of marital intercourse be said to exist between them if he remained alienated from the brightness of her faith by the darkness of detestable error? He reminds her that the husband without faith shall be saved by the wife who has faith, and that he will not cease by himself to pray for this. By his love as a father he begs her to send him information respecting her husband's progress and that of the nation subject to them, that he may render joyous thanks for the divine power, marvellously shown, to God the giver of all good things, and to blessed Peter, the prince of the Apostles, from whom he sends a personal blessing in a silver-framed mirror and an ivory gilt comb, which she is to accept with the same kindness with which it is sent.

King Edwin marched against the king of Wessex and punished his perfidy. He came back victorious, but would not on the spur of the moment, and without thought, receive the sacraments of the Christian faith; but he no longer served idols from the time he promised to serve Christ. Since then he continually heard from Paulinus the grounds of faith, and consulted the chief of his Witan, whom he thought the wisest, as to what he should do. But being himself a man of the greatest natural sagacity, he remained often alone, thinking over in his inmost heart what he ought to do, and considering the principles of religion.[1]

This was the time at which the letters of Pope Boniface V. reached him and his queen, Ethelburga. Paulinus was witness of his long hesitation. He saw the difficulty for a royal mind to accept the humility of salvation and bend to the mystery of the life-giving Cross; he was both using the words of human exhortation and having recourse to the goodness of God for the salvation of the man and of the nation which he governed; at last it may be believed that he learnt from a divine intimation to ask the king to accept

[1] Bede, ii. 9, translated.

a token which he had formerly received. So he came to the king in one of those silent communings with himself, and, laying his right hand on his head, asked if he acknowledged that sign. The king fell at his feet, and Paulinus, raising him up, said, "See, God has given you to escape your enemies; has bestowed on you the kingdom which you desired; will you give Him the third thing which you then promised? If you will bow to His will, which He declared to you by me, He will make you heir of His eternal kingdom in heaven."

The king assented, expressing the wish still to consult the chief thanes whom he most trusted, that, if they should agree with him, they might be consecrated to Christ at the same time with him in the fountain of life. The consultation which the king desired took place, and Bede has preserved for us the very words by which it appears that Edwin asked from his Witan, one by one, to give each for himself a decision as to this doctrine hitherto unknown, and this new worship of God which was being announced to them. And one who is called the chief of the priests answered the king's appeal by complaining how little he had got by his own zealous serving of their gods. Another of the chieftains followed the same course, but added these words: "O my king, the present life of man upon this earth, compared with that time which is uncertain to us, appears to be such as this: You, with your chieftains and officers, are seated at supper in winter-time; a fire has warmed the room, while outside the whirlwinds of winter storms and snows are raging, and a sparrow comes in at the one door, presently to pop out at the other. For the moment that it spends within, the tempest touches it not, but when that brief instant of serenity is passed, as it came from one storm it reverts into another, and slips away from your sight. So this life of man appears for an instant; but what follows it, or what went before it? Of both we know nothing. If, then, this new doctrine brings us anything more certain, it deserves to be followed." So the other chiefs and counsellors were disposed to pursue this leading of grace. But the chief of the priests added a desire to hear Paulinus himself speaking of that God whom he preached. The king assented, and when he heard Paulinus, the chief of the priests said, "I have long perceived that what we worshipped was nothing, for the more intensely I sought for the truth in that worship, the less I found it. But now I openly declare that in this preaching that truth is evident which is able to bestow on us eternal life, salvation, and beatitude. Whence, O my king, I propose that we give at once to the flames the temples and the altars which we have raised to no purpose."[1]

So King Edwin, with his council, assented to the preaching of Paulinus; the priest himself mounted the king's horse, which was strictly forbidden, rode into the enclosure of idols, cast his lance at them, and ordered them to be burnt. The spot where this happened is still shown at Godmundham, near York, where the priest, at the prompting of God, destroyed altars which he had himself consecrated. And King Edwin, with his Witan, solemnly accepted the Christian faith, and, in the eleventh year of his reign, on Easter Day, the 12th April 627, was baptized at York by Paulinus, in a wooden church which he had himself hastily built. He made that city the seat of his episcopate for Paulinus, his instructor and bishop. He afterwards built, by instruction of Paulinus, a larger church of stone, enclosing the former wooden structure. This was the beginning of York Minster.

From that time, during six whole years, King Edwin encouraged with his support the preaching of Paulinus, and the Northumbrian race showed such fervour that, on one occasion, when the bishop was visiting a royal villa where the king and queen were residing, he was given up to the continuous work of catechising and baptizing during thirty-six days. And King Edwin was so devoted to the faith that he persuaded the king of the East Angles to give up the worship of idols, and, together with his province, to accept the faith and sacraments of Christ.[2]

In the year 634 Pope Honorius, who had succeeded Pope Boniface V., addressed a letter to King Edwin. As the letter of Pope Boniface was addressed to Edwin while still a pagan king, upon occasion of his marrying a Catholic

---

[1] Bede, ii. 14, closely followed. [2] *Ibid.* iii. 17, p. 108.

princess, and urged him to put away the worship of idols for that of the Creator of heaven and earth, so this letter was addressed to him recognised as a most distinguished son by "Honorius the bishop, servant of the servants of God." He began by telling him that the ardour of his Christian faith in the worship of his Creator had shone far and wide, and become renowned in the world. "You recognise your kingship in that, having been taught to know your King and Creator, you show your belief in God by devotedly worshipping Him. And so, most excellent son, we entreat you, with the charity which belongs to us as a father, with constant prayer to maintain that vocation to His grace which the divine mercy has granted you. Occupied, then, constantly with reading the works of him who was your preacher, my Lord Gregory of apostolic memory, keep the teaching which he freely bestowed upon you constantly before your eyes, that his prayer may increase your kingdom and people, and present you blameless before God. What you have asked me to ordain for your bishops I grant without delay to the sincerity of your faith. I have sent the pallium to each of the metropolitans, Honorius and Paulinus, so that whichever of them be first summoned out of this world to his Maker, the other, by this our authority, may supply a successor. This we grant as well out of affection to your charity as because of the great distance between us, to show in all things our agreement with your devotion and accordance with your desire."

According to this Pope's decree, as Paulinus had been consecrated by Archbishop Justus, so Paulinus himself consecrated in the chair of St. Augustine Archbishop Honorius, the fifth and last survivor of the original band of monks. But before the letter of Pope Honorius reached King Edwin, he had closed seventeen years of a very glorious reign,[1] of which in the last six he had indeed fought for the kingdom of Christ, and falling as a champion in that service, he met with a death which the Church has considered a martyrdom. Two great persecutors of the Christian faith, Penda, the Saxon but heathen king of Mercia, and Cadwalla, the Breton-Cumbrian king, in profession a Christian himself, but in fact

[1] Bede, iii. 20.

most bitterly hating Saxons who became Christians, had fallen together with a large army on Northumbria, and utterly crushed King Edwin with his smaller force.[1] He fell on the field of battle, and Northumbria was put to fire and sword, Cadwalla, sweeping through its provinces for a whole year, massacring and torturing both women and children. His purpose was to efface the whole race of Angles from Britain; nor did he pay any regard to the Christian religion which had begun among them. Up to this moment, says Bede in 731, it is the Briton custom to count for nothing the faith and religion of the Angles, and to have no more communion with them than with pagans. The head of Edwin was taken to York, and afterwards laid in the church of St. Peter, which he had begun, and which his successor, King Oswald, finished. It was placed in St. Gregory's porch, from whose disciple Edwin had received the word of life.

So great was the ruin wrought by the Briton Cadwalla, that Paulinus had to fly with the widowed Queen Ethelburga and her daughter Eanfleda, and to take refuge in Kent, and when Rochester had lost its bishop, Archbishop Honorius and King Eadbald invited him to that see. There in his own time he passed to the kingdom of heaven with the fruits of his glorious labour. Having worked forty-three years for the conversion of England, in that church, says Bede, he left the pallium also, which the monk of the Cœlian monastery had received from the Pope of Rome. A full hundred years from the death of Edwin passed before that pallium, according to the original design of St. Gregory, was restored to the See of York in the person of Egbert.

But in a short time Northumbria received another king, who, on the death in 616 of his father, Ethelfrid the Ravager, with his brothers and a large retinue of young nobles, had taken refuge with the Scotti. There he continued in exile during the seventeen years of his uncle Edwin's reign. Since Columba's apostleship at Iona, the Scots and the Picts had become Christians;[2] and there Oswald, with his companions in misfortune, had learnt the Christian faith and been baptized according to the Celtic rite. When, after

---

[1] Bede, ii. 20.   [2] *Ibid.* xxxi. 3.

the death of Edwin, the tyranny of the Briton Cadwalla had wasted Northumbria, Oswald with a few followers prepared to attack Cadwalla at the head of his great army, having first with his own hands planted a great cross, and, with a loud voice, called on his men to pray for victory. Up to this day, says Bede of his own time, the spot where Oswald raised that cross is marked and held in great veneration. The Angles in their tongue call it Heavenfield. There after Oswald's death the monks of Hexham used to come to keep a vigil for him of many prayers, and to offer on the day of his death the victim of the sacred oblation.

Oswald gained a great victory and slew Cadwalla; and as soon as he obtained a kingdom, longing to gain for the Christian faith the whole people which he began to rule, he sent to those Scotti from whom he had received baptism, begging from them a bishop by whose doctrine and ministry the nation of the Angles which he was ruling might learn the gifts and receive the sacraments of the Lord's faith. And he shortly after received from them what he asked in the pontiff Aidan, a man of consummate gentleness and piety and mild rule, only wanting knowledge on one point, the keeping Easter on the right day; for this he kept according to the custom of the Scotti of the North and the Picts, though the Scotti who dwelt in the southern parts of Ireland had already learnt the canonical observance of Easter, at the monition of the prelate of the Apostolic See.

King Oswald acknowledged Aidan as bishop of all his kingdom, giving him Lindisfarne, as he himself desired, for the seat of his see. We can scarcely doubt that it was love to the island of Iona, from which he came, which led Aidan to choose another island, very similar in character, to become the spiritual metropolis of Northumbria. As bishop, he remained always a monk, not only in heart, but in the manner of his life. On this spot King Oswald[1] humbly and willingly listened to him, and sought with great care to build up and extend the Church of Christ in his kingdom. It was a fair sight to see when the bishop, not entirely acquainted with the English tongue, was at the work of evangelising, how the king with his chief thanes and ministers

---

[1] Bede, iii. 3, 18 lines translated.

served him for interpreter, for in his long exile he had perfectly learnt the Scottish language. Then day by day a number came from the Scottish region bent with great devotion to preach the word of faith to those English provinces over which Oswald reigned, and such of them as were of sacerdotal rank, to administer to believers the grace of baptism. So churches were built in different places, and the population joyously came to listen to the word. Possessions were bestowed by royal gift, and lands were set out for monasteries. The young English had their first teaching from Scotch preceptors, together with higher studies and observation of the regular discipline. For most of those who came were monks; Bishop Aidan himself a monk, as sent there from Iona, the monastery of which for not a little time was the citadel of well-nigh all the monasteries of the northern Scotti, and of all the Picts, and presided over the government of their people.

Aidan[1] was sent from Iona in the time of Abbot Segen, the fourth from Colomba, with the rank of bishop, to begin an English province in Christ. This was his life, far removed from the slackness of our times. All who went with him, whether tonsured or lay, had to meditate—that is, either to read the Scriptures or learn the Psalms. This was his daily work, and that of all with him wherever they came. And if it happened, which however was rare, that he was invited to dine with the king, he went with one or two clerics. After a slight refection, he hastened to leave with his party, either to study or to pray. It was by force of this example that religious men and women at that time took the custom through the whole year, with the exception of the fifty paschal days, to fast on Wednesday and Saturday up to three o'clock. When the rich were in fault, he would never for honour or for fear pass it over, but corrected them with severe reproach. To the powerful in the world he would never give anything except the food offered them in hospitality, but money gifts bestowed by the rich he either gave away for the good of the poor or apportioned to ransom those who had unjustly been made slaves. Many whom he had ransomed, when, after their ransom, he had made them

[1] Bede, iii. 5.

his pupils, he carried them forward by careful forming to sacerdotal rank.

King Oswald,[1] instructed, together with his people, no less by the life than by the teaching of a bishop such as Aidan, surpassed in power all his predecessors. He ruled over all the provinces of Britain which had four languages —the tongue of the Britons, of the Picts, of the Scots, and of the Angles. In the height of his power, nevertheless, which is wonderful, he was always humble, kind, and generous to the poor and to strangers. It is said that on an Easter Day the bishop had taken his seat at dinner with him when a great silver dish with royal food was set before them. The bishop was just lifting up his hands to bless the bread, when there came in suddenly the officer charged with succour to the poor, and informed the king that a great multitude from all quarters was sitting in the streets asking for alms from the king. Thereon Oswald ordered the banquet set before him to be given to them; and not only so, but broke up the great dish and divided it into small bits for them. At the sight the bishop at his side was so struck that he seized the king's right hand and said, "May this hand never grow old." His blessing bore fruit, for when Oswald had been slain in battle, his hand and his arm were cut off, and have remained hitherto incorrupt. In the royal city of Bamborough they are kept in a silver shrine in St. Peter's Church, and worshipped by all with due honour. It has been shown that the hand of the martyred king was so kept to the time of Henry VIII.[2]

Now Oswald,[3] the most Christian king of the Northumbrians, reigned nine years, and was slain in a great battle by that same pagan people and pagan king of the Mercians who slew his predecessor, Edwin. He was in his thirty-eighth year. His faith in God and his devotion were conspicuous by miracles, even after his death. In the spot where, fighting for his country, he was slain by pagans, up to this day cures of the sick, whether men or animals, cease not to take place; nor can we wonder that sicknesses are

---

[1] Bede, iii. 6, translated.
[2] Bollandists, August, vol. ii. p. 87; Montalembert, iv. 37.
[3] Bede, iii. 9, translated.

cured at the spot of his death, who during his life ceased not to care for the sick and the poor, to give them alms and to help them.

It was the general report,[1] and passed into a proverb, that Oswald expired uttering a prayer. For when he was ringed round with enemies, and saw that death was imminent, he prayed for the souls of his army; and the proverb ran, "God have mercy on souls, as Oswald said in falling." His brother and successor, Oswy, came a year after and rescued his head and arm, which the savage Penda, the pagan king of Mercia, had set on poles; the head he buried at Lindisfarne, whence, with the relics of St. Cuthbert, it was at length carried to Durham. The Church has placed him among her martyrs, and for hundreds of years he was enshrined in the Anglo-Saxon heart as the very ideal of a king, a saint, and a martyr.

On the death of King Oswald, who had ruled both the provinces of Northumbria, while, after a time of calamity, his brother Oswy took the northern part or Bernicia, the southern, or Deira, came to a prince of King Edwin's dynasty, Oswin, who, like both his predecessors, Edwin and Oswald, had passed years in exile.[2] Oswin was a man of majestic stature, of beautiful appearance, of agreeable address, of upright character, munificent alike to high and low; for his royal dignity in mind, in countenance, and merit he was beloved by all. The noblest from almost every province flocked to him. Among many virtues his humility was special. During his whole reign the monk of Iona, Aidan, who had become bishop at Lindisfarne, continued to pass on foot over the two great provinces, stretching from the Humber to the Clyde, which formed his diocese. He not only preached in the newly built churches, but went from house to house. King Oswin, when he came to his kingdom, was already a Christian. He had not, like Oswald and Oswy, been converted by the Celtic Scots, but he recognised Aidan as his bishop, and, as well as King Oswy, lived in great intimacy with him. Bede, who was born about twenty years after both Oswin's and Aidan's death, has preserved an anecdote of the king and

---

[1] Bede, iii. 12.   [2] *Ibid*. iii. 14.

the monk which sheds a bright light on the character of each.

Oswin had presented to Aidan a beautiful horse to aid him in the passing of rivers, or on any other occasion which required him to break his practice of going on foot. A little after the gift a poor man asking alms met him. The monk, leaping from horseback, ordered the horse, royally equipped as he was, to be given to the beggar; for indeed he was most merciful, cherishing the poor, a father of the miserable. This was told the king, and he said to the bishop as they were going in to dinner, "My lord bishop, why did you give to a beggar the horse of a king, which you were to keep for your own? Had we not many horses less costly, or other things fit to give to the poor, without your giving that horse, which I had chosen for your special property?" The bishop replied, "What are you saying, my lord king? Do you care more for the son of a horse than for a son of God?" And so they went into dinner. Now the bishop took his seat, but the king, as they had come in from hunting, stood with his officers at the fireplace to warm himself. As he did this, remembering the bishop's expression to him, he suddenly ungirded his sword and gave it to an officer, and falling hastily at the bishop's feet, begged to be pardoned, "for I will never henceforth say a word about this, or pass an opinion how much of my money you give to the children of God." The bishop at this was much alarmed, and, rising, instantly raised him up, promising that he had fully pardoned him, if only he would take his seat and be cheerful again. The king, yielding to the bishop's request, resumed his joyful manner, but the bishop became so dejected as to shed a flood of tears. When the attendant priest asked him in their own language, which the king and his household did not know, why he wept, he replied, "Because I know that the king will not live long, for I never before saw a humble king. That is why I perceive that he will be shortly taken out of this life, for this people is not worthy to have such a ruler."

But though Oswin was a man of distinguished piety and religion, Oswy, being of a rival though connected family, could not dwell in peace with him. Dissension broke out. Each levied an army. Oswin saw that his force was outnumbered. He thought it best to yield and preserve himself for better times. He dismissed his force, and, with a single knight, whom he deemed most faithful to him, retired to the house of a count, on whom likewise he entirely relied. But the count betrayed him to Oswy, who sent and put him to death, with the knight attending on him, who chose rather to be massacred with his lord than to take his life apart from him. It was a crime which struck general horror. This closed the six years of Oswin's reign in 651. But he gained the crown of martyrdom; and twelve days only after him the Bishop Aidan, who had so loved him, was called away to receive the perpetual reward of his labours.

Aidan had held the bishopric of all Northumbria, with his See at Lindisfarne, during sixteen completed years. He died at a royal villa, where he had a place to sleep in, leaning against the adjacent church. In this he was accustomed often to stop, and from it to go forth to his preaching on all sides. He had other like places in royal villas, for he had no possession of his own save his church at Lindisfarne and a few fields near it. They had raised a tent for him against the church, and here, leaning his head against the wooden buttress, he breathed his last breath. His body was carried to Lindisfarne and buried in the cemetery of the monks, and afterwards transferred to the right of the altar in a larger church built there in honour of St. Peter, with the veneration due to so great a pontiff.

Then Bede, after dwelling upon various miracles which he attributed to Aidan, sums up his whole character in these words:[1] "So much I have said of this man's person and his works; not praising or choosing in him his imperfect knowledge as to the keeping of Easter. That I much detest; but as a truthful historian simply record his deeds, praising in his actions what deserves praise, recording them for the benefit of readers—I mean his zeal for peace and charity, for continence and humility; the mind superior to anger and to avarice, despising at once pride and vainglory; the carefulness with which he fulfilled

[1] Bede, iii. 17, p. 145.

and taught the divine commands, his constant habit of study, his vigils, his authority, worthy of a priest, in refuting the proud and powerful, and equally in consoling the weak, his clemency in supporting and defending the poor. To put all in one word, from all which I have learnt from those who knew him, he took pains to omit nothing which he knew from the Gospels or the apostles, or the prophets ought to be done, but to carry it out in act to his utmost power. This is what I embrace and love in this bishop, for this is what I am sure was pleasing to God."

In 642, upon the death of his great brother, Oswald, King Oswy had succeeded to part of Northumbria, and after the death of his kinsman, so cruelly brought about by him, he ruled the whole. He had by Aidan's counsel demanded in marriage that Eanfleda, the daughter of Edwin and Ethelburga, whom St. Paulinus had taken away after her father's death for refuge to her uncle, Eadbald, king of Kent. Thus Eanfleda, the daughter of Edwin and the grand-daughter of Ethelbert, at once a Kentish and a Northumbrian princess, became, like her mother, queen of Northumbria, and, like her mother also, wife of the Bretwalda. In her husband's reign of twenty-eight years, from 642 to 670, she was a potent and a beneficent factor. She did not rest until she had induced her husband to let her found a monastery and a church at Gilling, in atonement for that unjust death which he had inflicted upon St. Oswin, that in it perpetual prayers might be offered both for the slayer and the slain. Eanfleda had fostered Wilfrid; it was by her counsel and her influence that in 648, at fourteen years of age, he had gone to the Abbey of Lindisfarne; and again she had encouraged his wish at eighteen to go to Rome, and had sent him to her cousin, King Erconbert, to speed him on his way. From the time that her abbey at Gilling was founded, Oswy showed such a zeal for the propagation and strengthening of the Christian religion, that he was reckoned among the kings who had best merited of the Church. Since Penda, the heathen king of Mercia, had killed King Oswald, he had not ceased during thirteen years to attack and ravage Northumbria. Oswy had in vain offered him all his treasures and jewels.

Penda's wish was to exterminate the whole Northumbrian race. "Since this heathen will not accept our gifts," said Oswy, "let us offer them to one who will accept them, to the Lord our God."[1] And he made a vow to dedicate to God, as a virgin, a daughter whom the Queen Eanfleda had just borne to him, and at the same time to give twelve domains to found as many monasteries. And so with a very small army he went to the encounter. It is said the pagan army exceeded his by thirty-fold; that they had thirty legions under most experienced captains. Oswald's own son, Prince Ethelwald, stood away from Oswy, and joined the enemy, who were going to fight against his country and his uncle, but kept apart to wait the issue in a safe place. The thirty leaders were almost all slain. The battle was fought by the river Broad Are, close to Leeds. Then King Oswy, to fulfil his vow in gratitude to God for the victory, gave his daughter Elfleda, scarcely a year old, to be dedicated as a nun, and supplied the land he had promised for twelve monasteries, which, giving up the study of worldly warfare for the exercise of the heavenly, should supplicate for the eternal peace of his nation. And Elfleda was taken to the monastery of Hartlepool, where Hilda was then abbess, who two years after built the monastery of Whitby. And under Hilda, Elfleda, that daughter of the king who was fourth in descent from Ethelbert, through her mother Eanfleda and her grandmother Ethelburga, first learnt the regular life, and afterwards succeeding Hilda as abbess, became its teacher, until, says Bede, completing fifty-nine years, that blessed virgin attained the embrace and marriage of the Celestial Spouse. At that monastery, Elfleda herself, her father Oswy, and her mother Eanfleda, and her mother's father Edwin, and many others of the nobility were buried in St. Peter's Church. This war King Oswy accomplished in the region of Leeds, in the thirteenth year of his reign, on the 15th November 655, to the great advantage of both peoples. For he delivered his own race from pagan devastation, and, by cutting off Penda, their perfidious head, converted to the grace of the Christian faith the nation of the Mercians and of the

---

[1] Bede, iii. 24, p. 159.

neighbouring provinces. Three years after Penda's death Oswy reigned over his Mercian kingdom and other southern provinces, and subjected almost all the nation of the Picts to the English kingdom. But Wulphere, son of Penda, speedily recovered his throne, and married the Kentish Princess Ermenilda, great-grand-daughter of Ethelbert; she, as queen of Mercia, became devoted to the spread of the Christian faith, who in her widowhood became third abbess of Ely, succeeding therein two queens, one of Northumberland, the other of Kent.

Finan, another bishop ordained and sent by the Scotti, succeeded Aidan as bishop at Lindisfarne in 652, and after ten years was followed by Bishop Colman. Of these three bishops, Aidan, Finan, and Colman, who sat at Lindisfarne, presiding over the Northumbrian kingdom for the thirty years from 634 to 664, Bede speaks [1] most highly, praising their poverty and continence. When they left, the only houses, besides the church, were very few, only what civilised life absolutely demanded. Money they had none besides their flocks. Whatever the rich gave them, they presently bestowed upon the poor. For neither money nor houses were needed to receive the great of the world, who never came to the church but to pray or to hear the Word of God. The king himself, when need was, came with only five or six attendants, and when he had finished his prayers went away. If they needed any refreshment, they were satisfied with the simple daily fare of the brethren. The whole solicitude of those teachers was to serve not the world, but God; their whole care to cultivate the heart, not the appetite. Accordingly at that time religion was in great veneration. Wherever a cleric or a monk came, he was received by all rejoicings as God's servant; if he was met on a journey, they flocked to him, bending their necks to be crossed by his hand or blessed from his mouth, and they gave diligent heed to his exhortation. On Sunday they flocked to church or monastery, not for the body's refreshment, but to hear the Word of God. If a priest came into a village, its people soon met together, and were careful to ask him for the word of life. For priests or clergy had

---

[1] Bede, iii. 25, p. 161; iii. 26, p. 168.

no other reason for visiting villages but to preach, baptize, tend the sick, and in a word to care for souls. They were so far from all the plague of avarice, that no one, except upon compulsion from the great of the world, would receive land and possessions for the building of monasteries. Such was the custom maintained for some time after this in the Northumbrian churches.

But in the year 664 the question concerning the proper time of keeping Easter and the proper tonsure came to a head. Those who came from Kent or Gaul charged the Scotti with keeping Easter contrary to the custom of the whole Church. Even in Oswy's own royal house, Queen Eanfleda, who had with her a priest keeping strictly the Catholic observances, might with her special household be keeping the Lenten fast, while Oswy had already reached the time of Easter, rejoicing with his portion of the household. The disagreement in Aidan's time had been tolerated, because while it was known that he could not keep Easter except after the rule of those who had sent him, yet in faith, in piety, in charity, he kept it after the manner of all saints, so that he was held in veneration by Honorius, Archbishop of Canterbury, himself. It touched also the two Northumbrian kings, since Oswy had been taught and baptized by the Scotti, knew their language perfectly, and was entirely in favour of what they maintained, while his son Alchfrid had for his teacher Wilfrid, who had learnt the true custom at Rome itself, and so Alchfrid knew that Wilfrid's doctrine should be preferred to all Scots' tradition. And had also given a monastery at Ripon, with land for forty families, which the Scotti, who first had it, would rather give up than yield their own custom, and Alchfrid had given it to Wilfrid as abbot, and then caused him to be ordained to the priesthood by Agilbert, who had then come to him from Wessex.

So it was resolved that a synod should be held in the monastery of Whitby,[1] of which Hilda was then abbess; and thither came the two kings, Oswy and Alchfrid, father and son; the bishops, Colman with his clerics out of Scotland, Agilbert with the priests Agatho and Wilfrid; James

---

[1] Bede, iii. 25-26.

the deacon, who had been under St. Paulinus at York, and Romanus, the Kentish priest in Queen Eanfleda's household; the Abbess Hilda with her party on the side of the Scots, in which also was the venerable Bishop Cedd, consecrated before by the Scots, who in that council was a most vigilant interpreter of both sides.

King Oswy began by saying that those who served God together should keep one rule of living, and that all who were expecting one kingdom in heaven should not disagree in the celebration of the heavenly sacraments; rather they should examine which was the truer tradition, and this was to be followed by all in common. Then he called upon his own bishop, Colman, to declare what was the rite he followed, and whence it had its origin. Colman answered that he had received from his elders, who sent him to be bishop where he was, the Easter which he kept, which all our fathers, men beloved of God, are known to have kept in the same way. And this way none should despise or reprobate, because it is said to have been that which was kept by the Apostle John, the Lord's specially loved disciple, with all the churches which he ruled. As he pursued this strain the king called upon Agilbert to put forth the way which he followed, and the authority from which it was derived. Agilbert answered the king by requesting that his disciple, Wilfrid, the priest—as he was of one mind with himself and with all the others there present who practised the Church's tradition—might speak for him, as he would explain his sentiments in the English tongue better than he could do through an interpreter. Wilfrid, receiving the king's orders to speak, began: "The Easter which we keep I have seen celebrated by all at Rome, where the blessed Apostles Peter and Paul lived, taught, suffered, and were buried. I have beheld it practised by all in Italy and in Gaul, which I went through for the purpose of study or of devotion. I have found Africa, Asia, Egypt, Greece, and the whole world, wherever the Church of Christ is spread, through different nations and tongues, doing this at one and the same time: all but these and the accomplices of their obstinacy—the Picts, I mean, and the Britons, with those from the two most remote islands of the ocean, and not the whole of these, who with foolish toil fight against the whole world." Here Colman spoke: "I wonder how you will call that a foolish toil in which we follow the example of so great an Apostle, who lay upon the Lord's breast, and whom all the world knows to have lived with the utmost wisdom." In answer to this Wilfrid went into a long discussion as to how the rule of keeping Easter was followed, which it would serve no purpose to quote, for the conclusion drawn by Wilfrid lies in the last words, when he addressed Colman thus: "If you and your companions, having once heard the decrees of the Apostolic See—nay, of the Universal Church, and these, too, confirmed by the sacred writing—disdain to follow them, beyond a doubt you sin. For supposing that your fathers were holy, is their small number from the corner of a distant island to be preferred to the Universal Church of Christ throughout the world? And if that Columba of yours was holy and powerful by his virtues—who is also ours if he was Christ's—could he be preferred to the most blessed prince of the Apostles, to whom the Lord said, 'Thou art Peter, and upon this rock I will build My church, and the gates of hell shall not prevail against it, and to thee will I give the keys of the kingdom of heaven.'"

As Wilfrid wound up with these words the king said, "Is it true, Colman, that these words were said by the Lord to Peter?" And he said, "It is true, O king." The king replied, "Can you produce any word of such power given to your Columba?" To which he said, "Nothing." The king rejoined, "Both of you agree without dispute that these words were specially said to Peter, and the keys of the kingdom of heaven were given him by the Lord?" They replied, "Yes, certainly." And he thus concluded: "And I say unto you, that this is that doorkeeper whom I will not contradict, but, so far as I have knowledge and strength, I desire in all things to obey his statutes, lest, when I come to the door of the kingdom of heaven, there be no one to open to me, if he turn away who is admitted to hold the keys."

These words of the king found favour with those who were sitting beside him, or standing, the greater with the less. They declined the less perfect institution, and hastened to transfer themselves to what they had learnt to be better.

In this Council Wilfrid appears as the champion of Catholic doctrine and custom, to which the king of Northumbria, who was likewise the Bretwalda of the Saxon confederation, and had originally been brought up at Iona under the Celtic customs, bowed his head with a decision so emphatic that the Celtic bishop retired from Lindisfarne. Bishop Colman,[1] seeing his teaching slighted and his party disregarded, returned to Iona, taking with him those who chose to follow him—that is, those who refused to accept the Catholic time of keeping Easter, and the Roman tonsure. There he meant to consider what course to take. This question was raised in the year of the Lord's Incarnation 664, the twenty-second year of King Oswy's reign, the thirtieth of the Scottish episcopate in an English province, of which Aidan counted seventeen, Finan ten and Colman three years.

Wilfrid by birth belonged to the highest Northumbrian nobility. He was born in 634, just after the untimely death of King Edwin had seemed to bring irreparable disaster on the Roman mission in the North of England. Bede,[2] being his junior by thirty-eight years, and engaged in study and writing during the last eighteen years of his episcopate, which he also survived for twenty-five years after Wilfrid's death in 709, came to know him intimately, and records that he was a youth of kindly disposition, whose character surpassed his age—so modest and so circumspect in all his conduct, that he was beloved, respected, and cherished by those older than himself as if he were one of them. He had lost in infancy a very pious mother; his father had married again. At thirteen years of age he preferred the monastic to the secular life. For that he needed not only his father's consent, but that of King Oswy, the chief of his nation. As a noble young Anglo-Saxon, he obtained from his father complete armour and a train of servants fit to present himself before the king. At the court he was presented by his friends to the queen, that Eanfleda, the daughter of King Edwin, and Queen Ethelburga, who in her baptism

[1] Bede, iii. 26, p. 167.   [2] Bede, iii. 28, p. 172.

in 626 became the first fruit of the Christian faith in the Northumbrian people. She was herself to bear that Elfleda —consecrated by Oswy before his great victory—the future Abbess of Whitby, where, in her widowhood, Eanfleda herself became a nun under her daughter. Wilfrid, the boy of thirteen, was of noble and striking aspect and of keen intellect. When he expressed to the queen his wish, she obtained from her husband the permission that he should quit the military service and enter the religious life. She intrusted him to a special friend of King Oswy,[1] an old warrior who cherished himself a desire for the cloistral life, and under such guidance sent him to Lindisfarne, at that time, in 647, the seat of Bishop Aidan, and the great monastic establishment of Northumbria. There Wilfrid, delivering himself up to the service of the monks, carefully studied to know and to practise all that belonged to monastic chastity and piety;[2] and being of sharp intellect, he very quickly learnt the psalms and certain books. He was not yet tonsured, but was marked out in no slight degree by the virtues of humility and obedience, which are more than tonsures; and for these both his elders and those of the same age cherished him with deserved affection. Now this youth of sagacious mind, while serving God during several years in this monastery, by degrees perceived that the way of virtue handed down by the Scotch was by no means perfect, and he mentally purposed to go to Rome, and to see what ecclesiastical or monastic rites were observed at the Apostolic See. Referring this purpose to the brethren, they praised it and encouraged him to effect it. Thereupon he went straight to Queen Eanfleda, as he was known to her, and by her advice and influence had been placed in that monastery, and he told her of his desire to visit the apostolic threshold. She, delighted at his purpose, sent him to Kent to her cousin, King Ereombert, with the request to forward him with honour to Rome. It was in the time of Archbishop Honorius, one of blessed Pope Gregory's disciples, a man instructed in the very depth of church matters. While this quick-minded youth was carefully learning what he was examining, another youth of the English nobility, named

---

[1] Montalembert, iv. 157. [2] Bede, v. 19.

Biscop, and surnamed Bennet, joined him there, with the same desire to see Rome.

His biographer, Eddius, notes that this desire to see Rome, which arose in the heart of Wilfrid studying at Lindisfarne under Celtic teachers, was the first time that it was kindled in a Saxon mind. Before the end of this century it became the chosen pilgrimage of the race, whose kings and queens sought to be buried under the shadow of St. Peter's, as Ina founded a Saxon quarter in Rome.

Wilfrid, coming to Canterbury in his opening manhood of eighteen, with the good word of Queen Eanfleda, was treated with great affection by King Ereombert. He kept him nearly a year, but at length sent him forward to Rome in company with Bennet Biscop, who was somewhat older, and more austere than himself. They journeyed together to Lyons, when Biscop went on at once to Rome. But Wilfrid was kept by the Archbishop,[1] who was charmed by the prudent language of the youth, by the grace of his beautiful countenance, his quickness of action, his consistency and ripeness of thought, so that he gave to him and his companions, so long as they were with him, everything which he wanted in abundance. For reading in his tranquil face the blessedness of his mind, he said to him,[2] "If you will remain with me, I will give you a neighbouring part of Gaul to govern, with the virgin daughter of my brother for wife, and I will hold you for an adopted son." But Wilfrid replied, "I have made a vow. Like Abraham, I have left my home and my father's house to visit the Apostolic See, and there to learn the rules of ecclesiastical discipline for the advantage of my nation, but, if God will permit, I will return this way and see you again."

Wilfrid went on his way,[3] with all his train, abundantly supplied by the Archbishop. When he came to Rome, he set himself to visit the churches, especially that church of St. Andrew[4] on the Cœlian Hill, whence St. Augustine and his troop of monks had come forth to their mission in England. And there before the altar he besought St. Andrew, by the love of that God whom he had confessed in his

---

[1] Bede, v. 19, p. 285.
[2] Eddius, c. 4.
[3] Bede, v. 19, p. 285.
[4] Montalembert, iv. 142.

martyrdom, to open his mind, and soften the rudeness of his Saxon tongue, and enable him to study, comprehend, and teach the eloquence of the gospel to the English nation. In his visits to the various churches, and the daily eagerness of his study, he obtained the friendship of a very learned and holy man, the Archdeacon Boniface, who was high in the counsels of the Pope, and who instructed him carefully in the four Gospels, the proper computation as to Easter, and many other things belonging to ecclesiastical discipline, which in his own country he had not been able to learn. Before he left Rome, Wilfrid was presented by Boniface to the Pope, who would seem to have been Eugenius, the successor of the martyred St. Martin.[1] The Pope, informed of his journey and his purpose in coming to Rome, laid his hand upon his head and blessed him.

Wilfrid, leaving Rome,[2] returned to the Archbishop at Lyons, with whom he stayed three years; from him he received the tonsure, and was treated by him with so great an affection that he thought of making him his heir. He learned much from very learned doctors,[3] and no doubt he might compare the teaching and the discipline in this, one of the most leading churches of Gaul, with that which he had received at Rome from the Archdeacon Boniface. The affection of the Archbishop for him increased daily. But this was broken up by the cruelty of Ebroin, Mayor of the Palace, who caused the Archbishop to be seized, to be dragged to Chalons, and there put to death. Wilfrid, being one of his clerics, insisted on following him, and, against every entreaty on his part, to suffer with him; "for," he said, "nothing is better than for father and son to die together and to be with Christ." While thus he was preparing himself for death, he was noticed by the captain of the executioners, who asked, "Who is that handsome youth preparing himself to die?" He was told, "An Angle from beyond the sea, of the race of those who have conquered Britain." And he ordered to spare him and let him go, for that nation of the Angles was then a great

---

[1] Eddius, quoted by Montalembert, iv. 143.
[2] Bede, p. 285.
[3] Eddius, quoted by Montalembert, iv. 145.

terror to many. And so, having buried his spiritual father, he returned to England, being reserved, says Bede, to be a bishop of the English nation.

Wilfrid returned to England. At this time King Oswy had associated with his kingdom his son Alchfrid. This prince conceived a great affection for him, gave him large land at Ripon, enabling him to build a monastery there; or rather, having given the land to monks of Celtic education, when they refused to celebrate Easter according to the Roman computation, and preferred to leave, he had transferred it to Wilfrid. Thus Wilfrid, coming from Rome with full instruction in Roman doctrine and practice, was placed by the Prince Alchfrid, as king of Deira, in a position of great influence. He was abbot, but not yet priest.[1] Not only did the king love the holy abbot, but all the people, noble and ignoble, counted him for a prophet, and the king, receiving a visit from Agilbert, bishop in Wessex, so recommended to him the humility, zeal, fervour, goodness, and sobriety of Wilfrid, that he ordained him priest, specially for the monastery of Ripon, "the king," says Bede, "desiring that a man of so much learning and religion might be attached to him specially and continually as priest and teacher."[2] This was before the Scottish sect had been eliminated by the decision given at Whitby; but after that, Alchfrid, with the counsel and consent of his father Oswy, begged that Wilfrid, being about thirty years of age, might be consecrated bishop for him. So he sent him to the Gallic king,[3] who sent him to be consecrated to Bishop Agilbert, for Agilbert had left Wessex and become Bishop of Paris. And Agilbert, with a large attendance of bishops, consecrated him at Compiègne. While he was thus absent, King Oswy, imitating his son's industry, sent to Kent a holy man, Ceadda, brother of that Bishop Cedd who had been in the Council of Whitby. Ceadda was priest in the monastery of Lastingham, near to Whitby. But when they got to Canterbury, they found Archbishop Deusdedit already dead, without as yet a successor ap-

[1] Montalembert, iv. 150, from Eddius.
[2] Bede, v. 19, p. 287.
[3] Abstract of Bede iii. 28, pp. 172-173, "to their own country."

pointed, and Ceadda had to go for consecration to Vini, in Wessex, who was at that time the only bishop in all Britain canonically consecrated. King Oswy had sent Ceadda to be consecrated as Bishop of York, and Ceadda, placed in the See of York, showed himself admirable both in belief and conduct, while in pastoral work he set himself to visit, not riding, but on foot, in apostolic fashion, towns and country, cottages, villages, and castles. For he was one of Aidan's disciples, made after his pattern, both in act and conduct, and he strove to bring up his own hearers according to Aidan's example and that of his brother Cedd. And Wilfrid, now a bishop, for, it would seem, his monastery at Ripon and for King Alchfrid's own household, brought by his teaching many rules of Catholic observation into the English churches. And so it was brought about that as the Catholic rule of life daily grew up, all the Scotch who dwelt among the English either yielded to them or returned to their own country. "Thus Ceadda at York and Wilfrid at Ripon were ordained bishops of the Northumbrians."[1]

At this time[2] the most noble kings of the Angles, Oswy of Northumbria and Egbert of Kent, took counsel together what was to be done for the state of the English Church. For Oswy, though educated by the Scotch, had come to understand truly that the Roman was the Catholic and Apostolic Church. And by the choice and consent of the Holy Church of the English nation, they took a priest named Wighard out of the clergy of the Bishop Deusdedit, a good man and fit for the episcopate, and sent him to Rome to be ordained bishop, so that, having accepted the archbishopric, he might be able to ordain bishops for the churches of the English through all Britain.

But Wighard, reaching Rome, was, before consecration, carried away by pestilence. In consequence, King Oswy received a letter to this effect from Pope Vitalian :—

"To the lord our excellent son Oswy, king of the Saxons, Vitalian the bishop, servant of the servants of God. We have received your Excellency's welcome letter, reading

---

[1] Bede, v. 24, p. 310, in his chronology.
[2] *Ibid.* iii. 29, p. 174, translated verbatim.

which we recognise the pious devotion and fervent love which you have for the blessed life; and since by the protecting hand of God you have been converted to the true and apostolic faith, you hope that as you reign in your own nation so you may reign in the future together with Christ. Blessed then is the nation which has merited to have a king so wise and a worshipper of God, and not only a worshipper of God himself, but one who studies day and night to convert all his subjects to the Catholic and Apostolic faith, for the redemption of his own soul. Who would not be delighted with such news?"[1]

Then he quotes to the king a number of prophecies foretelling such conversions in all nations, on which he says—

"See here, most excellent son, how it is clearer than the light prophesied, not only of you, but of all nations, that they shall believe in Christ, the Maker of all things. Therefore should your Highness, as already a member of Christ, in all things follow the pious rule of him who is perpetually prince of the Apostles, whether as to the celebration of Easter, or as to all things which the holy Apostles Peter and Paul have handed down. They, as two luminaries of heaven, illuminate the world: so does their teaching daily enlighten the hearts of men who are believers."

Then stating his regret for the death of Wighard, he says: "We have not yet been able to find, in accordance with the tenor of your letter, a man in all respects fittingly adorned to be sent to you for bishop, considering the distance to be traversed. As soon as such a person is found, we will send him with instructions to your country, that he may, by the divine help, eradicate from all your island every tare of the enemy, both by his word of mouth and his reference to the divine oracles."

The Pope further, speaking of the presents received from the king through Wighard, mentions the presents he had sent to the king, and especially "to our spiritual daughter your wife (that is, the Queen Eanfleda), over whose zeal the whole Apostolic See with us rejoices, as her works before God are fragrant and blooming. Let your Highness hasten as we trust, to consecrate all your island to Christ our God.

[1] From Bede, iv. 1, p. 180.

For, indeed, you have for protector our Lord Jesus Christ, the Redeemer of the human race, who will grant you all prosperity to multiply a new people of Christ, by establishing there the Catholic and Apostolic faith. For it is written, 'Seek first the kingdom of God and His justice, and all these things shall be added to you.' For He asks and has obtained that all His islands, as we hope, may be subjected to Him. And so we salute your Excellency with paternal affection, and constantly entreat the divine clemency that it may condescend to assist you and all yours in all good works, that you may reign with Christ in the world to come. May the grace from on high guard your Excellency in safety."[1]

The choice of an Archbishop of Canterbury put by the two kings of Northumberland and Kent on Pope Vitalian cost him no little pains. He urged Adrian, an African abbot, excellently instructed both in monastic and church discipline, and an accomplished master both of the Greek and Latin languages, to accept it. Abbot Adrian, with great labour, excused himself to the Pope, and presented another whose age and whose learning fitted him, as Adrian thought, better for such a work. This was a monk from a neighbouring monastery, named Andrew, who was in the opinion of all suitable. But the state of his health was an obstacle. Adrian was further pressed to take it himself, and thought of an Eastern monk then at Rome, of mature age, for he was sixty-six. Born at Tarsus, with a perfect knowledge of everything which one who had to exert the whole discipline of the Church should know, and possessing both languages and spotless in his moral life. Adrian brought such a man, named Theodorus, to Pope Vitalian, who chose him on condition that Abbot Adrian should attend him, to guide him in making the journey, and to carefully watch that he should not, after the fashion of a Greek, introduce anything against the faith into the Church over which he was to preside.[2] Theodorus had to be ordained subdeacon, and waited four months that his hair might grow sufficiently to receive the Latin tonsure. He was then consecrated by Pope Vitalian on the 26th March

[1] Bede, iv. 1, p. 178-179.   [2] Ibid. p. 179.

668, and so in May he was sent with Adrian to Britain.

They passed together to Marseilles, and then to Arles, where they gave commendatory letters from Pope Vitalian to Archbishop John, who kept them until Ebroin, Mayor of the Palace, gave them permission to proceed. Theodorus then went on to Agilbert, Bishop of Paris, where he was well treated and remained some time. He stayed also with the Bishop of Meaux, for the approach of winter led them to seek shelter where they could. While they were here, King Egbert learnt that the bishop for whom they had asked from the Roman bishop was in the kingdom of the Franks. Upon this he sent at once Redfrid, his ealderman, to bring him. Redfrid came, and, with Ebroin's permission, took him to the port of Estaples, where his weak health kept him some time, and thence he sailed to Britain. But Ebroin had kept Adrian through a suspicion that he bore some commission from the Emperor at Constantinople to the kings of Britain against the kingdom of which Ebroin had the chief rule. When satisfied that this was not so, he allowed Adrian to follow Theodore, who, on his arrival, gave him the monastery of St. Peter, where the Archbishops of Canterbury are buried. For the apostolic lord had charged Theodore, on his leaving Rome, to give Adrian a place in his diocese, where he might fitly live.

Bede says that Theodore arrived at his church the second year after his consecration, on the 27th May 669, a Sunday, and lived in it twenty-one years, three months, twenty-six days.[1] Presently he made a visitation of the whole island, wherever the Angles dwelt, for he was received and listened to most willingly by all of them, and disseminated the right order of living, the canonical rite of celebrating Easter, in which Adrian accompanied him and walked with him; and he was the first of the archbishops to whom the whole Church of the Angles yielded obedience. But because Theodorus and Adrian were abundantly learned as well in sacred as in secular knowledge, they gathered about them a crowd of disciples, and poured forth daily streams of salutary doctrine to irrigate their hearts; and, together with the sacred writ-

[1] Bede, iv. 2, p. 181.

ings, delivered to their hearers instruction in the metrical art, in astronomy, and in ecclesiastical computation. A proof of this is that up to my own time pupils of them survive who know the Latin and the Greek tongue as well as that in which they were born. Nor from the time that the Angles came to Britain have there been happier years, for they had most brave and Christian kings, a terror to all barbarous nations. The wishes of all men hung upon those joys of the heavenly kingdom of which they had but just heard, while all who desired to be instructed in these holy lessons found masters ready to teach them.

The chanting in church, which had hitherto been restricted to Kent, from this time began to be taught through all churches of the English; and except James, the deacon of St. Paulinus at York, Ædde was the first teacher of chanting in the Northumbrian churches, having been invited from Kent by Wilfrid, the first bishop of the English nation who learnt to communicate the Catholic mode of living to English churches.

So Theodorus in his universal visitation ordained bishops in the proper places, and by their help corrected any usages which he found not quite perfect. Thus, with regard to the Bishop Ceadda, whom Oswy had placed at York, when the objection of Theodore to the mode of his ordination was made, that bishop offered to discontinue his work. Theodorus contented himself with remedying his defective ordination. Ceadda, in obedience to his direction, was re-ordained, but he was removed from York;[1] and as the result of Theodore's visitation, Wilfrid was acknowledged Bishop of Northumbria. Ceadda had retired to his abbey of Lastingham, and Wilfrid at York was ruling the whole monarchy of Oswy; and because it was the custom of that bishop to carry on the work of the gospel rather on foot than on horseback, Archbishop Theodore enjoining him, whenever the distance was long, much against his will, to ride, with his own hand, in zeal and love for his work, helped him to mount, for he had found him to be a holy man. Wulfhere, who had succeeded Penda as king of Mercia, entreated Theodore to give him Ceadda for bishop, and he became

[1] Bede, p. 183.

Bishop of Lichfield, and as such he has lived for ages in the remembrance of his people. He is praised by Bede as a pattern of continence, humility, learning, prayer, and voluntary poverty, to whom he ascribes miracles.

In 670 King Oswy died, aged fifty-eight. At that time he was so touched by the Roman and Apostolic rule of life, that he purposed, if he recovered from the illness under which he was suffering, to go to Rome, and there to finish his life at the holy places; and he besought Wilfrid, as his bishop, to conduct him thither, promising to bestow great gifts on him. Thus Bede signifies that when Oswy's important reign of twenty-eight years terminated in 670, he was in perfect union with Wilfrid as the bishop of all his kingdom. The King Alchfrid has disappeared from history, while Wilfrid appears to have found in King Egfrid a patron as devoted as the former prince, and in Etheldreda, who had been Egfrid's queen for about ten years, a most munificent patroness, who had bestowed on him, to build a monastery and church, her own domain of Hexham, the dowry which her second husband Egfrid had bestowed on her, as her first husband had given her the domain of Ely. But her devotion to Wilfrid as bishop and guide of her life was great.

Bede mentions another fact, telling greatly on the formation of Christian life in England at the time of the Council of Whitby, in 664.[1] "There were at that time many of the nobles and of the middle-class of the English nation who, during the sitting of the bishops Finan and Colman, that is, in the years 651–664, left their island country and retired into Ireland, either for the purpose of sacred study, or to lead the life of continency. Of these, some presently bound themselves to a strict observance of the monastic rule; others prepared to go round to the cells of various teachers, giving their time to study. All these the Irish (Scotti) receiving with the greatest cordiality, supplied them with daily food without cost, with books also for their study, and with gratuitous instruction." Among them he mentions two young noblemen of great ability, named Adilhun and Egbert. "The first had a brother equally dear to God, who also afterwards came to Ireland for study, and, after

[1] Bede, iii. 27, p. 171.

being well taught, came back to England, was made a bishop in Lincolnshire, and for a long time most nobly governed the church. These two, Adilhun and Egbert, were together in the monastery of Rathmel, both in danger of death from the great mortality prevailing, which had struck down most of their comrades. Egbert had gone out from the infirmary to be by himself, and to think over his past life, entreating of God that he might not die until he had made up for the past negligencies of his boyhood, or been more abundant in good works. And he had made a vow to live on in a foreign land, and not return to England; for besides the canonical time of chanting, he would daily recite the whole psalter for the divine praise, and every week pass a day and night fasting. His tears, prayers, and vows finished, he went back and found his comrade asleep. He began to sleep himself; but presently his comrade woke up, and looking at him, said, 'O brother Egbert, what have you done? I was hoping that we should enter together into eternal life, but know that you will receive what you asked for.' He had learnt this in a dream. Adilhun died that night, but Egbert lived long after, became a priest, spent a life full of good works, and died lately, in 729, at the age of ninety. I learnt what I have recorded from a very venerable priest, who heard it from Egbert himself." It was this Egbert whom Bede records to have succeeded in a matter in which every one else had failed. In the year 716 the monks of Iona received the Catholic instead of their old Celtic rites, at his teaching. It was about eighty years since, at King Oswald's request, they had sent Aidan as bishop to teach the English; and now the man of God lived there thirteen years, after consecrating the island with, as it were, a fresh dawn of union and peace; and on Easter Day, 729, he there died after celebrating mass, and the joy of that supreme festivity, which he had begun with the brethren to whom he had brought the grace of unity, he completed, says Bede, with our Lord and the Apostles, and the other citizens of heaven, where he ceases not to celebrate it without end.

Bede considers it worthy of special note how the monks of the Scottish nation, who dwelt at Iona, together with the monasteries subject to them, received, by God's help, the rightful keeping of Easter and the canonical tonsure. The father and priest Egbert, beloved by God, and to be named with every honour, came to them from Ireland. He had kept, it would seem, that vow of living in a foreign land which he had made in 664, when he was seventy-five, down to 716.[1] "As a teacher he won hearts, while he was most devoted in executing what he taught. He was most joyously welcomed at Iona, and by his words succeeded in changing that tradition which had come to them from their fathers. Of this tradition it may be said in the Apostle's language, they had 'a zeal of God, but not according to knowledge.' And Egbert taught them the celebration of the chief solemnity in the Catholic and Apostolic manner under the figure of a continuous crown, alluding in these words to the Roman tonsure, which he taught them to accept; and it is evident that this took place by a wonderful dispensation of goodness, that because that nation freely, and without grudging, took the pains to communicate to the English nation the knowledge of God which it possessed itself, it also afterwards reached the perfect rule of life in those things in which it had been deficient by the English nation. Whereas, on the contrary, the British who refused to unfold to the English that knowledge of the Christian faith which they possessed, after the English people were already believing, and had in all things the rule of the Catholic faith, continue inveterate and halting in their steps, and show their heads without a crown, and venerate Christ's solemnities without the society of Christ's Church." It may be added that Wilfrid pleaded this cause at the Council of Whitby in 664, before the Bretwalda of the English, whom he convinced; and that an English pilgrim from Ireland, seven years after Wilfrid's death, in 716, was the person ordained to restore Iona and its monasteries to unity.

After the first visitation of the English dioceses by Archbishop Theodore came the first Council. The king of Northumbria, Oswy, the great Bretwalda, preparing to make a pilgrimage to Rome, died, and left his son Egbert heir to his kingdom.[2] In Egbert's third year Theodore convoked

---

[1] Bede, v. 22, p. 303.   [2] Ibid. iv. 5, p. 189.

a council of bishops, together with those many teachers of the Church who both knew and loved the canonical statutes of the Fathers. When assembled, he set before them, for strict observance, with such a mind as became a pontiff, all that concerned the unity of the Church's peace. This is the text of the synodical action :—

"In the name of our Lord God and Saviour Jesus Christ, the same Lord reigning for ever and governing His Church. It pleased us to meet according to the sacred canons, for the purpose of considering matters necessary to the Church. We met on the 24th of September in the place called Hertford. I, Theodore, however unworthy, named by the Apostolic See Bishop of the church of Canterbury; our brother in the episcopate, Bisi, Bishop of the East Anglians; our brother in the episcopate, Wilfrid, Bishop of the Northumbrians, was present by his deputies; our brothers in the episcopate, Patta, Bishop of Rochester, Lutherius, Bishop of the West Saxons, Winfrid, Bishop of the province of Mercia. When we had each taken our seats in order, I said, 'I beseech you, most beloved brethren, for the fear and love of our Redeemer, that we all treat together what concerns our faith, that whatever has been decreed and defined by the holy and approved Fathers be kept stainless by us all.' And when I had finished this prologue, I asked each one of them, in order, if they agreed to keep what has been of old decreed by the Fathers. To which all our episcopal brethren answered, saying, 'It is entirely our pleasure, all of us, with most willing and ready mind, to keep what the canons of the holy Fathers have defined.' I forthwith presented to them that same book of the canons, and from that book showed them ten headings which I had marked as being most necessary to us, and I begged that they might be most strictly received by all.

"The first was, that we all keep together the holy day of Easter on the Sunday after the fourteenth day of the first month.

"The second, that no bishop invade the diocese of another, but be content with the government of the people intrusted to him.

"The third, that in the monasteries consecrated to God,

no bishop may at all disquiet them, nor take away by force anything which is theirs.

"The fourth, that monks do not pass from place to place, that is, from monastery to monastery, unless by leave of their own abbot, but remain in the obedience which they promised at the time of their conversion.

"The fifth, that no one of the clergy leave his own bishop and go about in general, nor that he be received, if he go anywhere, without commendatory letters from his own bishop. If, being received anywhere, he do not, when invited, return, both the person who received him and the person received be subject to excommunication.

"The sixth, that foreign bishops and clergy be content with such hospitality as they meet, and that no one may perform any sacerdotal act without permission of the bishop in whose diocese he is recognised to be.

"The seventh, that a synod be convoked twice a year; but because many causes hinder it, all agreed that we meet once a year, at the beginning of August, in the place called Cloveshoe.

"The eighth, that no bishop ambitiously prefer himself to another, but that all acknowledge the time and order of their consecration.

"The ninth, that many more bishops be made as the number of the faithful increases; but we put off the present treatment of this matter.

"The tenth for the married: that no one have any but a legitimate marriage; that no one commit incest; no one leave his own wife, except for what Holy Gospel says, because of fornication. But if any one expel his own wife, joined to him in legitimate marriage, if he be a good Christian, let him be united to no other, but remain as he is, or be reconciled to his own wife.

"So these heads were treated of by us together, and defined, that no scandal of contention may arise hereafter from any one of us, or any other things be spread abroad by any, and it seemed good that every one of us, by subscription of his own hand, should confirm what had been defined. The statement of our agreement I dictated for our notary to write. Whoever, therefore, in any way attempts to infringe this our sentence, which is according to decrees of canons, confirmed also by our consent and the subscription of our hands, let him know that he is severed from every sacerdotal office and our society. May the divine grace preserve in safety us who are living in the unity of His holy Church."

Bede in a solemn manner marks as an epoch the holding of this Council, which was coeval with his own birth. He illustrates such incidents as these.

In the year 667 a monk of Tarsus happened to be at Rome. He was sixty-six years of age, still a layman, not knowing the English tongue. He was called forth by the successor of St. Peter, and received from him the commission to go to England as Archbishop of Canterbury. A few years before, Pope Martin had been kidnapped in his own Lateran cathedral, and carried a prisoner to Constantinople by an Eastern emperor, the patron of a heresy which that Pope had resisted and censured in a Council which he had called against it, and for this, after a series of outrages, he was martyred. Pope Vitalian, his second successor, consecrated the monk of Tarsus, and sent him forth, accompanied by another monk, an African, whom he charged to attend upon the new Archbishop. So the two monks, the first an Asiatic, the second an African, passed through France, and Egbert, king of Kent, hearing of their arrival in the kingdom of the Franks, sent his ealderman to conduct the new Archbishop to Canterbury. The Archbishop, when arrived in England, appointed his companion, as soon as he was set free from his detention by Ebroin and had rejoined him, to be Abbot of St. Peter's monastery in Canterbury, as his bosom counsellor. He then held a visitation of the several dioceses in the Saxon Heptarchy, correcting whatever he found to be wrong. Thus, at York, seeing a defect in the ordination of Ceadda, he instructed that he should be re-ordained; he established Wilfrid, whom he found bishop at Ripon, to be Bishop of Northumbria at York, and afterwards transferred Ceadda to Lichfield. He then held at Hertford, in 673, the first Council of the English Church, making provision for the seven kingdoms as belonging to one Church. Thus Canterbury, by the hand of a Greek monk who was ordered to it by the Pope, fulfilled the place marked out by St.

Gregory in its institution seventy years before, and in its first century began to draw the seven Saxon kingdoms to the acknowledgment of one Church co-extensive with England, a great preparation for the absorption of the seven fluctuating territories in one indivisible kingdom. And so the hierarchy of St. Gregory was the corner-stone of England's unity. One monk sent expressly by a Pope laid it; another monk, sent equally by a Pope, at the distance of one human life, built it up, attesting its unity with the Church of the whole world in the authority which he thus exercised, an authority bestowed upon him by "the servant of the servants of God," and acknowledged by the Bretwalda of the Anglo-Saxon confederation.

CHAPTER VII

THREE NUNS OF ODIN'S RACE—HILDA, ELFLEDA, AND ETHELDREDA

THREE martyr kings had contributed in no slight degree to this result. Bede has expressly traced the beginning of the Christian faith in his own country, Northumbria, to its King Edwin, while still a heathen Saxon, seeking a wife from the house of King Ethelbert. He had gained Ethelburga, the daughter of the first Christian Saxon king, and of the descendant of Clovis, Bertha, on the condition that he would treat her as a Christian queen with full enjoyment of the mass and the presence of a bishop, to sanctify herself and her household.

Her daughter, Eanfleda, born in 626, became the first Christian of Northumbria; and Edwin, of his own full choice, after consultation with his Witan, was baptized with them at York by that bishop of his household, one of the monks who had either come with Augustine to England or joined him afterwards from the monastery on the Cœlian Hill, dear to every English heart. Edwin was crowned with martyrdom, and the Christian faith which Ethelburga had brought with her was threatened with extinction in Northumbria, and the young Eanfleda was carried away by her mother, the widowed Ethelburga, for refuge with her uncle, Eadbald. The former queen of Northumbria, in her widowhood, founded an abbey at Lyminge.

But another martyr king was raised up for Northumbria. Oswald was brought back from his exile with the Scots. He had been taught by them the Christian faith, with the Celtic customs derived from Ireland. Oswald's first act was to plant a lofty cross with his own hand, and call his comrades to worship before it; and the spot from that time became consecrated ground for English hearts; and his second act was to entreat his educators, the monks of Iona, to send him a bishop, that he might win his people to the Christian faith. In obedience to that summons, the monk-bishop Aidan came, and during the seven years of Oswald's reign, from 635 to 642, was the soul of Oswald's government. At the end of that time King Oswald also, like Edwin, was crowned with martyrdom, and the singular glory attached to his name was that the very moment of his death was expressed by the proverb, "O God, have mercy upon souls, as Oswald said when he was dying."[1] He died at thirty-eight years of age, and his work seemed but half done.

Then succeeded his brother Oswy, and a cousin of a rival house, Oswin, who divided Northumbria between them; and Oswin's piety, valour, and goodness are described in terms which equal those given to Oswald. The monk-bishop Aidan was his bosom friend, as he had been of Oswald. They carried on the work of converting the heathen Saxons with joint forces. But one day, in Oswin's presence, at the banquet beside him, Aidan became sad and silent, and when his attendant remarked it, Aidan replied in the Irish tongue that Oswin the king was too good to live; and in fact, he was put to death by the king who was his cousin and rival, as well as the brother of Oswald; and the monk-bishop died but twelve days after the murdered king, whom he had so loved, and who had so much loved him. But Oswin in his short time had also gained the crown of martyrdom.

And now in this history, which is almost without a parallel as being the history of three kings, converts from heathenism, royal in their whole conduct, devoted to their faith, and martyrs for the faith which they had brought to their subjects, an incident ensued which crowns a great record with an unexpected surprise. Oswy, the brother of Oswald, gained, by the murder of Oswin, the half of Northumbria which he had coveted. But he had for his wife that Eanfleda, the daughter of Edwin and of Ethelburga, the granddaughter of Ethelbert and Bertha. From her very birth she was marked to bring a blessing: first of all to her father, for in delight at her mother's safety, through

[1] Montalembert, iv. 32, quoting Bede, iii. 9, 12.

the prayers of St. Paulinus, he promised to leave idolatry, and as a pledge of his promise intrusted her to Paulinus, and so she was baptized on the holy day of Pentecost, 626, the first of the Northumbrian race, together with eleven others of her household. She also was the youthful queen of Oswy,[1] the patroness to whom St. Wilfrid owed both his education at Lindisfarne and then again his first visit to Rome. She mourned over the death of a kinsman, which took place by the order of a husband, and she drew that husband to consent to her founding a monastery and a church at the spot where his crime had been committed, that prayers might daily be said for the victim and for the slayer. That daily offering was heard, and Oswy's reign lasted twenty-eight years, and when he died in 670, he died with the desire to end his days at Rome under the guidance of St. Wilfrid. The youth whom his queen had singled out for protection was then bishop of all his dominion. The Archbishop whom he had sought from Pope Vitalian had been chosen by that Pope and had been welcomed by him as Archbishop of Canterbury, was received in visitation throughout England, was giving England a standard of doctrine, and uniting its bishops as rulers of one church. And the reign of Oswy the slayer had been as favourable to the growth of the Church and the unity of nascent England as the reigns of the three martyr-kings, in whose honour the mass is still said. Of Queen Eanfleda it remains to say that she bore to her husband Oswy that daughter, Elfleda, who, at her birth in 655, was vowed by her father Oswy to God in gratitude for the victory over the heathen Saxon, Penda. For Penda had slain both King Edwin and King Oswald, and for a whole generation persecuted the Christian Saxons of Northumbria. Elfleda fulfilled her father's offering: she succeeded St. Hilda as Abbess of Whitby, and the mother, Eanfleda, closed the years of her widowhood as a nun under her daughter's rule.

In that great host of noble Saxon women who became mothers of the English race, Eanfleda is conspicuous as daughter, as wife, as mother, as queen, and as nun. In her the Merovingian blood of Clovis, through her grand-

---

[1] Bede, ii. 9, p. 93.

mother Bertha, was far surpassed by the blood of her grandfather Ethelbert, fifth in descent from the pirate Hengist, but first Christian king of Odin's race, a race which, from the time of Ethelbert, produced more of both sexes who embraced the monastic life than has been given to any other royal house.

In A.D. 634 began the work of the three Celtic monk-bishops Aidan, Finlan, and Colman, invited by these Northumbrian kings to be bishops of their realm, and to convert their people to the Christian faith. Their see was at Lindisfarne, the barren island on the eastern coast of Northumbria, chosen by Aidan and his friend Oswald in final remembrance, as it would seem, of that other island in the western archipelago of Scotland which once gave the faith it brought from St. Patrick to the sons of Scotland, and yet remains the burial-place of so many kings and chieftains. The three bishops carried on their holy work, loved, supported, and laboured with, by the three Northumbrian kings, Oswald, Oswin, and Oswy. Bede records them with unstinted love and admiration, excepting only certain Celtic customs, in which their strict followings of the tradition drawn by St. Patrick from Rome, in his own time, led them to differ as to the great rite of keeping Easter. The better informed Apostolic calendar had established, in Bede's own time, a great and universal canon. But words can scarcely surpass the encomium which Bede pays to the self-denying tenderness of their charity, to the severity of their discipline, exceeding, in some points, that of the monks of Canterbury, to their apostolic labours in traversing on foot the entire district of their diocese, stretching from the Humber to the Clyde. In the thirty years from 634 to 664 the holy life of these monks spread widely veneration for the faith which they brought. Aidan was ever a monk, not only in heart, but also in life.[1] Almost all his fellow-labourers who came from Ireland or Scotland were monks like himself. All followed together the cœnobitic rule of their order and their country. A hundred years after Aidan the system he had established at Lindisfarne was still in full vigour. As in his time the bishop himself was head

[1] Montalembert, iv. 22, quoting Bede's Life of St. Cuthbert.

of the community on the island, or, if he was not, he remained subject, as monk, to the abbot's authority, chosen by the community itself. The priests, the deacons, the chanters, and the other officers of the cathedral-church were all monks.

Aidan[1] threw himself especially into the work of education. From the beginning of his mission he drew to him twelve young Englishmen whom he brought up with the greatest care for the service of Christ. One of them at least became a bishop. Every church and every monastery which he founded became at once a school, wherein the children of the Angles received, from the monks who came with Aidan, an instruction pushed as far as that of the great Irish monasteries. On the purchase of slaves he bestowed chiefly the gifts of munificent Anglo-Saxons, to save those who, in Bede's expression, had been unjustly sold; which means, probably, those who were not foreign prisoners, nor had been condemned to servitude as punishment for some crime. For the Saxons, and also the Celts, did not shrink from selling their brethren, or their children, like cattle. Aidan carefully instructed the slaves whom he ransomed, put them among his disciples, and often raised them to the priesthood. Thus the monks fought with barbarism and slavery. In that time of friendship between the noble Oswald and no less noble Oswin and Aidan, day by day fresh gifts of land, due to their generosity or that of Northumbrian thanes, swelled the patrimony of the monks and the poor; new missionaries from Scotland or Ireland helped on the work of Aidan and Oswald, preaching and baptizing neophytes. James also, the deacon of St. Paulinus in past time, remained at York. As a disciple of St. Gregory, he joined the teaching of music to the lessons of religion, and was to the North a master of ecclesiastical chanting in the Roman manner.

King Oswald went to Wessex to choose a bride. In so doing he helped to convert the king, her father, and became his godfather at baptism, while he carried off the princess Kineburga to continue his line in Northumbria. He had been powerful in the conversion of Wessex to the faith by thus supporting her king.

[1] Montalembert, iv. 26, translated. References to Bede.

But not only was the monastic life that institution by which the three monk-bishops, aided by the kings Oswald, Oswin, and Oswy, went on to convert Northumbria and Mercia; the noblest virgins of the Anglo-Saxon race had chosen that life with special predilection. Not martyr-kings and monk-bishops only have written their names in the Christian history of their country, but the daughters of Odin, as soon as they heard the name of Christ, the life of His mother, and the example of both, fell in love with the birth of Bethlehem and the house of Nazareth, and chose not the future of a Valhalla, but a heaven where the Virgin-born and the Virgin-mother shone the brightest in a host who served God in company with angels, and had aspired by grace to that unbroken communion with their Maker which belonged to angels by their creation as spirits. The honour which had not been wanting to the Teutonic women in that imperfect tradition of their original race wherein the preaching of Christ found them, led them to clasp eagerly the higher honour to be brides of Christ; and as the German marriage had retained a greater purity in the perpetual association and faithfulness of husband and wife than other yet unredeemed races, so the perfect following of Christ, which the virginal life opened to them in becoming Christians, drew them with a greater attraction than has happened to softer and less energetic races. Where in the Christian history do we find, at the very first conversion of a people, such names as Hilda and Ebba, Etheldreda and Elfleda? Did not Ethelburga, carrying the faith to Northumbria, then left in early widowhood by Edwin, take refuge with her brother King Eadbald, and retire also from his court to found a monastery at Lyminge, being the first of Anglo-Saxon[1] women to take the veil, and where she finished her life? The Saxon Penda, heathen persecutor and destroyer, fell at eighty years on the field of battle, true to his old character. But from him sprung favourite daughters of the Church, St. Kineburga espousing Aldfrid, king of Northumbria, but remaining a virgin, and becoming a nun, and St. Kineswitha, wooed by Offa, king of Essex, but inducing him to become a monk, and St. Eadburga,

[1] Bede, p. 114, in note.

Abbess of Dorchester, while a fourth daughter, Wilburga, founded with her husband the monastery of Chertsey. Penda's son, Merwald, ealderman of the Mercians, gave him three grand-daughters, St. Milburga, Abbess of Wenlock, St. Mildreda, Abbess of Minster, St. Milgitha, nun at Canterbury. Penda's son Wulphere was king of Mercia, and married Ermenilda, and both in nineteen years of royalty did their utmost to convert their people. And Ermelinda in her widowhood followed her mother, Sexburg, as third Abbess of Ely, while her daughter Wereburga, another grand-daughter of Penda, was Abbess at Weeden, at Trentham, and at Hanbury, and finally succeeded her mother as fourth Abbess of Ely. Her brother, Coenred, Ermenilda's son, was king of Mercia in 764, and a monk at Rome in 709. Oswald and Oswy, each in his day Bretwalda, and great converters, by their personal labours as well as by their example, were sons of Ethelfrid, the Ravager, the heathen king who brought down an army on the Christians of Cambria, after they had not listened to St. Augustine, and slew the multitude of monks at Bangor monastery who prayed for their people, but had never shown the least willingness to convert the Saxons who had taken Britain. Oswald and Oswy had likewise a sister, sought for in marriage by the Scottish king. But Ebba rejected his suit, and chose rather in the neighbourhood of her brother's royal city of Bamborough, to be Abbess of Coldingham, to help St. Etheldreda in her flight from her husband when he recalled his permission to leave him. Ebba was the friend of St. Wilfrid, and powerful in her intercession for him to be restored to his see. Was not, in the sister of the two sovereigns Oswald and Oswy, the preference of the virginal life to a royal marriage an example which would strike all ranks of Anglo-Saxon maidens? Was not her noble and holy life, at the head of a great sisterhood during thirty years, such a commendation in palace and cottage as might touch every heart? She was the daughter of Ethelfrid the Ravager, and of Acha, the sister of King Edwin, and so united in her person the two rival lines which contested the double domain of Bernicia and Deira, making up Northumbria. Her monastery of Coldingham just reached the northern limits of that realm which her brothers won—in the part also which her nephew Egfrid was afterwards to lose, as Edwin, her uncle, had given his name to the capital of Scotland, which his posterity was not to keep. The Abbey of Coldingham and the Castle of Edwin—the Edinburgh of to-day—marked the bounds to which the dominion of the Angles then reached.

Yet Ebba was not the only abbess of royal lineage. There was another great-niece of Edwin, who came back with him in 617, when her race was restored from exile. Let us hear what Bede, in part her contemporary, has written of her.

"In the year of our Lord's incarnation[1] 680, the most devout servant of Christ, Hild, abbess of the monastery called Streaneshalch—that is, the Isle of the Lighthouse—after the many heavenly works which she did on earth, was taken away from the earth to receive the rewards of heavenly life on the 17th of November, being sixty-six years old. If her life be divided into equal parts, she spent most nobly the first thirty-three years in secular dress, and more nobly consecrated the following equal number of years to the Lord in the monastic life. For she was noble too in birth, being daughter of King Edwin's nephew, by name Hereric. She also received, together with that king, by the preaching of Paulinus of blessed memory, the first bishop of the Northumbrians, the faith and the sacraments of Christ, and preserved them spotless even to the time when she merited to reach His vision.

"Now when she determined to leave the secular habit and serve Him alone, she retired into the province of the Eastern Angles, for she was akin to that king, and she wished, if she could bring it about, to leave her own country and everything which she possessed, to go into Gaul, and to lead a foreign life for the Lord in the monastery of Chelles, in order the more easily to merit a perpetual country in heaven. For her own sister, Heresuid, mother of Adwulph, king of the East Saxons, was at this

[1] Bede, v. 23, p. 221.

time subject in that same monastery to the regular discipline, and was waiting there for the eternal crown. Touched by her example, she too remained in that province a whole year, with the intention of foreign pilgrimage. Then she was called back to her country by Bishop Aidan, and accepted ground for maintaining one family on the northern side of the river Wear. There, with very few companions, she led for one year the monastic life.

"After this she was made abbess in a monastery named Hartlepool, which had been made not long before by a devout servant of Christ named Hein. This is said to have been the first woman in the Northumbrian province who, by consecration of Aidan the bishop, took up the purpose and the dress of a nun's habit. But having continued not long at that monastery, Hein retired to the city Calcaria, called by the English Kalkacester, and there fixed her dwelling. Now Hild, the servant of Christ, was set over the rule of that monastery, and presently took pains to order it in all things by the regular life as she was able to learn it from learned men, for both Bishop Aidan and all the religious who knew her, on account of her inborn wisdom and love of the divine service, were wont carefully to visit her, to treat her with earnest affection, and gave her diligent instruction.

"When, then, she had presided several years over this monastery, greatly intent upon the institution of the regular life, it was her lot to undertake also to build and set in order the monastery in the place called Streaneshalch. She employed herself actively in the work thus laid upon her. For she instituted this monastery also with the same rules of the regular life as those with which she had governed the former one. She maintained here also a very strict watch over justice, piety, and chastity; above all, over peace and charity. So, after the example of the primitive church, no one there was to be rich, no one in want, everything was to be common to every one, since nothing was the property of any one. Her foresight was so great that not only people of middle station sought counsel from her in their necessities and found it, but kings and princes also not unfrequently. She made her subjects so to study the reading of the divine Scriptures, so to exercise themselves in righteous works, that very many could easily be found there who were fit to undertake ecclesiastical rank—that is, the duty of the altar.

"In fine, we afterwards saw five become bishops out of this monastery, and all these men of singular merit and sanctity. They are Bosa, Ætla, Ofsfor, John, and Wilfrid. Of the first, I said above that he was consecrated Bishop of York; of the second, it is a short intimation that he was ordained to the bishopric of Dorchester; of the two last, one was Bishop of Hexham, the other of York; of the third one, we would say that he had devoted himself in each of the Abbess Hild's two monasteries to the reading and study of the Scriptures. Then, desiring increase in perfection, he came to Kent to Archbishop Theodore of blessed memory. After studying some time the sacred writings, he was bent also to go to Rome, a thing at that time esteemed a matter of great virtue. On returning thence to Britain, he turned aside to the province of Worcester, which King Osric then ruled. And there, preaching the word of faith, and also showing himself an example of life to those who saw and heard him, he remained a long time. Then the bishop of that province, named Bosel, was so infirm that he was unable to fulfil the office of bishop. On this account he was by the judgment of all elected for the episcopate, and by order of King Ethelred ordained by Wilfrid, the bishop of blessed memory, who at that time administered the episcopate of the Angles of Middle England, for Archbishop Theodore was then already dead, and no one yet appointed to succeed him. In this province a little before—that is, before the man of God Bosel—a man of the greatest energy and learning and of excellent ability, named Tatfrid, was chosen bishop from the monastery of the same abbess, but was carried off by a premature death before he could be ordained.

"But not only did this handmaid of Christ and abbess, Hild, whom all who knew her for her signal piety and grace were wont to call Mother, live to all with her in her own monastery as an example of life, but likewise served for an occasion of salvation and correction to a great many far away whom the happy report of her industry and virtue reached. A dream was to be fulfilled which her mother, Bregusuid, saw in her infancy. For when her husband, Hereric, was in banishment under Cerdic, king of the Britons, where also he died of poison, she saw in a dream as if he whom she sought with all diligence was suddenly taken away, and no trace of him appeared anywhere. But after seeking him most carefully, she found suddenly under her vest a precious necklace. Gazing at it earnestly, it seemed to glitter with so great a brightness that all the corners of England were filled with the grace of its splendour. That dream was truly fulfilled in her daughter of whom we are speaking, whose life presented examples of the works of light not only to herself, but to many who had the will to live well.

"Now when she had ruled this monastery for many years, it pleased the kindly Provider of our salvation to try her holy soul with a long infirmity of the flesh, that, after the example of the Apostle, her virtue might be made perfect in infirmity. For she was struck with fevers, and began to be wearied with severe heat, and for six continuous years did not cease to suffer from the same trouble. In all this time she never omitted either to give thanks to her Creator, or to teach in public and in private the flock intrusted to her. For, instructed by her own instance, she warned all of the duty obediently to serve the Lord during the body's health, and in adversity or in infirmities of the limbs ever faithfully to render thanksgiving to the Lord. So then in the seventh year of her infirmity the pain turned inwards, and she came to her last day, and about cockcrow, when she had received the viaticum of sacrosanct communion, the handmaids of Christ in the same monastery being round her, she was urging them to keep the gospel peace with each other and with all; in the midst of her entreaty she saw death joyfully, or rather, to use the Lord's words, she passed from death to life."

Bede then goes on to speak of another nun in a monastery thirteen miles from Whitby who had a vision at the moment of her death. She was in the dormitory awake when she suddenly heard the sound of the bell which called the nuns to prayer, or to be present at the passing of a sister; the house appeared unroofed and all filled with light, and while she was gazing steadily at this, she saw in the light itself the soul of God's servant carried to heaven in the midst of angels. She hastened to the prioress, who summoned all the sisters to the church to pray for the soul of their mother. While they were so praying the rest of the night with early dawn, brethren came to them from the monastery at Whitby announcing St. Hilda's death, which they said they already knew. They found that the vision corresponded to the hour. "And so by a beautiful union of things God brought it about that while the one witnessed her departure from this life, the other recognised her entrance into the perpetual life of souls."[1]

Bede describes the thirty years life of St. Hilda as Abbess of Whitby, which ran from 650 to 680, as a light to the whole land, which shone not only on those who lived under her rule or knew her by personal intercourse, but on a great number who only heard of her by report. His words convey incidentally the great dignity which in that first age of Anglo-Saxon conversion surrounded the quality of abbess and the virginal life. She had brought from Gaul the institution of the double monastery, not only that of the female community in a house apart by itself, but of the male community in another house, of both of which the abbess was superior. When the Eastern monk of Tarsus, St. Theodore, became Archbishop of Canterbury, he knew not this discipline by his knowledge of the East, and did not approve it, though he left it standing, as having an experienced position. The rank held by abbesses was part of the special Anglo-Saxon veneration for women when seen in the light which a virginity consecrated to God bestowed. "We[2] are astonished at the crowd of neophytes of both sexes who spring from all the races of the Heptarchy to take the vow of perpetual continence. No one of the new Christian nations seems to have furnished so great a number, and with none does Christian virginity seem to have exercised a more prompt and sovereign ascendancy. Nowhere do we see nuns surrounded with so much veneration and clothed with

[1] The words of Bede.   [2] Montalembert, v. 241-243.

so undisputed an authority. The young Anglo-Saxons, initiated at first in the cloistral life in the Gallo-Frank monasteries, which were prior in time to all those in England who had given themselves to God, had need to return to their island to learn their own value in the eyes of their compatriots.

"The Anglo-Saxon conquerors looked with a tender and astonished respect on those noble maidens of their race, who appeared to them encircled with a halo unknown to them, of a supernatural grandeur, of a power at once divine and human, victorious over all the passions, over all the weaknesses, over all the covetousness of which the germ had only been too highly developed by the conquest. Such a respect showed itself at once in the national laws, which concurred in placing under the safeguard of the severest penalties the honour and the liberty of those to whom the monuments of Anglo-Saxon legislation granted the title of the Lord's betrothed, the brides of God.[1]

"When one of these holy maidens found herself invested by the choice of her companions or the nomination of the bishop with the right to govern and represent a numerous community of those like herself, the chiefs and the people of the Heptarchy recognised in her without difficulty all the liberties and all the attributes of the loftiest rank. Abbesses, for example, such as Hilda, Ebba, and Elfleda, had very readily an influence and an authority which rivalled that of bishops or the most venerated abbots. Often they had the train and the bearing of princesses, especially when they were sprung from royal blood. They acted as on an equality with kings, bishops, and the greatest lords; and as the rule of enclosure seems not to have existed for them, they are seen to go everywhere as they thought fit. We may cite the appointment given by Elfleda, as Abbess of Whitby, to St. Cuthbert in the island of Coquet, and the festival to which she invited that holy bishop for the dedication of a church situated on one of her manors. They would be present at national and religious solemnities, and even, like queens, take part in the deliberations of national assemblies, and attach their signatures to charters which marked the

[1] "Godes Bryde;" Thorpe's Ancient Laws of England, ii. 188.

result. The three-and-twentieth article of the famous laws or *dooms* of Ina assimilates in certain respects not abbots only, but abbesses to kings and the greatest personages of the land. In the Council of Beccancelde, held in 694 by the metropolitan and the king of Kent, the signatures of five abbesses figure in the midst of bishops, after decrees the purport of which is to guarantee the inviolability of the property and the liberties of the Church."

The name of Elfleda, the second Abbess of Whitby, is every way fitted to be joined to those of St. Ebba and St. Hilda. She came into the world at the time her father Oswy was about to win that great victory over the heathen Saxon Penda, king of Mercia, which finally turned the scale in favour of a Christian England. Before the battle her father vowed to give her as a virgin to the service of God, and to erect twelve monasteries—six in Deira and six in Bernicia. He went with a very small army against a great one. "They say," writes Bede, "that the pagan force was thirty times greater, but he trusted in Christ for his leader; and the thirty dukes were almost all slain."[1] This was in the year 655; and Bede, in the year 731, sums up all the years of the Elfleda so vowed. That daughter of a king first learnt the discipline of the regular life, then became its teacher, until, having completed in 715 the number of fifty-nine years—of which thirty-four were spent in succession to St. Hilda as Abbess of Whitby—"the blessed virgin reached her Heavenly Bridegroom." Thus Elfleda at her great monastery of Whitby was abbess and princess also, as Hilda had been.

St. Bede marks especially the day of St. Theodore's arrival in England[2] as Archbishop of Canterbury on the 27th May 669, and his immediate visitation of the whole island, "wherever the English races dwelt;" their cordial acceptance of him and obedience to him, with the Abbot Adrian at his side; his establishing bishops "in the proper places," and his correction of anything wrong. He notes also that Wilfrid had returned from his consecration at Compiègne, and had ordained priests and deacons in Kent before and until the arrival of the Archbishop. St. Theodore's visita-

[1] Bede, iii. 24, p. 159.   [2] *Ibid.* iv. 2, p. 181.

tion ensued, and he found Ceadda, by King Oswy's appointment, bishop at York, and following Aidan's mode of life, but the Roman customs. Yet he also found a defect in his ordination by Bishop Wini. Ceadda submitted entirely to him, offering to resign his work as bishop, but he contented himself with re-executing his ordination. Ceadda retired to his Abbey of Lastingham,[1] and Wilfrid administered the episcopate of the church of York, and likewise of all Northumbria, as well as the Picts to the uttermost extent of King Oswy's dominions. It was the time when the primate, admiring the zealous activity of Wilfrid as he went over his vast diocese on foot, insisted upon his riding on the occasion, and helped him on horseback with his own hand. St. Theodore, also, at the request of Wulphere, son of Penda and king of Mercia, who had married the princess Ermenilda, daughter of King Ercombert of Kent, afterwards moved Ceadda to the episcopate of Mercia. There Ceadda lived at Lichfield with seven or eight brethren, with whom, when resting from the labour of preaching, he used to pray and study. The ten years following this establishment of Wilfrid at York by the primate was the time of his great prosperity. The king, Oswy, was only prevented by illness and death from going in person with him to Rome to visit Pope Vitalian, who had sent him a primate so welcomed by all men. Wilfrid himself was vigorously superintending his very large diocese. But his former friend, King Oswy's son, Alchfrid, had given him a large domain in land at Ripon, on which he built his Benedictine monastery, and over this he was abbot. At Oswy's death, his son Egfrid had succeeded him, and Egfrid had for ten years been married to the Queen Etheldreda, that East Anglian princess renowned above all of her day for her beauty, piety, and beneficence. Wilfrid had succeeded in establishing with the new king, Egfrid, the same authority and influence which he had obtained in the last years of his father, King Oswy, and also with the former

---

[1] See the passage in Bede, v. 19, p. 237: "Ceadda, virsanctus, tribus annis ecclesiam sublimiter regens, dehinc ad monasterū sui, quod est in Læstingaei, curam secessit, accipiente Wilfredo episcopatum totius nordanhymbrorum provinciæ."

prince and king, Alchfrid, who has disappeared from history. Moreover, the Queen Etheldreda considered him more than any one in his diocese. As a proof of this, she had bestowed on him her dower lands, the gift of her husband Egfrid, at Hexham, on which Wilfrid built a monastery and church so costly and beautiful that it had the reputation of being the finest structure north of the Alps. The land given at Hexham extended twelve miles in length by three in breadth. Here, too, he was abbot as well as bishop of Northumbria. The Queen Ermelinda of Mercia also was his firm friend, the near kinswoman of Queen Etheldreda, and afterwards to be her second successor at Ely. It was five years after Wilfrid's appearance at the Council of Whitby when he came into this great position; he was then, in 664, thirty years of age. His eloquence and power of speech had moved King Oswy, the Bretwalda, in spite of his Celtic education at Iona, to admit the authority which Wilfrid claimed for Peter as prince of the Apostles, and to declare that the doorkeeper of the kingdom of heaven should claim and receive his homage rather than those who had preached and converted so many in his kingdom by mission from St. Columba. Oswy had by no means disregarded the admirable life and example of these missionaries. They were monks of the most strenuous and self-denying discipline. They followed the rule of Iona, but with a severity almost exceeding the rule which St. Augustine and those after him carried on at Canterbury. The effect of Oswy's decision on Wilfrid's pleading at Whitby was to lead Bishop Colman to give up his diocese and retire at first to Iona, which some other missionaries would seem to have done; but the greater part who had been instructed by them, as, for instance, Ceadda and his brother Cedd, would seem to have conformed to the Roman custom. Wilfrid is admitted to have been the first to establish in the north the Benedictine rule, and he was closely followed in time by St. Bennet Biscop, who had been joined by Pope Vitalian with the Abbot Adrian, and charged to accompany the new primate to England, and had afterwards founded his double monastery at Wearmouth and Jarrow by munificent gifts of land from King Egfrid.

At the beginning of this time of great prosperity and influence Wilfrid would be thirty-five years of age. From his early youth the great impression made by his personal beauty and the grace of his address, united with a devotion which was proof against every trial, are dwelt upon by contemporaries. The Queen Eanfleda, her cousin King Ercombert, the Archbishop of Lyons, whose martyrdom Wilfrid tried to share, the son of King Oswy, Prince Alchfrid, the abbess-princesses Ebba and Elfleda, the queens Etheldreda and Ermelinda, the kings Oswy and Egfrid, are all recorded to have been won by the external dignity and the inward worth of a man whom the fervent eloquence of a great orator and historian has entitled "the eldest born of an invincible race, the first Englishman." Indeed, in following as far as the recording history of contemporaries will allow the long forty-five years of Wilfrid's episcopate, there is no occasion on which he can be found to have failed in duty, to have shrunk from trial, hazard, or self-denial, to have been a slave to vainglory or a victim to self-love, to have tried for increase of dignity rather than gaining of souls. The youth who shrank from marriage when offered with corresponding youth and a dowry of dominion because he had made a vow to serve St. Peter, sacrificed himself also to maintain in her resolve one who had vowed herself to the virginal life, and kept it in spite of a double marriage. He also carried with him to his latest breath the devotion of a number of houses which he had himself created and built up in the Benedictine rule. In these he had the double merit—one of establishing the rule itself, the other of attracting the individual members to it by the force of his life and example.

St. Etheldreda had been for ten years the wife of King Egfrid when he succeeded his father Oswy in 670. Egfrid, says Bede,[1] was a very religious man, equally distinguished both in mind and act. Etheldreda had been married for a short time before, but she was wife of Egfrid during twelve years, living with him all that time, yet glorious for her unspotted virginity. "And Wilfrid, the bishop of blessed memory," says Bede, "replying to my own question, whether

---

[1] Bede, iv. 19, p. 214.

that was so, because some had doubted it, averred to me that he was certain of it; for Egfrid had promised him a great amount of both lands and wealth if he could persuade the queen to live with him in conjugal intercourse. Nor is it to be doubted that even in our age such things have been, which in a former age faithful historians record now and then to have taken place, by the gift of one and the same Lord who promises that He will remain with us to the end of the world."

But the result of Egfrid's application to Wilfrid was that the great bishop learnt from Etheldreda that she had been married to both husbands against her will, and had kept herself faithful throughout to a previous vow of continence. She had often petitioned the king to allow her to retire from the world and pursue in a monastery the sole service of Christ, the true King. At length with great difficulty she obtained King Egfrid's consent, and went to the Abbey of Coldingham, of which Ebba, the king's aunt, was abbess. There she received the veil of nun from Wilfrid the bishop; but she was pursued by Egfrid, and after a series of marvellous escapes, took refuge in her own great property in Ely, on which she built a monastery, and was established as abbess there by Wilfrid himself.

Thus, in the year 672, Etheldreda, having been twelve years married to Egfrid, in the last two of which, after King Oswy's death, she had been queen of Northumbria, had carried out her original vow, which dissolved her never-accomplished marriage, and Egfrid had taken Ermenburga for his wife. During many years after this event Wilfrid had his seat at York, making his rounds on foot or on horseback over his immense diocese. He continued to set up monasteries, encouraging the Benedictine rule. These he made places of general education, in which everything was taught which was valuable for the life of that age; so that the students might either serve God in the regular life, if that were their choice, or take the king's service as soldiers. They were taught music and likewise architecture, for which Wilfrid became famous. To his Abbey of Hexham he brought masons from Canterbury, or even from Rome. The whole conversion of the northern country during the thirty years of the three Celtic bishops, from 634 to 664, had been conducted by monks, but from the Council at Whitby, in the last-named year, Wilfrid had prevailed in carrying out the Catholic custom, to which he had made the Celtic preponderance give way. St. Theodore at his visitation found nothing to complain of in their doctrine. Thus things went on until 679; but from the time that St. Etheldreda became abbess at Ely, King Egfrid appears to have taken more and more offence at Wilfrid. His wife Ermenburga stirred him up to continual jealousy of the wealth, influence, and vigour of Wilfrid, who was bishop over all his dominion. It would appear that St. Theodore in the year 679 was moved to divide into three the great diocese which Wilfrid during ten full years had administered by Theodore's own authority, given to him expressly by Pope Vitalian. When Wilfrid came back after a temporary absence, he found himself without a see. He claimed justice both from the king, Egfrid, and from the Archbishop; but neither would listen to him, and he thereupon appealed to the judgment of the Holy See—that is, he appealed to the actual Pope, who was St. Agatho, against an unjust exercise of the authority which ten years before Pope Vitalian had conferred on the Primate whom he had appointed and sent to Canterbury. And this, at the distance of eighty years from the coming of St. Augustine, was the first instance of that appeal which later on in Norman times St. Anselm and St. Thomas, both themselves Archbishops of Canterbury, had to exercise.

Wilfrid determined to carry his appeal to Rome in person, and left Northumbria accompanied by a large train both of monks and laymen. He left, says his biographer Eddi, many thousands of his own monks in the hands of the new bishops, who belonged to the Celtic school, while he had given to all his monks the rule of St. Benedict. He passed by two great monasteries, that of Ely, where St. Etheldreda always received him as her own bishop. There the ex-queen of Northumbria had established a great monastery on the dower-land which her first husband had bestowed upon her, and which for seven years she was to rule with the greatest exactitude of the regular life and the highest character for holiness and goodness. It was the last time she was to receive the bishop whose firmness had enabled her to carry out her own original purpose, and whose steadfast support had maintained her throughout. He passed also that other monastery of Medhampstead, which was to change its name of the Home in the Marshes for that of the prince of the Apostles, and, under the name of Peterborough, receive from him, when he came back, the guarantee of its safe continuance given him by Pope Agatho.

Then Wilfrid, embarking, was cast by the wind on the Frisian coast, where he had the glory to be the first Anglo-Saxon who took part in the conversion of the kindred Teuton race. During several winter months he was engaged in preaching every day, being received with welcome both by the king, Aldgils, and the people. "He preached Christ to them, instructing many thousands of them in the word of truth, and washed them from the stains of their sins in the fountain of the Saviour. He was the first to begin there the evangelical work which afterwards Willibrord, Christ's most reverend pontiff, completed with great devotion."[1]

But Ebroin, Mayor of the Frank Palace, had sent to the Frisian king a promise under oath of a bushel of gold coins if he would deliver to him either the Bishop Wilfrid alive or his head. The king, in a great banquet which he gave to the envoys of Ebroin and to Wilfrid with his train, read this letter aloud to them, tore it in pieces, and cast them into the fire. Eddi, who witnessed the scene, gives us the words he used to Ebroin's envoys—"Go, tell your master what you have seen, and add my words, May the Creator of all things rend up, destroy, and consume those who perjure themselves to their God and keep no faith with man."

Wilfrid at this time in his monastery of Ripon was, during thirteen years, maintaining a young Northumbrian boy, brought to him in childhood by the mother. This was that Willibrord, reserved by God to carry on after the example of his teacher that conversion of the Frisian race with which his name has been for ever connected.

In the spring Wilfrid pursued his way to Rome through

[1] Bede, v. 19, p. 287.

Austrasia, and found a sovereign who had formerly enjoyed his hospitality at Ripon.[1] This was Dagobert II., who in his infancy had been dethroned by Grimoald, Mayor of the Palace. He had been stealthily sent to Ireland, and found refuge in a monastery. In 673 the Austrasian lords, wishing to escape the yoke of Ebroin, the master of Neustria and Burgundy, invited back the already tonsured prince. It was Wilfrid whom they besought to bring about his return, and Wilfrid it was who gave him a great reception in his monastery at Ripon, and sent him forward on his way with many gifts and a good escort. Dagobert showed his gratitude, not only by an affectionate welcome, but by earnestly pressing Wilfrid to accept the bishopric of Strasburg, then vacant, and the greatest of his kingdom.

Wilfrid declined, and went forward to Lombardy, where he was kindly received by Berechtaire, then king of the country. There also his enemies at home had pursued him, and his life was saved by a king, barbarian in race, but already Christian. He said to Wilfrid, "Your enemies in England have promised me great gifts if I would prevent your journey to Rome, for they consider you a fugitive bishop. My answer to them was this—In my youth I was an exile, dwelling with the king of the Avars, a pagan, who swore to me before his idol that he would never deliver me up to my enemies. Some time after this they sent to offer this pagan king a bushel of gold coins if he would deliver me to him. He refused, saying that his gods would sever the thread of his life if he broke his oath. How much more would I, who know the true God, not lose my soul to gain the whole world." Upon this he gave Wilfrid and his train an honourable escort to conduct them to Rome.

St. Wilfrid reached Rome at a moment of the greatest interest in the history of the whole Church, when St. Agatho, a Sicilian monk, was Pope, and was about to close a deadly struggle in which, during forty years, the Byzantine emperors had sought to overthrow the faith of the Church by the Monothelite heresy, which they had espoused. Wilfrid had left Rome more than twenty years before, an almost unknown man. In the interval he had become the bishop of

[1] Montalembert, iv. 266-268.

the largest see in England, and had spread, to the best of his power, the Benedictine rule in a number of monasteries founded by him. He had also become the champion of Roman authority in the Congress of Whitby, held before Oswy, Northumbrian king and Bretwalda. He was now appealing to the Pope from an irregular act of his own archbishop's, specially chosen, consecrated, and sent by his predecessor twelve years before. While St. Agatho showed himself disposed to hear the plaint of the Bishop of York, he likewise showed great consideration for the Archbishop of Canterbury. The Pope had already specially invited him, as Primate of England, to attend the Council which he had summoned at Rome against the Monothelite heresy. From this Theodore had on account of age excused himself; but he sent a monk charged with violent accusations against St. Wilfrid, and Hilda, the princess-abbess of Whitby, had sent messengers with the like complaints.

Pope Agatho brought this whole affair of St. Wilfrid's appeal to him before his court of fifty bishops and priests, held in the Lateran Church under his own presidency. The Pope said, " Wilfrid, Bishop of York, is at the door. Bid him come in." The bishop being introduced, asked that his case should be read before the whole court, and said, " I, unworthy Saxon bishop, have fled for refuge to this impregnable citadel, because I know that the rule of the sacred canons outflows from it to all the churches of Christ. My bishopric, in which I have sat for more than ten years, has been invaded. I have been convicted of no fault, but three bishops have been put into my place. I do not venture to accuse Archbishop Theodore, because he has been sent from this Apostolic See. I submit myself absolutely to the Apostolic judgment. If I am to return to my see, I beg only that those who have usurped it may be expelled, and if the number of bishops is to be increased, that they may be selected by a council from the clergy."[1]

Pope Agatho thereupon greatly praised the conduct of Wilfrid, in that, seeing himself unjustly deposed from his see, he did not seek to resist through the secular power, but " referred himself to the canonical help of St. Peter,

---

[1] See Mansi, xi. pp. 183-184; Montalembert, iv. 270.

prince of the Apostles, from whom we derive, promising to accept the decision which St. Peter, whose office we discharge, should by our mouth enact;" and the whole council reported, "We decree that Wilfrid the bishop take up the bishopric which he lately held, and that the bishops whom he chooses for his helpers, with the consent of the council to be held there, be ordained by the archbishop, and that those who in his absence, contrary to rule, were put into the episcopate, be expelled.'

Pope Agatho further ordered Wilfrid to take his seat among the 125 bishops who, by his invitation, were sitting at Rome to prepare the way for the sixth General Council. St. Theodore had been invited to attend this Council, which took note of the affairs of the English Church. It prescribed a new division of bishops, in which it did full justice to the archbishop's wish to increase their number, and ordered that the metropolitan should have twelve suffragans duly elected and ordained, of whom no one should intrude upon the diocese of another. Thus the Pope and Council charged St. Theodore to complete the work of St. Gregory and St. Augustine by convoking a general assembly of the Anglo-Saxons, "wherein, in conjunction with the bishops, the kings, the chief thanes, and the faithful of rank, he might search out what he should find the best for all the English provinces and the whole people."

Moreover, Bede [1] expressly states that Pope Agatho not only summoned Wilfrid to this Council, but enjoined him at the same time to declare his own faith and that of the province or island from which he had come, and being found together with his people to be Catholic in his faith, this also was entered in the deeds of that synod: '"Wilfrid, bishop dear to God, of the city of York, appealing to the Apostolic See for his own cause, and absolved by this power from matters certain and uncertain, and with the other 125 bishops in synod placed in the seat of judgment, made confession of the true and Catholic faith for all the region of the north, the islands of Britain and Ireland, which are inhabited by the Angles and Britons, as also by the nations of Scots and Picts, and ratified this with his subscription."

[1] Bede, v. 19, p. 287.

Wilfrid remained some months at Rome, and concerned himself to obtain pontifical privileges for two great English monasteries, though not in his own diocese, those of Peterborough and Ely. He had obtained that for Ely at the desire of the Abbess Etheldreda, but received at Rome the news of her death. Of all who were attached to him, she was the one whose trust in him created between them the completest union, and what he had suffered in maintaining her cause was the bond of closest affection. She had been for seven years abbess of the convent which, when he sanctioned the invalidity of her marriage, he had encouraged her to raise on her own great estate at Ely. It ranked in importance with the monasteries of the royal abbesses, Ebba and Hilda. She was even queen of Northumbria, not waiting for widowhood to become a nun, but after twelve years of marriage exerting her right to decline a bond which she had never with free-will accepted. And she had made herself a name which was to be remembered above all others of her sex during the nine centuries of English Catholic faith; for she was the most popular of English saints, and both men and women in all these generations had merged her name of birth into that softer name of Audrey, which betokened not only reverence, but a sort of domestic love. As in all the converted nations, the Saxon children of Odin bear the palm in their choice of the virginal life, so she bore in their own mind the palm among them; for being a king's daughter, endowed with beauty which brought suitor after suitor to her feet, compelled against her will to accept the first rank, the friend of St. Cuthbert as well as of St. Wilfrid, venerated by two husbands who were only allowed to give her their name, she was not content to spend on the building and forming of monasteries two great estates, but, in the full lustre of a beauty which lasted to her dying day, she became as abbess the most perfect of nuns, the most self-denying to herself, the fullest of loving-kindness to others. What Bede has not hesitated to say of her we may venture to quote.[1] "She was carried off suddenly to the Lord in the midst of her people, seven years after she had held the rank of abbess, and according to her own

[1] Bede, iv. 19, p. 215.

command was buried in a wooden coffin in their midst, in the usual order. She was succeeded as abbess by her sister, Sexburg, who had been wife of Ercombert, king of Kent. When she had been buried sixteen years, that abbess resolved to disinter her bones and translate them in a new coffin to the church. And she bade some of the brethren search for a stone out of which they could make a coffin. They went on board a boat, for Ely itself is a district surrounded with water and marsh, and has no big stones in it. And they came to a deserted small town, not far off, which in the English tongue is called Grantchester, and near its walls they found a coffin most beautifully made of white marble, with a lid also of the like marble closely fitting. So understanding that their journey had been favoured by the Lord, they brought it back thankfully to the monastery.

"But when the body of the sacred virgin and bride of Christ had been brought to open day out of the grave, it was found as incorrupt as if she had died or been buried upon that day, as Bishop Wilfrid and many others who knew of it attest. But with more certain knowledge, the medical man, Cynifrid, who was present both at her death and when she was raised from the grave, was accustomed to relate that when she was ill she had a very great tumour under the breast, 'and they told me,' he said, 'to make an incision in that tumour to let out the bad matter in it. This I did, and she seemed for two days to be somewhat better, so that many thought she might get well. But the third day the old severe pains came back; she was snatched suddenly from the world, and changed death for perpetual health and life. And when, after so many years, her bones were to be raised from the grave, and a tent was spread over, and the whole congregation of brethren on the one side, and sisters on the other, stood chanting psalms, while the abbess herself had gone inside with a few to raise the bones and wash them, suddenly we heard the abbess from within proclaim with a loud voice, 'Glory be to the name of the Lord.' Presently after they called for me to come inside the door of the tent, and I saw the body of God's sacred virgin raised from the grave, and lying on a couch like one asleep. But when the covering on the face was removed, they showed me the wound made by my incision healed, so that, instead of the open and gaping wound with which she was buried, the smallest traces of a cicatrice then appeared.' But also all the foldings in which the body had been wrapped appeared unstained, and so fresh that they seemed to have been put that very day on her chaste limbs. They say that when she was suffering from this tumour and pain of the cheek or neck, she was much pleased with this kind of infirmity, and was accustomed to say, 'I am quite sure that I deserve to carry on my neck the weight of this pain, on which when a girl I remember carrying very heavy necklaces; and I believe that heavenly goodness willed me to have pain of the neck, that so I may be absolved from the guilt of my excessive levity, when a red tumour and burning heat disfigure my neck, to make up for gold and pearls.' Now by the touch of the wraps surrounding her, evil spirits were expelled from bodies possessed by them, and other infirmities were in many cases cured. They relate also that the coffin in which she was first buried saved pain to the eyesight in some cases; when patients prayed leaning their head against it, they presently lost the pain or the darkness of their sight. So the virgins washed the body, draped it in new robes, and carried it into the church, and placed it in the sarcophagus brought, where to the present day it is held in great veneration. It is wonderful that a sarcophagus so fitting the body of the virgin was found, as if it had been made on purpose, and a place for the head cut separately, answering exactly to the size of hers."

Bede adds to this narrative a Latin elegy which he had composed many years before "to the praise of that queen and spouse of Christ."

Etheldreda, queen of Northumbria, resigned her crown, and was sanctioned by Wilfrid, Bishop of Northumbria, after full examination of her case, which she set before him, in becoming first a nun, in doing which she took refuge with the king's own aunt, the Abbess Ebba, at her monastery of Coldingham. Flying thence, because the abbess felt that she could not protect her from the reviving passion of her nephew, King Egfrid, she was able through many difficulties, which the popular devotion kept for ages in remembrance, to escape to Ely, where Wilfrid further sanctioned her founding an abbey and becoming its first abbess. As such she lived seven years, from 672 to 679. She was succeeded by her elder sister, Sexburg, who had been wife of Ercombert, grandson of St. Ethelbert, and most zealous in the destruction of idolatry. Among their children was Ermenilda, wife of Wulphere, son of the pagan persecutor Penda, and king of Mercia from 656 to 675. Queen Ermenilda was zealous in her endeavours to spread the Christian faith, and in her widowhood succeeded her mother as third abbess of Ely. That convent had the singular lot of receiving three queens for its first three abbesses. Nor was the fourth less illustrious, as St. Werburga followed her mother, Ermenilda, and having been abbess first at Weedon, then at Trentham, thirdly at Hanbury, being fourth in lineal descent from Ethelbert, became fourth Abbess of Ely.

Among Bede's most valuable and most attaching works is a notice which he has left us of the five abbots who first governed the monasteries of Wearmouth and Jarrow, to the discipline of which he was indebted for the formation of his character, as he further owed his learning to the peace and undisturbed tranquillity of their institution and to their treasured library. He begins with the founder.

"The religious servant of Christ, Biscop,[1] surnamed Bennet, by the help of grace from above, built a monastery in honour of the most blessed prince of the Apostles, Peter, near the mouth of the river Wear, to the north, for which Egbert, the worshipful and very pious king of that people, gave him land and assistance. During sixteen years he carefully ruled that monastery with the same zeal with which he had built it, amid numberless toils from the journeys which he made or the infirmities he suffered. He was sprung from a noble English stock, but with no less nobility of mind devoted himself to gain for ever life in company with the angels. Being already at the court of King Oswy, and by his gift possessing a landed estate suitable to his rank, at the age of twenty-five he disdained

---

[1] Historia Abbatum, &c., p. 316.

a perishable in order to obtain an eternal inheritance; he despised this earthly warfare with corruptible payment, preferring to be in the service of the true King, and merit to have a perpetual reign in the celestial city. He left home, relations, and country for Christ and the gospel, to receive a hundredfold and possess eternal life. He rejected children of the flesh that he might be able to follow the Lamb who shines with the glory of virginity. Being predestined by Christ to educate sons for Him in spiritual doctrine, who were to dwell in immortal life, he rejected the fathership of mortal offspring.

"Thus he made a first journey to Rome in 653 to behold and worship with his own body the spots where the bodies rested of those blessed Apostles with desire of whom he was ever kindled. Returning soon to his country, he ceased not to love and venerate those institutions of ecclesiastical life which he had seen, and to preach them to such as he could. At this time King Oswy's son Alchfrid was purposing to go to Rome to worship the Apostolic threshold, and wished to have him for companion. When King Oswy preferred to have his son remain in his kingdom, Bennet Biscop in his youthful zeal went again with great speed to Rome in the time of Pope Vitalian of blessed memory. As before, he imbibed with delight not a few lessons of holy knowledge, and after a few months he went to the island of Lerins, gave himself to the monks there, received the tonsure, and took on him the regular discipline and vow of monastic life. After two years, instructed completely in this, again carried away by his love for Peter, prince of the Apostles, he determined to return to the city consecrated by his body.

"At this time Egbert, king of Kent, had sent from Britain Wighard, elected for the office of bishop. He had been sufficiently trained in all ecclesiastical instruction by the Roman disciples in Kent of blessed Pope Gregory. King Egbert had wished him to be consecrated at Rome for his bishop, so that having a prelate of his own nation and tongue, he might, with the people his subjects, be more perfectly imbued both with the mysteries of faith and the language in which they were couched, when these should be received, not through an interpreter, but by the tongue and the hand of a kinsman and a tribesman. This Wighard came to Rome with all his train, but died of a sudden attack before he received the pontificate in A.D. 667. But the Apostolic Pope, fearing lest the religious deputation of the faithful to him might lack its due fruit by the death of those deputed, took counsel, and elected from his own people the archbishop to send to Britain—that is, Theodorus, qualified both by secular and ecclesiastical learning, and that in both languages, Greek and Latin. He gave him for colleague and counsellor a most energetic and prudent man, Abbot Adrian, and because he saw that Bennet was a man wise, industrious, religious, and of noble rank, he commended to him the bishop, when consecrated, with all his people. He enjoined him to give up the pilgrimage which he had taken for Christ's sake, and, in view of a greater good, to return to his country, bringing to it a teacher of truth such as he had carefully sought out, to whom, both in his journey thither and in his teaching there, he might serve as interpreter and guide. It was done as he bade. They came to Kent: were most graciously received. Theodore ascended the bishop's seat. Bennet received the government of St. Peter's monastery, of which later Adrian was made abbot.

"After two years' government of this monastery he went on a fourth visit to Rome, and either bought there, or received by gift of friends, a large number of books of the divine learning, which he brought back with him. When he reached Northumbria again, and its king, Egfrid, he told him all that he had done since in early life he resigned his country. He did not conceal the ardour of his religious zeal; how he had studied at Rome and in all parts the Church's rule and the monastic institute; he made known how many sacred volumes, how large a number of relics, whether of apostles or of martyrs, he had brought; and he acquired such favour and intimacy with the king that he gave him at once land enough for seventy families out of his own domain, and charged him to build there a monastery to the first pastor of the Church, which was built in the year 674, the fourth of Egfrid's reign.

"Not more than a year after its foundation, Bennet went over to France, and brought back with him masons, who built a stone church after the Roman fashion, which he had always loved, and he worked so hard out of love for St. Peter that within a year the roof could be put on and mass said. When the work was approaching completion he sent for glaziers from France, whose art was hitherto unknown in England. Everything needed for the ministry of the altar and church, holy vessels and vestments, not being able to find at home, that religious purchaser brought from parts beyond the sea.

"But what he could not find even in Gaul, that active provider for the ornaments of his church brought by a fifth journey from Rome. First, a vast multitude of books of all kinds; secondly, an abundant grace of relics of apostles and martyrs to serve many English churches; thirdly, he bestowed on his monastery an order of singing and chanting, and ministering in the church according to Roman institution, having asked and accepted from Pope Agatho, John, the archcantor of St. Peter's and abbot of St. Martin's, whom he brought to Britain—a Roman to Englishmen—to be the future teacher of his monastery; and John coming thither, not only delivered orally to his pupils what he had taught at Rome, but also left much written, which hitherto has been kept out of gratitude to him in the monastery's library.

"Fourthly, Bennet brought no mean gift, a letter of privilege from the venerable Pope Agatho, accepted with the permission, consent, desire, and entreaty of King Egfrid, in which the monastery he had made should be absolutely safe and free for ever without interruption. Fifthly, he brought pictures of holy likenesses to adorn St. Peter's Church, which he had built, such as the likeness of the blessed Mother of God and ever-virgin Mary; of the Twelve Apostles to adorn the central vault; of the Gospel history to decorate the southern wall; the Apocalyptic visions of St. John to adorn the northern. Thus they who entered the church, however ignorant of letters, wherever they cast their eyes, would ever behold the aspect lovely, though but in images, of Christ and of His saints, or would watchfully retrace the grace of the Lord's incarnation, or would carefully examine themselves in that trial of the last judgment which they saw before their eyes.

"King Egfrid had been so delighted with the building of the monastery at Wearmouth to St. Peter, that he gave further land to St. Bennet, fit for the maintenance of forty families, to build a monastery to St. Paul at Jarrow, on the Tyne, six miles off from the former. This monastery was provided in a similar way with the older. Each had an abbot, under St. Bennet, in his frequent absences. At length Bennet himself wasted away with a long illness of three years. Often and often he charged the monks of his two monasteries to keep the rule which he had established. 'You are not to suppose,' he told them, 'that I have out of my own head produced these decrees. I have learnt all this out of the seventeen monasteries which, in all my many wanderings, I have found the best, and delivered it to you for safe maintenance.' He enjoined that the very noble and rich library, necessary for the instruction of the church, which he had brought to them from Rome, should be carefully maintained, and not scattered. He many times repeated to them his charge that, in electing the abbot, they were to choose not his family, but his fair life and upright teaching. I tell you of a truth, that of two evils I would far rather that God, if He so judged, should reduce this spot, in which I have planted a monastery, to an eternal solitude, than that my brother by the natural tie, who we know has not entered the path of truth, should succeed me as abbot in ruling it. Beware, then, my brothers, how you ever seek a father for race, or for any other outward quality; but, according to the rule of the great Abbot Benedict, according to the terms of our privilege, in the assembly of your congregation inquire with common counsel who is fitter and worthier for such a ministry by the merit of his life and his repute of wisdom, and whom all, with an unanimous search of charity, choose for the best. Call upon the bishop, and beg that he may be established as your abbot with the usual benediction. They who in a carnal order generate sons after the flesh must seek carnal and earthly heirs for a carnal and earthly inheritance; but they who bear spiritual sons to God from the spiritual seed of the Word must have all their actions spiritual. Let them count among their spiritual children that one the greater who is endowed with an ampler grace of spirit. So earthly parents are wont to consider their first-born the beginning of their children, and in partitioning their inheritance give him the preference.'"

Bennet Biscop died in January 690, sixteen years after he had founded the first of his two monasteries at Wearmouth. He had already seen two of his abbots die, one of them, Easterwin, a kinsman of his own, formerly an officer in the king's court before he became a monk, who died when he was absent in his last journey to Rome; the other, Sigfrid, chosen by the monks to succeed him. He also died four months before St. Bennet, who then appointed Ceolfric abbot of both monasteries. Ceolfric ruled with the same remarkable care and zeal. He obtained from Pope Sergius the same privilege which St. Bennet had obtained from Pope Agatho. Ceolfric left at his departure in 716 from his monasteries to Rome about six hundred brethren. He died on his journey three months afterwards, forty-three years since he had been associated with St. Bennet, at the time when, as Bede has written, "he began to build his monastery in honour of the most blessed prince of the Apostles, and Ceolfric was to him an indivisible companion, working with him and teaching with him the regular monastic institution."

We learn the conversion of England from one man contemporaneous with it, fully informed by so many actors in that work, and the most scrupulously honest of historians. He assures us in the narratives which we have quoted from him, that this great victory over paganism was the exclusive work of the monastic life in the two sexes. The character which St. Gregory the Great had impressed on the whole movement was continued throughout the century. The monk-bishop whom the martyr-king Oswald summoned from Iona to convert his subjects, and no less the two bishops who succeeded him, together with those who worked under them, and planted the faith by their labours, their preaching, and that life which made both labours and preaching fruitful, were monks. At the same time with them came the royal nuns who presided as abbesses at Coldingham, at Whitby, and at Ely, and who showed how deeply the Anglo-Saxon maidens shared the conviction which stirred the other sex. The monasteries which they represent in chief arose on all sides.

"All the bishops of the Heptarchy came out of monasteries. Monks exclusively formed the clergy of the cathedrals, where they lived in community with the diocesan prelate for their chief."[1] That was the very instruction given to St. Augustine for Canterbury by St. Gregory himself. "During a century at least they acted exclusively for secular or parochial clergy. The monasteries were the homes whence the missionaries went forth to go to the rural stations, where they baptized, preached, and celebrated all the ceremonies of worship. Thither they returned to restore themselves by study and prayer. Rural parishes came but slowly, encouraged by Archbishop Theodore in the south, by Archbishop Egbert and Bede in the north. Thus monasteries served Christian England a long time, not only for cathedrals, but for parishes. Most of the cathedrals preserved their monastic character even after the Norman conquest. The decrees of the Council of Cloveshoe in 747 are the first authentic documents which prove as a general fact the distribution of lay lands into districts administered by priests subject to bishops, not connected with churches situated on lands dependent on monasteries, and served by priests subject to abbots. These churches, where the priest was always attended by a deacon and several clerics, are sometimes called little monasteries."[2]

The hundred and fifty years during which Saxon life carried out in Britain the traditions and practices in which the children of Odin were nurtured, had swept away all marks of the former Briton church. The only three relics[3] remaining were Glastonbury, always a great centre of Celtic devotion; the little church close to Canterbury, where Queen Bertha used to pray; and the fragments of a British church discovered in the brushwood at Evesham in laying the foundations of the new abbey, the consecration of which

---

[1] Montalembert, v. 153-155.   [2] Lingard, i. 151-161.
[3] Montalembert, v. 155.

was St. Wilfrid's last public work. So much the more wonderful was the ardour of those same children of Odin in propagating, after the coming of St. Augustine, the same faith which had previously vanished before them. "There never was any people who embraced religion with a more fervent zeal than the Anglo-Saxon, nor with more simplicity of spirit. As the monks at this time attracted all the religious veneration, religion everywhere began to relish of the cloister."[1] "It was frequent for kings to go on pilgrimages to Rome or to Jerusalem on foot, and under circumstances of great hardship. Several kings resigned their crowns to devote themselves to religious contemplation in monasteries—more, at that time and in this nation, than in all other nations and in all times." "The monastic institution, then, interwoven with Christianity, and making an equal progress with it, attained to so high a pitch of prosperity and power, as in a time extremely short to form a kind of order, and that not the least considerable, in the State."[2] "There was no part of their policy, of whatever nature, that procured to them a greater or juster credit than their cultivation of learning and useful arts. It is certain that the introduction of learning and civility into this northern world is entirely owing to their labours."[3] "They were cultivated in the leisure and retirement of monasteries, otherwise they could not have been cultivated at all; for it was altogether necessary to draw certain men from the general rude and fierce society, and wholly to set a bar between them and the barbarous life of the rest of the world, in order to fit them for study and the cultivation of arts and science."[4] "It is by no means impossible that for an end so worthy—the introduction of Christianity —Providence on such occasions might have directly interposed. The books which contain the history of this time and change are little else than a narrative of miracles. It is sufficient to observe that the reality or opinion of such miracles was the principal cause of the early acceptance and rapid progress of Christianity in this island."[5]

Monks approaching all the kingdoms of the Heptarchy,

[1] Burke, pp. 282-283.   [2] *Ibid.* p. 264.   [3] *Ibid.* p. 271.
[4] *Ibid.* p. 274.   [5] *Ibid.* p. 263.

one after another, as missionaries, remained there permanently as bishops, pastors, preachers; by degrees they subdued the British soil and covered it with their establishments.[1] Their work was slow and difficult. They had storms; they had revolutions. The Jutes after Ethelbert's death fell back in Kent; twice there were apostasies in East Anglia. The old British Christians pursued with fury the Saxons becoming Christians, as in Northumbria; and the heathen Saxon, Penda spent thirty years of his life in alliance with them against those of his own race who were being converted. All these difficulties were gradually overcome by the self-denying and patient perseverance of the monks who derived their mission from Iona. They did not use violence in the work of conversion. King Edwin, consulting with his Witan before he received baptism at York, and weighing carefully the doctrines which he was going to receive, pictures also the history of the sixty years of which he stands at the head; and at the same time he marks the conjunction of the secular authority with the spiritual from the beginning. Bishops and abbots sat in deliberation beside kings and thanes. At Whitby the very assembly which determined under the Bretwalda the reception of Roman rather than of Celtic customs as to the time of celebrating Easter, was held in the convent of the royal Hilda, attended by thanes as well as by bishops and priests. It is, in fact, the image of a Parliament, the meeting together and sitting beside each other of the spiritual and the temporal powers, and a discussion in common such as never can be seen in the city founded by Constantine, nor in the councils collected by Byzantine emperors.

The union which thus grew up between the Church and the State was the offspring of the monastic spirit. The liberty which reigned within the walls of the monastery between the fathers, who gave implicit obedience to the abbot whom themselves had chosen, and who were called by him to consultation in every important matter, formed an element henceforth in the temporal government of kingdoms. The blessing of St. Benedict had overflowed his monastery, and made all the ranks of a society which he had formed in

[1] Montalembert, v. 147.

every part of the countries claimed by him for his own. The lords who owned vast lands, and the people who cultivated these lands under them, had in large numbers embraced, by their own free choice, the spiritual life under the Benedictine rule. The result was that the secular life itself became capable of higher aims than it had known in Constantine's empire. Another standard had educated the race out of which Charlemagne arose. We may take Wilfrid and Bennet Biscop as choice specimens of a class which became very numerous first in Gaul, from the time that St. Maur went forth from Monte Cassino with the blessing of his patriarch and settled on the banks of the Loire. Then, following on St. Augustine's mission, the same wonderful expansion of the monastic life appeared in England, and presently St. Columba entered into the tent of St. Benedict. Wilfrid and Bennet Biscop were Anglican nobles, knights by race, of whom in their natural condition kings were proud, mates of thanes and ealdermen. Wilfrid is said to have left thousands of monks behind him when he appealed to Pope Agatho in 680. Bennet Biscop, in his sixteen years, from 674 to 690, constructed monasteries which had six hundred monks when Ceolfrid, the teacher and friend of Bede, left them to go to Rome in 716. They planted the Benedictine rule in the North of England; and in the twenty-two years of the Primate chosen and sent at the request of the Bretwalda Oswy by Pope Vitalian, the rule which had originally gone from St. Gregory to Canterbury coalesced for all England with that which came from the missionary work of the Celtic teachers. But see the great part which the Teuton women took. Ethelbert had been married for many years to his queen Bertha, the Merovingian daughter of Charibert, king of Paris. Before he bowed his head to the banner of Christ, he weighed, meditated, and calmly accepted the change from Odin to Christ. Consider the line which followed. By Queen Bertha he had his daughter Ethelburga, who carried the Christian faith into the household of the Northumbrian King Edwin. That king also weighed and meditated before he yielded to the preaching of Paulinus. Carried away to speedy martyrdom, yet to him was given a daughter, Eanfleda, whose life as queen of Northumbria runs

T

as a golden thread for eight-and-twenty years through the reign of her husband Oswy; and they too have a daughter, that Elfleda given by her father in her infancy as a thanksgiving to God for the great victory over the heathen Penda, after which his children made Mercia Christian; and Elfleda at six-and-twenty years of age succeeded Hilda as Abbess of Whitby: four women—Bertha, Ethelburga, Eanfleda, Elfleda, mother, daughter, grand-daughter, great-granddaughter—whose names are woven into the history of Christian England. Not only was Ethelburga the mother of a great offspring, but her brother Eadbald, who had given her in that marriage to King Edwin, reigned most nobly [1] after his conversion by St. Lawrence; and his son Ercombert was the first king of the Angles who had the idols destroyed in all his kingdom and ordered the forty days fast of Lent to be kept. He espoused Sexburga, daughter of Ina, king of the East Angles. One of their daughters, Earcongotha, became of great renown as Abbess of Faremoutier; and this gives occasion to Bede to note [2] the close connection there was between the first English monasteries and those which had already sprung up in France, descending from St. Martin or St. Maur, or the great Irish missionary St. Columban. Thither in their first conversion the Anglo-Saxons sent their daughters to be educated, and for espousal to the Heavenly Bridegroom; so that France became the cradle of English nuns. That wonderful growth which was about to burst out in England was specially fostered by the communities on the banks of the Marne and the Seine, such as Jouarres, Faremoutier, Andelys, and Chelles. The double monasteries, carefully separated from each other, of monks and nuns, but under the government of one abbot, passed from France to England. Earcongotha was another great-grand-daughter of Ethelbert, and her sister Ermenilda, queen of Mercia for many years, became in her widowhood third Abbess of Ely, and was succeeded by her daughter Werburga as fourth Abbess of Ely, being fourth in descent from Ethelbert. But the number of great Anglo-Saxon women who either began or ended as nuns is so large that I shrink from the attempt to record them. It is enough to bear in

---

[1] "Nobilissime," says Bede.   [2] Bede, iii. 8; Montalembert, v. 259.

mind the most illustrious of them all, that Etheldreda whose name of Audrey shone as a light through so many centuries of English history. When the first in rank of all English women left the throne of the most powerful king to become a nun—when the bishop most persuasive, the observed of all observers, the champion of Rome and establisher of the Benedictine rule in the North, received and sanctioned her renunciation of the world, which he could only do because she had refused her consent to the conjugal life at its beginning, they joined together the natural reverence for women which had dwelt in the Teutonic race with that respect for the virginal life shown in the consecration of it by the Church's ritual. The historian of the monks of the West records what ensued on that example: "Not to mention bishops, abbots, monks, solitaries, we count from the seventh to the eleventh century twenty-three kings, and sixty queens, princes, or princesses, issuing from the different Anglo-Saxon dynasties, among the saints recognised by the Church. No other nation has ever furnished an equal contingent."

Etheldreda was niece of Hilda through her sister Hereswitha, and great-niece of Edwin. Wilfrid and Bennet Biscop were nobles of Edwin's kingdom. This conversion of the race of Odin was specially fostered during that seventh century from the time that Pope Boniface V. wrote to encourage Edwin in the rejection of idolatry, and Pope Honorius congratulated him on leaving it, and Pope Eugenius welcomed Wilfrid and Bennet Biscop, and Pope Vitalian found a Primate for them, and Pope Agatho confirmed Wilfrid's appeal, and Pope Sergius found Rome already a place of Saxon pilgrimage. The same historian declares how, " in transforming the manners and beliefs of the Anglo-Saxon conquerors, the monastic missionaries altered in nothing that native genius of the German race.[1] They were able to make a nation of Christians more fervent, more generous in alms, more submissive, and more attached to the Church, more magnificent in their munificence to monasteries, more fruitful in saints of both sexes, than any other contemporaneous nation. But they deprived it of no public virtues, no one of its rude and energetic instincts. They retrenched no

[1] Montalembert, v. 193.

particle of its manly nature; infringed in nothing that independence and boldness which have remained to this day its distinctive mark."

Thus the seventh century is marked to England evermore as the time of its conversion to the Christian faith. And this conversion is brought about by a new and most energetic race deserting that life of Odin which had been its portion during several hundred years. During the hundred and fifty years in which it had occupied this island it had followed the tradition in which it was nurtured. It had indulged in perpetual war, slaughter, and plunder, not only with the Britons whom it had invaded, but with other bands of its own tribes, for so the Valhalla which it worshipped on the other side of the dark valley required. To such a race those who came to preach Christ bore no weapon; they unsheathed no sword; they shed no blood. They exhibited a Redeemer - God who suffered, and who was born of a maiden - mother, and they carried in their own flesh the tokens of the one and of the other. What ensued remains for ever a marvel, a miracle which none can deny, and greater by far than raising the dead to life, healing the paralytic, or causing the blind to see. For a great multitude of all classes listened to this teaching, and imitated in their own persons the teachers. Monks came to teach them, and monks they became. Mothers and daughters were told of the spotless Mother, and they became like her in their mode of life. It was preached to them in the words of one who himself saw and studied the Fathers of the Desert:—"Christ is come of a virgin: O ye women be virgins, that you may become mothers of Christ." They believed and obeyed.[1] This with a certain portion of the population, sufficiently large to be endowed by the kings, queens, and nobles with such public and private lands as made them in no long time a power in the State. But their own choice of life, the following a strict rule in prayer, in food, in the discipline which makes a house, combined with the declining the tie of marriage, the following a direct imitation of their Lord, made them a standard of excellence, an example ennobling the more

[1] St. Gregory Nazianzen, Sermon on Christmas Day, 380.

common course of the world around them. But in that self-same century wherein England was thus gained there arose a power which designedly set itself to destroy the monastic life. The Caliphs of Mohammed recognised in the monk not only the professor and practiser of the faith which they most opposed, but the manner of life the most hostile to their own example and practice. The founder of their misbelief had shown this abhorrence in all his conduct, and all those who owned him for their prophet derived from him a relentless persecution in both sexes of the life which consists in a special imitation of Christ. While Aidan and Finian and Colman were gathering their proselytes in the glens and valleys of Northumberland, Omar was destroying thousands of Christian churches in the wide regions which his armies occupied, and carrying into infamous captivity multitudes of nuns. As England was lifted up to the divine life, its lustre sank in Syria, Mesopotamia, and North Africa. The land of the Fathers of the Desert relinquished the light which had shone on them so brightly three hundred years before, while it rose to kindle for many centuries the unquenchable torch of piety and learning in more lasting homes through Gaul and the British Isles, and presently on the yet heathen land of Arminius, the land of Saxons unreclaimed, which caused Augustus to cry out for his legions, but accepted Boniface, the Anglo-Saxon monk, for the chief of its hierarchy.

CHAPTER VIII

ST. BONIFACE, APOSTLE OF GERMANY

BEDE dwells very strongly upon the great strengthening of the Church in England wrought by Archbishop Theodore in the twenty-two years of his primacy, which ran from 668 to 690. He stemmed, so far as lay in his power, the many irregularities which had sprung up in different parts. Some of these may well be ascribed to the seven or eight kingdoms into which the land was divided; not to mention that in this time the various regions of England were only more or less converted. Of these, Sussex was among the last, and it was converted by the action of St. Wilfrid, who had been most irregularly expelled from his own diocese of York, then embracing all Northumbria, by the anger of King Egfrid, exasperated against the bishop after the surrendering of his throne by his queen Etheldreda. And here it is remarkable that Archbishop Theodore, whose authority in general had been exerted to bring about one order and observation of the universal canonical rules among his bishops, had for some unexplained reason allowed himself to depose Bishop Wilfrid, to divide his diocese into three, without even hearing him, and even, what is still more strange, when Wilfrid had returned from Rome, and was restored by the judgment of Pope Agatho I., had suffered King Egfrid first to imprison him and then to continue the privation of his see. But Wilfrid, retiring from York, carried his episcopal action and all his vigour and heroic endurance of wrong into other parts. He added to his crown by converting and civilising the wild Saxons of Sussex. In due time King Egfrid was killed in battle; his second wife, in her widowhood, was converted from an enemy to a friend of Wilfrid. The Primate, Theodore, confessed his wrong done to Wilfrid, desired to have him for his own successor, a desire which did not move Wilfrid's assent to it; and Wilfrid came back to York, and lived to be again a great Northern bishop, to protect again and support all his houses of Benedictine monks, to suffer a second persecution from another king of Northumbria, to appeal again to another Pope, John VI., and once more to be restored by him after a solemn judgment, so that he died at last in his place, the man of unconquered resolution, spotless in life and heroic in charity, whose forty-five years as bishop, since he fought the battle of Rome before the Saxon Bretwalda at Whitby, to his death as both bishop and head of many Benedictine abbeys among his brethren in 709, can scarcely be surpassed in the annals of the whole episcopate; that perpetual ten thousand who form the personal guards of our Lord through all the ages, at present nineteen centuries, of His conflict with the world.

It is in St. Theodore's primacy that we have marked for us the first rise of a commencing parochial administration; hitherto the cathedrals were ruled by bishops, who lived as monks with their clergy, according to the original institution of Pope Gregory. Further, the monasteries, as established by Wilfrid and Bennet Biscop, supplied a great number of monks who, from them, visited the country round them, preaching, instructing, baptizing, tending the sick; while the female monasteries, such as those of Whitby, Coldingham, and Ely, embraced a great number of nuns. But gradually thanes were converted and built churches, they gave part of their land for the maintenance of these churches, and on these priests were settled by the several bishops.[1]

The chief resource of the bishops to obtain such mass-priests lay in the cathedral monastery, where the clergy were carefully instructed in their duties and trained in their exercise. These communities formed the principal seminaries for the education of the clergy. Here, with the assistance of the best masters, the young ecclesiastics were initiated in the different sciences which were studied at that period, while the restraint of a wise and vigilant discipline

---

[1] See Lingard, i. 148–161, in which pages he describes the first institution of mass-priests in district churches, holding under the bishops, not under monasteries.

withheld them from the seductions of vice, and enured them to the labours and the duties of their work. According to their years and merit they were admitted to the lower orders of the hierarchy, and might, with the approbation of their superior, aspire at the age of five-and-twenty to the order of deacon; at thirty to that of priest, but not unless their services were actually required for the performance of some office to which they had been appointed. By ecclesiastical law no mass-priest could be instituted; by both ecclesiastical and national law none could be removed, without the consent of the bishop. In the language of the time, the mass-priest was wedded to his church, and could not be divorced from it but for a reasonable cause, and by his own judge. It was in his church that he ought to be daily found at the seven canonical hours, to sing the praises of God, and to pray for himself, for his flock, and for all Christian people. The baptism of infants was particularly recommended to his care. He was to be ready to administer that sacrament at all hours; to see that it was not delayed beyond a certain time after the birth, and to compel the parents to offer the child soon afterwards to the bishop for confirmation. Attention to the sick was another important branch of his duty. He was to visit them frequently, to hear their confessions, to carry and administer to them the eucharist, and then to anoint them with the last unction. In the tribunal of penance—an institution which formed the most difficult of his duties—he was advised to weigh with discretion every alleviating or aggravating circumstance, that he might apportion the penance to the offence; and in aid of his own judgment, he was advised to consult and follow the directions of the Penitential.

A mass-priest was not appointed without a deacon to attend upon him; and at least two other clerics of minor orders would be found in his household; he was therefore never left solitary, nor exposed to the dangers which such a condition would entail. He had to instruct these in he Latin language and in ecclesiastical learning; and not only them, but generally also the children of his parishioners. "Mass-priests," says the authority, "shall always have at their houses a school of learners, and if any good man will trust his little ones to them for lore, they shall right gladly receive and kindly teach them. Ye shall remember that it is written: 'They that be learned shall shine as heaven's brightness, and they that draw and instruct many to righteousness shall shine as stars for ever.' They shall not, however, for such lore, demand anything of the parents, besides that which the latter may do of their own will."[1]

The mass-priest was strictly confined to a life of continency, a regulation equally practised and enforced by the Roman and the Scottish missionaries. This discipline was based on the doctrine of Christ in the Gospel, that His disciples must be ready to renounce the gratifications of sense, to forsake parents, wife, and children, through the love of Him; and on the reasoning of the Apostle that while the married man is necessarily solicitous for the concerns of this world, the unmarried is at liberty to turn his whole attention to the service of God. Hence it was inferred that the embarrassments of wedlock were hostile to the devotion of a mass-priest. His parishioners, it was said, were his family, and to watch over their spiritual welfare, to instruct their ignorance, to console them in their afflictions, and to relieve them in their indigence, were to be his constant and favourite occupations.

As to the Anglo-Saxon Church, every doubt as to the discipline established in it by the Roman missionaries from the very beginning must be removed by the answer of St. Gregory to St. Augustine, according to which only the clerics who had not been raised to the higher orders, and who professed themselves unable to lead a life of continency, were permitted to marry. Ceolfric, the Abbot of Wearmouth in Bede's time, and Bede himself, and his friend Egbert, the Archbishop of York, are equally agreed in this. The words of Egbert are:[2] "Clerics not in holy orders may take wives, that is, neither presbyters nor deacons; but priests must on no account take wives." "During more than two hundred and fifty years from the death of Augustine these laws respecting clerical celibacy, so galling to the natural propensities of men, but so calculated to enforce an elevated idea

[1] Thorpe, ii. 414, quoted by Lingard, p. 154.
[2] Lingard, Anglo-Saxons, i. 161.

of the sanctity which becomes the priesthood, were enforced with the strictest rigour; but during part of the ninth and most of the tenth century, when the repeated and sanguinary devastations of the Danes threatened the destruction of the hierarchy no less than of the government, the ancient canons opposed but a feeble barrier to the impulse of the passions; and of the clergy who escaped the swords of the invaders several scrupled not to violate the chastity which, at their ordination, they had vowed to observe. Yet even then the marriage of priests was never approved by the Saxon prelates, and as often as a transient gleam of tranquillity invited them to turn their attention to the restoration of discipline, the prohibitions of former synods were revived, and the celibacy of the clergy was recommended by paternal exhortations, and enforced with the severest penalties."

Our Saxon ancestors, in the century of their conversion by bishops and priests who were monks, far from imagining the presence of a woman in the house of a mass-priest, "made an improvement on the severity of the fathers assembled in the great Council of Nice, and even female relations were forbidden to dwell in the same house with a priest."[1] Their books, still extant, say: "God's priests, and deacons, and God's other servants, that should serve in God's temple and touch the sacrament and the holy books, they shall always observe their chastity." "If any man in orders, bishop, priest, monk, or deacon, had his wife ere he were ordained, and forsook her for God's sake, and they afterwards return together again through lust, let each fast according to his order, as is written above with respect to murder." "If priest or deacon marry, let them lose their orders." "To every servant of God, who should serve God in chastity, it is forbidden that he have in the house with him any relation or kind of woman for any kind of work, lest he, through temptation of the devil, sin therein."

By these acts of legislation the Anglo-Saxons of Bede's time, specially the first Archbishop of York, who was chosen to inherit the dropped pallium of St. Paulinus, and from

---

[1] See Lingard, i. 160, who quotes these passages in the Anglo-Saxon language from the authorities.

whom the whole line of York descends through centuries, from age to age, receiving as he did from the Roman Pontiff his credentials, marked that it was one body with the whole Western Church, whose discipline in this most important point of priestly purity—the special *sacerdotal* mark and signet—it upheld and avowed. Of the twenty-four Popes who sat in the See of Peter between the first Gregory and the second, his like, and, in the judgment of Baronius, well-nigh his equal, there was no one more distinguished than Sergius, who sat in the last thirteen years of the seventh century, and no one defended and fostered the young English Church more than Sergius. In his time Anglo-Saxon kings and princes made pilgrimages to Rome. If Wilfrid and Bennet Biscop between 650 and 660 risked their lives in doing this, as in those same ten years a Pope laid down his life by imperial judgment at Constantinople for defending the Christian faith in the person of Christ at Rome—if those two, both leaders and introducers of the Benedictine Order, were the first of their country to introduce this pilgrimage as an act of worship, it became in the last decade of the century, when Sergius sat in the papal chair, a not unusual act of piety. The fifth descendant of the once great Emperor Heraclius, the Emperor Justinian II., had called a Council in the Dome Chamber of his palace, and as he had summoned it himself, so he arrogated the power to confirm it, whereas his father, the Emperor Constantine the Bearded, had but a few years before thought it the duty of Pope Agatho to convene the Sixth Council, and when he died begged Pope Leo II. to confirm it. But Justinian II. did not stop his innovations here; not only did he sign his name in the imperial vermilion writing at the head of this Council, but under his own name he had lines written for what he esteemed his *own* five patriarchs; and he sent the canons to Pope Sergius, requesting him to sign his name between that of the emperor and that of the Archbishop of Constantinople. In that year, 692, the three Eastern patriarchs of Alexandria, Antioch, and Jerusalem had for fifty years fallen under Mohammedan domination. Among the canons which Justinian II. had first confirmed and then required Pope Sergius to sign, canons altering the ancient immemorial practice of the Church respecting the celibacy of the clergy were introduced. By these canons[1] the continuing practice of their marriage, as it had been made before ordination, was allowed to priests, deacons, and other spiritual persons, and conjugal intercourse between them permitted, while to bishops such permission was not allowed.

Pope Sergius refused the demand of Justinian II. to sign these Trullan canons of discipline. As a consequence, the emperor sent his chief guardsman to Rome with the charge to carry the resisting Pope to Constantinople, where the lot which had befallen his predecessor, Pope Martin, from the emperor's grandfather, Coustans II., awaited him likewise. But people and army rallied round the Pope, and the guardsman had to fly for refuge under the Pope's bed in order to save his own life. It was the whole discipline of the Western Church which Pope Sergius saved in refusing his subscription to the demand of the Eastern emperor that he should assent to abuses introduced by this exclusively Eastern Council. Three years before, Cadwalla, the king of Wessex, had laid down his throne, and at thirty years of age came to Rome to receive baptism from this very Pope Sergius. He lived but a few days afterwards, and was buried in the atrium of St. Peter's.

Thus the discipline respecting the marriage of the clergy, which the Anglo-Saxon canons attest, and which the Anglo-Saxon practice carried out for two hundred and fifty years after their Church was founded, was the universal rule of the Western Church, and bore the witness of a daughter to it. It comes as a pendant to that marvellous choice of the monastic life shown by both sexes of the Anglo-Saxon people in their first conversion, when the children of Odin became the children of Christ; and the race which in their old inherited patriarchal religion showed a multitude of captive women who sacrificed their life rather than their chastity under Roman cruelty, now produced such a flock of Christian converts, who embraced the life of Christ and His mother as no other Northern people showed.

This maintenance of sacerdotal chastity was not the peculiar institute of one Pope, but the rule of all, brought down

[1] See Hergenröther, "Leben Photius," i. 217.

from the ancient fathers, belonging equally to Italy, France, Spain, and Ireland, as well as England, recognised in the penitentials of Archbishops Theodore at Canterbury and Egbert at York. England was converted in the seventh century mainly by monks and nuns, but not at all by married priests, a degradation first introduced as a sequel of Danish massacres, and entailing the deepest dishonour on those who suffered themselves to fall under it. Every practice of the ancient Church, from the Council of Nice onwards, was violated by such an ignoble presence in a priest's household, instead of the deacon who attended on him, and the clerics who assisted the regular celebration of divine worship, and the seven hours of daily prayer in the district churches established by the bishop in proportion as the possessors of land were converted.

Pope after pope, at the risk of life, resisted the attempt of the Byzantine emperors to force this alteration of the old discipline on them as guardians of the Western Church's rule of life. The guardsman of Justinian II. was not only foiled, but glad to escape with his life under the Pope's protection. But such disgrace in that time of seven revolutions, which all but destroyed the Byzantine throne, did not prevent the usurping emperor, Apsimar, ten years later, to commission another Exarch, by name Theophylact, to carry away Pope John VI. to Constantinople, that he might be induced to give that consent to the Trullan canons which Pope Sergius had refused. This attempt also miscarried, through the energy of Italian troops defending the Pope. Again, in the very last days of the reign which Justinian II., "the man of the nose split,"[1] had recovered, he summoned Pope Constantine in 710 to visit him. That Pope had at his right hand, as deacon and counsellor, his future successor, Gregory II., and the effort of the emperor to get the canons of his own unrecognised Council received again failed. Pope Constantine returned to Rome in safety, and thither presently, by another usurper, the head of Justinian II., having been cut off, was sent in a box to prove to all men that the race of Heraclius was extinct, having passed through five generations, in which the masters of Constantinople had lost

---

[1] *Rhino-tmetos* was his Greek appellation.

half their empire beneath the sway of a new religion, and that new religion, true to its own character, persecuted what remained with internecine hatred. Afterwards, when Leo III., the seventh in that series of emperors raised by revolutions, had for ten years exercised a stable authority, he not only attempted to bend the resolution of that great Pope Gregory II. to maintain the existing rule of the Church as to the sacredness of the sacerdotal life, but five times tried to sacrifice the Pope's life, in which attempt every time he failed. It was through such perils that Sergius and the succeeding popes maintained intact that rule of the Western Church in accordance with which the conversion of England was brought about, chiefest and most by the exemplary sacrifice of both sexes in the Anglo-Saxon race when they embraced the monastic life, and then by the mass-priests placed by the bishops through their dioceses, who during centuries were faithful to their practice of celibacy.

Pope Sergius was a Sicilian monk of Palermo, a natural subject of the Eastern empire; he was succeeded by John VI., another subject of the same; and then by John VII., a third subject; fourthly, by Sisinnius, a Syrian; fifthly, by Constantine, also a Syrian. These five popes lived in times of the utmost danger, and equally resisted those whom they esteemed their lawful emperors, and whom they obeyed in all which they considered lawful commands. Thus, Pope Constantine acceded to the imperial invitation to go to the emperor at Constantinople, that same emperor, be it remembered, who tried to carry off Pope Sergius into captivity, and when this failed tried to take his life. They all resisted the tampering of the emperor with the discipline of the Church in the important point of clerical celibacy, not as a new thing, but as it had come down from past ages. "No sooner had the succession of Christian princes secured the peace of the Church than laws were made to enforce that discipline which fervour had formerly introduced and upheld. The regulations of the canons were supported by the authority of the emperors; by Theodosius the priest who presumed to marry was deprived of the clerical privileges; by Justinian his children were declared illegitimate."[1] These Popes were under that absolute rule over Italy which Justinian gained by conquest, and exercised by his institution of Exarchs. At this time that rule had gone on during a hundred and forty years, and had been the source of perpetual suffering and ignominy to Italy.

Bede testifies to the important action of Pope Sergius on the English Church in other matters also. Cadwalla, king of Wessex, out of exceeding reverence to St. Peter, as Bede, in quoting his epitaph, writes, "left all for the love of God, that he might as a guest behold Peter and Peter's See, in his conversion changed rejoicingly his barbarian rage, and with it his name, as Sergius the bishop ordered, naming him Peter, when himself his father in the fountain of regeneration." In the next year Archbishop Theodore died, and Beretwald, Abbot of Reculver, being chosen in his stead, Pope Sergius confirmed to him the primacy over all Britain.

Just at the same time, the year 692, St. Willibrord, whom Wilfrid had received as a child and nurtured at Ripon,[2] made his pilgrimage to Rome, "that he might enter upon the work of evangelising the heathen, which he had longed after, with the permission and blessing of Sergius, then ruling in the Apostolic See. He hoped also to obtain from the Pope relics of apostles and martyrs, so that having destroyed the idols in the heathen nations to whom he was to preach, he might have ready relics of saints to put there in the churches which he would dedicate to them. He also desired either to learn there or to receive a great many things which a business of such magnitude required." In all these matters having obtained his wish, he returned to preach. His brethren in Frisia had selected Suidbert to be their bishop. He was sent to Britain, and Bishop Wilfrid, driven from his diocese at that time, was an exile in Mercia, and he consecrated Suidbert, because Archbishop Beretwald had not yet returned to his see, having gone abroad to be consecrated by the Gallic metropolitan, Godwin. Suidbert carried on his episcopate in Frisia, and was given by Pepin, Mayor of the Palace, an island in the Rhine,

[1] Lingard, i. 157.   [2] Bede, v. 11, p. 264.

on which he built a monastery. There for some time he led a life of the greatest continence, and there he died.

But Wilfrid's pupil and foster-child, Willibrord, was sent forward by Pepin to Rome,[1] where Sergius was still Pope, with the request that he might be consecrated bishop for the Frisian people. This was fulfilled in the year 696, when Pope Sergius consecrated him on St. Cecilia's day, in her own church, and changed his name to Clement. He stayed fourteen days in Rome, and was then sent back to his mission. "Now Pepin gave him for the seat of his cathedral an illustrious castle of his own, named Wiltburg, which in the Gallic language is called Trajectus (Utrecht). Here that most reverend pontiff built a church, preaching far and wide the word of faith and recalling many from error. He built many churches in those regions and constructed some monasteries. Afterwards he himself appointed other bishops in those regions out of the brethren who had come to preach either with him or after him, of whom some already sleep in the Lord. But Willibrord, surnamed Clement, venerable for his advanced age, for he is passing the thirty-sixth year of his episcopate (and Bede was writing this in 731), and after manifold struggles in his heavenly warfare, he is sighing with all his soul for the rewards of the divine remuneration."

St. Willibrord survived long after these words of Bede, for St. Boniface, who was not only his friend, but for some time partner in his mission, declares in his 97th letter,[2] that he was a missionary for fifty years, up to extreme old age. So that St. Willibrord during fifty years, from 696 to 745, ten years after the death of Bede himself, was engaged in converting Frisia, in all which he executed his commission from Pope Sergius as Archbishop of Utrecht.[3] It was the hand of St. Willibrord, the Anglo-Saxon missionary sent from Rome by Pope Sergius, which baptized in 714 Pepin, the son of Charles, the son of Pepin, Mayor of the Palace, that Charles Martel whom Pope Zacharias was to name Patricius of Rome, and that Pepin whom the

---

[1] Bede v. 11, p. 266.
[2] See the Note 29 in Bede, p. 266.
[3] Alban Butler's Life, on November 7.

magnates of France exalted to be king in the stead of the degenerate Merovingian, according to the judgment of the same Pope Zacharias, and whom St. Boniface, named by him Archbishop of Mainz, crowned king of France in 752 at Soissons, inaugurating the Carlovingian monarchy, which was then further consecrated by Pope Stephen at St. Denis.

These are some acts of that Pope Sergius who defended the Church's liberty in maintaining the sanctity of her own ministry, who preserved England to be converted by monks and nuns and priests, such as the practice of many hundred years had already handed them down; priests such as St. Augustine and his companions, such too as Bishop Aidan, and all those who were with him and his companion bishops from Iona. To this conduct of Pope Sergius was due the unblemished glory of the first Anglo-Saxon century.

But St. Willibrord was likewise the special link of connection between the two great men of purely Anglo-Saxon blood, one of whom was made from Rome the instrument of spreading the Benedictine rule for the conversion of England, and the other made equally from Rome the head and founder of that hierarchy to which Germany owes itself—St. Wilfrid and St. Boniface.

The first appearance of St. Boniface at Rome was in the year 718, three years after the accession of Pope Gregory II., when the Emperor Leo III. had obtained full possession of the Byzantine crown. Gregory himself was of patrician blood, nourished in the old Roman traditions. He it is whose letters I have elsewhere quoted to that monarch, asserting the right of the Church to carry out her own worship in venerating the images of our Lord, of His holy Mother, and of the saints and martyrs, which had come down through centuries, against the purpose to abolish them, which Leo had borrowed from his inveiglement in Jewish and Saracen impiety. But this was some ten years after the act which I am about to record. Gregory II. had two great purposes in view—one to keep the Italians in their duty to the emperor, while he would not sacrifice their rights nor give up the keys of Rome to the Lombards; the other was to assure the Christian adoption of the youthful Northern nations.[1] At this moment an Anglo-Saxon monk appeared in his presence, drew forth from his mantle a letter from his bishop, Daniel of Winchester, and humbly waited for the answer. The Pope looked on him with cheerful countenance, gazing into him with smiling eyes. He heard from the account given to him that the name of the monk was Winfrid, that is, the Peace-winner; that he was nearly forty years of age; that he was born at Kirton, in the kingdom of Wessex and county of Devon, and had been instructed in sacred and profane literature in the monasteries of Exeter and Nutschell. His repute for learning had caused him to be asked to teach in convents, and to be called to share in the counsels of bishops; but he had already been drawn by that ardour for the mission abroad which had laid hold of Anglo-Saxon monasteries. He had gone to Frisia, but at that moment war had broken out between Rathbod the Duke and Charles Martel. The young missions had been disturbed and Winfrid went back to England. Now he came a second time abroad to visit Rome and have his vocation confirmed. The Pope, after frequent interviews, conferred on him full powers in the following words:[2]—" Gregory, servant of the servants of God, to the priest Winfrid. The pious purpose of your zeal, kindled with the love of Christ, and the proofs which you have given us of your faith, demand that we should call you to partake our ministry of dispensing the divine word. Learning then that from your childhood you have studied the sacred letters, and that, urged by the fear of God to make use of the talent intrusted to you, you went forth to diffuse among the unbelieving nations the mystery of the faith, we felicitate you upon your piety, and will aid you in this grace. Since, then, you have had the modesty to submit your desire to the advice of the Apostolic See, as a member which awaits its movement from the head directing the whole body, in the name of the indivisible Trinity, by the immovable authority of the blessed Peter, prince of the Apostles, to dispense whose doctrine by authority is our office, we order that you carry the kingdom

---

[1] This narrative is drawn from Ozanam's *Civilisation Chrétienne chez les Francs*, vol. ii. p. 171. See the Letters of Gregory II. in Mansi.

[2] Mansi, xii. 234. Ozanam's translation, with some corrections.

of God to all the unbelieving nations which you shall be able to visit, and that you pour into these uncultivated souls the preaching of the two testaments with the spirit of virtue, love, and sobriety. Further, we will that you watch over the observance of the baptismal rite, according to the form which will be drawn up for your use by the chancery of the Holy See. Whatever you shall want, having once begun the work, take care to make known to us. Fare you well."[1] This was given on the 15th May, in the third year of the reign of the Emperor Leo.

At this first visit Winfrid stayed long enough in Rome to make himself well familiar with the place, containing for him, a Northern of Teutonic blood, so many wonderful thoughts, a storehouse of the grace of God in past times, to which he was looking for further graces. Of these the words of the Pontiff were to him a guarantee. Winfrid had looked again and again on the loving countenance and smiling eyes of Gregory; he had looked also on that statue of Peter in his own church which Leo the emperor afterwards wrote to the Pope he would abolish, and received the Pope's answer that all the nations of the West looked up to him as a god; and Winfrid, as son of one of those nations, did what forty generations of men have done since his time. He laid on his head St. Peter's foot, as a sign that they did homage, each in his day, to the living Vicar of Christ, in whom Christ reigns, and conquers, and commands.

Then Winfrid, fortified by the Pope's word, went on his journey northward. In the capital of Lombardy, Pavia, King Liutprand, albeit that he longed for thirty years to get possession of Rome, received him hospitably, and bestowed gifts on him. Then Winfrid crossed the Alps and came down on Germany, his land of promise, the land which was to own his influence from the source of the Rhine to its mouth, from the Alps to the Elbe's entrance into the Northern Sea. He passed through Bavaria, Thuringia, and Eastern France, carefully noting the peoples, according to the instructions of the Holy See. He found Frisia again, and Willibrord, its bishop, working in it with the favour of the people, now

---

[1] This letter is given in Mansi's collection, vol. xii. p. 234. I have translated Ozanam's faithful rendering of it.

inclining to the Franks. Winfrid seconded the bishop during three years, as he was destroying pagan sanctuaries and raising churches. St. Willibrord wished Winfrid to share his episcopate, but from this Winfrid shrunk back. He rather chose to go on to nations still more wanting his aid. As he was stopping at a monastery near Trier, and expounding to the community a passage of Scripture during a repast, a young man of fifteen named Gregory, of royal descent and great hopes, was so enthralled by his words as to declare that he would never leave him, and became one of his most attached and distinguished disciples. Winfrid went on to Thuringia, a country then ravaged by wars, where he had to work with the labour of his hands. At length he succeeded in gathering up some scattered Christians, in correcting the manners of the priests and the belief of the faithful. The peasants came to hear a man who spoke their language and ventured into their forests. Many became Christians; many deserted the idols to which they had fallen back. Two brothers, Detdie and Deorwulf, whom he had gained from paganism, gave him one of their lands called Amonaburg. There he built a church and a monastery. Next he advanced into Hesse, where he baptized several thousand barbarians just approaching the Saxon frontiers. He sent a disciple, Binne, to give account to the Sovereign Pontiff of the fruits obtained, after which he made a second mission to Rome himself.

The Pope had invited him, and after his coming received him in the Basilica of St. Peter's, heard from him all that he had done, and asked for his profession of faith. This Winfrid made up with great care, and wrote out. When the Pope learnt the great number of converts, and his urgent need for more assistance, he declared his intention to make Winfrid a regionary bishop, that is, without definite limit of jurisdiction, but having liberty to carry the faith where he should find men fit to receive it. On St. Andrew's Day in 723, he consecrated Winfrid himself; and as he had changed a Saxon name before to Clement, so he changed Winfrid the Peace-giver into the equivalent Bonifacius. In that name he shines as martyr in the Church's everlasting roll. A certain oath had been taken since the time of Pope

Gelasius, then more than two hundred years. This may be recorded as forming the future oath of the German hierarchy, and already forming that of the hierarchy in the English Church, more lately founded than Gelasius by St. Gregory. To the second of that name Boniface upon his consecration swore:[1]—

"In the name of our Lord God and Saviour Jesus Christ, in the sixth year of the Emperor Leo's consulate. I, Boniface, by the grace of God bishop, promise to you, blessed Peter, prince of the Apostles, and to your vicar, blessed Pope Gregory, and his successors, by the Father, the Son, and the Holy Ghost, the indivisible Trinity, and by this, thy most sacred body, to keep the whole fidelity and purity of the Catholic faith, to persist by the help of God in the unity of that faith, on which all the salvation of Christians without doubt depends. I will in nothing at any one's persuasion consent against the unity of the common and universal Church; but, as I said, I will in all things show my fidelity and sincerity and agreement with you and the interests of your Church, to which the power of binding and loosing has been given by the Lord God, and to your aforesaid vicar and his successors. But if I come to know of any prelates acting against the ancient rules of the holy Fathers, I will hold with them no communion or intercourse, but rather, if it be in my power, prevent them; if not, I will immediately report it faithfully to my Apostolic Lord. But if, which God forbid, I were to attempt to act in any way against this my promise, either by my own prompting or that of others, let me be found guilty at the eternal judgment, let me incur the punishment of Ananias and Sapphira, whose purpose was to defraud you of their own goods, or who ventured to tell a falsehood. This statement of my oath I, Boniface, humble bishop, have written by my own hand. I depose it on the most sacred body of St. Peter: so have I expressed, as prescribed, my oath, with God for my witness and judge, which I promise to keep."[2]

From time to time, and through the ages, the Popes use a particular word to express the fabric of the Church's unity; something within which all are safe, while without it they

---
[1] Mansi, xii. 235.   [2] Transcribed from Mansi, xii. 235.

are liable to collapse and perish. That word is *compages*, or the structure. The engagement thus solemnly taken by each bishop at the time he is consecrated appears to me the most adequate fulfilment of this word and its meaning. It at once marks out what the Universal Church alone is, as well in its doctrine or mass of belief as in its material fabric or its communion. It equally marks out what every so-called *national* church is *not*. A national church may try to make such an engagement on the part of bishops a part of its discipline, substituting only for the spiritual head the temporal sovereign, and will term, it may be, the breaking such engagement on the part of an individual high treason. Or again, a sovereign enjoying the fulness of temporal power may act through what he shall choose to term a "Holy Synod," comprehending in itself bishops as well as laymen, but deriving from himself, and wielding under that name, his own imperial authority. But in both these cases the engagement belongs only to something of civil extent and right, and neither in the mass of doctrine nor in the material fabric concerns the Universal Church, and the person of him to whom that Church has been committed, with the power of binding and of loosing divinely bestowed. Thus we hear that bishops from Pope Gelasius, A.D. 492–496, to Pope Gregory II., A.D. 715–731, took this oath; and the Church's *compages* lasted unbroken when new countries such as Britain and Germany were taken into its fold. The living structure of minds preserved it whole. But when an attempt was made to attach the structure to the person of an earthly king, it broke up, until what had been unity, both mental and material, became a by-word of heresy and schism, in which literally every man claimed to have an *opinion*, and no one went beyond an *opinion;* and neither man, nor woman, nor child would submit to be taught the one *creed* of the Christian Church.

But to the Anglo-Saxon monk, whom he named Boniface, together with the hand and word which conferred upon him the unction of bishop, and in return for his oath, Pope Gregory II. gave protection, support, and counsel, and a book in which the canons of the Church were marked, and questions which Boniface, in the circle of his action, would have to solve. He entered into the family of the Roman Pontiff, that brotherhood of all Christendom, which centres in his person and radiates from him. This privilege, in that year 723, Boniface received, and it was renewed to him continually under Popes Gregory III., Zacharias, and Stephen III.

Pope Gregory II. wrote six letters[1] intended to assist the new bishop in the work of converting the people to whom he should be sent. One was to Charles, already Mayor of the Palace, to whose dignity he recommends his brother Boniface, as approved in faith and morals, consecrated by him bishop, and instructed in the statutes of the Apostolic See, over which, by authority of God, he presides. Boniface is charged by him to preach to the peoples of the Germanic nation, to such as dwell on the eastern side of the Rhine, still in the error of heathenism or clouded over with ignorance. He asks the protection of the Duke Charles against any enemy, "since you know," he adds, "that it is God to whom you will show this favour, who had foretold that He will consider Himself received by those who receive His apostles, marked out to bring light to the heathen."

A fuller letter addressed by "Gregory the bishop, servant of the servants of God, to all bishops, priests, deacons, dukes, castellans, counts, or all Christians fearing God," begins:[2] "Moved by the great solicitude for the matter of thought put under our charge, we know that populations in parts of Germany, or on the east bank of the Rhine, are wandering in the shadow of death, under persuasion of the old enemy, and, with the seeming of Christians, are in slavery to the worship of idols, while others have not even the knowledge of God, nor have been washed by holy baptism, but as pagans, like brute beasts, do not recognise their own Maker; and we have judged it necessary for the illumination of both these classes in the preaching of the true faith to send the bearer of these letters, Boniface, our most reverend brother and our colleague, as bishop, that he may inform them of

---

[1] These letters are to be found in Mansi, xii. 238-242. I have quoted from them in parts.

[2] "Solicitudinem nimiam gerentes pro speculatione nobis creditæ."—Mansi, xii. 238.

the doctrine of this Apostolic See, that, out of love to our Lord Jesus Christ and reverence to His Apostles, you may receive and cherish him, and supply his needs."

In another letter to all the Thuringian people he tells them to obey Boniface as their bishop and honour him as a father, "for we have not sent him for any temporal lucre, but for the gain of your own souls."

To all the people of the Old Saxons he writes: "Our brother and fellow-bishop, Boniface, is a faithful minister and fellow-servant in the Lord, whom I have sent to you for this very purpose, that he may know your circumstances, and console your hearts with his exhortation in Christ; that you may be freed from diabolical deceit, and aggregated to the adoption of sons, and escaping eternal condemnation, may possess eternal life."

Nor is the mission thus given to Boniface at all indefinite. In this, as in every case, the Holy See acts upon a certain rule and order, which as it had been carried out in Britain in the Church wherein Winfrid had been educated, so it enjoined him to apply to the Old Saxon race to which he was approaching as St. Augustine had applied it to the New Saxons.

In another letter, "Gregory the bishop, servant of the servants of God, sends greeting to his most beloved sons in the Lord, the clergy, the magistracy, and the commonalty of Thuringia. Making no delay to your well-directed desires, we have ordained as bishop for you our brother and fellow-bishop, Boniface. We have given him in charge never to make illicit ordinations, nor admit to sacred orders either one who has been twice married, or one who had married other than a virgin, or one illiterate, or one vitiated in any bodily part, or one who had undergone public penitence, or one liable to any municipal claims or any condition, and marked in consequence; but if he find any such already, he must not advance them. He must on no account receive Africans, everywhere pretending to ecclesiastical orders, because some of them are Manicheans, others often rebaptized. Let him be careful not to diminish, but rather increase church furniture, or whatever belongs to property. Out of the income of the Church, or the offerings of the faithful, let him make four parts—one to keep for himself, one to distribute to the clergy according to the business of their occupation, a third part to reserve for the poor and strangers, and a fourth for church buildings; of all which he will give an account to the divine judgment. Ordination of priests or deacons he will know are to be celebrated only on the fasts of the fourth, seventh, and tenth months, also at the beginning and middle of Lent on the Saturday evening. The sacrament of Holy Baptism must be given only at Easter and Pentecost, except when in urgent danger of death; lest men should perish eternally, such remedies are to be supplied. Now you are to obey devotedly one who observes the precepts of our see, that the body of the Church may be blameless and approved, through Christ our Lord, who lives and reigns with God the Father Almighty for ever." This letter is dated in the seventh year of the Emperor Leo III., four years before the Iconoclast usurpation had broken out, but when the Saracens had already advanced into Spain. They show in living words how, at the beginning of the eighth century, the gaze of the Popes was fixed in hope and confidence on the Northern nations, and how they watched to provide them with certainty of doctrine and undeviating practice; and that as Gregory the first sent a monk, the prior of his own monastery, from Rome to convert that branch of the Saxons which had conquered England, so Gregory the second sent another monk from England, a converted Anglo-Saxon, to convert the Old Saxons, still in the bosom of their forests, still, to use his own words, not knowing even their Maker.

Thus he begs the Thuringians to give up idolatry, because "the Son of God, Himself true God, came down from heaven, was made man, condescended to suffer and be crucified for us, was buried, and rose again, ascended, and charged His disciples to go and make disciples all nations. Therefore it is that we, desiring for you to rejoice for ever with us, where there is no end of joy, no sorrow, nor bitterness, send you our most holy brother Boniface to teach you the faith of Christ. Obey him, therefore, in all things, and honour him as your father; observe him and act, and you will be safe, you and your sons, for ever; build him likewise a house where he may dwell as your bishop, and churches wherein you may pray, that God may pardon your sins and give you eternal life."[1]

If we reflect upon the contents of these Papal writings[2] issued in the year 723, being both letters of guidance and conveying full powers, we may note in them the constitution of the German Church in its essential foundations. In these it has continued for more than eleven hundred years to our own days, with the blessing of God. These foundations are, first, the German Church is no national church, but is founded in the closest connection with the See of Peter. The German Apostle has sworn to him the closest unity in a solemn oath, and in a book given to him in his consecration as bishop received the statutes of the Universal Church as the norm of the constitution and government of the German Church. In the letters giving him full powers he received not only the charge to convert the heathen, but likewise to bring back to Catholic order Christians who had lapsed from it. Secondly, the German Church was to be not one divided from the State, but, with all its independence, to subsist as a community united with it for the maintenance of temporal protection. For this, Gregory II. recommended Bishop Boniface to the protection of Charles Martel, the Frank Mayor of the Palace, who then stood at the head of the Frank realm; for this he recommended the Apostle of the Germans to the magnates of Thuringia. Thirdly, although the See of Peter could not then, in the yet undetermined ecclesiastical circumstances, mark out a definite diocese to Bishop Boniface, and so the Pope writes only in general to the German bishops that they should accept Boniface as their fellow-bishop and support him with everything necessary; yet the future direction of the primatial See of Boniface is already pointed out, since the Pope marks for him the lands of Germany lying eastward from the Rhine as his sphere, without nearer description, in opposition to Neustria and Bavaria, and in this the allowable national establishment of the German Church is prepared beforehand.

[1] Mansi, xii. 241, translated.
[2] Winfrid Bonifacius, by Dr. von Guss, p. 90, translated.

Boniface left Rome with the Papal blessing in the year 723, and went to the court of Charles Martel, presented to him the Pope's letter, and asked for his protection.[1] He was kindly received by Charles, who gave him a letter of protection signed with his own hand and seal, and addressed to the bishops, dukes, counts, governors, officers, faithful, and friends. To these the Mayor of the Palace announced that he had taken Bishop Boniface under his strong protection, and should any grievance against him arise which the law could not settle, he and his people should come to the court in peace and good condition, and no man should show him opposition or utter condemnation.

The Christian faith had penetrated into Hesse, but was mixed up with remains of heathenism, offerings under sacred trees, foretellings, witchery, and enchantments. To meet all this[2] one speaking action of Boniface has been recorded for us, which is the more telling because of the light which it throws upon the ancestral religion then prevailing among the nations whose passage to the Christian faith we are now recording. The religion in Ireland when St. Patrick came, in England when St. Augustine came, in Germany when St. Boniface came, was a worship of the powers of Nature in woods and streams and fountains, in caves and hills, and in creatures supposed to haunt these, the offspring of men's kindled imagination. Now such a holy oak, which they called Thor's Oak or the Thunder Oak, stood in the parts where Boniface came. At the feast of Thor a great number of heathens had been drawn together. In the midst of these Boniface, attended by his disciples, appeared with axe in hand. He approached the gigantic tree and struck it; scarcely had he dealt on it a few strokes when a gigantic wind arose, seized on the vast crown of the tree, and tore asunder the four great trunks into which it was divided. The tree fell to the ground, the heathen looked on astonished and paralysed with fear. Boniface had conquered their gods. They pressed round him for baptism. The Anglo-Saxon monk carried among them the decision of St. Gregory the Great to make what had been heathen sanctuaries into

---

[1] Dr. Von Guss, p. 92, translated.
[2] *Ibid.*, p. 94, from Boniface's Ep. 13, Jaffé.

Christian. What had taken place at Godmundham in Yorkshire was repeated in Hesse. Boniface, with the counsel of his brethren, determined to build a house of prayer out of the four trunks of Thor's Oak, and this he consecrated in honour of St. Peter, announcing thereby his relationship and duty to St. Peter's See. "That man," said an old Life, "full of the Spirit of God, forthwith built renowned monasteries and distinguished basilicas, and altars also for divine sacrifices, in the places whence he had expelled those vanities, and decreed that the name of the living God should be worshipped in the very spots where the natives had hitherto worshipped dead idols." A spot where Woden yielded to Christ in the preaching of St. Boniface was not far from where in after ages the beautiful church of Marburg should for centuries bear the shrine of that Elizabeth, the Hungarian princess and Thuringian duchess, whose charity carried her, a widow in the bloom of youthful beauty, to all the height of sanctity, to put off her royal robes for a nun's humble costume, and dying at twenty-four, to be held as the patroness of her country before the God whom she had served in His poor with the utmost devotion.

The contest of Boniface with false believers and reprobates who frequented the court of Charles Martel, as well as with unconverted heathen, was severe. He is believed to have built many more churches in provision for his thousands of believers than is recorded in certain history, and it is a historic fact that he chose spots to which the people in heathen times had had recourse. The Pope had repeatedly enjoined him to build churches and monasteries, and in his letter to the Thuringians had recommended them to furnish him with dwellings. In his wandering life he would not yet need a stately cathedral, but such temporary structures as might serve for the nurture of his converts, and be of such a character as St. Benedict's son would choose.

For help to his pastoral care he applied to England. He and his companions were no longer enough for his needs, and especially for education of the female sex he required nuns. The son of St. Benedict wrote to that Order, flourishing in England, and not in vain.[1] He had since his departure

---
[1] Von Guss, pp. 107, 111, 113.

from England maintained a constant correspondence with prelates and monasteries. About the year 728 a number of learned monks had been drawn to him to take part in the work of education. More numerous yet were the nuns, of whom Lioba, from the double monastery of Wimburn, is famous. Boniface gave her as abbess the convent of Bischofsheim, which soon flourished under her guidance, and produced a crowd of abbesses and teachers for other houses. She won not only the affection of those under her rule, but the favour of the great, as of Pepin and his sons, of Hildegarde, the queen of Charlemagne. Boniface, without whose counsel she did nothing, esteemed her (who was also his kinswoman), so highly that he desired for her to be buried beside himself at Fulda.

So a number of learned and devoted Anglo-Saxon monks and nuns laboured under direction of St. Boniface in Hesse, Thuringia, and Franconia for the regeneration of the Teuton race. He found liberal help from the great and rich for the foundations which he needed. He founded them all in union with the Roman Church. Even for such points of liturgy and discipline as he might himself decide by his weight as bishop he consulted the Holy See, to silence by such authority those who sought to make division. St. Boniface sent a number of such questions, giving information of the progress of his mission, by a priest to Pope Gregory II., who answered him on November 22, 726.

Pope Gregory II., who so greatly furthered the conversion of Germany, ended a glorious pontificate in February 731. His successor, Gregory III., was chosen unanimously at the funeral. Boniface immediately sent him a deputation, and besought a succession of the favour which had attended him, and a continuance of all those good works which Gregory II. had given him instruction to execute. At the same time he informed the Pope of the work of conversion going on. We have four letters of the Pope which bear witness to his reply.[1] One is thus addressed:—"Gregory, servant of the servants of God, to our most reverend and holy brother Boniface, our colleague as bishop, sent by this holy Apostolic See to illuminate the nation of Germany, or the nations

[1] Mansi, xii. 277-282.

dwelling all about in the shadow of death, lying in error. Great was our congratulation, on reading the letter of your most holy brotherhood, to find that many had been turned by you, through the grace of our Lord Jesus Christ, from gentilehood and error to the knowledge of the true faith. And as we are taught by the divine instruction in parables that he to whom five talents were intrusted gained also other five, we applaud, with the whole Church, gain in such commerce. Therefore of right have we sent you the gift of the sacred pallium, that, receiving this, you may clothe yourself with the authority of blessed Peter the Apostle; and we order that, by God's will, you be ranked as one of the archbishops." He then enjoins that this be used either in saying mass or in consecrating a bishop, and that as numbers increase, " you be bound by rigour of the Apostolic See to ordain bishops, with religious care that the episcopal dignity do not become common." Another letter is addressed to all bishops, priests, and abbots, begging them to receive " our brother bishop Boniface, who was sent by our predecessor Gregory, the bishop of holy memory, to preach in the parts of Germany: let your love bestow aid upon him for the sake of Christ, acknowledging His promise given in those words, ' He who receives a prophet in the name of a prophet shall receive a prophet's reward, and he who receives a just man in the name of a just man shall receive a just man's reward.'" A third letter, addressed to all the chiefs and people of the provinces of Germany, reminds them that the Pope has renewed the charge given to Boniface, and begs them to receive in the Church's ministry the bishops and priests whom Boniface ordains by the apostolic authority committed to him. It charges them also to abstain from all heathen worship, diviners, soothsayers, sacrifices of the dead, auguries from groves or fountains, phylacteries, incantations, poisoners, ill-doers, and sacrilegious observances, such as take place in your regions. A fourth letter is addressed to the bishops of the provinces of Bavaria and Allemannia. Its purpose is that they should fittingly receive Boniface as representing the Apostolic See. "For it is fitting that you know that our brother and fellow-bishop Boniface, bearing our place, should be received with due honour in the name of Christ; that you should take up from him and worthily hold the ecclesiastical ministry with the Catholic faith, according to the custom and norm of the Holy Catholic and Apostolic Church of God, over which, by the pre-eminent grace of God, we preside, as by apostolical authority he has been marked out by us." "That wherever he charges you to meet for the celebration of councils, whether on the banks of the Danube or in the city of Augsburg, or wherever he think fit, you be found ready, in the name of Christ, that we may learn by his mandate of your meeting."

It is to be noted that Pope Gregory III. thus appointed Boniface archbishop and bestowed on him the pallium just at the same time, A.D. 732, that he raised Egbert, brother of the king of Northumbria, to whom Bede dedicated his History, to be Archbishop of York, thus restoring, after a hundred years' interval, the design which Gregory the Great had originally intended at the time of sending St. Augustine. The pallium of York is specially due first to the Pope who made Canterbury, and secondly to the Pope who made the primacy of Germany.[1] Thus Boniface, the Anglo-Saxon convert, who, with the pallium given at Rome, founded the Sees of German bishops in Bavaria and Allemannia, and himself became their primate in Mainz, was a Roman missionary. By his hand Rome constructed the hierarchy which made Germany one nation, and his see retained its primacy for more than a thousand years. So Rome sent the monk who became Archbishop of Canterbury by mission of the first Gregory, and, by his prevision, led the English hierarchy for nine hundred years.

It would seem that Boniface did not, for some years, exercise all the authority of founding sees thus given to him in 732. Perhaps the wars in which Charles Martel was engaged, and other incidents, caused him to delay this placing bishops where the number of Christians required them, until his third journey to Rome, in 738.[2] Boniface was then approaching sixty years of age; he had never personally met Pope Gregory III. He now came with a large train of clergy to consult the apostolic authority on all matters which concerned him as legate of the Holy See.

[1] Von Guss, p. 135.   [2] Hergenröther, i. 467.

The Pope received him with honour, and he stayed a longer time communicating his designs for organising the Franco-German Church, visiting also the holy places and the tombs of martyrs, and commending his own churches to their prayers.

When he left Rome in 739, he took with him Papal letters in which also the bishops of Bavaria and Allemannia were invited to meet him in a synod. Duke Odilo invited him to Bavaria, which he divided into four bishoprics—Salzburg and Freiting, and Regensburg and Passau. Then in Thuringia and Hesse he established, in 741, four bishoprics—Würzburg, Buraburg, Erfurt, and Eichstatt. For the first three he asked and obtained the confirmation of Pope Zacharias.

In one year, 741, the three great actors in human events were taken away—the second last emperor, Leo III., in June; Charles Martel, the Mayor of the Palace, who wielded the whole Frank power, in October; and in November, Pope Gregory III., whose wisdom and courage during ten years had maintained, without faltering, the unequal conflict with the wickedness and cruelty of the Byzantine. The Lombard King Luitprand was on the point of seizing Rome when Pope Zacharias was chosen and consecrated the same day, without waiting for the approval of either exarch or emperor. This was the third of the three great Popes who placed the utmost confidence in St. Boniface. He, as legate of the Holy See, worked for the unity of Germany by holding councils both in Germany and in France in concert with Pepin and Carlomann, who, as Mayors of the Palace in Austrasia and Neustria, had succeeded to the power of their father, Charles Martel, when he died Duke of the Franks. His military rule had not been favourable to Church order, and Boniface had to write to Pope Zacharias that for eighty years no national or provincial council could be held in the realm of the Franks. During this time it is doubtful whether even diocesan councils had been held in the Church's provinces of Mainz, Cologne, and Trier. In Bavaria, Boniface had already, in 740, worked in unity with the Duke Odilo, so that by direction of the Holy See he had held a council. Carlomann, in the first year of his government, had invited

Boniface to him, and besought him to hold a council in his kingdom.

We possess the letters which Boniface addressed to Pope Zacharias, and the answers which the Pope sent to them. They are full of instruction as to the terrible hazards which beset the Church as the kingdom of Christ, and human society itself at that time.

These are the words in which our countryman, Winfrid, the Anglo-Saxon of Devonshire, addresses at his accession the ninety-third Pope, who was a Greek by descent, but born in Calabria, a subject of the Eastern emperor, like nine other Popes preceding him from the accession of Pope Agatho. Zacharias, in the providence of God not known to Boniface when he thus wrote, was to be the last of the subject Popes, and to be succeeded by pontiff-kings.[1]

"We confess, O Lord and Father, that since we have heard by messengers how Gregory, pontiff of the Apostolic See, of venerable memory, the predecessor of your apostolate, was delivered from the bondage of the body, and departed to the Lord, we have not heard of greater joy and gladness, for which, with outstretched hands, we give God thanks, than that the most high Arbiter has granted your benignant Fatherhood to rule the system of canonical law and to direct the helm of the Apostolic See.[2] Therefore, as bowing our knees before your feet, we earnestly entreat, that like as we have been devoted servants and subject disciples of your predecessors, in behoof of St. Peter's authority, so we may merit to be servants and obedient subjects of your piety and tender rule of the canons. Thus we hope to preserve and spread the Catholic faith and the unity of the Roman Church, and to invite and incline to obedience to the Apostolic See whatever hearers and disciples God may give me in this my office of legate."

Next he declares to the Pope that he has founded three episcopal sees in Germany, of Würzburg, Buraburg, and Erfurt, which he begs to be confirmed by the authority of his apostolate. He proceeds:—

---

[1] Mansi, xii. 312.
[2] "Quod clementem paternitatem vestram altissimus arbiter canonica jura regere et apostolicæ sedis gubernacula tene e concessit."

X

"Be it likewise known to your Fatherhood that Carlomann, Duke of the Franks, sent for me, and besought me for that part of the kingdom of the Franks which is in his power to begin to collect a synod, and promised me, concerning his wish, to correct and amend somewhat of the Church's religion, which now, for a long time, that is, not less than sixty or seventy years, has been trodden under foot and scattered. If he have the will, by God's inspiration, to fulfil this, I need to have and to know the counsel and the command of your holy authority, that is, of the Apostolic See. For the Franks, as elders say, for more than eighty years have not held a synod nor had an archbishop, nor founded anywhere or renewed the canonical rights of the Church."

Then he proceeds to expose at length the ruinous and scandalous disorders which had infected sees far and wide, and if he is to meet and remedy these, which involve the acts of bishops, as well as of all orders inferior to them, he says, "Because I am known to be the servant and the legate of the Apostolic See, my word here and yours there must be one and the same." He asks that the authority given to him by Pope Gregory III., to name his own successor, may be repeated by Pope Zacharias, as will be seen presently to have been done. He goes on even to represent scandals which were said to have been seen at Rome, and which he entreats the Pope not to allow.

The Pope sent a detailed answer to this letter. It is addressed, "To our most reverend and holy brother Boniface, the Bishop Zacharias, servant of the servants of God."[1]

In the first place, he confirms the establishment of bishops in the three cities mentioned by Boniface. Next, "as to the request of Carlomann, our son, to you, to hold a synod in a city of his dominions, because all ecclesiastical rule or discipline has been utterly abolished in that province, which is too deplorable, because through a long time no synod of bishops[2] has been held, this we willingly grant, and order to take place. For neither what is priesthood,[2] nor what is done by those who call themselves priests,[2] is known."

As to the third point he writes, "When you sit in the

---

[1] Mansi, xii. 316.   [2] Sacerdotum, sacerdotium.

council, with Carlomann beside you, whatever may be the rank of the delinquents set before you, whatever ecclesiastical rule you see them to have exceeded, have the canons and statutes of the Fathers in your hands, and determined according to what you are taught by them."

As to his request to be allowed to appoint a successor in his lifetime, the Pope could only allow it when death appeared instant, and he might then send such an one to be ordained at Rome. "This we allow to no one else, which under stress of charity we have thought fit to grant you."

In another letter,[1] written after the council held by Boniface, the Pope says: "You have shown us how God has touched the hearts of our most excellent sons, Pepin and Carlomann, that by divine inspiration they strove to be your companions and aids in preaching;" and he sends the pallium for the three metropolitans at Rouen, Rheims, and Sens, whom Boniface had appointed. And in a third letter, in reply to the question whether Boniface had the right of preaching in Bavaria, which Pope Gregory III. had given him, Pope Zacharias writes: "We do not diminish but increase what our predecessor granted, and not only in Bavaria, but likewise in the whole of the Gauls; so long as the Divine Majesty continues your life the office of preaching as our legate is laid upon you; study to reform spiritually to the rule of rectitude anything that you find contrary to the Christian religion or the statutes of the canons."

Perhaps the authority which Pope Zacharias was then exercising in the Frank realm, and the confidence which he bestowed on Boniface as his legate, are most amply shown in the answer which at this time the Pope addressed to the questions submitted to him by Pepin, Mayor of the Palace. It is in the year 744; the Pope still cites the year of the reigning Eastern emperor, in sign of being his subject. The address runs: "To the most excellent and Christian lord, Pepin, Mayor of the Palace; to all the most beloved bishops of churches; to the religious abbots; and to all princes seated in the region of the Franks, who fear God: Zacharias, Bishop of the Holy Catholic and Apostolic Roman Church, sends greeting in the Lord. Grace and peace be ministered

[1] Mansi, xii. 322, 325.

unto you by God the Father Almighty, by our Lord Jesus Christ His only Son, and by the Holy Spirit."

The Pope says: "As our aforesaid son, Pepin, after consultation with you, has requested of Us to give an answer to all the heads mentioned, We have set forth in our answer what by God's inspiration We are able by apostolic authority to decree, according to what We hold as handed down from the holy fathers and sanctioned by authority of the sacred canons."

The Pope, in the twenty-seven headings which follow, treats of what concerns the ecclesiastical life in all ranks, from metropolitans downwards, in monks and nuns, in widows, in what concerns marriage, and the faults therein of which men or women are guilty. In these documents, bishops, priests, and deacons who were married before they received orders, according to the ancient rule, may not continue the married life, and if they do, are to be removed from ecclesiastical office. Other clerics are not so compelled, but the custom of each church to be observed.

The scrutiny of the Pope, therefore, as asked for by the Mayor of the Palace, with the bishops, abbots, and lay princes who joined in his request, touched the most secret springs of life. And when, a few years later, the Mayor of the Palace put before the Pope the solution of a question importing the utmost moment both to himself and to France, as to whether it was lawful to change the deputed authority of a great subject, who wielded, in fact, the whole power of the State, into the supreme authority of a sovereign who enjoyed the title without exercising the duty, it is plain that he went to one whose position was already acknowledged as equal to the weight which was put upon his judgment; while the connection of Pope Gregory III. with his father, Charles Martel, in sending him the keys of St. Peter's sepulchre, justified the application; and again the complete assent with which the judgment was accepted and acted upon bore witness to the need which called it forth. Both the answer to the questions in the document just quoted, and the decision which moved the magnates of France to take the Carlovingian instead of the Merovingian race for their ruler, attest the completeness of the Papal authority in Gaul before the Byzantine despotism then pressing on the Pope had been relinquished. In another letter to Boniface at this time[1] the Pope speaks of that intimate bond of charity by which, though absent in body, he is ever with him in spirit. He refers to the decisions which Pepin, as Mayor of the Palace, had requested him to send respecting the sacerdotal order and the salvation of souls. Though Boniface was already instructed as to what he had decreed, still he had complied with Pepin's request. He desired these "apostolic documents" to be read before the council of bishops in the presence of Boniface, to whose direction he commits the matters in question. "Act, therefore, most beloved brother, in the ministry committed to you; receiving from Almighty God the reward of your work, may you attain eternal life."

In a letter to a number of bishops,[2] among whom are those of Rouen, Spires, Würzburg, Meaux, Cologne, Strasburg, he says, "You have in our stead to confirm your affection, and work together with you for the Gospel of Christ, our most holy and reverent brother, Archbishop Boniface, legate of the Apostolic See."

Already, on the 21st April 741,[3] Boniface had held the first council of Germans, at which the new bishops of Würzburg, Buraburg, and Eichstatt attended, as well as the bishops of Cologne and Strasburg, and others. Great reforms were here enacted. Another council was held at Leptino, still further extending these reforming enactments. Boniface had, in agreement with Pepin, carried his activity also into Neustria, where the metropolitan authority had been almost extinguished, and provincial synods interrupted for eighty years. Boniface replaced the metropolitans at Rouen, Rheims, and Sens. Boniface, as legate of the Holy See, held in March 744 a great council at Soissons of twenty-three bishops, whose canons were also published as civil law. Of these the Apostle of the Germans sent a report to the Pope, and asked of him instruction and direction, besides their confirmation.[4]

---

[1] Ep. viii., Mansi, xii. 334.   [2] Ep. xi., Mansi, xii. 344.
[3] The facts following are drawn from Hergenröther, 467-469, with frequent translations.
[4] Hergenröther, p. 469, translated.

Boniface undertook nothing without the Papal Chair; he took counsel of it not only in important, but in proportionately slight matters. Herein his reverence for St. Peter's Chair, his sense of his own humility, the example of the Apostle of England, Augustine, worked upon him. Further, the difficulty of his position, the many who opposed him, not only with heathen errors, but with Arian also. The questions of the great archbishop to four different Popes touched on the most various subjects.

Boniface, by a resolution of the spiritual and civil powers together,[1] received in 746 Mainz as the seat of his metropolitan dignity instead of Cologne. This new metropolis, confirmed by the Pope in 748, had under it the bishops of Utrecht, Tongern, Cologne, Worms, Speier, Augsburg, Chur, Constance, Strasburg, Würzburg, Eichstatt, Buraburg, and Erfurt.

The poor monk who, thirty years before, quitted Friesland after fruitless labour, had as spiritual father won great populations for the gospel by his courage, his trust in God, his unwearied work. He was archbishop and papal legate, with extended powers over both Austrasia and Neustria. He had converted numberless heathen, organised the Church, abolished many abuses, restored the holding of councils in the Frank realm, and laid the foundation for morality and civilisation among the Germans. But all his life was one unbroken series of toils and struggles. Seducers of the people, teachers of false doctrine, criminal priests, jealous and ambitious bishops encompassed and hindered his path. Much which he had built up was cast down. That did not frighten him. He built up again what had been cast down. He overcame all obstacles by endurance. He restored union, and sought to secure firm structure to his foundations; to protect bishops from the robbing and mishandling of the worldly great, both by binding them closely together with the head of the Church and with the Frank kingdom. To that kingdom he gave fresh lustre by carrying out the decision, which only the authority of the Holy See enabled Pope Zacharias to give, when he pronounced that the race of Clovis, having held the crown of the Franks since 486,

---

[1] Hergenröther, p. 470, translated.

might in its utter degeneracy be made to yield to that better race which for more than a generation had borne its burden. So the Papal legate, who had been trusted by four Popes, and had conveyed to them all the sorrows and trials of the people which he was called to instruct, executed the mandate of the nobles of France, and crowned at Soissons in 752 Pepin, Mayor of the Palace, as Charles Martel his father, and Pepin d'Heristal his grandfather, had been. And Pepin, according to the ancestral ceremony in electing the king, was thrice carried on the royal shield around the ranks of his electors, and became what Pope Zacharias had declared that he might be, and what Clovis had been— King of the Franks.

Among all the deeds of Boniface in the thirty-seven years of his apostleship, from 718 to 755, I would note his devotion to the monastic order in both sexes. He chose them to make his labours faithful. At first he carried with him Anglo-Saxons, both monks and nuns, who followed him out of devotion, and placed themselves at his command. They served his schools, they attracted his converts, they taught his doctrine. He called to him successive troops of them from his own country; no less he drew them from those to whom he preached. He made Lioba, his English kinswoman, from her abbey at Wimburn, an abbess in Germany. So one of his happiest scholars[1] was Sturm, a noble youth from Bavaria, whom his parents had given to him for education. Abbot Wigbert of Fretzlar had formed him, and then he was made a priest. It was the wish of his heart to have a monastery of his own. Boniface encouraged this wish, for he considered monasteries as colonies on ground scarcely won, fortresses in newly converted districts, workshops and centres for new undertakings. He sent Sturm with two companions into the desert of Buchonia to find a suitable place for the desired monastery. Fulda was the result. After a long search, he found a spot of which Boniface approved. Sturm became abbot of the new house, which became to Boniface his favourite sojourn, where he could find refreshment in his many toils. The monks kept severely St. Benedict's rule. At Sturm's death in

[1] Hergenröther, i. 470, translated.

799, the monastery had four hundred members beside the novices. Fulda was the most effective place of education for the German clergy, and rivalled St. Gall and Reichenau in piety, knowledge, and art. Here was a rich seminary for future harvest.

Boniface did for St. Benedict in Germany at least as much as St. Wilfrid did in England. He made the children of the patriarch his brethren and his sisters, his companions and fellow-labourers in life and in death.

But the man who surrounded himself with men and women of Anglo-Saxon race in his work of preaching abroad did not forget his country at home. He who was legate over France bent the same watchful eyes over the course of the Church in England. Throughout the whole of his career he had kept a most constant intercourse with the prelates and monasteries in England, and in 746 he addressed a letter to Cuthbert, then Archbishop of Canterbury, in consequence of which that archbishop called a council at Cloveshoe. At this council he presided, and it was attended by all the bishops of England, and by Ethelbald, king of Mercia, with his chief dukes.[1] The Archbishop presiding brought before them "letters of the Pontiff, the Apostolic Lord, Zacharias, venerable in the whole world, which were read with great diligence, as by his apostolical authority he commanded, and were plainly recited first in Latin, then in our own tongue. In these that illustrious Pontiff warned familiarly the inhabitants of every rank and condition in this our British island, and lovingly entreated them; while he declared that the sentence of anathema would fall on those who despised what he said, and persisted in ill-doing. After reading the admonition contained in these words, the bishops, who are set by God over others to teach with authority, fell to mutual exhortation, and considered their own office of instructing others in the serving of God, as set forth in the bright mirror of the blessed Father Gregory's homilies and the canonical decrees of the holy fathers."

It is not possible for the archbishop, the bishops, and the king and nobles of a country to show a more complete

---

[1] See Mansi, xii. 395; and Lingard, i. 111.

ST. BONIFACE, APOSTLE OF GERMANY

recognition of the supreme authority of the Pope than did they who convened and attended this council. "They enacted thirty-two canons of discipline for the reform of the clerical and monastic bodies, the greater uniformity and regularity of the public worship, and the general encouragement of piety and devotion."[1]

In the letter which led to the convocation of this council, this is what an Archbishop of Mainz, in the middle of the eighth century, writes to an Archbishop of Canterbury. He is giving an account of a meeting of his suffragan bishops just held at Mainz. "There lies upon us a greater solicitude for churches, and care of their populations, than upon other bishops, on account of the palliums intrusted to us and received, while they are only charged with their own dioceses. Now in our synodical assembly we decreed and confessed that it was our will to maintain to the end of our life the Catholic faith and unity, and submission to the Roman Church; that it was our will to be subject to St. Peter and his vicar; to convoke a synod every year; that metropolitans should ask for their pallium from that see, and in all things desire canonically to follow the commands of Peter, that we may be numbered among the sheep of his charge. And we all agreed to that confession, and subscribed and sent it to the body of St. Peter, prince of the Apostles, which the clergy and Roman pontiff received with gratulation. We ordered that every year the decrees of the canons, and the rules of the Church, and the norm of the regular life should be read in synod and be received. We decreed that the metropolitan who had been exalted by the pallium should exhort the rest, admonish and inquire who is careful for the salvation of the people, or who a negligent servant of God. We forbade huntings, chasing with dogs in woods, and keeping hawks and falcons. We ordered that every year every presbyter should give in Lent an account of his ministry to his bishop, whether about the Catholic faith, or about baptism, or about the whole order of his ministry. We ordered that every year each bishop should carefully visit his diocese, confirm the people, teach the whole mass of them, inquire into and prohibit pagan

[1] Lingard, i. 112.

observances, diviners or soothsayers, auguries, phylacteries, incantations, or all Gentile filthiness. We interdicted the servants of God from wearing pompous dress, warlike habiliments, or arms. We ordered that it belongs to the metropolitan, as appointed in the canons, to investigate the conduct of the bishops subject to him, and that of their people. He is to advise the bishops, when they come from a synod, that by meeting in their own diocese the presbyters and abbots they make known and charge them to observe the precepts of the synod. And each bishop, if unable to correct or amend anything in his own diocese, should lay it in the synod for correction, before the archbishop and all openly, just as the Roman Church, when we were consecrated, bound us even by oath,[1] that if I should see bishops or people deviating from the law of God, and should be unable to correct them, I should always faithfully point them out to the Apostolic See and the Vicar of St. Peter for emendation. For thus, if I mistake not, all bishops are bound to make known to their metropolitan, and he to the Roman pontiff, anything for the correction of their people which is impossible for themselves. And so they will be free from the blood of lost souls."

This statement of St. Boniface, solemnly made to the Archbishop of Canterbury of his day, is more than a hundred years before the false Decretals appeared. It has been the fashion of some to attribute to them an increase of Papal authority which existed long before them. This letter testifies the anachronism which they have committed.

Boniface had no rest in his great activity as preacher of the faith, as founder of new churches and monasteries, as metropolitan of thirteen bishops, as restorer of the lapsed ecclesiastical order of things.[2] One thing especially tried him as his years increased—the number of disciples whom he had drawn from the cloisters of England, whom he would leave exposed to all the risk of exile and persecution among a half-barbarous people.[3] He wrote to Fulrad, Abbot of

---

[1] A reference to the episcopal oath, as given above.

[2] Hergenröther, p. 471, translated.

[3] Ozanam, ii. 212, drawn from the letters of St. Boniface to Fulrad, translated.

St. Denys, and counsellor of Pepin, in these terms:—"I conjure you, in the name of Christ, to accomplish the work which you have begun, that is, to salute in my name our glorious and amiable King Pepin, to thank him for all the charitable works which he has done for me, and to tell him that it seems probable to me and to my friends that my infirmities will soon put an end to my temporal life. Therefore supplicate our great king, in the name of Christ the Son of God, to kindly inform me, while I am still alive, what he intends to order for my disciples after me. For almost all are foreigners, and many are priests, and charged in many places with the serving of churches. Others lead the religious life in monasteries, and have been destined from their childhood to the teaching of letters. There are also old men who have long laboured with me. They all cause my disquietude, and I desire that after my death they may have the advice and protection of your piety, and be not scattered like sheep without a shepherd, and that the people who touch the pagan frontiers may not loose the law of Christ. I therefore earnestly pray you, if God will, and your clemency approve, to have instituted in this charge of people and churches my dear son and fellow-bishop, Lull; and I hope, if God will, that the priests will find in him their superior, the monks a doctor of the rule, and the Christian people a faithful preacher and pastor. I urge it specially because my priests on the frontier of the heathen lead a very poor life. They have bread, but they cannot find clothes, nor maintain themselves in these spots for the good of their people, if they have not advice and support, as I have endeavoured to give them. If the piety of Christ inspire you to consent to my prayer, please to inform me by my own messengers or by your letters, that so by your kindness I may rejoice, whether I live or die."

He obtained from Pope Stephen III. and King Pepin permission to cede his archbishopric to his beloved Anglo-Saxon disciple Lull, and gave to him the entire charge, especially to complete the Thuringian churches and to build a basilica at Fulda. "For me, I shall begin my journey, for the day of my departure is approaching. I desire to go, and nothing can turn me from it. Therefore, my son, prepare everything, and place in the chest of my books the shroud which shall cover my old body."[1] He took with him the Bishop Eoban of Utrecht, the priests Walter and Wintrig, the deacons Hamund, Skirbald, and Bosa, and the monks Waccar, Gundwaccar, Illesher, and Bathowulf, and all went together down the Rhine to Utrecht. After resting a while, they began to evangelise the country, and many thousand men, women, and children received baptism. One day, the 5th of June, the Archbishop's tent had been planted near Dockum, on the banks of the Burda, separating Eastern from Western Friesland. The altar had been prepared, and the holy vessels for the sacrifice, for a great number had been called together to receive confirmation. After sunrise a rout of barbarians, armed with lance and shield, suddenly broke into the plain and fell on the camp. They had sworn together to kill the enemy of their gods. The servants seized their arms and prepared to defend their masters. But the Archbishop in the first tumult of the attack came out of the tent surrounded by his clergy, carrying the reliques, which never left him. "Give up the struggle, my children," he said; "remember that the Scripture teaches us to return good for evil. For this day is what I have long desired, and the hour of our deliverance is come. Be strong in the Lord; hope in Him, and He will save your souls." Then, turning to the priests, deacons, and inferior clergy, he said, "Brethren, be firm, and fear not those who can do nothing to the soul, but rejoice in God, who prepares you a dwelling in the city of the angels. Regret not the vain joys of the world, but pass boldly this short passage of death, which leads you to an eternal kingdom." Then the furious band fell on them and slaughtered them; and rushing into the tents, found nothing but reliques, books, and wine kept for the holy sacrifice. With so little to pillage, they turned to slaughter each other.

The body of St. Boniface was found; beside him was a book mutilated and stained with blood, which seemed to have fallen from his hands. It contained several short works of the fathers, among them the writing of St. Ambrose on the Blessing of Death.

---

[1] Ozanam, ii. 215, from Willibald: De Passione Sancti Bonifacii.

CHAPTER IX

THE HOLY SEE FROM ATTILA TO CHARLEMAGNE

> "Rise, then, thou chief of Empires and the last,
>   Later there can be none;
> Rise, *first* of Empires, since the whole world's Past
>   In thee lives on.
> Ride forth, God's warrior, armed with God's command
> To chase the great Brand-wielder with the brand
> To the Asian deserts back and wastes of burning sand."
> —AUBREY DE VERE.

LET us go back a moment to that passage in history to which I am scarcely able to cite an equal in human things, that meeting between Attila, the scourge of God, at the head of his destroying hosts, and St. Leo the Great, attended by a few priests, and coming to stop his advancing course.

The declared purpose of Attila was to descend upon Rome and sweep it from the earth with the Mongol besom of erasement. We know not what passed; we know only what ensued. The conqueror, who had ravaged vast countries without mercy, and looked upon the disappearance of Rome before him as the seal of universal triumph, acknowledged Leo to be the messenger of the God whose scourge he entitled himself. He withdrew his army and retired away, and left Rome, which had no army to defend it, unassailed. And Leo returned, and forthwith received the official request of the fourth General Council, that of Chalcedon, to confirm it; and the entreaty of the Eastern Emperor Marcian, with that of his wife, the virgin-saint Pulcheria, grand-daughter of the great Theodosius, and sole heiress of his spirit, to the same effect. And he complied with this request of the Council on the one hand, and of the emperor on the other, by ratifying its doctrinal decrees, while he rejected, together with other canons, that canon for the exaltation of the See of Constantinople which his legates had not approved. He had in former years, on the annual festival of St. Peter and St. Paul, proclaimed to the assembled bishops of Italy how Rome, under the guidance of the Apostles Peter and Paul, "from the mistress of error became the instructress of truth, being made by the sacred See of St. Peter the head of the world, as a holy nation, a chosen people, a priestly and a royal city, and having a rule wider through a divine religion than through an earthly domination." For this city he had gone as ambassador to Attila, and saved it by his word and the dignity of his person from immediate and utter destruction. Returning to it, the Church in her great Council, and the emperor behind the Council, owned Leo to be all which he had said to the bishops of the West. The bishops of the East used to him words true in their application to the Pope, but true of him alone when they addressed him, "as intrusted with the Vine by the Saviour Himself." Yet even this was not all; he was to see the Western emperor perish by the result of his own infamous crime, and the empress, whom he had sacrificed, call from Carthage to avenge her own wrong an army of Vandal spoilers led by the worst of Arian pirates. Once again his single unarmed presence saved his city from burning.

Pope Leo before Attila, and again before Genseric, proclaims the fall of the Roman empire in the West, as the homage of the council proclaims the full truth of all his doctrine. Rome ceases for ever to be the imperial city, but begins to be the spiritual instead of the secular capital. The life of which he had spoken to the bishops at their yearly meeting on St. Peter's Day from that time forth generated the city which out of its material ruins produced the spiritual empire.

In these events we see the universal pastorship of St. Peter accepted by the whole Church, and that pastorship acknowledged to reside in St. Leo, as the successor of the whole line of Roman bishops from St. Peter to himself. And further, the preservation of the city of Rome from destruction by the conquering Attila through the action of St. Leo in meeting him and turning him back; and after three years another conqueror in actual possession of Rome, submitting to similar action on the part of St. Leo so far as to limit himself and his invading army to the plunder of the city, refraining from the lives of the inhabitants. The situation thus created is at once the end of the Western empire, the dethronement of Rome as its civil capital, but the full acknowledgment of its bishop as the head of the whole episcopate, as what the degenerate grandson of Theodosius, while still Western emperor, termed him, "chief of the episcopal coronet," encircling the earth—*principem episcopalis coronæ*.

Such, then, was "the new world in which the Pope stood from the year 455, and he stood in it for three hundred years."[1] From that time Rome existed only because St. Leo had twice saved it. Through the three hundred years it continued to exist only because it was the See of St. Peter's Primacy. The particular act which we are now contemplating is "the creation of a body of States whose centre of union and belief was the See of Peter. That is the creation of Christendom proper."

Let us consider first the position of St. Leo when Genseric had left the spoiled and plundered Rome, carrying off with him the miserable Eudoxia and her captive daughters, the elder of them forced at once to espouse the Arian Vandal Hunserich. Leo survived about five years, in which he beheld the appointment and extinction of two phantom emperors, Avitus and Majorian. St. Leo outlived Majorian for three months. It was the fourth Western emperor whom he had seen murdered in six years and a half. He left Ricimer, half a Sueve and half a Visigoth, in possession of Rome. The twelve hundred years of victory which Roman tradition had assigned to Romulus and Remus were completed. He had seen Stilicho and Aetius in turn assassinated by the son and the grandson of the great Theodosius for saving the empire; and in Ricimer began the domination of foreign soldiers of fortune, various in their native tribes, but all Arians in misbelief.

Thus St. Leo closed the old world, which he had set forth to the bishops who met his call on St. Peter's Day from all parts of Italy. The new world which he opened, in the name of the two Apostles, the patrons of the Rome which

[1] Vol. vi. p. 54.

he had so celebrated, lay in the hands of Arian predominance. The emperor of the West was pronounced by the Roman Senate, at the bidding of Odoacer, to be extinct; his imperial insignia were carried to Zeno at Constantinople, and Zeno, somewhat later, despatched Theodoric to take possession with his Ostrogoths of Italy, that he might be turned aside from the Byzantium which Constantine had founded for the head of his Christiam empire. Odoacer and Theodoric, equally Arians, had civil mastery over the Apostolic see which lasted fifty years. But even this does not express the whole subjection of the Apostolic See; for the Emperor Zeno, now sole master of the Roman name, had a bishop of great enterprise, whose character both ruled and inspired him, and who thought the subjection of Rome to Arian masters, who were also Northern invaders, had brought about the time for Byzantium's bishop to acquire predominance, as the residence of the emperor over St. Peter's See, in infidel captivity. And so for thirty-six years, from A.D. 484 to A.D. 520, arose the Acacian Schism. The Bishop of Constantinople had behind him the Emperor Zeno; when he died, Anastasius succeeded, says the Greek document, to his wife and the empire. He reigned from 491 to 518, carrying out to the utmost the plans of Acacius. These two emperors made every attempt to overthrow the spiritual independence of the Church, both in the East and in the West. Thus five Popes, Felix, Gelasius,. Anastasius, Symmachus, and Hormisdas, are engaged at once with spiritual and civil enemies, with imperial schism striving to overthrow the old constitution of the Church, as established at the Council of Chalcedon, both in doctrine and government, and with Arian predominance, crowned in Theodoric, the ablest of the Northern invaders. No one can read with unprejudiced eyes the acknowledgment to Pope Hormisdas by the Eastern prelates and the emperor of all for which he and his four predecessors had been contending without wonder at the perseverance crowned with such a result. It was that the whole East, emperor and bishops, proclaimed that "the solidity of the Christian religion rested entire and perfect in the Apostolic See." [1]

[1]. Vol. v. p. 168.

That Arian predominance, which was, as it were, crowned in the person of Theodoric, was to fall with him; but its fall was preceded by violent acts. Theodoric, as king of Italy, required Pope John I., as his subject, to undertake an embassy to the Eastern emperor, Justin I. He went, being the first Pope who had visited Constantinople. He was received with the highest honour and many gifts, but returning, never escaped alive from the dungeon of Theodoric at Ravenna. The tyrant died shortly after the victim, but a Gothic rule followed for about ten years. A short-lived sovereign, the Gothic Theodatus, required his subject, Pope Agapetus, in the year 536, to go for him to Constantinople. He went, and did great things, deposing the heretical patriarch Anthimus, but he died there himself. And Justinian was the cause of a new state of things coming to pass. He began the Gothic war, and Belisarius, being his general and in possession of Rome, took upon him to depose the Pope Silverius and appoint Vigilius in his stead. And then began a dominion in which, for more than two hundred years, the Byzantine emperors became lords of Rome, not with that temporal sovereignty which the Theodosian house represented, but as lords of a conquered province and ruling a garrisoned city. The first-fruits of such a dominion were seen when Pope Vigilius was summoned by Justinian, as his subject, to Constantinople, as Theodoric had ordered Pope John I. and Theodatus Pope Agapetus to go thither. Vigilius was the third Pope so called to obey as a subject. He obeyed very unwillingly, and during eight years was treated with gross indignity by a monarch so great in his capacity of civil legislator as Justinian. Vigilius escaped at last, with the dignity of St. Peter's successor acknowledged and persecuted, to die on his way back to Rome.

But now a double tyranny from the time of Justinian is imposed by the Byzantine emperors on the Popes. At the end of the Gothic war the Exarchal viceroyalty is riveted on them. That chain is doubly linked. The civil subjection is complete. Not the Pope only, but Italy, is treated as a captive who has no rights; who has not even the feeble defence of being his master's property, but, as a distant province is treated as a scapegoat to save the lord from nearer and therefore more precious loss. Throughout these two hundred years, Byzantium, which had already turned the Goth upon Italy, saves itself from Northern invaders by suffering Italy to be plundered until the Caliphs of Mohammed are sent to work her resurrection. Yet this is only half the servitude under which the See of St. Peter works on enduringly. In all that time, the acknowledged civil subjection is made the instrument for attempting incessant attacks on the spiritual supremacy. By his hold on Vigilius as a subject, Justinian had kept him a captive in his hands; had impeded him in his rights with regard to the Fifth Council; had created fears in the bishops around him as to his freedom in spiritual action. After thirty years, his great and wise successor, Gregory, had need of the utmost exertion of all his authority to heal the schisms which the overbearing dominion of Justinian had scattered among disturbed bishops.

The lordship over Rome, which began under Belisarius in 536, and was completed by Narses in 553, lasted for more than two hundred years; giving the Eastern emperor the means of exercising a double tyranny over the Apostolic See—one tyranny which the Pope acknowledged, in that he was a civil subject in an absolute monarchy; the other that he was exposed to see his guardianship of the faith incessantly attacked by the struggle of an emperor to place the seat of spiritual power, like that of civil power, not in the city of Peter, but in the city of Constantine. At the beginning of the sixth century, Acacius, shortly before the bishop of Constantinople, and his four successors, had been excommunicated, and the solidity of the Christian religion declared to rest in the Apostolic See, yet at the end of that century St. Gregory found another bishop of Constantinople ready to assert that he was universal bishop, and to be made a patriarch by the law of Justinian, though Pope Gelasius had declared that the Roman, the Alexandrian, and the Antiochian Church alone possessed that dignity.[1] One after another Byzantine bishops are thrust forward by Byzantine emperors, first to obtain control over the bishops of Alexandria and Antioch, preceding them in age and rank,

[1] See vol. v. p. 115.

and then, with the authority so gained, to put themselves on equal rank with the See of Peter. The effort does not cease, and the means of using it in the Exarchal viceroyalty scarcely alter, down to the times of Leo III. and his son Constantine Kopronymus, when at last King Pepin, for the love of Peter, breaks the chain which had enfolded every Pope from the time of Simplicius under Odoacer to Pope Stephen III., and the Pope becomes sovereign in his own city where the Lombard Aistulph would have made him a subject to the successor of the first invader, Alboin.

Therefore St. Leo, from Attila and Genseric, began a new world, and it continued such in its identity of effort until Pope Leo III. had placed a greater than Theodoric, a nobler than Justinian, and a purer in belief than this succession of adventurers who had soiled the seat of Constantine and Theodosius, to be "Charles Augustus, crowned of God," first the example and then the teacher of Christian monarchy, whom "the chief of the episcopal coronet" chose to be his defender and advocate.

But from the time that Belisarius exercised the sway of a conqueror, and installed Vigilius to do the will of an empress at Rome, the whole line of Popes was subject to the strain of absent lords, who acknowledged their primacy while they sought every means afforded by their captive civil position to encumber its action. From the martyrdom of Pope Silverius in 540, to Pope Zacharias in 741, thirty-three Popes are counted, of whom no one but endured the enmity of the Byzantine sovereign. Besides the one design in which all these sovereigns were engaged, which was to set up their own bishop, as conveying to all Eastern bishops their will, the Pope was exposed to the perpetual interference of that Exarch whom St. Gregory so plaintively has described to us as his worst enemy. The Exarch usually plundered the Holy See at a vacancy; strove to interfere with the election; delayed its announcement at his pleasure. St. Gregory's own consecration followed six months after his election. That of Zacharias was the first set free from the degrading condition which the Northern invasion, after the removal of the Western emperor, had set upon the Holy See, and which Justinian and his successors used to the utmost and perpetuated. There are no less than four great battles which the Popes, thus fettered, underwent, and in which only the intrinsic virtue dwelling in St. Peter's See enabled them to prevail. There was the first battle, in which Acacius, being bishop of the city which was the imperial residence, strove, by the help of two successive emperors, Zeno and Anastasius, not only to make subject to himself the older Eastern patriarchates, but to make a captive Rome lose her spiritual primacy. There was the shameless exhibition of bare power by which Justinian sought to enthral that one Pope who had unduly gained his great pre-eminence. There was the conflict against the Monothelite invasion, carried on for more than forty years of the seventh century, which caused the martyrdom of one Pope and the persecution of ten immediate successors of Pope Honorius, while four bishops of Constantinople aided to the utmost their emperor in his attempts; and in the eighth century there was another contest of more than forty years, in which two emperors, Leo and Kopronymus, tried to overthrow the whole tradition and settled habit of the Church, aided, as usual, by their Byzantine bishops. Had one of these thirty-three Popes failed in their duty, as one bishop of Constantinople failed after another, the Church would have yielded to the world, the salt have lost its savour, and been trampled under foot.

Let us pass for the present to the especial work done by one of these Popes at a time of the greatest stress, when he anticipated not the rise of a new world, but the foundering of the old, yet provided, as the father of monks, for the peril and the need of the coming age.

When Gregory, against his own will, and in spite of every effort, was placed in the See of Peter, that Northern inundation had raged for 150 years. Since Leo's time Rome had become a city of ruins, in which he was to keep guard day and night against the ever-ready Lombard, aided by the treacherous Exarch. Yet amid plague and inundation the patrimony of the Church in Gregory's hands never ceased. We know, by the aid of his existing letters, kept with greater success than those of any Pope before him, how his unwearied eyes travelled over the whole earth, discovering and righting every wrong. From him we have learnt in their fullest detail the deeds of his own Roman Benedict. And perhaps of all his acts the dearest and most precious to posterity is that dedication of his father's house to the rule of Benedict, and that sending forth forty monks from it to traverse France, and present themselves before a Saxon king to announce the Gospel. It was a hundred years since Clovis had accepted the Christian faith, and, amid numberless crimes and scandals, his race of Franks had been faithful to that one thing. But from end to end of that land the very noblest of the Teuton race, both men and women, had, in the midst of penance, poverty, and solitude, raised in deserts, forests, and wilds those homes of Benedict and Columban which ended in creating a new France. And while this vast and wide conversion was proceeding, Gregory sent his missionaries into a yet more savage land. It is precisely the period which includes the first and second Gregory, that is, the years from 590 to 731, wherein the vast number of religious houses arises in France. The man who, above all others of his time, fosters and encourages the spirit of Benedict, is the Pope Gregory. The act of his which proclaimed most sensibly to all the world the value which he assigned to the monastic spirit is the mission which he gave to St. Augustine, and which he called upon the Gallic bishops and the civil rulers, especially the famous Queen Brunehaut, to further to the utmost of their power.

When Augustine the monk and his brethren, with the figure of our Lord borne at their head, appeared before the Saxon Ethelbert, surrounded by his thanes and barons, the two powers, which for four hundred years contested the possession of the new Europe yet to be created, were in visible presence before each other. Two lives struggled for mastery—the life of Odin and the life of Christ. That of Odin had been in full action for centuries, since the first father of the Asars had left the precincts of the Eastern sea, and carried those who followed him to the fastnesses of their Saxon land. In the hundred and fifty years since Hengist and Horsa had driven their pirate boats into Roman soil in England, the Christian Church had retired before them, fleeing for refuge into the Welsh mountains and the wilds of Strathclyde. The last bishops, those of London and York, had left their few remaining people, and a vague belief in mountains, streams, and forests, peopled with vague and uncertain fairy or diabolic forms, dwelt in the legends which Odin brought with him. Their future was the place where human blood, shed with bravery but without mercy, gained an entrance for the slaughtered warrior. The thanes and barons by the side of Ethelbert were faithful to his person; they heard his purposes and gave him their counsels. The land of Britain they had divided into at least seven domains, continually changing in extent, encroaching on each other or retiring with incessant slaughter. In each of these they gave a sort of royal homage to such as, like Ethelbert himself, were descended from Odin, and made a sort of royal family, forming in each generation alliances with each other, and selecting one of these chiefs to be for his life Bretwalda of the Saxon confederation. They cherished with fidelity certain hereditary principles and customs which they had brought with them from the North. In accordance with these, they were freemen, and even self-governed, so far as having a king and obeying him; they were also consulted by him, and as he was *royal*, so were they *noble*. Their marriage was that of one man with one woman, an original mark of descending tradition, in which they were nearer to inherited custom than the Greeks and Romans of their day. These indeed regarded themselves civilised, while the others were but savages. But the children of Odin were in this respect what Odin had been, whereas the children of Theseus and Romulus were in rapid descent from that comparative purity which indicated their nobler origin. The companions, then, of Ethelbert, in their hundred and fifty years of English sojourn, had vigorous elements of civil life stirring in them —monarchy, free government, mutual fidelity, courage, and fearlessness; perhaps even the expectation of a vague futurity; a sense also of justice and right, but yielding perpetually to force. Before them shone in their presence, borne by unarmed men, the figure of the Saviour of the world, the Virgin-born, the God who preached from the Cross. The demeanour of that Saxon chief who then gazed on the bearers to him of a new faith was one not often surpassed in history. He considered their words; he watched their actions; he observed the habits of their life from day to day. He said that the words they told him were opposed to what he had heard all his life; that he must think over them, and would finally judge of them as they appeared to him. And the result was that he accepted their faith, was baptized by them, left his people free to embrace or to reject what they said, and at the ensuing Christmas witnessed ten thousand of his people becoming Christian like himself.

This is what Pope Gregory has himself recorded in letters still remaining. From that time forth the land whence the Christian Church, having existed with its full ministry for, say, three hundred years, and been compelled to depart, saw the Anglo-Saxon race, which had compelled that departure, resume the full Christian faith; saw monks spring from those monks; bishops gradually partitioning their spiritual charge among the seven kingdoms; raising in them monasteries and nunneries; ruling their clergy according to the discipline of monks; forbidding a woman to live in the houses of mass-priests; and raising, finally, in each parish a church, where the Christian worship was practised seven times a day. This was, in brief, the result of that venture whereby, in the concluding years of the sixth century, Pope Gregory, watching daily for thirty years over his own life and the lives of his people against the heathen Lombards when they broke into Italy, despatched from his father's house, which he had made a monastery, the mansion on the Cœlian Hill, a troop of forty monks to traverse France, and plant the Gospel once more in a Britain which from Christian had become heathen.

Thirty years later we have brought before us a conversion repeating, as it were, that of Ethelbert, in the character both of the chief and of his companions. A valiant man had risen of the race of Odin to be king in the extreme north of England. No man of such might had acquired so large a dominion. As yet he and all his people were pagan. At that point of time King Edwin sought an alliance with Ethelbert's son, the king of Kent. Eadbald had at first disregarded all Christian precept, and married Ethelbert's second and young wife after his father's death. But he had become a Christian penitent and fervent in faith, and he gave the hand of his sister, Ethelburga, to the Northumbrian king on condition that she was attended in her new home by a bishop with his household, and enjoyed full liberty to practise her religion. Edwin even promised that he would accept the religion of Ethelburga if, upon inquiry with his Witan, he found it the more worthy of God.

The princess came, and was to Edwin what her mother, Bertha, had been to Ethelbert. And long spiritual conflicts ensued between the king and Paulinus, the bishop, one of the forty Roman monks. And the fifth Pope from St. Gregory, Boniface V., wrote to King Edwin conjuring him from the order of the world to accept the Creator of all things and to cast away his idols. King Edwin was given to solitary thought and long reflection. A king of the south, a king of Wessex, had sent a messenger to him, who was conversing with him, and sought to assassinate him with a poisoned dagger upon Easter Day. He was saved by the devotion of a guard, who interposed his body and was slain.

In one of those conversations which Paulinus held with the king, seeing Edwin's hesitation, he followed a divine impulse, laid his hand on the king's head, and asked him if he acknowledged that sign. The result was that the king had again an earnest conference with his thanes, and afterwards with them solemnly accepted the Christian faith, and was baptized by Paulinus at York in the newly-built church of St. Peter. That was the begining of York Minster.

The renunciation of Odin and the acceptance of Christ was then as marked in the case of Edwin and his thanes as of Ethelbert and his thanes. And the daughter whom Ethelburga presented to her husband was to be that famous Eanfleda who in after years came back to be queen of Northumbria, made her husband, from one once a murderer of his friend, a Catholic Bretwalda, and who nurtured St. Wilfrid, sending him first to the monastery of Lindisfarne, and afterwards to learn all the teaching of St. Peter at Rome. So three chosen women, Bertha, and her daughter

Ethelburga, and her grand-daughter Eanfleda, appear in the history of England, the first-fruits of those noble women who brought the Christian faith to the land which had become heathen.

But there are two others also, so singularly great and good, and passing out of heathenism straight into the deeds of heroes and the crown of martyrs, that I cannot pass them silently in this connection. What English pulse should not beat higher at the thought of Oswald and of Oswin, as I have already recorded them? The standard of the Cross, which Oswald reared with his own hands when he came into the North from Iona, became a tree of blessing for nine hundred years, until desecrated by the crimes of the wife-murderer; and the blood of Oswin, shed by a cousin, had virtue, through the penance of Eanfleda, to become a robe of expiation, in which her husband, Oswy, gains from the successor of St. Peter an Eastern monk as Archbishop of Canterbury, to join the north and south of England in the completion of St. Augustine's work.

But how strong and decided was the choice of these men, how fully they measured the interval between Christ and Odin, we see by the very large part which the monastic spirit and life bore in the whole conversion of the land. It is as marked in the three monk-bishops, Aidan, Finan, and Colman, as in Augustine's original band. Every minister whom they drew around them, whether in the race which they brought from Iona, or in those whom they gathered from the people to whom they were preaching, were monks, just as the bishops who came from Canterbury lived with their clergy as monks. Pope Sergius saved them from accepting the degradation attempted in the Dome-hall of the palace of Constantinople by Justinian II., the fourth descendant of Heraclius. The Anglo-Saxon clergy were not served by wives; the Anglo-Saxon land was converted by monks and nuns.

Moreover, it was so converted precisely at the time when the infamous life with wives and concubines of Mohammed, in the ten years of his professed prophetical office, was followed by the equally ignominious lives of the Caliphs, who really set up his empire. They followed with peculiar hatred and laboured destruction religious houses, both male and female, in the East, exactly in those seventy years when the children of St. Benedict and St. Columban were planting them in the West. St. Gregory had died twenty years before the first Saracen pestilence had been breathed on the world. Mohammed was then the faithful servant and agent of his wife, but Gregory had in three things given an impulse to the monastic race which it had not before received. First, he had in his own person accepted and practised it; secondly, he had sent out a mission for the conversion of a nation which was intrusted to it; thirdly, he had in his Roman council, as Pope, passed decrees establishing the rules which should be observed by bishops in their dealing with monasteries and convents. In the hundred and fifty years which had passed from St. Leo to St. Gregory, the monastic order had greatly increased; and from St. Benedict's time the rule had passed from the divergencies on minor points which had first prevailed, according to the experience of those who instituted any house, and the wise moderation of St. Benedict had tended to prevail everywhere in the West. The veneration of so great a Pope as Gregory for the Roman noble who had witnessed all the sufferings of Italy in the Gothic war had greatly encouraged the propagation of his houses. He who wrought a new world while he was despairing of the old, visibly breaking up, had unconsciously to himself prepared a race whose energy, courage, and devotion were to lay the deep and strong foundations of an Europe in process of formation. At the Council of Chalcedon religious houses were mainly under the rule of individual bishops; in the time of Gregory they had passed beyond the concern of particular dioceses. The mere spread of the Benedictine houses over France would require that an authority swaying the whole country should make arrangements for them in common which would tend to establish one rule. The further spread in England, and the great part they played in Ireland, would carry this still further. No man can tell exactly when all the houses which sprung, directly or indirectly, from St. Columban completely and singly received the Benedictine rule, but all without force, and by the final persuasion of the superior result accomplished by it, did so receive it. And no doubt the action of St. Gregory, which we have been noting, had a large part in this reception.

The venture, then, of Gregory first planted by his monastic mission the life of Christ in Britain instead of the life of Odin. That which was great and strong in their old life remained, but mercy, self-denial, and the Cross came upon them. The sisters of kings who were martyrs became virgins. King Oswy dedicated a newly-born daughter of his wife Eanfleda to God on the occasion of overcoming with a small force the heathen Saxon Penda, king of Mercia, who so long slaughtered the Christians, and from whom sprung so large a number of Christian converts. Elfleda, the daughter so dedicated, became the second Abbess of Whitby in succession to Hilda; and Werburga, fourth in descent from Ethelbert through Eadbald, Ercombert, and Ermenilda, became fourth Abbess of Ely, succeeding the three queens, Etheldreda of Northumbria, Sexburga of Kent, and Ermenilda of Mercia.

It is, then, in this seventh century that not only the religion but the realm of England grew up. The teaching of the monastic life furnished the standard upon which the whole fabric of government, whether civil or religious, was based. England was not a State before it was a Church, but the Christian faith was present at the birth of civil England. It preceded the State in other countries, took it up and moulded it here. It was the gift of Rome to it. Augustine came in the name of Rome. When he said that he was sent by Gregory to announce Christ, he named to those who had been outlaws and pirates themselves a great and venerable name. His first act was to take a long journey to the distant city of Arles in order to receive from its archbishop, by the direction of the Pope, that sacred office of bishop which was needed for the full exercise of his authority. His mission was not insular, but the outcome of a word which had already gathered many nations into one. The Saxons knew themselves to be of one race indeed, but of seven different divisions, which constantly waged war with each other. Whatever the religion they assumed was, it clearly was not national. They learnt from the very beginning the essential difference between Church and State, and, in fact, during the whole Saxon period of four hundred and fifty years down to William the Norman, the relation between Church and State was clear to the Anglo-Saxon mind. The solidity and entireness of the union between the Two Powers was never shaken. It sprung from the Gregorian conversion of England—was part itself of that conversion.

Gregory's first step was to create something which spoke of a State while it created a Church. He gave to Augustine the status of an archbishop. While his diocese only reached over a part of one small kingdom, he ordained that he should have twelve suffragan bishops, and even another metropolitan like himself, who, as soon as circumstances were ripe for such a development, should likewise have twelve suffragans, and each of these having the pallium from the body of St. Peter, should tend by their very appointment to the unity of a kingdom. That, indeed, was their work. In an incredibly short time, before the death of Archbishop Theodore, these bishops radiating from Canterbury penetrated into the Saxon kingdoms and drew them together. York, it so happened, was the last, yet St. Bede witnessed his own friend, the brother of the king, promoted to that office, and linking the south with the north.

From the beginning of the two converted countries, Ireland and England, the people, through the hierarchy formed by the Church, rise to the highest office, and are mated on equal terms with the noblest born in their civil rank, and sit with them in consultation on affairs of state. Thus Wilfrid and Bennet Biscop are nobles, high in favour with their sovereigns, before, by the permission of their sovereigns, they embrace the monastic state. That everywhere is the action of St. Gregory's Church. It was one of those pregnant actions out of which he drew the still shapeless Europe.

Herein Parliaments have their origin. Episcopal councils lead to National Chambers. The congress at Whitby is an anticipation of Parliaments; bishops become peers by their landed possessions held directly of the Crown, while from the beginning they retain their full ecclesiastical position. The concurrence of the Two Powers marks the whole Saxon period. As the king and his thanes were together in the case of Ethelbert and of Edwin and of Oswy, so king, thanes, and bishops continued together. At his first council Archbishop Theodore marked the presence and required the attestation of each bishop, and in their spiritual work they voted alone, but the sovereign also assented to the work when done, as part of the civil law, while their enactment was accepted by the Pope as part of what the Church held throughout her whole domain. Pope Vitalian, who had sent Theodore, and that at the instance of Oswy, the Bretwalda, kept watch also over what he did as sent. This was the Church's work—that is, the work of the Roman See everywhere. The Spanish councils of Toledo bore witness to this in the sixth and seventh centuries; the capitularies of Charlemagne in the eighth. The English councils and courts in Anglo-Saxon legislation, and Alfred, the hero-king, was the most loyal of Catholics in the restoration of his kingdom after the Danish ruins.

The empire in the East never admitted what we mean by a Parliament. The autonomy of the Church, so far as it existed legally from Constantine, A.D. 323, to the Emperor Leo, A.D. 474, was the remaining tradition and existing exercise of the Church's original position before Constantine, not the union of the ecclesiastical and secular chiefs, the *principes* spiritual and civil debating together things common to Church and State. The time of St. Gregory first witnesses, as his action produces, that in the West. The Eastern absolutism repudiated it always.

When the Christian faith came to the ancient civilisations of Syria, Egypt, Constantinople, and Rome, it was not so received into the inmost mind as it was in the monasteries which we have recorded as founded either in the vast region of France by the children of Benedict and Columban, or in the British island by Gregory's mission, reinforced by the monk-bishops from Iona. Herein lies a radical difference between the civil State which sprung up in England in the first century after A.D. 597, and the State which existed in Justinian's empire, A.D. 527–565. In the ten years A.D. 630–640, Palestine, Syria, Egypt, after being long trampled on by despotic power in Constantinople, surrendered their seven centuries of Christian faith. Antioch, Alexandria, and Jerusalem became chiefly Mohammedan. Twelve hundred years have passed in that most miserable captivity; the Saracenic ruin advanced on with portentous strides, and by the year 700 the strong walls of Constantine's city were the only great bulwark remaining against the yearly reiterated attack of those who denied the Christian faith altogether, and specially outraged Christian morality. They were repulsed by the help of the Greek fire rather than by Christian courage. But at that very time multitudes of Teuton men and women, by their voluntary acceptance of Benedictine life, saved France for the Christian faith, rejected and expelled the Arian misbelief. And in that same time Anglo-Saxon monks and nuns made Britain Christian and Catholic in heart and marrow, as the people of Heraclius and Justinian, and Constantine's contemporaries had never been. The conversion which he inaugurated left an ancient State in which the whole body politic had been formed and grown up in heathenism and idolatry; the conversion which Gregory had planned and begun, established on fixed principles, and which his successors carefully superintended, while Archbishop Theodore, sent direct from one of them, made it conterminous with England, took up a nation of pirates and freebooters and transformed society by making it Christian in its very roots. Augustine and Paulinus, Wilfrid and Cuthbert, Bennet Biscop, Willibrord, and Aldhelm, Beda and Boniface, were great agents in this. The number of kings, queens, and princesses of Odin's race who monachised shows how that new life had penetrated into the Saxon blood. Only we must remember that the Saxon conversion was but part of a vast movement. The great annalist of the Benedictine rule notes the extraordinary fertility of its second century, the importance and greatness of the work done by the monks, and that in reference to the Mohammedan aggression. It is time to note the effects, spiritual and civil, of the *Common Life*. The general assumption of this by the Northern invaders in France, and Spain, and Italy, and then in Britain, helped by the devoted Irish race, and lastly in Germany, from the time of the Saxon Boniface, I count to be the basis on which Europe has been built; and as Benedict the Roman was the great builder, so Gregory the Roman inspired and blessed the building.

I have now pursued the religious life in a course of historical sketches during four hundred years, from Antony, its patriarch, in the deserts of Egypt, to Boniface, legate and counsellor of the Roman See. And Boniface, the Anglo-Saxon, the Papal benediction stirring his Teuton nature within him during more than thirty years, carried everywhere the rule of St. Benedict in the border-land of Gaul and Germany. The life which was celebrated by St. Athanasius, the great champion of the Christian faith in the fourth century, and studied with careful attention, and then with zealous practice, by St. Basil and his bosom friend St. Gregory, has spread with a most wonderful development among the sons and daughters of Teuton race. They have first overthrown the Roman empire in Gaul and then embraced its religion. I wish to search as closely as I am able into the nature of a fact which this series of events has forced upon my mind. The fact which I search into is, that the monastic life constitutes a society more deeply Christianised than that which subsisted in Constantine's empire.

Athanasius, after five banishments and many hairbreadth escapes of his life from the persecution of the Roman emperors Constantius and Valens, bestowed upon the West the Life of Antony, whom during many years he had known, loved, and venerated. His work stirred a multitude of minds, kindling intensely their spirit, as did, somewhat later, the Confessions of St. Augustine, who, indeed, was one of those awakened by it. But the life thus portrayed was then practised in one of the outlying provinces of the Roman empire. Its author thought it a marvel that a man who lived in a desert approached with difficulty could become known even before his death to Constantine and the emperors, his sons, and to many of their subjects. From that time forth, and through the exertions of the greatest saints, as well as the most renowned among them for their gift as preachers and writers, the life begun in Egypt was propagated in Palestine and Asia Minor and in the chief cities of the empire, first in the East, but gradually in the West. I have introduced St. Augustine and St. Jerome as marking its presence at Rome, and Pope Liberius as recording in St. Peter's the profession of the virginal life by the sister of St. Ambrose, and the praise which that Pope expressed for it. During the continuance of the empire the monastic life in both sexes was to be found widely spread. It formed, however, still numerically a small proportion of the population. As long as the fabric of Roman government and civilisation continued unimpaired, the growth went on of those who sought a retreat from the seduction of unchristian life in discipline, penance, and regular devotion. But in the time we are now traversing we witness quite a different state of things—different in that society itself is constructed on a new basis.

Let us take the seventh century, and a passage in it from one who has specially studied it.[1] The mission of the Irish in Austrasia was, above all, to extend and regularise monastic institutions. The example of Columban and his companions was a delight to bold spirits, formed a leading to the timid, and turned, we may say, in the same direction the whole effort of Christian society. The spirit of the solitaries at Luxeiul was gaining the world, and made itself felt in the Church and in the State. St. Elicius and St. Amandus do not think they have completed the conversion of Flanders unless they cover it with monasteries. Their disciples people the two abbeys of Ghent, those of Tournay, those of St. Ghislain and Marchiennes, of St. Tron and Lobes. The Carlovingian family of great civilisers marks itself already by the number of its foundations. The widow and daughters of Pepin of Landen, Ita, Begge, Gertrude, take the veil, form communities at Nivelles and Andane, and in order to instruct in singing psalms the virgins whom they assemble, call in more Irish masters. Later, Pepin of Heristal and Plectrude open to other Irish pilgrims St. Martin of Cologne, found in the same city St. Mary of the Capitol and Sustern in the diocese of Maestricht. In these institutions we find something else than the terror of the dying, or a great criminal who tries for the safety of his soul by the prayers of others,

---

[1] Ozanam, ii. 117-120, translated.

and particularly more than thousands of lives consumed in a cloister's inertness and the weariness of never-ending psalmody. We may trace there religious inspiration first of all, but also a design of wise policy. The abbeys of the seventh century, with their population of three or five hundred monks, were like so many fortresses whose walls stopped the incursions of unbelievers. They stationed themselves from the banks of the Somme to those of the Rhine, girdling Austrasia from the north, separating it from the heathen countries, and lastingly enclosing it in the extended frontier of Christianity. The abbeys were immovable colonies in the midst of a population otherwise transitory. Societies which did not die, did not abdicate like bishops, did not let themselves be carried away in the train of kings, and resisted better than they both fraud and violence; these societies, obedient, chaste, and laborious, astonished the barbarians, had a hold on them by benefits, and at length kept them fixed, which went far to civilise them.

Abbeys have been considered as schools of profane and sacred science; they were at the same time schools of industry and agriculture, which preserved in their workshops all the arts of antiquity, and were as obstinate as old Romans in pushing on the cultivation of deserts. With them also we see begin that innovation of Christian time, female education. After the cœnobitic city of Kildare, founded by St. Brigitt, where an abbess and a bishop governed together two great communities of monks and nuns, double monasteries had spread in Ireland, and later in Austrasia, where we find those of Nivelles, of Maubeuge, and those of Remiremont. Men and women lived there quite separate, but under one law. At Remiremont the abbot had the spiritual government; at Nivelles and at Maubeuge the abbess seems to have kept it. A discipline which suited the admirable purity of Irish manners would not be so well preserved among the Franks. But the female monasteries multiplied. The pastoral crosses of their abbesses found respect with the neighbouring lords. Their libraries became enriched with classical writings. Their nuns ranked with chroniclers and poets. Equality of minds, which the old wisdom had not pursued, was to reappear in monasteries,

z

and so find its way into families. These grave foundresses of the seventh century, who had only thought of educating a few hundred barbarous young women, began the education of the most chivalrous and polite people in the world.

The conversion of the Franks of Austrasia drew with it that of three peoples who fell under their dependence—of the Allemans, the Thuringians, and the Bavarians.

I have been for some time busied with two great events—the one, the conversion of Ireland by St. Patrick in the fifth century; the other, the conversion of England by St. Augustine, beginning at the end of the sixth, and extended to almost every part by St. Theodore, who died in 690. These are national conversions. In the former, a Celtic people, pagan from the earliest of its records, accepts the Christian faith; in the latter, a Teuton people, pagan likewise, and worshipping like the former the powers of nature, accepts the same faith. In both the acceptance is voluntary; in both, likewise, for the first time in Christian history, it is effected by monks and nuns. Not only has St. Patrick brought with him from Rome and from France the monastic institute, which he had witnessed in all its vigour, but he had fixed it in the hereditary Irish genius; it has filled vast monasteries with its offspring, and sent them to Scotland and England to draw the yet heathen people to their own life and faith. St. Augustine is a monk, leading a troop of monks, who come from the centre of Rome, with mission from the Pope himself; and when they take root, the Pope commands the archbishop, whom he names as primate in that newly acquired country, to live as monk with his clergy, carrying on the life which the Church had inherited from the Apostles at Jerusalem. Then the children of St. Patrick from their monastery of Iona listen to the invitation of an Anglo-Saxon convert to send him a monk-bishop to convert his people. For thirty years, three bishops, all monks, and using monks to convert the heathens to the faith which Patrick brought, join all the power of the monastic spirit with that same spirit which had lived on at Canterbury; and Rome completes her work by sending another monk from St. Paul's city of Tarsus to establish bishops who shall direct the whole land under the rule of Canterbury. And in that conversion of England Anglo-Saxon women take an active part. The daughters and sisters of princes are found to preside over convents; and the noblest of them all has created a name imperishable in history, as leaving the chief throne, which was then that of Northumbria, with the sanction of her bishop, to live a nun among her sisters, on the ground which a husband only in name had given as a bridal gift.

It is hard for the mind to realise the immense extent to which the monastic spirit was poured out in both sexes over wide regions. That great civil fabric which the Roman empire had reared was in St. Leo's time reduced to ruin. An Arian invader from the North requires the Roman Senate to declare a Western emperor needless. Another Arian invader from the East supplants him, and in the name of the Eastern emperor rules Italy and a great dominion besides with independent force. But his skill is impotent in the end to join the Roman mind with the Gothic arm. Rome herself passes by conquest under a delegated viceroyalty; and the Popes for more than two hundred years have to maintain themselves by the intrinsic power of their primacy. They fight a desperate battle against the Eastern tyranny, playing the champion to the Monothelite heresy. In the midst of this struggle, St. Benedict gathers in the Samnite mountains his rule of life. He sends a favourite disciple to the banks of the Loire with the measure of bread and of wine, out of which to produce a race which shall reject marriage and live on labour, prayer, and study. This was in the year 543. In the time of St. Boniface we are at the distance of two centuries, and we find that the life which St. Martin had already founded at Tours, and St. Honoratus had planted at Lerins, and St. Cæsarius at Arles, and others in Marseilles and elsewhere, had spread everywhere in Gaul. The race of Clovis, gaining France, but giving it no one State—by which we mean a realm free from division, with fixed and stable boundaries, and uniting a people within a country —was expiring in ignominy. The voice of Peter gave it a death-blow, and made a race sovereign which he had already raised to the patriciate of the Roman See, and called to be the defender of its primacy. But the greater marvel is that God has raised out of this conquering race of Franks men and women who, by incessant acts of freewill, have renounced their wealth as conquerors, and their free agency as subjects, for the life which St. Benedict introduced to them, and St. Columban widely propagated. It has gone from one, end of France to the other. It has vaulted from Rome to Ireland, and again from Rome to Britain; it has taken possession of these countries; and out of races which have been notorious for internecine cruelty among each other in their pagan state, a multitude have left their own land to win to the Christian faith those who were still pagans. Irish missionaries have left their country to convert Anglo-Saxons, and both Irish and Anglo-Saxons to convert Teutons, and they worked this conversion, not when those Teutons revelled in the richness of Roman civilisation, in such a life as the cultivated fourth century showed in so many consular or patrician homes, such as Paulinus and his wife retired from, but when the land was quaking in uncertainty. They who came to convert were in poverty and nakedness, in the life which did not live by human means, the life of Benedict in the Samnite mountains, the life which St. Ouen and his brethren chose instead of king's palaces. It was this life which enabled St. Boniface to work with Pepin and Carlomann in restoring the sees of their dominions from the terrible disorder into which they had fallen in the last two generations of the sluggard kings. Thus Trier, Cologne, and Mainz, recovered the position which they had held in the great unfallen Roman empire; and not that only, but the word of Pope Zacharias had joined to them the thirteen sees over which the province of the Anglo-Saxon primate Boniface extended. His pupil Sturm carried for him that life through the woods to Fulda, and no one of his eleven Anglo-Saxons failed him on the trial-day at Dockum; and Lioba, once a nun at Wimborne, after her long career as German abbess and her years of labour for him, was joined with him, as he wished, after the death of both, in her rest at Fulda. And Germany was made as Erin and England were made, and the three great daughters owned Rome for one mother.

Reviewing the time which passes from St. Gregory's entrance on the Roman See in 590 to the consummation of St. Boniface in his martyrdom of 755, what is the scene presented to us? One, I think, of which no other time presents a result so wonderful. We have the vast extent to which the monastic order has been embraced by men and women in the great region of what had been the Roman empire, and we have the vast extent to which the countries bordering on the southern coast of the Mediterranean Sea have ceased to be Christian; and have also, with the fiercest heat of intolerance, proclaimed their intention to destroy the Christian faith, and especially the monastic order within it. I wish to consider these two events in their bearing on each other.

Let us cast a glance upon this mortal duel which has been going on during thirteen centuries, the duel between the life of Nazareth as seen in Benedict, when, in the solitude of Subiaco, as images of his former social life at Rome came to tempt him, he threw himself into the thorns, and clasped with them the cross, and the life of Mohammed with his Egyptian slave, or with the wife of his adopted son, threatening with infamous captivity all whom he conquered.

Herein the seventh century surpasses the fourth and fifth. Pope Liberius accepted and blessed the sister of St. Ambrose in her profession of the virginal life before him in St. Peter's. Pope Gregory sent forth forty monks from the abbey which he had founded in his father's palace to convert a nation of pagans, the most cruel then known, for they had made a slaughter-house of a once Christian country. This marks the difference of the times. All Roman grandeur had perished in the vast domain at the centre of which Liberius spoke. But from the midst of those ruins another Pope saw the Common Life tacitly gathering its spiritual conquests. The monastery in which Benedict caused his rule to live was everywhere. The seventy-two instruments of good works which he drew up for its inhabitants fixed their minds upon the divine life of faith.

I will only cite the two first and the three last as a specimen. The first runs: "In the first place, to love the Lord God with all one's heart, all one's soul, and all one's strength." The second: "Then one's neighbour as oneself." The three last: "To pray for one's enemies in the love of Christ; to make peace with an adversary before the setting of the sun; and never to despair of God's mercy."[1] In the home which the abbot constructed for city and for desert alike, he assigned to every member his special work. No one was left idle or to intrude into the function of another. But the common property and business of all were the seventy-two instruments of good works. Every son and every daughter of the Northern invasion who accepted Benedict's measure of wine and measure of bread as the food of the body, accepted the seventy-two instruments of good works as the food of the soul.

The life which went on outside those monasteries was that of a wild hunting for the lords of the soil, and a scanty agriculture for those who worked as their vassals. All sorts of hardships and sufferings were inflicted by the one and endured by the other. But the monastery which supplied its own wants had first of all the worship of God for its daily work, and the care of its neighbour for its second thought. Cities had perished in abundance, and the fields once surrounding them lapsed into deserts. But of the new cities and towns which in lapse of time arose in France, three-eighths bore the names of monks, and the great forests learnt to become their choicest territories and most fruitful gardens of human food.

But the monastery, each of which worked this effect for its own neighbourhood, carried the missionary spirit everywhere. We know not to what degree the diocese of each bishop since the time of St. Leo had practically receded in actual extent, or how many parochial districts had lapsed before the progress of foreign inroad. That the destruction had been very great we have every reason to believe. It was in the dwelling together produced by the cœnobitic rule that all the great missionaries of whom we have spoken —Wilfrid, Bennet Biscop, Cuthbert, Aldhelm, Boniface—

[1] Rule, pp. 31-37.

looked for the propagation of the spirit to work the conversion of others—looked for the training of the missionary himself. Thus Wilfrid in his monastery at Ripon received Willibrord a helpless child, and after years of discipline and training sent him forth a trainer of others. Thus he followed the example of Wilfrid, preaching in Frisia. And Rome, by Wilfrid's hands, made him a bishop. So Boniface found him, and worked with him during three years, and was besought to join. But he rather went forth with an express and greater mission from Rome, and founded a host of monasteries and convents as the Legate of four successive Popes, and thus he becomes the chief of a great hierarchy for more than a thousand years.

Of the work in France, let us judge by these as the sample of a multitude of examples.

Bishop Ouen,[1] whose influence and concurrence had bestowed on the diocese of Rouen the two powerful abbeys of Fontenelle and Jumièges, is attached to Columban by a remembrance dating from his earliest years. The great Irish monk was everywhere marked by his love for children and the fatherly kindness he showed them. At the time of his exile, and during his journey from the court of the king of Neustria to that of the king of Austrasia, he had stopped at a castle situated on the Marne, belonging to a Frank lord, the father of three sons—Adon, Radon, and Dadon—two of them still very young. The mother brought them to the holy exile for his blessing. That blessing brought them happiness and ruled their life. All the three at first, like the whole youth of the Frank nobility, were sent to the king's court, that is to say, the court of Clotaire II., then of his son, Dagobert I. These two for a certain time reigned alone over the three Frank kingdoms. The eldest of the three brothers, Adon, was the first to break with the grandeurs and pleasures of secular life. He built on his inherited estate, upon a height looking down on the Marne, the monastery of Jouarre, which he put under the rule of Columban, and where he became monk himself. Almost at once, by the side of that first foundation, there sprung up another community of virgins, which was to

[1] Montalembert, ii. 586-596.

become much more illustrious, and be associated a thousand years later with the immortal memory of Bossuet.

Radon, the second of the brothers, who had become Dagobert's treasurer, followed his brother's example, and, like him, gave up his portion of his father's inheritance to found another monastery, also on the banks of the Marne, called after his name Reiul, the contraction of Radolium.

There was still the third, Dadon, afterwards called Ouen. He had become dearest of Dagobert's lieges, the chief in his confidence. He had even become his Guard of the Seal, with which, in the usage of the Frank kings, all edicts and acts of the public authority were sealed. He did not the less follow the example of his brothers, and that inspiration which Columban's blessing had breathed on their young hearts. He looked in the forests then encompassing Brie for a spot suitable for the foundation which he sought to create and endow. At last he found it near a torrent called Rebais, a little south of the sites chosen by his brothers. It was a clearance shown to him during three successive nights by a cloud shining in form of a cross. There he built a monastery, which kept the name of the torrent, though Ouen first gave it the name of Jerusalem, as a symbol of the fraternal peace and contemplative life which he meant to reign there. It was there he wished, like his brothers, to finish his life in retreat. But neither the king nor the other lieges would consent. He had to continue some time longer at the Merovingian court, until the day when he was chosen bishop, at the same time as his friend Eligius, by the unanimous consent of clergy and people.

He held through the whole province of Rouen a sort of sovereignty at once spiritual and temporal, for he had obtained a privilege from the king of Neustria, according to which no bishop, abbot, or count, or any other judge, could be put there without his consent. During the forty-three years of his pontificate he changed the face of his diocese by covering it with monastic foundations, one of which in Rouen itself has kept his name, being consecrated to art and history by that marvellous basilica, a monument at this present moment the most popular which Normandy contains.

But Ouen had not left his dear foundation of Rebais

without a head worthy to preside over its future. He would have it filled with the spirit of the great saint whose memory remained always so dear to him. So he brought from Luxeuil the monk who seemed to him best to personify the institution of Columban. This was Agilius, the son of that lord who had obtained from the king of Burgundy the gift of Luxeuil for the Irish missionary. Agilius, like Ouen and his brothers, had been presented when quite a child for the blessing of Columban in his father's dwelling, and then intrusted to the saint to be brought up in his monastery. Here he had taken the religious habit, and gained the affection and confidence of the whole community. While he was associated with the mission of Columban's successor with the heathen Warascians and Bavarians, his renown was great in all the country of Frank domination. Wherever he had passed, at Metz, or Langres, or Besançon, he had excited universal admiration by his eloquence and the miraculous cures due to his prayers. All the cities wanted him for their bishop, while the monks of Luxeuil looked upon him as their future abbot. It required a written order of Dagobert to make him come out of the monastery, which seemed his true birthplace, and bring him at first to Compiègne. Here he was received with great ceremony before all the court, and the government of the new abbey placed in his hands, with the consent of the bishops and the lieges assembled at the palace. Twelve monks of Luxeuil came in with him, and were soon joined by a great number of noble lords, as well of the royal train as of the neighbouring parts, so that Agilius counted eighty disciples, and among them the young Philibert, who was to carry the Columbanic tradition from Rebais to Jumièges. All together gave themselves up to the labour of clearing the soil and the duties of hospitality, with a zeal which made all the new monasteries so many colonies of agriculture, so many sure places of succour for travellers in those vast provinces of Gaul. Their work was to raise up these at last from that double ruin which Roman oppression and barbarian invasion had brought down on them.

Irish missionaries, then abundant in Gaul upon the track of Columban, traversing it to carry to Rome the homage of their burning devotion, willingly stopped at the gate of a monastery where they knew that they would meet a pupil and admirer of the great saint of their nation. Then Agilius gave them in abundance the good wine of the banks of the Marne, so that sometimes he exhausted the provisions of his house. A graceful story tells us his watchful charity in a still more attractive light. One winter evening the abbot, having spent his day in receiving guests of a higher rank, was passing through the different offices of the monastery. He had reached that part which received strangers, special for the reception of those in want, when he heard outside a feeble and plaintive voice, as of a man crying. Through the wicket of the door, in the evening dusk, he caught sight of a poor man, covered with sores, lying on the ground, and craving to be admitted. He turned to the monk who was by him, crying, "See, in the midst of other cares, we have neglected our first duty. Go quickly and get him something to eat." Then, as he had upon him all the keys of the house, which the porter brought him every evening after the stroke of compline, he opened the fold of the great door with the words, "Come, brother, we will do for thee all thou wantest." The leper's pains prevented him walking, so he took him on his shoulders, carried him in, and placed him on a seat by the fire. Then he went to get water and a towel to wash his hands, but when he came back the poor man had disappeared, leaving behind him a delicious fragrance, filling the whole house, as if all the aromatics of the East and all the flowers of spring had poured out their odours.

These sweet effusions of charity were blended under the rule and influence of Columban with the most vigorous virtues, as well in the female as the male sex. During that same journey from Neustria to Austrasia, the illustrious exile, before reaching the house of St. Ouen's father, had stopped with another family allied to this, then dwelling near Meaux. Its head was a powerful lord named Agneric, whose son Cagnoald had been from his boyhood a monk at Luxeuil, and accompanied the abbot in his banishment. Agneric held the dignity which is translated by the term "the king's guest," and his king was precisely that Theodebert to whom Columban was repairing. He received that illustrious banished man with joyous emotions, and would be his guide during the rest of his way. But before they set out he begged Columban to bless all his house, and on this occasion presented to him a quite little girl, only known to us under the name of Burgundofara, a name which indicates at once her high nobility and the Burgundian origin of the family, as meaning the noble baroness of Burgundy. The saint gave his blessing, but at the same time vowed her to the Lord. History does not mention if it was with the consent of her parents, but the noble young girl, when she reached marriageable age, thought herself bound by this engagement, and resolutely opposed the marriage which her father wished her to contract. She became sick and was near dying. At this moment the Abbot Eustasius, Columban's successor at Luxeuil, was coming back from Italy to give an account to Clotaire II. of the mission with which that king had charged him to his spiritual father, and passed by Agneric's villa. When he saw the young dying girl, he reproached the father with having broken the engagement taken to God by the saint whose blessing he had asked for. Agneric promised to leave his daughter to God if she were cured. Eustasius obtained the cure, but hardly had he gone away to Soissons than the father, disregarding his promise, wished afresh to force his daughter to the marriage she rejected. Then she escaped, and took refuge in the cathedral of St. Peter. Her father's people followed her with orders to tear her from the sanctuary and menaces to kill her. "You think, then," she said to them, "that I fear death. Try it on the pavement of this church. How happy should I be to give my life in so just a cause to Him who gave His own for me." She held out till the return of the Abbot Eustasius, who finally carried her off from her father, and obtained from him the grant of a domain whereon Burgundofara was able to found the monastery called after her name Faremoutier. Like the queen Radegonda, a century before, she added a community of religious organised by her brother. Her example drew many recruits among the wives and daughters of the Frank nobility, whom her cousins had gained in their own sex for their monasteries of Jouarre and Rebais. That corner of Brie thus became a sort of monastic province holding of Luxeuil. Burgundofara lived there forty years, observing faithfully the rule of Columban, and she was able to maintain it courageously against the perfidious suggestions of the false brother Agrestine. He came to try to draw her into the revolt against Eustasius and the traditions of their common master. "I will have," she told him, "none of thy novelties; and as to those from whom thou detractest, I know their virtues; I have received from them the teaching of salvation, and I know that their instructions have opened to many the gate of heaven. Depart hence at once and give up thy foolish notion."

Of her brothers, the elder, Cagnoald, became afterwards bishop of Laon, the younger bishop of Meaux. He gave up his patrimony to found monasteries to receive Anglo-Saxons, who, in their recent conversion, flocked to the Franks. Many of their daughters came to take the veil at Faremoutier. Those first-born of that great Christian family which was breaking out in Britain seem to have been specially received and formed in the communities on the banks of the Marne and the Seine; at Jouarre, Faremoutier, Andelys, and Challes. Burgundofara had quite a colony of Anglo-Saxons. There St. Hilda of Whitby wished to be. Bede says that her sister, Hereswida, queen of East Anglia, in that same convent submitting to regular discipline, was at this time expecting the eternal crown; Earcongotha, sister of the queen-abbess Ermenilda, and, like her, third in descent from Ethelbert, died abbess of Faremoutier in 700. Of her Bede says, "A child worthy of her parent (King Ercombert of Kent), a virgin of great virtues, serving the Lord in the monastery built by that most noble abbess Fara."[1]

We must here note a most signal and wonderful service which these monasteries, in both the sexes, conferred upon the world. By this seventh century the men and the women who had followed the example of the first Fathers of the Desert in so many provinces of the Roman empire, and now, in that great part of what had once been the

---

[1] Bede, iv. 25; iii. 8.

Roman empire, but had now little trace of orderly government left, had substituted free and self-chosen labour for labour servile and compelled. They worked in obedience to abbot or abbess, as those holding to them the place of Christ, with a willingness which the slave had never shown, and, in the nature of things, never could show. The destruction of agriculture in Italy had long been ascribed to the perpetual encroachment of slave labour. Thus *latifundia* had ruined the spirit of the early Romans, such as the ballads spoke of in the famous times when the consul, leading his citizens to battle, after his year of office held the plough in his own fields. In that famous scene depicted by St. Gregory, where the Gothic chief who had been bidden to travesty his commander fell detected before the sitting Benedict, he paid homage to that great transformer of labour who planted his house in the desert to meet every need of daily life for the tenants he collected in it, and taught them to exist when the single priest fled before the invader. In numberless instances the labour thus undertaken had transformed the outward state of the country, and the *latifundia*, after becoming woods and wilds in the slave-time, became the richest marvels of fruitfulness under the abbot's cross.

This was in the character of the labour itself; but what of the character of those who gave it? In the fourth century the princely mansions of the great Roman landlords scattered through the provinces contained a multitude of freedmen and freedwomen, too often concealing under even Christian names lives which rather presented the features of Roman civilisation than of Christian discipline. Now monks and nuns replaced the *libertini* and the *libertinæ*, who had been the instruments and victims of Rome's worst time under a Nero or a Domitian. In that way the terrible inundation from the North, after destroying the civilisation which Tacitus loved, and which commanded mankind under Trajan and Hadrian, led to the formation of a new society. The entirely wonderful extension of the monastic life led to the creation of so vast a number working under Benedictine conditions, that a new standard for a loftier human nature was erected in the countries wherein they rose. The house constructed by Fara, who was ready to die on the floor of the church rather than be compelled against her will to marry, was the fruitful beginning of other houses wherein the like spirit dwelt. The sister of that Etheldreda who raised the great house of Ely on the marriage dowry given by a husband only in name, followed in Sexburga, King Ercombert's widow; by him she had two daughters. One, Ermelinda, after helping to convert Mercia as its queen, became third Abbess of Ely; the other, Earcongotha, was herself Abbess of Faremoutier. The substitution of such inhabitants of monasteries for the *libertini* and *libertinæ* of Neronian times is the full accomplishment of monastic life, to which I attribute the springing up of a Christian Europe. A moral character in labourers never known before was by degrees spread everywhere.

Another result was that which more than anything humanised barbarism itself. It was not one host which in settled battle-array broke into France and Spain, and beat down all before it. It was a perpetual succession of small bands out of many various tribes. They came as raiders; the leaders were no better than the soldiers. Their object was plunder. One after another they came, bringing desolation each on a small sphere—ready to fight with others who came near and narrowed their bounds of depredation. How was a kingdom to come out of this? It was a Julius Cæsar who tamed Gaul, not a Clovis, or a Clotaire, or a Dagobert. But in the houses of Benedict or of Columban one spirit dwelt. They had endurance beyond that of soldiers in the field, but they had the love of brethren for those around them. Among their instruments were—to keep death daily before one's eyes; to keep guard at all times over the actions of one's life; to know for certain that God sees one everywhere. When houses from end to end of France lived on these rules, and lived for the one purpose of spreading such a faith, that cohesion by degrees replaced in the country the original fraction of the barbarian mind. The Teuton did not lose his dauntless spirit; he kept it, but implanted on it brotherly love. Barbarism in the land of Arminius never entirely expunged its original sin; never to this day has become one land; never accepted with full obedience and trust the *missi* of Charlemagne. Thus its greatest race failed at last with the most utter ruin, and the prince of poets was constrained to say of its flower when beheld in Paradise itself—

> "Quest' e la luce della gran Costanza,
> Che del secondo vento di Soave
> Generò il terzo e l'ultima possanza."
> —PAR. iii. 118.

But Benedict did not so fail as a third and last potentate; his five hundred years, with the blessing of St. Gregory, generated Europe; and the seventh century, with its numberless sorrows in the eighth, could produce a patricius who should rescue Rome, and breed an "Augustus, crowned of God," to bind together barbarism and lift its leaders into Christian monarchy.

And so it was that out of this long travail of three hundred years, showing no sign but of destruction and descent, from these undisciplined regardless raiders the forming of Christian nations began. In the midst of all these the See of Peter lived; the bishops who had to deal during many generations with Christian kings in name, rulers in fact, often worse than heathens to their wives and children, as St. Gregory of Tours sadly mourns, appealed continually to that see as the fountain of truth for the supernatural life, likewise as the seat of political knowledge and Roman experience and steadfastness in the civil domain. When Fara and those she fostered became nuns, when her brothers became monks and bishops, both learnt in the cloistered life, its settled habits, and obedience given to God, a temper and character unknown to them in their natural condition. By receiving the monastic they became capable of the civil Christian rule. The first Saxon century which I have been describing shows this. Oswy at the Whitby congress marked the transition from his first to his ultimate rule of action, and his thanes with him learnt the demeanour of Christian nobles. He took all that the monk-bishops of Iona had brought and taught of good when he said, on hearing the words of Wilfrid corroborated by his own Bishop Colman—the Saxon king was simple and straight-minded—" Do both of you agree," he said, " that these words were specially said to Peter, and the keys of the kingdom of heaven were given him by the Lord ? " They replied, " Yes, certainly." And he answered, " And I say unto you that this is that doorkeeper whom I will not contradict, but, so far as I have knowledge and strength, I desire in all things to obey his statutes."

The whole Saxon period is summed up in these words; the whole monarchy which Alfred at length ruled was the development of St. Gregory's Canterbury and Oswy's decision.

The race of Clovis had not put off the original turmoil of barbarism sufficiently to make France. They gave way to Mayors of the Palace who could produce a Charles Martel, a Pepin, and a Charlemagne, when the See of Peter had touched them, and out of the Church's defenders had created the Christian throne. The Christian throne came of that extreme misery in which Benedict saw the peasant crouching before the Goth, looked upon the intruder, and marked the limit of his time and power, and when Gregory took upon himself on the throne of Peter the life which Benedict had put into tangible shape, and out of it wrought a Christian kingdom in the land where barbarism had destroyed one. Thus he anticipated Mohammed's whirlwind of sensual force which was to sweep through the East. Having seven emperors in the last years of the seventh century and the first of the eighth, through seven revolutions all but destroys the Byzantine throne, until the rude hand of a soldier risen from the ranks terminates that convulsion at last in Leo III. And he, as soon as he was well established, attempted to take possession of the Church of God, as he had seized on Constantine's ensanguined seat. Those years from 685 to 715 proved that Justinian's empire could not longer nurture either subjects who respected lawful authority or monarchs who upheld Christian rule. Antioch, Alexandria, and Jerusalem, in their sudden fall and apostasy, showed that they were ripe for the sensual morals and the despotism of Mohammed. Against them the rule of St. Gregory, in the race trained and cultivated by Benedict, had formed an adequate and enduring rampart. The Mohammedan flood swept without pausing from Cæsarea, once and for centuries the Christian city of St. Basil—over the Egypt of the Desert Fathers, and over St. Augustine's Africa to the extreme west. But the monk of Tarsus tarrying at Rome, and sent so wonderfully by Pope Vitalian at the request of King Oswy, the Bretwalda, to fill the See of Canterbury, had during this very time of that flood's outpouring completed the conversion of a new race. That race had taken Christ for Odin, and maintained their family under the example of Nazareth. The Teuton as a Benedictine was in kept reserve against the Saracen voluptuary; the monastery in the West, over the great realms of Gaul to its utmost northern limit, and Britain to Edinburgh, left the harem to a degenerate East and the justice of a sovereign who reigned at Bagdad. The two forms of life showed themselves on one side in Charlemagne, on the other in Haroun Alraschid, while the diminished Byzantines kept half their debased empire between these two sovereigns utterly antagonistic. This momentous contrast came precisely from the hand of Rome, and was instant at the time of the great martyrdom of St. Boniface. That legate of four Popes had in the Pope's name crowned the new race in Pepin. Only three years after the new Primate of Christian Germany died a martyr's death. The spreading of monasteries had been for thirty years his special work. The monarch whom he crowned listened to the prayer of an exiled Pope, beat back the intrusive Lombard, and placed a free Pope in a free Rome. The very son whom that Pope had blessed as a youth and declared Patricius of Rome, like his father, Pepin, lived to complete the work of the regeneration of France, by subduing, after a war of thirty years, that stubborn Saxon power which had so long refused Christian conversion. Leo and Kopronymus, his son, after abusing to the utmost the imperial power, which only a new revolution, after many previous, had put in their hands, had to surrender the oppressed and mistreated Italy. The last and some of the most cruel and disgraceful deeds of Kopronymus were the calumnies with which he sought to lessen the monastic life among his own people. The Carlovingian race, on the contrary, protected and maintained everywhere the Benedictine rule which had gained France. It is in these houses men

2 A

and women were trained in obedience as subjects, and wisdom as counsellors to monarchs. The men who in their lives during long years carried out the seventy-two instruments of good works, when they dwelt in sufficient numbers throughout those sacred fortresses to form a leaven of the population, made that new France, and that new England, and that new Germany. In these Christian monarchies became possible, because, they were constructed from below with Christian subjects. This was the outcome of three hundred and fifty years from St. Leo the Great to Pope Leo III. This is why I have said that St. Leo stood, after confronting and repelling Attila, in a new time, which received at length its coronation when the greatest man of the Teuton race, who mounted on his knees the steps of St. Peter's, received also on his knees, in the greatest of Christian basilicas, the charge to bear the standard of Christ as emperor of the Romans, to reconstruct that empire which a degenerate senate at the bidding of an Arian condottiere declared to be unnecessary, but to reconstruct it according to the model of Christian polity and law, which the head of the Christian people delivered to him. For it was the word of Leo III. which made Charles, "the crowned of God," Augustus.

It was only fifteen years after the death of St. Leo, during which time Rome had been more cruelly sacked by Ricimer than in the same century by Alaric and by Genseric, that the condition of servitude was entered into under which the Popes laboured. I have said that in this condition of servitude they passed through four conflicts of extraordinary severity and peril, and passed through with a victory due only to the spiritual power with which God had invested them as vicars of Christ. Two of these conflicts I have delineated at length in a former volume, only pointing to them briefly at present. The first of these was concentrated in the Acacian Schism and the Arian predominance from 476 to 526. The second began immediately after on the exarchal viceroyalty. As to the duration of this, I have only traversed the first half, and the second half contains the more dangerous and extreme conflict. Herein the whole power and enmity of the Byzantine ruler is twice exerted against the See of Peter. Justinian created for his bishop a patriarchal throne instead of that bishopric of the royal residence which alone Pope Gelasius allowed, while he asserted the original Petrine triad of Rome, Alexandria, and Antioch to be alone in possession of patriarchal thrones. Justinian passed, and another of the many changes on that throne, as dangerous to monarchs as corrupting to bishops, ensued. Heraclius was called from the West to dethrone the monster Phocas, and, having accomplished it, prepared a race as tyrannical. His grandson Constans was able to filch a Pope from the Lateran church itself, judge him by the senate of Constantinople, and cause him to perish of hunger in the Crimea. It was this race of Heraclius which for forty-six years, from 636 to 680, strove to impose their Monothelite heresy on the Popes, and, if the Popes had yielded, upon the whole Church. It was the position of the Popes as subjects in a garrisoned provincial city which enabled Byzantine rulers to inflict on them this trial. And if the civil subjection had carried with it the spiritual supremacy, if one of the ten Popes immediately succeeding Pope Honorius had yielded or flinched, when four patriarchs of Constantinople enabled those emperors to do their work by supplying their false doctrine with language adequate to express it, Byzantium would have accomplished the destruction of the Christian name and faith. But the Popes won this third battle, and not one of them failed. And in that third battle was contained also the Saracenic life; the harem fought the monastery. And this side of the conflict touched England most sensibly. The second Justinian attacked not only the doctrine of St. Leo, which the Pope defended and maintained, not only the authority which all the East had acknowledged when it set its hand to the statement as a formulary of communion, that "in the Apostolic See the solidity of the Christian religion rests entire and perfect." Justinian II. aimed to make the Pope one of *his* five patriarchs, and wished him to sign his name as such *after* the emperor's, confirming a council, when his own father had expressly attributed that power of confirmation to the Pope alone. But one thing more that same Justinian II. attempted. He strove to make the clergy rescind their perpetual discipline down to that time of an unmarried celibate priesthood. The great Pope Sergius refused both one attempt and the other. It was to this Pope Sergius that the Anglo-Saxon kings came in pilgrimage. It was by this Pope Sergius that the Anglo-Saxon Church, as a province of the whole Western Church, carried on their original discipline, and did not allow the presence of a woman in a mass-priest's house. It was this Pope Sergius who, in thus acting, maintained the conversion of England as wrought by monks and nuns.

When, then, the Saracens had not only conquered the three Eastern patriarchs, and made the whole former Roman territory to the straits of Gibraltar their own, but also crossed over to Spain and vanquished the Christian government of the land, upon the Monothelite contest of dogma was jointed also the question whether the Christian or the Saracenic life should prevail. From the time of Mohammed's presumed prophetic call in 622, the era of his religion, the moral life which he had himself preached and practised worked for mastery. He largely imposed it on the East; he strove to make it prevail in the West. At the time of the martyrdom of St. Boniface in 755, St. Benedict's rule had obtained that it should not prevail in the West, and the vast multitude of Christian houses had gained the victory which St. Gregory's mission of Augustine had heralded. The Virgin Son of the Virgin Mother triumphed in the life which He had Himself instituted upon earth. That is the second victory by which the Popes made Christendom; their example, their precept, and their rule had, out of the Teutonic ancestral tradition, the rude but valiant mass which had known only Irminsoul, drawn the men with whom Godfrey won back Jerusalem, the women whose first-fruit was Etheldreda, whose perfect form was St. Teresa.

But the fourth battle of the captive Popes, the Popes who died as St. Martin or resisted as St. Sergius, remains to be mentioned. The Sixth Council, confirmed by St. Leo II. in 682, with an Eastern emperor and his patriarch who were both orthodox, seemed to have put down the Monothelite heresy as well as the imperial tyranny. Both arose again. The double contest in religion and in civil life reappeared, and that for the long period of fifty years. The eighth century began with such Christian discomfiture that the southern shore of the Midland Sea had become Mohammedan instead of Christian, and that the emperor in Constantine's city, instead of guarding the See of Peter, called Pope Constantine to visit it with the view of subjecting him. The time of the utmost trial had arrived: an Eastern revolution had sent to Rome the head of the tyrant Justinian II., and had lifted to its throne a race of despots more savage and erring than he had been, who was the great-great-grandson and the worst offspring of Heraclius. The emperor Leo III. complicated his struggle with the Saracen by attempting to add to his imperilled crown the government and to control the doctrine of the Christian Church. Then God raised up to His Church at the utmost need three Popes of extraordinary wisdom, resolution, and fortitude, the second and the third Gregory, and Zacharias. No contest can be imagined more unequal than that which the emperor Leo III., holding all military power among Christians in his hand, forced in the year 726 on Pope Gregory II. That contest, in all its double civil and religious aspect, lasted fifty years, from 726 to 776. Leo III. seized in all his empire the patrimonies with which St. Gregory the Great, and so many Popes succeeding him, had fed a desolated Rome. By his sole *ipse dixit* he severed ten provinces from their original attachment to the See of the Western patriarch, and added them to the patriarchate of his own bishop. Further, he sent a fleet and army which tried to destroy Ravenna, and issued his command to capture Rome and carry away the Pope. During twenty years three Popes preserved Italian allegiance to him and to his son. At last Pope Zacharias sanctioned the Mayor of the Palace to assume the name as well as to hold the power of the king of the Franks, and the mandate of the new king rescued Pope Stephen from vassalage to a Lombard Aistulph, and the See of St. Peter from an emperor Kopronymus, and broke for ever the exarchal viceroyalty. Byzantium forfeited the Italy on which she had so trampled for two hundred years, and her emperor ceased to wear that Western crown which, from the fatal era of 476, he had so abused. The Iconoclast contest, like the Monothelite, was at once of dogma against heresy and of right against tyranny. By it the mission which the great heart of St. Gregory had devised met with its full accomplishment. The Christian faith and the Christian life survived together in the Benedictine discipline, which closed at length the destruction of 350 years. And the work of St. Leo the Great, who repulsed Attila, was completed in his successor, St. Leo III., who crowned Charlemagne; and that clear assertion of the Divine Incarnation which the great letter of the former had set forth was established by the latter to be the heart and centre of the Christendom which his coronation of the great Western champion secured against the insurgent Mohammedan imposture of doctrine and degradation of morality.

Thus the new era, which the first Leo began in weakness and sorrow, which continued during 350 years of terrible destruction, an era without its equal in the convulsions brought upon civilised life, had a termination in the third Leo. From his act, which a Pope alone could execute, date five hundred years in which a new Europe, resting on the joint labour and union of religious and civil chieftains, sprung up, and was exhibited in a series of Catholic nations. Of these, St. Peter's See, as it had been the creator, so it was the guide and crown. No symbol of it, as regards at least its secular idea, could be more telling than when the figure of the great emperor, without in his imperial robes, and within them in his garb of sackcloth, was discovered sitting on his throne in the vault of his cathedral at Aix-la-Chapelle. Five hundred years of growth and decision which followed that wonderful act of Leo III. were followed by a second five hundred years, which have tried to impair, and even to dissolve, the union of civil government and of spiritual belief, and the world trembles at the thought that a convulsion may be in store for unbelief which may recall, or even surpass, that which attended the breaking up of the great empire.

Three lines of temporal government came into clear light by the act of St. Leo III. The first was that accomplished by the Christian Church, which created in Charlemagne a monarch on Christian principles, not a monarch of the Augustan line, ruling simply by strength of arm, and welding separate and rival nations together, as from Augustus to the great Theodosius, by superior discipline, equal law, and conquering arms, but a monarch who received the code of law so perfected, and the canons of the Church meeting every need of Christian life, from the hand of the Vicar of Christ, a monarch who both kept the Pope's faith and guaranteed his throne.

Over against him stood a monarch who ruled with absolute power as the heir and successor of a pretended prophet, whose realm had been constructed entirely on that pretence, who ruled because an angel had falsely been supposed to order him to take for his own a son-in-law's wife, and to take, not for wives, any captive in war who fell into his hands. Haroun Alraschid at Bagdad is the living example in the presence of Charlemagne of such a ruler, and his dealing with a trusted vizier the measure of his justice, and of the justice shown in the thousand years of the rule which succeeded him.

The third line of government which dated from that act of Leo III. is that sovereign of Constantine's Byzantine succession which, with divided and decimated empire, lived on yet for 650 years. They claimed to be Roman, but had nothing Roman save the pretension of the Roman eagle worked on the purple buskins decorating the feet of despotic power. The Christian faith which Constantine had found and respected, they had from the time of the Acacian Schism tampered with and strove to dominate. The boldness with which the emperor Leo III. had done this resulted in the loss of Italy and the deliverance of the Pope from civil tyranny. And the subsequent six centuries ended in a still greater overthrow, when the matchless city, which had so long resisted the Mohammedan assault, yielded at last, and became the prey of the government which had succeeded to the throne set up at Bagdad, and the principles of misgovernment and unbelief which have been its unfailing inheritance.

INDEX

AGATHO I., Pope, hears in council the appeal of St. Wilfrid, 274; decrees that he is Bishop of York, 275; requests Wilfrid to sit in his council at Rome, 275; grants him privileges for the monasteries of Ely and Peterborough, 277.

Aidan, the monk-bishop, sent from Iona, his daily work, 226; held the See of Northumbria sixteen years, 230; his character by Bede, 230; was the soul of Oswald's government from 635 to 642, 255.

Ambrose, St., his description of his sister's profession as a nun to Pope Liberius in St. Peter's, 83-85.

Antony, St., his life in the Desert of Egypt to his 105th year, described in detail by St. Athanasius in the year 365, 4-53.

Athanasius, St., publishes his Life of St. Antony, 55; is long with Pope Julius I. in refuge at Rome, 55; great effect of his Life of St. Antony, 57; bearing of his Life on the first appearance of the monks, 58.

Augustine, St., his testimony to the anchorites and cœnobites of his day, 60-63; as a priest he sets up a monastic house, 63; as a bishop, one of his own clergy, 64.

Augustine, St., a monk who came in the name of Rome, 347; the incidents of his conversion, 193-198; its character, 206.

BASIL, St., his account of the effects of the monks on himself, 66; his monastic life in Pontus, 67; his picture of monastic discipline, 67-70; what a monk's demeanour should be, 70-73; his encounter with the apostate Julian, 73.

Bede, St., his birth, labours, and life, 212-213; his last day, 211-212; Burke's estimate of him, 213; value of his History, 215-216; no such history of any other single nation existing, 221; his history of the five abbots, 280-285.

Biscop, St. Bennet, his life told by St. Bede, 280-285.

Boniface, St., his first appearance before Pope Gregory II., 305; who gives him a mission to convert Germans, 306-307; learns at Rome to be fortified by the Pope's word, 307; visits again Archbishop Willibrord at Utrecht, 308; visits Thuringia and Hesse, 308; consecrated a regionary bishop by Gregory II., 308-309; binds himself to the Pope by oath, 309; carries six letters of the Pope to Germany, 311; these letters, in A.D. 723, give him full authority in Germany, 314; is received by Charles Martell, 315; cuts down Thor's oak, 315; derives great help from monks and nuns in England, 316-317; becomes legate of Pope Gregory III., who bestows the pallium on him in A.D. 732, 319; establishes bishops in France and Germany under Pope Zacharias, 321; holds councils with the Duke Carlomann, 322; restores the Church in the French provinces with him and his brother Pepin, 323; receives Mainz as seat of his dignity as Metropolitan, 326; his devotion to the monastic order in both sexes, 327; his letter to Cuthbert, Archbishop of Canterbury, 328; which produces the Council of Cloveshoe, 328-329; his own great Council at Mainz, orders the Church of that day, 329; applies to King Pepin for his Anglo-Saxon fellow-workers, 330; whom he had consecrated as king in A.D. 752, 327; resigns his archbishopric to Lull, 331'; descends the Rhine, and is martyred on its banks, with all the Anglo-Saxons in his train, 332.

Boniface V., Pope, his letter to King Edwin, 218; and to Queen Ethelburga, 219.

Bossuet, what he says of the rule of St. Benedict, 132.

Burke, the state of Saxon Britain the worst of all, 204; his praise of St. Bede, 213; religion everywhere began to relish of the cloister, 287; kings going on pilgrimage to Rome or Jerusalem, 287; the great extent of the monastic institutions, 287; without monasteries there would have been neither learning, arts, nor science, 287; in such a case miracles may have been given for an end so worthy as the introduction of Christianity, 287.

CASSIAN, St., his great house at Marseilles, his life, 102.

Cæsarius, St., Archbishop of Arles, 101; his rule for the monastic life, 101.

Christ and Odin in presence before Ethelbert, 341-342; and before Edwin, 344; and before Oswald and Oswin, 344; and in the whole monastic mission sent by Gregory, 347.

Chrysostom, St., his comparison of royal power with the life of the monk, 77-83.

Cloveshoe, Council of, called by Cuthbert, Archbishop of Canterbury, A.D. 747, attended by the king of Mercia, his thanes, and all the bishops of England, 328.

Columban, St., his life and labours, 149-162.

Colman, third monk-bishop, answers for Iona at Whitby in 664, 235; rules during three years, and retires after Oswy's decision, 236-237.

EANFLEDA, the queen, summary of her acts as wife, mother, queen, and nun, 254-257.

Ebba, St., royal abbess, sister of two kings, 260.

Edwin, king and martyr, seeks alliance with the king of Kent, 218; is saved from an assassin and has his child baptized, 219; is converted by Paulinus, 220; is converted with his Witan, 222; receives letters from Pope Boniface V., 219, and Pope Honorius, 222; dies in battle after six years' championship of the Church, a martyr, 224.

Elfleda, daughter of Oswy and Eanfleda, dedicated by her father at her birth, 267; second Abbess of Whitby for thirty-five years, abbess and princess, 267.

Ercombert, king of Kent, grandson of St. Ethelbert, most zealous in destruction of idolatry, husband of Sexburga, father of Ermelinda, Abbess of Ely, and of Earcongotha, Abbess of Faremoutier, 280.

Ermelinda, queen of Mercia, succeeds her mother as third Abbess of Ely, 269.

Ethelreda, St., Queen of Northumbria, foundress and abbess of Ely, 268; sanctioned by St. Wilfrid to become a nun, 271; her history, and disinterment incorrupt, 277-280; her name melted to Audrey, a household name to English women for eight hundred years, 200.

Eugenius I., Pope, blesses St. Wilfrid at his first coming to Rome, 240.

FINAN, second monk-bishop, preaches in Northumbria ten years from 652, 233.

INDEX

GREGORY of Nazianzen, St., united with Basil in his life as a monk, 74; terms the life of St. Antony by Athanasius a code of the monastic life in the form of a narrative, 56.

Gregory of Nyssa, St., on virginity as the perfection of the incorporeal nature, 74–76.

Gregory the Great, his birth about 540, 191; accepts the rule of St. Benedict and watches over its extension, 191; the sole promoter of England's conversion, 192; enjoins St. Augustine and his monks to persevere, 193; commends them to the bishops and the queen in France, 194; they go in his name before King Ethelbert, 194; Ethelbert receives the Christian faith as sent by Gregory, 195; Gregory orders Augustine to be consecrated bishop at Arles, 196; orders the Bishops of London and York to receive the pallium, and each to preside over twelve bishops, 197; gives Augustine no authority over bishops of Gaul, but commits all English bishops to him, 198; records the conversion at the first Christmas of 10,000 Angles, 198; himself attests the mission from Rome as sent by him, 199; the nine Christian centuries of England date from him, 200; in his letter to Mellitus directs old temples to be reconsecrated, 201; orders bishops to live with their clergy as monks, 202; is made by St. Bede "to hold the first pontificate in the whole world," and the English to be "the seal of his apostolate," 208; his appointment of the primacy in Canterbury is established in St. Theodore, 212.

Gregory II., Pope, St., his mission of St. Boniface, 306; changes his name and consecrates him regionary bishop, 308–309; gives him letters for Germany, 311–314.

Gregory III., Pope, St., gives St. Boniface the pallium, 318; makes him his legate, 319.

Guizot, three Teutonic peoples occupying Gaul, Burgundians, Visigoths, and Franks, 137; nature of the Teutonic invasions, 137–140; merit of the Franks in stopping fresh inundations of barbarians, 140; two hundred and fifty years of Merovingian rule had not made a State in Gaul, 148; its unsettled and shifting kingdoms, 149; a picture of the Church's unity and the confusion of human things, 151–154; how the six Councils of the Church give one legislation which the empire can no longer give, 153–155.

HERTFORD, Council of, the first, 249; its canons, 250–252.

Hilarion, St., his life and following of Antony, 95.

Hilda, the royal abbess, her life, 262–267.

Honorius I., Pope, letter to King Edwin as a Catholic, 222; grants to him the pallium for York, 223; grants that the head of English peoples be for ever in Canterbury, 205–206.

JEROME, St., his commendation of Pammachius as a convert monk, 64.

LERIN, the rise and effect of its monastery, 99–101.

Leo, St. Leo the Great, the world which he saved from Attila, 333; the Council whose doctrinal decrees he confirmed, 333; the whole episcopate naming him as "intrusted with the Vine by the Saviour Himself," 334; preserves Rome a second time from Genseric, 334; causes it to exist during 300 years as the See of St. Peter's Primacy, 335; which is completed at the end of 350 years by his successor, St. Leo III., 372–374.

Leo III., Pope, St., the thousand years and the three monarchies which date from his act, 374-375.

Liberius, Pope, his spotless character attested by St. Basil, St. Ambrose, St. Epiphanius, and Pope Siricius, 85.

Lingard, Anglo-Saxons, the eight English kings pilgrims to Rome, 119; Saxon value of the life of chastity, 200; condition of the Saxons in England in their heathen state, 204; discipline of the Anglo-Saxon Church, 207, 208; the archbishop the connecting link with the Pope, 209; change in the monastic discipline from the Desert to the Anglo-Saxons, 226; what he thought of Bede's history, 215; cathedrals preserving their monastic character, 286; the gradual growth of mass-priests in district churches, holding under the bishops, not under monasteries, 295-296; a deacon and two clerics attend on each mass-priest, 296; strictly confined to continency, 297; the marriage of priests never approved by Saxon bishops down to the Danish inroads, 298; no marriage of bishop, priest, monk, or deacon allowed, 298; quotes the Emperors Theodosius I. and Justinian I. as maintaining this law, 302.

MARTIN, St., of Tours, his devotion to a monk's life, 85; founds monasteries at Ligugé and at Marmoutier, 87; his ascetic life described by his pupil Sulpicius Severus, 87.

Möhler, his "Mönckthum" quoted, 85, 104, 106; his judgment of the Life of Antony by Athanasius, 57.

Montalembert, names given by the monks to their monasteries, 157; Merovingian munificence and wickedness, 143.

OSWALD, king and martyr, plants a great cross and wins a kingdom, 225; asks for a bishop from Iona, and receives Aidan at Lindisfarne, 225, 226; rules over four languages, 226; bestows alms profusely, 227; prays in the act of dying in battle, and is held a martyr, 228.

Oswin, king and martyr, assists Bishop Aidan in his preaching, 228; bestows his own horse on him, 229; is murdered by his rival Oswy, 230; and is esteemed a martyr, 230.

Oswy, king and Bretwalda, espouses Eanfleda, 231; reigns with her twenty-eight years, from 642 to 670, 231; gains a great victory over Penda, and dedicates his infant daughter for a nun, 232; calls the Congress of Whitby, 234-237, and accepts the authority of St. Peter as decisive, 236; makes Ceadda Bishop of York, 242; acknowledges the Roman to be the Catholic Church, 242; applies to Pope Vitalian to find and send an archbishop to Canterbury, 243; receives St. Theodore as archbishop from him, 246, and at his appointment St. Wilfrid as Bishop of Northumbria, 246; beseeches St. Wilfrid to conduct him to Rome, but dies before, 246, 247; is drawn throughout his reign by his queen, Eanfleda, to the Catholic Church, 256.

PACHOMIUS founds the first monastery at Tabennæ, on the Nile, about 325, 1; another for his sister, 2, who is said to have had four hundred nuns in it, 87.

Patrick, St., nature of his conversion of Ireland, 203; its chief incidents and its time, 181-200.

Paulinus, St., converts King Edwin, 220, by whom his preaching during six years is encouraged, 222; receives as Bishop of York the pallium from Pope Honorius, 223; retires with Queen Ethelburga and her daughter Eanfleda to Kent, 224.

RADEGONDE, queen and saint, her history, 144-145; during forty years nun at the Holy Cross of Poitiers, 145; tries to tame the Merovingian princes, 146; her burial by St. Gregory of Tours, 147; follows in her enclosure the rule of St. Cæsarius at Arles, 147; her life a mixture of saints and monsters, among whom she is the most austere of penitents and most charitable of saints, 148.

SERGIUS I., Pope, a monk of Palermo, maintains the law of celibacy in the West against the Trullan innovations of Justinian II., 302; receives the pilgrimage of King Cadwalla to Rome, and confirms Archbishop Beretwald at Canterbury, 303; consecrates Archbishop Willibrord in 696 at Rome, 304; preserves the discipline of the Anglo-Saxon province of the Church, and of the whole Church, 371.

Sexburga, wife of King Ercombert, then successor of her sister, and second Abbess of Ely, 280.

THEODORE, St., a monk of Tarsus, stopping at Rome, selected by Pope Vitalian, consecrated and sent as Archbishop of Canterbury, 244; received in A.D. 669, makes visitation of the whole island, 245; ordains bishops in their proper places, 246; holds the first Council, 250; summary of his acts, 252-253, 267.

VITA COMMUNIS, what it is, 174; compared with marriage, 175; makes the supernatural home, 176; instrument to overcome barbarism, 177; acceptance by the Teutonic race makes France, 178; its effect in making a Christian Europe, 351; its diffusion during the continuance of the Roman Empire, 351; its advance in the seventh century, 352-353; its part in *national* conversions, Irish and English, 354; the life of Benedict an utter antagonism to the life of Mohammed, 357; the monastery substitutes the free labour of monks and nuns for the servile labour of *liberti* and *libertinæ*, 365; monastic cohesion overcame barbarism, 366; the mortal duel of 1300 years lies between the harem and the monastery, 357, 364, 369, 371, 372.

Vitalian, Pope, his letter to King Oswy, 242; chooses an archbishop of Canterbury, 244; selects Theodorus, a monk of Tarsus, consecrates him, and sends him to England, 244; assigns him as colleague Abbot Adrian, and also Bennet Biscop, 282.

WERBURGA, daughter of Ermelinda, fourth Abbess of Ely, fourth in descent from Ethelbert, 280.

Wilfrid, St., born in 634, of the highest Northumbrian nobility, 237; obtains at thirteen his father's consent to take the monastic life, 237; is sent by Queen Eanfleda to Lindisfarne Abbey, 238; obtains from her to be sent through King Ercombert to Rome, 239; goes with St. Bennet Biscop to the Archbishop of Lyons, 239; visits Rome and is presented to the Pope, 239; wishes to suffer martyrdom with the Archbishop of Lyons, 240; is made abbot at Ripon, establishing a Benedictine house, 241; is appointed at Whitby Congress to conduct the Roman cause, 235; King Oswy yields to his exposition of St. Peter's authority, 236; is ordained Bishop of Northumbria, 242; and so rules the whole monarchy of King Oswy, 246; reverenced by King Egbert and his queen, Etheldreda, 248; is summoned by St. Theodore to the first Council at Hertford, 249; is given by Queen Etheldreda her dower land at Hexham, 268; sanctions her becoming a nun, and abbess at Ely, 271; Wilfrid supplies a complete education in his monasteries, 272; is deposed from his diocese in 679, and appeals to Pope Agatho, 272; preaches in Frisia, 261; is restored by Pope Agatho as Bishop of York on appeal, 275; sits among the bishops at Rome and attests the faith of Britain and Ireland, 276; when banished from York, he converts Sussex, 294; his forty-five years of episcopate unsurpassed in lustre, 295.

Willibrord, St., a foster-child of St. Wilfrid at Ripon, 303; consecrated by Pope Sergius in 696, for fifty years Archbishop of Utrecht, 304; baptizes in 714 Pepin, son of Charles Martell, who was crowned king of France in 752, 304; the link between St. Wilfrid and St. Boniface, 304.

ZACHARIAS, Pope, St., letter to him of St. Boniface, as his legate, 321; he confirms the bishops appointed by St. Boniface, 322; answers the questions propounded to him by Pepin, Mayor of the Palace, 323; appoints Mainz to be the seat of the German Primate, 326; authorises Pepin to become king of the Franks, 327.

THE END

Printed by BALLANTYNE, HANSON & CO.
Edinburgh and London

www.ingramcontent.com/pod-product-compliance
Lightning Source LLC
Chambersburg PA
CBHW051246300426
44114CB00011B/916